Chile: The Crime of Resistance

CHILE
The Crime of Resistance

BY

SUZANNE LABIN

First edition
Published 1982
by the Foreign Affairs Publishing Co Ltd
139 Petersham Road, Richmond, Surrey TW10 7AA
England

Printed in Great Britain
by Brown Knight and Truscott Ltd
Dowgate Works, Tonbridge, Kent

ISBN 0 900380 32 2

By the same author

1951 — STALINE-LE-TERRIBLE, panorama du régime soviétique (*SELF*, Paris)
1954 — LE DRAME DE LA DÉMOCRATIE (Horay, Paris)
1957 — Les Entretiens de Saint-Germain : LIBERTÉ AUX LIBERTICIDES? (*Spartacus*, Paris) couronné par le Prix de la Liberté
1959 — LA CONDITION HUMAINE EN CHINE COMMUNISTE (*La Table Ronde, Paris*)
1960 — IL EST MOINS CINQ (*Berger Levrault*, Paris)
1961 — VIE OU MORT DU MONDE LIBRE (*La Table Ronde*, Paris)
1962 — COMPÉTITION URSS/USA (*La Table Ronde*, Paris)
1964 — LE TIERS-MONDE ENTRE L'EST ET L'OUEST. Vivre en dollars et voter en roubles (*La Table Ronde*, Paris)
1964 — VIÊT-NAM, RÉVÉLATIONS D'UN TÉMOIN (*Nouvelles Editions Latines*, Paris)
1966 — MENACES CHINOISES SUR L'ASIE (*La Table Ronde*, Paris)
1967 — 50 ANNÉES DE COMMUNISME (*Berger Levrault*, Paris)
1969 — LE PETIT LIVRE DE MAO : la guerrilla paie (*La Table Ronde*, Paris)
1970 — HIPPIES, DROGUES ET SEXE (*La Table Ronde*, Paris)
1975 — LE MONDE DES DROGUÉS (*France Empire*, Paris)
1979 — LA VIOLENCE POLITIQUE (*France Empire*, Paris) couronné par le prix Henri Malherbe
1980 — CHILLI, LE CRIME DE RÉSISTER (*Nouvelles Editions Debresse*, Paris)
1981 — Israel, Le Crime de Vivre (Nouvelles Editions Debresse)

CONTENTS

Chapter		Page
	Foreword by Brian Crozier	vii
	Introduction	ix
I	The Historical Background	1
II	Introducing the Characters in the Popular Front	10
III	Chronicle of Mr Allende's Reign	30
IV	The Political Rot Sets in—Legality Flouted	40
V	Violations of Freedom of Expression	50
VI	Regimentation of the People	62
VII	Despoiling the Citizens	72
VIII	The Violent Path to Socialism	82
IX	Economic Disaster	102
X	Moral Rot	117
XI	Popular Opposition	126
XII	The Political Opposition	146
XIII	The Final Abyss	155
XIV	The Lessons of the Allende Experiment	171
XV	Foreign Intervention in Chile? Against Whom? In Whose Interests?	184
XVI	Repression under Pinochet	199
XVII	The Present Political Situation	217
XVIII	The Economic Recovery under Pinochet	229
XIX	The Campaign against Pinochet—A false Symmetry	248
XX	The Crime of Resistance	260
	Index	273

FOREWORD

THE INTERNATIONAL LEFT thrives on myths and is well supplied by the enormous propaganda machine of the Soviet Union. Until the military coup of September 1973 in Chile, the great emotive myth had been the imperialist image of the United States in Vietnam, but it had become difficult to sustain the Vietnam myth after the American withdrawal, which followed the Paris agreements early that year. The fall of Mr. Salvador Allende in Chile came therefore as a providential gift to the Communist myth-makers.

During Mr. Allende's three years in power, Chile was plunged into economic chaos, galloping inflation and violent anarchy. The Cuban embassy in Santiago became the main centre for Fidel Castro's subversive activities in the "southern cone" of South America, extending to Argentina and Uruguay. The myth of the great socialist experiment in Chile nevertheless took precedence over the uncomfortable facts, and Santiago became a shrine for left-wing pilgrims from all over the world. On returning after one such pilgrimage, for instance, Mr. François Mitterrand, now President of the French Republic, declared that the Chile of Mr. Allende presented a model for Socialism in France.

When General Augusto Pinochet Ugarte and his companions intervened to rescue the Chilean people from the criminal follies of the Allende experiment, the myth took on a new dimension. Henceforth General Pinochet and his regime became the dominant hate-symbol for the military repression of "democracy"—until the "repressive" regime in El Salvador relegated them to second place.

Mme. Suzanne Labin, the author of this illuminating study, is one of the world's leading demolishers of ideological myths. As long ago as 1950, she drew merciless opprobrium and invective upon her head with her book *Staline-le-Terrible*, exposing the horrors of Stalin's regime at a time when it was still fashionable to think of him as the hero of the Great Patriotic War, scourge of Hitler and protector of the Soviet people.

Since then, she has distinguished herself as a champion of freedom, who has never lacked the courage to look behind the flattering images of the propagandists, in China as well as in the USSR and elsewhere.

In her new book, now presented to the English-speaking world, she does what very few writers on contemporary themes bother to do, by delving into Chilean history. She chronicles the advent of Mr. Salvador Allende's coalition on a minority popular vote, and the rapid ruin of the country which followed. She does not shirk the necessary job of investigating the widespread charges of brutality against the Pinochet regime, and demonstrates that apart from early excesses in the heat of the aftermath, most of them are palpably false.

Scrupulous as she is in her respect of verifiable facts, Suzanne Labin wields a highly readable and original polemical style. As a bilingual specimen myself, I am very conscious of the difficulties of preserving the flavour of the Labin style in English translation. Between them, the two translators—Geoffrey Lawman and Ann Elwell—have, I believe, pulled it off. The outcome is an English version of an important book which will cause many men and women of good will to cast fresh eyes upon the Pinochet experiment, which has brought peace and prosperity where disorder and poverty had reigned.

Brian Crozier

London, January 1982

INTRODUCTION

THIS STUDY IS AN ATTEMPT to carry out the most difficult task in the whole ideological debate, that of reinstating the true facts once the public has been induced by massive propaganda to accept as proven truth what is, in fact, blatant falsehood.

I can bear personal witness to the difficulty of the task, and to the persecution and suffering one is exposed to if one tries to swim against the tide of propaganda once its bias has become generally accepted. In 1950, at a time when all shades of political belief throughout the world agreed that the Soviet Union was a "progressive" regime whose merits far outweighed its defects, I had reached the conclusion that it was in fact one of the bloodiest tyrannies in history. I published my findings, irrefutable ones, in a book called *Staline-le-Terrible*. This was immediately greeted by a shower of abuse, and those whose ideals and values were most closely threatened by Communism were the loudest in accusing me of slandering it. 25 years later Solzhenytsin's revelations burst on the world, confirming point by point everything I had written, including the Gulag phenomenon, the extent and horror of which I had described in terms identical to his own.

It is my earnest hope that the public will by now have drawn the correct conclusion from this and will be more ready to give a welcome to books that set out to unmask the huge hoaxes that Communism keeps foisting on the world. In the case of Chile two contrary myths have been foisted on us. The Allende government that impoverished, oppressed and starved the people has been presented as though it were the hero of some improving but sentimental novel, the first to work the miracle of establishing a "Socialism with a human face", carrying out far-reaching reforms in perfect legality and with the consent of the whole people, and bringing about a rapid improvement in material prosperity. On the other hand Pinochet, who saved the country from famine and terror, has been abused and calumnied to an extent that has seldom been equalled in the long annals of misrepresentation, to the point where even the most fair-minded are convinced that his regime is a fascist one.

I went to see Chilean reality on the spot, and assembled a copious dossier on the Allende and Pinochet regimes. It is this personal contact and evidence, and the analyses based on them, that form the substance of this book. Just as it was true that Stalin, despite the popular belief, was a tyrant who plunged his people into misery, it is my hope that unbiased readers will now be forced to admit that, despite the popular belief, it is true that the Allende regime was an almost total disaster for Chile. They will see that the three Allende years brought the country nothing but violence, illegality, spoliation, shortages, censorship, black market and repression—including the brutal crushing of many strikes declared by *the very workers* whose interests the regime claimed to be defending—culminating in the tense dramatic days of September 1973, during which Chile felt itself sliding into the ultimate twin horrors of famine and terror. The unbiased reader will also come to agree that the Pinochet coup d'état came as a response to the anguished expectations of a whole people, and that even the most blameless of democrats, ex-president Frei, thanked Pinochet publicly for his action. The reader will note, too, that while the regime set up by Pinochet is indeed an authoritarian one, without political parties or parliament, and this is regrettable, it is nevertheless one which has made life liveable for its people, and is in no way fascist.

Several motives influenced me to undertake once again—this time on behalf of Chile—the thankless task of proving to people that they have been lied to.

Firstly, I hate in any case to see a falsehood winning. It is for me a sign of degradation and corruption in society, and I cannot tolerate this for very long without reacting.

Secondly, what has happened in Chile has particular importance for my own country, France. For we too have as our Government a popular-front alliance of Socialists and Communists, and one capable of winning not just 36% of the votes, as did Allende in 1970, but 51%, and with full executive powers. The leader of this front, Mr. François Mitterand, told us all, after a visit he made to his comrade Mr. Allende, that his goal was to set up a Chilean-style Socialism in France, thus refurbishing the illusion that it is possible to build a "Socialism with a human face" by following a legal and democratic path. And millions of Frenchmen still believe that this is what Allende did in fact achieve in Chile, and long to repeat his achievement in France, totally unware of the blood, sweat and tears that such a Socialism cost the people of Chile. Frenchmen in particular must therefore be brought to see what such a face and such a path really mean.

They must realise too that it was no crime for the Chileans to resist a total Communist takeover of their country, even by military force, even though another means would have been preferable. But no other method was left open once the left-wing parties in the country had committed the folly of legally bringing into office a Marxist coalition which immediately surrounded itself with a para-military force of

15,000 foreigners, including 12,000 armed Cubans, thus rendering any restoration of legality impossible by peaceful means. The lesson that recent events in Chile have for us in France is that the worst fate that can befall a country is to fall under *Communist domination*, and that we are entitled to do everything possible to prevent this apparently irreversible process from taking place. *If we do not want to be driven to calling on a Pinochet, we must not put on the throne an Allende.*

I have a further reason for writing this book: I find it particularly saddening to see Chile, a country so beloved of the gods, becoming a target for the hatred of mankind.

I have been round the world 16 times myself, and I find it hard to think of a more attractive country and, what is more, such an unlikely, totally unexpected one. Once one has reached the top of the Andes, one's next step would seem to land one directly in the Pacific Ocean. And then one becomes aware of this exiguous foothold clinging to the edge of the continent—a long ribbon of land, narrow as a thread, stretching for 2,700 miles between ice-peaks and sea. It is a natural showcase for the finest exhibition of natural beauty the world can offer: from the palm-trees, luxuriant flowers and scented tropical air of the north; through many-coloured deserts dotted with isolated forts, a lunar landscape unequalled by Sinai or the Sahara; then at the centre the great fertile plains, green and welcoming, a Normandy set against the majestic backdrop of peaks of Himalayan grandeur; further south a region of deep forests, emerald lakes and toy-like conical volcanoes capped by eternal snows, which could give even Switzerland lessons on how to compose a landscape; then 700 miles of magnificent fjords like some southern super-Norway; and finally the utter flatness of the pampas, with its unending grasslands, its sheep, its winds and its fireflies, stretching towards the South Pole.

The population that pursues its daily round against these enchanting backgrounds is a civilised one, largely of European stock, noted for its beautiful women and hard-working men, brisk and lively, given to good-natured joking and full of indomitable courage. Their cultural level equals that of France, their honesty that of Switzerland, their civic responsibility that of England. As to their personal pleasantness of manner, this has no equivalent anywhere else in the world. They are on Christian-name terms with you before they've known you for five minutes, and your new acquaintance will refer to himself or herself in terms such as "Your friend thinks that . . .", and will henceforth greet you with a kiss at each meeting, and scour the city to find you the newspaper or the car you need. The television announcer, calling his reporter in New York, says to her live on the screen: "Hallo, darling . . .", to which she replies: "Johnny! How are you, sweetheart . . .?" Their speech abounds in diminutives. To tell someone to "turn right" would seem to them curt to the point of churlishness; a passer-by showing you the way will almost sing his directions to you with the words: "Take a nice little turn to the dear little right" (*una vueltita a la derechita*).

Not that the Chileans have always had an easy time of it. Their country is indeed beautiful, but by no means easy to get a living from. Only a sixth of its land surface is cultivable. The distances are enormous, and the ubiquitous mountains an obstacle to communications. There are frequent and devastating earthquakes, and the rainy season falls at the wrong moment for the crops. And as if these natural difficulties were not enough, men had to build the Panama Canal, thus ruining the old trade route round Cape Horn, and the discovery of synthetic nitrates reduced a whole vast and prosperous region of the country to a burnt wasteland. To get the better of so many hostile factors, the Chileans have had to show more courage, endurance and resourcefulness than the famous conquerors of the Far West in the far more hospitable northern hemisphere.

In addition to the courage and pleasantness of her children, Chile has a further reason for pride: from 1830 until Pinochet's time the country has experienced very few of the pronunciamentos that occur so frequently in the rest of Latin America. Once it was past the growing-pains of independence, Chile had been a state based on law for nigh on 150 years, and thus had been continuously democratic for as long as France. Universal suffrage which they have had for longer than the French, respect for the law, freedom of public debate and the independence of the judiciary are deeply rooted in the traditions of this politically mature people, a fact of which they are justly proud.

It is a strange paradox that this lovely country should be the stage for a political drama of such magnitude. It is almost as though the battle of Verdun had been fought in the park at Versailles. And yet it is a fact. It was in this narrow corridor of the "good life", stretching peacefully between the mountains and the sea, forgotten by the headlines, its only claim to fame being the silent witness of a century and a half of solid achievment, that there took place, over a period of less than five years, a series of tragic events as far-reaching in their consequences for the world's destiny as any of the great crises of Europe and Asia. These events have brought us face to face with some of the most critical problems of current politics: Is there such a thing as a democratic path to Socialism? Can economic collectivisation co-exist with political freedom? Has a people the right to escape from slavery through the intervention of its armed forces? Is a democracy bound to tolerate in its midst parties hostile to liberty? Are violence and hunger the only possible forces that can spur us into changing our social systems?

You, the reader, want to discover what the response of a courageous nation was to these questions (sometimes at the price of its own blood); may be this is why you are reading this book.

CHAPTER I

THE HISTORICAL BACKGROUND

From 1810 to 1914

THE REVOLUTIONARY PROCESS that prised Chile loose from the Spanish crown and culminated in complete and final independence on 12 February 1818 began in 1810, at approximately the same date as in other Latin American countries and, as with them, was made much easier thanks to the Peninsular War, then raging in the home country. The more enlightened Chileans had grown tired of obeying orders from Madrid. They convened a "Cabildo' (liberation committee) in Santiago, and on 18 September 1810 (a date whose anniversary was to become Chile's National Day), this committee forced the Spanish governor to resign, and set up in his place an autonomous governing junta. Just as in most Latin American countries this initial upheaval was followed by a long period of unrest: dictatorships, violent discord, a Spanish reconquest, the campaigns of generals O'Higgins and San Martín, who once again expelled the Spaniards, and further economic and political upheavals. Finally, in 1831 President Prieto called on Mr. Diego Portales, a conservative politician of distinction, who in 1833 established a strong though authoritarian constitution. This provided for a Congress with two chambers, a President elected on a property-qualification suffrage (the property qualification was abolished at the end of the century), Catholicism as the state religion, and separation of the executive and legislature, the executive having the most weight.

On this basis, and without becoming president himself, Mr. Diego Portales brought civil peace and prosperity, based on free enterprise, to the country. The armed forces were kept strictly subordinate to the civil power, and this made Chile unique on the Latin American continent. Mr. Diego Portales was assassinated in 1837, but he had given such strong roots to his creation that it survived his death. Chile's political structure had been given its basic shape.

Mr. Diego Portales was an outstanding representative of the Chilean ruling class of the time, a kind of *aristocratic bourgeoisie* that combined the productive energies of the bourgeoisie with the culture and refinement of an aristocracy, and which possessed the rare gift of imposing order without oppressing those over whom it ruled. This was the class that had been the driving force behind the movement for independence, and it gave Chile a succession of highly distinguished presidents, the most notable of whom were Bulnes, Montt, Pérez, Santa Maria and Arturo Alessandri. As a social group, this class has a certain similarity to the plantation owners of the southern United States as they might have been without slavery. Since then, it has been one of the rare ruling elites in the world that has not needed to have a guilty conscience because of its privileges, education and power. Moreover, it has never sought to buttress its collective ethos by adopting any monolithic class ideology; in fact it soon divided into conservative and liberal trends—in European terms, die-hards and Voltaireans. Mr. Portales instilled into his class the conviction that the purely defensive role of the military should always be subordinated to the civil power, the only force within society empowered to initiate action, always provided that access to the latter was by merit. These unusual "barons", who put in as much work themselves as they demanded from others, developed, too, under the influence of immigrants from Germany, who came in in considerable numbers during the presidency of Mr. Bulnes, a remarkable knowledge of and respect for the law, and this became as it were their code of honour. In all matters, written rules were the first things to be consulted. If these did not supply the answer, they were expanded and supplemented, and if they left room for conflicting views, the task of arbitration was entrusted to learned judges, whose independence was held to be sacrosanct.

Under the leadership of these remarkable heirs of Spanish hidalgos and Prussian organizers, the country developed peacefully, despite the three wars in the 19th century against Peru and Bolivia, all of which the Chileans won in a series of brilliantly fought land and sea battles. Thanks to these Chile gained her far northern provinces, to the loss of which Peru and Bolivia are still not reconciled. Apart from this, there was an uninterrupted expansion of roads and railways, agriculture and industry all over the country. Attracted by the healthy climate and the free yet orderly public life, hard-working immigrants continued to arrive in a steady stream from all over Europe. Some of them settled on dry, rocky land and struggled to bring it under cultivation. Indeed, the exotic and colourful names of these newcomers have led to the kaleidoscopic variety of names to be found today in the Chilean telephone directory. In 1850 copper was discovered, and soon became the principal source of the country's wealth.

However, this is not to say that everything was idyllic. Like all other countries, Chile experienced social and political struggles, but they remained within the bounds of the law. The only grave crisis took place in 1891, when President Balmaceda wanted to establish an authoritarian presidential regime. The Congress rebelled, and was supported by the navy. These two joint forces based themselves on the north and began military action against Balmaceda who, for his part, also raised and armed volunteer troops. The regular army remained neutral in this conflict. 10,000 lives were lost in the ensuing civil war, which ended with the defeat and suicide of Balmaceda. Admiral Montt, who had skilfully led the legalist forces, took his place as president, and was immediately confirmed in office by a free election. Once further elections had brought in a constitutional congress, the navy returned to its quarters and normal political life was resumed. One new factor, however, was a notable strengthening of the power of the legislature, and this tendency was confirmed 30 years later when the new balance of power, corresponding to that in the American system, was written into the 1925 constitution, the second in the country's history, and which remained in force until Pinochet.

However the period during which this second constitution came into existence was one of unrest; indeed, the years 1924–1932 were called "the second anarchy", (the first had been that following independence and which Mr. Portales had brought to an end). During this "second anarchy" Chile witnessed, though on a reduced scale, the sort of political ups and downs that the more enlightened Chileans had thought only happened in the other countries of Latin America. On 5 September 1924 a "kid-glove" coup d'état took place: General Altamirano, who had become prime minister under pressure from the army, dissolved Congress. The president in office, Mr. Arturo Alessandri, who had appointed the general, was obliged to flee. Shortly afterwards a second coup was carried out by discontented populist officers, who objected to Altamirano's considerable weakness. Next, president Arturo Alessandri returned from exile, passed the 1925 Constitution and brought about the election of a new Congress. This was followed by further military intrigues which resulted in colonel (later general) Carlos Ibañez del Campo becoming president, and led to Alessandri's second departure abroad. After a remarkable modernisation programme, Ibañez was forced to resign, this time as a result of strikes, violent student demonstrations and defections within the circle of his closest supporters. Next, Mr. Montero was legally elected president, but was overthrown on 4 June 1932 by a further coup d'état in which military and civilians were equally involved and which was instigated by a major in the air force, Marmaduke Grove, who was a socialist. There ensued the curious episode of the "Socialist Republic", which lasted 100 days and was toppled by a further minor coup. The people had soon grown tired of Grove, and after a short period of uncertainty the President of the Supreme Court took over the national presidency provisionally and organised new elections which Arturo Alessandri won hands down on 24 December 1932. The "second anarchy" was over, and the constitutional order thus re-established was to continue unbroken for 41 years.

Another peculiar feature of Chilean history which the nation's writers have emphasized with pride is that the Indians who inhabited the country, the famous Araucanos, were unusually difficult to tame. They had already held their own against the Incas' attempts to subjugate them, and had established an autonomous social order and a culture of their own. These Araucanos inflicted on the Spanish conquistadors the only defeat the latter suffered in South America. They never submitted, and kept up the struggle until the middle of the 19th century, when president Montt finally granted them a special status which is still in force today. This fierce resistance by the Mapuches ("Araucanos" is the name they were given by the Incas) influenced Chilean history in two ways. From a moral point of view it toughened the character of Chileans *of both races* and instilled a tradition of courage and pride into civil life. Racially, the refusal of the Indians to let themselves be integrated reduced cross-breeding within the Chilean population.

From 1914 to 1964

The first World War brought great prosperity to Chile, due to record sales of copper and foodstuffs to the belligerents. It also swelled the numbers of the middle class, who began to act as a counterweight to the aristocratic bourgeoisie, and found its political expression in the radical party. Towards 1920, Chile had reached its present social stratification, comprising, below the upper and middle classes, whose distinctive features in Latin America are their initiative and culture, three clearly distinguishable classes among the ordinary people: a hard-working peasantry cultivating land that did not belong to it; a skilled urban working-class, fully class-conscious and already organised into trade unions; and, right at the bottom, drifting between the countryside and the outskirts of the towns, a vast class of illiterate poor doing all sorts of jobs or none at all. This lowest social stratum, which then formed a quarter of the population, still constitutes the country's greatest social evil. The extensive sector of the economy that it still occupies remains as under-developed as the poor countries of Asia, while the rest of the nation is at roughly the same level of development as mediterranean Europe.

The dominant life-style is strongly European. When speakers in Paris talk well or badly, they are applauded or hissed in Santiago. Modern Chile very soon developed a political spectrum similar to that of France: a Communist Party strictly obedient to Moscow, a Socialist Party that began by being reformist, but became Marxist in 1948 and Leninist in 1967, a radical party which was masonic, progressive and anti-clerical; then, after the Second World War, at the same time as its sister parties in Europe, a standard Christian-Democratic party was formed. All these parties of the Left ate year by year into the support of the two traditional right-wing parties, the conservatives and the liberals, who nonetheless remained powerful and merged in 1966 to form the so-called "National Party" of today. The backdrop to this has been forceful and long-standing activity by the trade unions. The themes discussed, the positions adopted and the jargon used are part of a political game which is an exact replica of European politics, so that a budding politician from Paris, of whatever political tendency, would feel perfectly at home in pursuing his career if he were transplanted to Santiago.

As early as 1938, barely two years after France, Chile had its first Popular Front, formed, like the French one, by an alliance of the radical, socialist and communist parties with the support of the unions. In the presidential elections of 1938 the Front brought its candidate, the radical Mr. Pedro Aguirre Cerda, to power, with 39% of the votes. This first experiment was cut short by the untimely death of the president, who was replaced temporarily by a government of neutral caretakers. But in the next presidential elections, in 1942, the Popular Front stood once again, and its candidate, Mr. Juan Antonio Rios, again a radical, won with 41% of the votes, that is, with increased support. President Rios, however, was an honest radical and a serious statesman who had no wish to implement Marxist doctrine in the economic field, and he was all the keener to keep his allies at a distance since under Mr. Ampuero's leadership the Socialist Party had grown considerably more extremist. Dissatisfied with what they thought of as Rios' "weakness", the socialist-communist bloc succeeded in imposing as candidate in the next elections a man with more "backbone", Mr. Gabriel Gonzalez Videla, a populist orator who even promised to have Communists in his cabinet if he were successful. He was elected at the end of 1946, with 42% of the votes (again with increased support) and kept his word.

However Mr. Videla had in fact too much backbone. Within a few months he realized that his communist ministers were concerned only with infiltrating the various public offices and the unions and stirring up public opinion by ceaselessly outbidding the government with extravagant promises. In short, he discovered to his cost the reality of Communism: the meaninglessness of signatures at the bottom of alliance agreements, which the Communist concludes solely in order to further his own cause. The day came when President Gonzalez Videla decided that "enough is enough". He dismissed his communist ministers. Shortly afterwards, on 30 September 1948, he passed through congress a "Law in defence of democracy" which, for the first time in the history of Western-style democracies, rules that it is *contrary to* and not *in conformity with* liberty to allow parties seeking the destruction of freedom to organise themselves; and with perfect logic he outlawed the Communist Party.

The Party remained underground for ten years from 1948 to 1958, until a new, independent president, elected in 1952, Mr. Carlos Ibañez del Campo, the ex-dictator of the troubled years of 1929–1931, put into practice the famous theory according to which it is disgraceful for a democracy to defend itself; abolished the law and once again legalized the Communist Party. For this he has never been forgiven by Chile's right-wing voters, who were in no doubts as to where they stood. In the 1958 elections, they managed, after three radical presidents, to bring into office their own candidate, Mr. Jorge Alessandri, the prominent son of the famous leader of the beginning of the century. But the Popular Front had still made a leap forward, winning 44% of the votes.

Mr. Alessandri's term of office, despite its many and varied achievements, failed to bring about a long-term swing back to the right. There were two main reasons for this. Firstly there was the considerable development of the Christian-Democrats under the impetus of Mr. Eduardo Frei's leadership, during which the party moved to the left. Secondly, there was a strong slide to the left too within the radical party, under the influence of communist infiltrators. This took place in the 1960s, a period during which a "cultural revolution" throughout the world brought to the fore the attitudes, values, enthusiasms and catch-phrases of the so-called "progressive" intelligentsia. This trend turned out to be as influential in Chile as anywhere else, for the country has always kept in step with major movements in Western public opinion. In 1964 Mr. Eduardo Frei was elected president with 56% of the votes, an unusually high figure for Chile.

It must be noted that a proportion of this support came from right-wing voters. Faced with the threat of a Popular Front government (the Front had been increasingly successful in previous elections, and had scored particularly well in a by-election at Curico a few months before the presidential elections), the right-wing parties, after first backing a prominent radical hostile to the left, Mr. Julio Duran, finally rallied behind Mr. Frei with Mr. Duran's consent. Mr. Frei thus became the standard-bearer of a kind of national anti-Marxist coalition. Thanks to Mr. Julio Duran's participation in this coalition, the electoral support enjoyed by the Popular Front, represented by Mr. Allende, decreased to 39% of the votes.

The presidency of Eduardo Frei

Mr. Frei's term of office, from 1964 to 1970, immediately preceded that of Mr. Allende and was in some respects its precursor. It is thus worthy of our closer attention.

Mr. Frei's first concern was to break with the right-wing parties who had helped him to power; he did this by paying public tribute to the very Marxism that he had been given a mandate to prevent, and by condemning the very social order he had been elected to defend. (He is not the only politician to have followed this line.)

Like all initially Catholic movements of the period, the Chilean Christian Democrats were intoxicated by the heady slogans of left-wing politics. They seemed to be competing as to who could prove himself more anti-capitalist, more popular and "progressive" than the rest.

On 26 February 1970 the Christian Democrat Minister of Education declared that Lenin was the greatest man of the century and belonged to the whole of mankind. The order of the day was to build "Socialism without the class-struggle". Copper was nationalized by buying back the mines from the American companies who were operating them. A social security system like that of France was set up. Those trade unions that had allowed themselves to be merged in the Communist-controlled CUT (*Central Unica de Trabajadores*) received every mark of the regime's approval. The universities were staffed by more and more progressive professors, the churches by left-wing priests. And as though to prove that going to Mass did not prevent one from being "emancipated", nothing was done to hinder a remarkable upsurge of eroticism and pornography (a phenomenon which until then had played only a very marginal role in Chilean life). Agency after agency was set up to plan the economy.

Last but not least, under the well-known slogan of "All land to those who work it!", a start was made on a great land reform by confiscating (with compensation) all estates of more than 80 "basic" hectares. (This would average around 200 acres. But the basic hectare is a variable area, designed to take account of the productivity of different soils, since this varies considerably from one area of the country to another.) These lands were distributed without payment to the farmers who worked them. All those who worked on a given estate received a share, and this often resulted in individual plots that were ridiculously small. To counter this fragmentation, the new owners were encouraged to form co-operatives, but these soon got bogged down in bureaucracy. This breaking-up of the land into small plots was carried out as a matter of principle, without any regard for the minimum area necessary for efficient cultivation with modern machinery. Nor, more generally, was any technical help provided to enable the new owners to maintain existing yields, let alone increase them. It is thus fair to say that the reform was introduced primarily for political reasons rather than for economic ones.

Many of the middle classes gave in to the new fashion and moved to the left, in the belief that it was in that direction that the wind of history was blowing in our century. But in their inmost hearts they were hoping that this wind would not carry them too far off course and would not turn into a hurricane. But this is what it often does for it is not the wind of historical inevitability, but that of hatred.

We can state this in other words by saying that leftism nowadays is not a political programme but a passion, and as such it tends, like any fever, to rise irresistibly to its highest temperature, its maximum intensity. Mr. Eduardo Frei's presidency proved no exception to this rule. The usual microbes of the leftist fever swiftly started to divide and multiply. The Christian Democratic party itself was split when its extremists broke away to form the MAPU (*Movimiento de Acciôn Popular Unificada*—Movement for Unified Popular Action), 30 degrees to the left of the parent party. A further split, 30 degrees further to the left, gave rise to the Christian Left under the leadership of Mr. Jacques Chonchol, who would later become one of the most frenzied mob-orators of the Allende era.

With these two successive shifts of 30 degrees plus 30 degrees, leftism had reached its extreme limit, and the process of hiving off secessionist groups from the main body of Christian Democracy came to an end. But other groups emerged outside it, in an infernal dance whose centrifugal force constantly threw off new bodies of extremists from its edges. The most notable of these was the MIR (*Movimiento de la Izquierda Revolucionaria*, or Left Revolutionary Movement), which was to play a very important role as a ginger-group under Mr. Allende, and which had come into existence principally as a reaction to the slowness with which the agrarian reform was being introduced. In fact the considerable expense involved in compensating the former landowners was acting as a brake on the reform. And so the MIR began, on its own initiative, to carry out forced expropriations without any indemnification, the first beginnings of the famous "tomas" (or seizures) which later, under Mr. Allende, were to swell into a mighty flood carrying with it incompetence and bloodshed. The MIR quickly duplicated its illegal extortions in the countryside by hold-ups and other terrorist outrages in the towns, and the helpless Frei government did nothing, committed as it was to currying favour with the left.

Meanwhile the traditional parties of the left continuously moved to more extreme positions in an effort to outbid the already advanced left-wing stance of the Frei government. If a politician is marked out and praised merely according to the position he occupies in the political spectrum, without having to back up his words by actions, he will naturally gravitate towards a position where he will be right in the limelight and from which he can shout loudest: and that means, in this case, as far to the left as possible. Throughout Mr. Frei's term of office one thus saw a veritable stampede by the parties and public personalities towards this privileged position, which had come to be regarded much as was Parnassus in ancient Greece. This seems to me to be an appropriate point at which to review the principal movements of the Marxist left-wing as they were at the end of Mr. Frei's presidency, and during their heyday, when they set their stamp on the Allende years; they changed very little over this period, except that the characteristics we are about to describe became more aggressively and openly marked.

CHAPTER II

INTRODUCING THE CHARACTERS IN THE POPULAR FRONT

The Communist Party

WE MUST GIVE CREDIT where it is due. At whatever point in its history we examine the Popular Front—at its origin as far back as 1938, at every major turning-point in its strategy, and at the very centre of its programme—we shall always find the Chilean Communist Party, the party whose General Secretary is that perfect *apparatchik* Mr. Luis Corvalan—the man who, when the military coup took place, was found hiding under his bed, and whom General Pinochet exchanged in 1977 for the Soviet dissident Mr. Vladimir Bukovsky.

The Chilean Communist Party is the oldest and most experienced Communist Party of Latin America, and the most faithful to Moscow. As early as 1912 Mr. Luis Emilio Ricabarren, a man of exceptional qualities, had founded a workers' movement on European lines. The impact of the Russian revolution led him, like so many others, to affiliate his group to the Communist International. The Chilean Communist Party, thus formed, derived considerable benefit from the immense intellectual and moral prestige of its founder. In 1923 Mr. Ricabarren went off on the customary pilgrimage to the USSR. Shortly after his return, he committed suicide for reasons which have remained a total mystery. No one knew whether it was the result of disillusionment or not; he left nothing in writing behind him to show what effect the Bolshevik regime had had on him.

This doubt as to the reasons for its leader's suicide made it possible for the Communist Party to continue to operate while claiming to be the heirs of Mr. Ricabarren. It quickly became a model of organization, discipline and unconditional obedience to the Moscow line. It was one of the rare Communist Parties in the world to give unreserved approval to the Hitler–Stalin pact. This approval went very far, as we can see from the fact that the Peruvian, Mr. Eudocio Ravinés, sent by Moscow to head the Chilean party, did not bother to conceal his support for Hitler, and even received subsidies from the Nazi embassy in Santiago (according to the revelations made by Mr. Marcos Chamudez in his book *Una Advertencia Americana*—An American Warning). This Mr. Ravinés was moreover a strange figure, a complex and many-sided character, a talented and arrogant adventurer. After a hectic career in which he took part in many of the Latin-American upheavals of the time, he made a spectacular break with Communism and set down in writing some fascinating revelations about it. Another communist leader, the Mr. Marcos Chamudez we have referred to above, also broke away from the orthodoxy of the party and published memoirs crammed full of revealing information about the true nature of this pro-Soviet party.

After the Second World War, the Chilean Communist Party took on its definitive shape, one very similar to that of the French C.P. It had between 30–40,000 members, 50% of whom were working class, organized in cells and districts. It was extremely militant, had a large stiffening of paid officials, and was so organized that it could "go underground" at a moment's notice; it possessed ample funds, its propaganda reached into all milieux, its structure was of the rigidly monolithic type euphemistically called (here as elsewhere) "democratic centralism". Its unremitting demagoguery was couched in a wooden and pedestrian language, it had a vast network of hidden contacts inside every political and cultural milieu and within the government ministries, and had heavily infiltrated the trade unions. However, although it dominated the leadership of the CUT (*Central Unica de Trabajadores*—a merger of a number of trade unions), thanks above all to the ability of the president of that organisation, Mr. Figueroa, a veteran Bolshevik, it never managed to win complete control of the intermediary levels, a third of which remained under the control of trades unionists of other political persuasions. The Chilean Communist Party, too, had less grip on the teachers and intellectuals than had the French Communists. But apart from these differences it continued, like its French counterpart, to follow the Moscow line with total fidelity whether that line was being laid down by Stalin, Khruschev or Brezhnev.

Nothing more needs to be said about a party that was no more than a mindless and obedient puppet in the hands of its leaders. However, I will add a brief note about its most famous hero, the Chilean communist poet Mr. Pablo Neruda (he has, indeed, been cut down to his true stature by a real poet, Mr. Ricardo Paseyro, in the French magazine *L'Express* of 28 June 1980). Here is the ode Mr. Neruda dutifully composed after the death of the bloodthirsty maniac Stalin:

> Stalin is our noontide
> The maturity of mankind and of the people . . .
> He teaches all men
> To grow tall, to grow tall . . .
> His structure
> Of wholesome breed and unbending steel . . .
> Malenkov now will carry on his work.

This little masterpiece succeeds in achieving the rare feat of bringing together in one lyrical effusion the utmost pinnacles of vapidity, falsehood, servility and opportunism. Mr. Paseyro quotes other examples, and numerous ones, of Mr. Neruda's asinine insipidities, which a shameless and unbridled campaign of publicity has tried to pass off as poetry. We may add that there was no deed too contemptible for Mr. Neruda to stoop to when it came to obeying the orders of his party. In company with the painter Mr. Siqueiros, he called for the assassination of Trotsky. Later he called for President Nixon to be murdered. His last book, which came out shortly before his death, had as its title *Incitement to Nixonicide*. He did his best to besmirch the reputations of a number of respected public figures chosen by the Communist Party as targets, including his fellow South American writers, and even Boris Pasternak. All this went hand in hand with a life of luxury, theatrical ostentation and megalomaniac insolence. Mr. Pablo Neruda was not without talent, but was nevertheless a prototype of all those court scribblers whom the party machine transfigured into revolutionary bards and succeeded in foisting upon a world gullible enough to swallow every piece of communist trickery.

The Socialist Party

Founded in 1931, this party at first differed little from its European counterparts. Apart from a small core of serious-minded workers, it was composed in the majority of primary school teachers, large numbers of civil servants and white-collar workers, a few skilled craftsmen, idealistic young members of the bourgeoisie and some farmers, and it filled them with progressive ideas. Its stance at its inception was thus reformist, rather like its French counterpart under Mr. Jaurès. But this moderate line meant that the powerful Radical party could easily steal its thunder and attract away many of its potential supporters. Consequently the Socialists moved further and further towards Marxism, and their leader, Mr. Ampuero, an untrustworthy character but an effective public speaker, managed to persuade the 1948 Congress to declare that the Chilean Socialist Party was *Marxist-Leninist*. This brought about the party's *exclusion from the Socialist International*—a highly significant fact, little known abroad, and which Mr. François Mitterrand was careful not to mention when giving the impression that the Chilean Socialist Party he was proposing as a model to his French listeners was the same sort of party as its European sisters. Strangely enough, those Chilean Socialists who left the party after this swing towards Leninism only managed to form quite small social democratic groupings. However, thanks to Mr. Arturo Ibanez, they exercized an influence inside the trade unions, where a non-Maxist Labour tradition survived, and was to play an important part when the time came for resistance to Mr. Allende.

The Chilean Socialist Party, with some 15,000 members in 1970 did not have a quarter of the Communist Party's organizational strength. However, following a characteristic pattern, it had far greater electoral support. During the 1960s it was the Socialist Party that developed into the principal hotbed of a headlong process of subversion, gleefully boasting that it was "outflanking the Communist Party on the left". The armed struggle had become the raison d'être of these Socialists, dubbed by Chileans the *termocêfalos*, literally "hotheads" (but the term, newly invented in Spanish, had so much more force than its long-standing English and French equivalents). At the Chillan conference, the Socialist Party handed itself over body and soul to its doctrinaire lunatic fringe, sometimes called "theosophists of guerilla warfare". The conference declared that recourse to revolutionary violence, seen as both "inevitable and beneficial", was *obligatory*. And this is the party which was later to be rapturously hailed as establishing Socialism by legal means!

The leader of the extremist wing who won the day at Chillan was later to be elected General Secretary of the Socialist Party at the Congress of La Serena, shortly after Mr. Allende's accession to power, and was frequently in the news under the name of Mr. Altamirano. This individual was to play as important a role as that of Mr. Allende himself, and is thus worth examining more closely, for he is a perfect exemplar of the generation that brought so much folly and misfortune to Chile, and elsewhere.

He was a patrician, the son of a wealthy and long-established family of the bourgeoisie, educated in the smartest schools of Chile and Europe, familiar with every pleasure from fine food and palatial hotels to pretty women, with a taste for abstract art and avant-garde cinema. It so happens that I dined at his house, though by that time it belonged to friends who had bought the property from his wife, who had stayed in Chile. It is a large house, modern and luxurious, with a beautiful garden and a swimming-pool, in the most fashionable neighbourhood in Santiago. By a mixture of qualities that seems contradictory, but which is revelatory of a whole era, this aristocrat was at the same time a passionate advocate of "power for the people". His articles, his speeches, his gestures and his plans were all pitched on a level of rabble-rousing frenzy. He was under a compulsion to feel himself a revolutionary and iconoclast, always driving ahead to the next intensification of the revolutionary process and indeed incapable of consolidating the gains of the here and now. Indeed, he clearly had no interest in accomplishing any project that would be of benefit to the workers; his sole concern was to juggle with doctrine in the abstract, for the sheer pleasure of it, paying no heed to the realities of the situation, to present himself as the most intransigent conceivable enemy of the established order. He would have been tormented with shame at the idea that anyone else had outdone him in the vilification of the existing order of things. In his directives to all levels of the Socialist Party hierarchy, written in February 1972 (which came to light during the military coup d'état and were published in the White Book), Mr. Altamirano explains that: "The institutions, codes of law, legal procedures, and the bodies for research and administration set up by the bourgeois state and its officials are totally incapable of serving us in the establishment of a socialist society. All such products and remnants of a hateful and out-of-date class regime are incapable of adaptation; they must be *destroyed by force*, and this will sweep away at the same time the whole of the present constitutional order. The sooner this is done the better. In this way the inevitable violence will cause least damage."

Here we have the background to what leftists throughout the world delightedly hailed as "the legal path towards Socialism". Another example of this was provided by Mr. Altamirano's chief disciple, the socialist deputy Mr. Mario Palestro, when in a resounding speech delivered in the Chamber on 9 July 1973 (quoted in *El Mercurio* of the following day) he declared: "We are not going to drop our pants before the instigators of civil war ... And why shouldn't we take the war to the Barrio Alto" (the rich quarter of Santiago) "so that those who get shot aren't workers and peasants? ... To those who object that statements like those I am making at this moment are a serious matter, our reply, repeated a thousand and one times, is that they are a true forecast of what is going to happen in our country."

By an historic irony it was this very Mr. Palestro who in October 1970 had the job of bringing Mr. Allende the Socialist Party's agreement to the famous *Statute of Guarantees*, the democratic guarantees Mr. Allende was to sign in order to make sure of the votes of the Christian Democrats which opened his way to the presidency.

Another noteworthy follower of Mr. Altamirano, Mr. Jaime Faivovich, who became governor of Santiago, had demanded that the programme of the Popular Unity front should include revolutionary tribunals and execution squads.

During an exile—and a very comfortable one—that lasted six years, Mr. Altamirano had plenty of time in which to reflect in depth on the ignominious collapse of all that he had preached for. Moreover, during that interval, the world had been shaken by Solzhenytsin's revelations about the Gulag phenomenon. One might have expected the fever of this hothead to have abated somewhat, and that a few seeds of realism might have taken root in his mind. Far from it. In the autumn of 1979 his book *Chili: les raisons d'une défaite* (Chile: reasons for a defeat) appeared in France. What were these reasons? Had the Popular Unity Front (UP) gone too far in its use of violence? Not at all—it had not gone far enough! The fault for this lay at the door of those UP leaders who "had not learned the simplest lesson in the Marxist copybook, which teaches that the overthrow of the bourgeois class can only be achieved through the *maximum use of force* . . . including that of open warfare", and that this must be directed, as Lenin realized, "by a party of steel, monolithic and disciplined". As one can see, there is no sign here of any second thoughts; the same old frenzy is spinning round as madly as ever in his brain.

Mr. Altamirano will stand as the prototype of a new breed thrown up by our times: the *Stalinist socialist*, or *the Marxist Goebbels*. This imprisonment within their own hell is of the very nature of fanaticism. But what excuse can we make for our liberal world as it continues to lavish approving smiles on such a raving madman whose dearest wish is to annihilate that world in blood, or for the bourgeois publishing houses who eagerly snap up such texts and turn down any anti-communist work?

Mr. Altamirano's work was brought out by Flammarion in their series 'The Rose in the Fist', to which Mr. Mitterrand has also contributed, and whose title was conceived to illustrate all the promise hoped for from the Socialism of "Let a hundred flowers bloom". But the Socialism it offers us, far from being floral, is an infernal one.

The Radical Party

The combined strength of the socialist and communist parties would not have been sufficient in itself to bring the Popular Front to power in Chile, any more than in France. The radical party, radically transformed by its extremists, was the essential lever that toppled the whole left into the UP.

It had previously been a traditional party, respectable and respected, with its principal power base among the progressive middle classes who, as early as the end of the 19th century, had begun to compete for power with that top stratum that I have called "the aristocratic bourgeoisie", and which was organized into the conservative and liberal parties. Very similar to the French radical party, masonic and anti-clerical, an advocate of free enterprise and against economic collectivism—"its heart to the left and its wallet to the right", as its detractors said—it was in fact a party in love with noble and humanitarian ideals, a scrupulous upholder of the rule of law, for whom the state played the role of impartial arbiter above the social classes, and it was active in promoting a non-religious and compulsory public education system. It was a relatively undisciplined body, with room in its ranks for political opportunists as well as eminent statesmen, but it stuck firmly to the principle of the subordination of the armed forces to the legitimate civil power, and it epitomised a characteristically Chilean sense of civic responsibility, prudent and yet ready to welcome social progress.

The party's swing towards leftist Socialism was to come about as a result of two concurrent factors, the general spread of the left-wing virus in the 1960s and a process of infiltration and undermining by the Communists. One is reminded of the path followed by the president of the Radical Party in France, Mr. Edouard Herriot, who believed that Communism belonged to the "family of the left", refused to oppose it; surrounded himself by a circle of brilliant wits sprinkled with communist agents, a coterie that became his personal court and his frame of reference in moral and intellectual matters; allowed himself to be invited by the Soviet authorities to make ostentatious tours through the Potemkin villages of the USSR; heaped fulsome praise on Stalin's regime during the darkest hours of his tyranny; turned himself into one of the most notable follow-travellers of the Soviets, and crowned it all by pronouncing an extravagantly laudatory funeral oration for that bloodstained maniac Stalin, an oration that ranks among the most shameful examples of Western praise of Stalinism.

Now the Chilean Radical Party had its own Mr. Herriot in the person of its chairman Mr. Anselmo Sule. He followed the same course, adopted the same attitudes and made the same speeches as Mr. Herriot. It was he who engineered the rapid swing of his party to the left, with the full connivance of the numerous concealed Communists in its ranks. Starting in 1950, one wing of the Chilean Radical Party specialized in a new type of fellow-travelling, including visits to communist countries followed by eulogistic reports, the systematic slanted presentation of Soviet manoeuvres in international politics so as to show them in the most favourable light, and making themselves the accomplices of Communism by their chairmanship of a number of cryptp-communist organisations (as Mr. Hermes Ahumada did in the case of the Chile-Bulgaria Committee, Mr. Carlos Morales Abarzua for the Chile-North Korea Committee, Mr. Juan Martinez for the Chile-Red China Association, Mr. Armando Holzapfel for the Chile-East Germany Association, Mr. Enrique Silva Cimma for the Chile-USSR Committee, and so on). Young Chilean radicals provided a considerable contingent of agitators and special envoys for the notorious World Federation of Democratic Youth and its Berlin Congress, one of the communist machine's biggest showcases for purveying propaganda to a gullible public.

This accelerated swing leftwards found its expression within the structures of the Radical Party. At the 1965 congress, the left wing, led by Mr. Hugo Miranda, Mr. Patricio Valdes and above all Mr.

Anselmo Sule, won majority control by a cynical misuse of mandates worthy of Stalin himself, and immediately began to make life impossible for the party's traditional wing, which under the outstanding leadership of Mr. Julio Duran, had dug their heels in and were opposing totally the swing to the left. For four years the party was torn by internal dissension until, at the 1969 congress, the majority in favour of Socialism summarily *expelled* Mr. Julio Duran's moderate fraction from the party in a Bolshevik manner totally alien to radical tradition. Mr. Duran consequently set up a new party called the Radical Democratic Party, a group which by its honesty and high ideals was destined to exercize far more influence than its numbers warranted. As for the 1969 radical congress, its resolutions might have been written by Mr. Jean-Paul Sartre. And, following its leftist metamorphosis, the radical party *was accepted as the representative of Chilean Socialism by the Socialist International!* That body, which had thought that by rejecting Mr. Altamirano's party, the one officially called "Socialist", it had shut the door on the fleas of Marxism-Leninism, had thus in fact let in its flies by the window.

To complete the picture, it is worth noting that the radicals of Mr. Anselmo Sule's tendency obeyed the same law that we have seen in operation for the Christian Democrats: as they moved to the left, they gave birth to extremists even further to the left than themselves, thus splitting the party. This was the origin, for example, of the PIR (*Partido de la Izquierda Radical*, or Left Radical Party). All this rumpus quickly disgusted the old rank-and-file members of Mr. Sule's party, and during Mr. Allende's reign these gradually joined the democratic opposition. Even the PIR, under Mr. Balfro's leadership, finally turned against Mr. Allende and worked for his downfall. Mr. Sule's original Radical Party was by then no more than an empty shell, with a faded label bearing its old and prestigious title still sticking to it.

We recommend all members of centre parties anywhere in the world, and particularly those who feel attracted towards an alliance with Marxists, to take seriously to heart the sad but salutary lesson of the disintegration of the Chilean Radical Party

Other Left-wing Groups

With the MAPU (Movement for United Popular Action), the Christian Democratic Left and the MIR (Movement of the Revolutionary Left), we are moving into the troubled and stormy waters familiar to all of us since the events of May 1968. By their origin, life-style, inflated rhetoric and feverish violence, these groups were identical to all those that flourished under the same banners in the slogan-chanting destructive demonstrations of that month in Paris, Berkeley, Tokyo, Rome, Hamburg or Stockholm. The only difference was that under the aegis of the UP in Chile these long-haired groups acquired room to manoeuvre, the means to back up their action, and a much wider audience. The MAPU and the Christian Democratic Left were accepted as full partners in the Popular Unity front, and were given seats in the government. The MIR remained outside the government, but established close links with it, and provided it with the cheerleaders and rowdies it needed. One of the leaders of the MIR, Mr. Andrés Pascal Allende, was the nephew of the new president himself (the son of his sister Laura, herself a socialist M.P. of the Altamirano clan); another of the MIR's leaders, Mr. Marambio, held no less a rank than that of chief of the GAP, Mr. Allende's praetorian guard, a post of such intimiate confidence that Mr. Allende would certainly not have entrusted it to a member of MIR without realizing all that this implied in identity of aims.

The MIR was in fact a *military party*, organized in a pyramid with cells of five members at its base, operational rather than deliberative in purpose, with an all-powerful central committee at the top. It had created three ancillary organizations, each one specializing in illegal expropriations and revolutionary agitation in different milieux: the MPR (*Movimiento de los Pobladores Revolucionarios*), which worked among the *"pobladores"*, the dwellers in the shanty towns; the FTR (*Frente de los Trabajadores Revolucionarios*, or Revolutionary Workers' Front), operating principally among the workers in the industrial belt of Santiago; and the MCR (*Movimiento de Campesinos Revolucionarios*, or Revolutionary Farmers' Movement), which concerned itself with dispossessing the landowners. The stewards responsible for maintaining order at an MIR demonstration were helmeted and jackbooted guerilla fighters armed with revolvers, while the MIR troops marching past flew distinguishing pennons, just like fighting units, from the end of the hardwood staves tipped with steel points, such as the North Korean partisans used. After the military coup, the secret premises of the MIR were found to contain not only considerable stocks of arms, but in addition a whole arsenal of bogus official stamps for producing false papers. A detailed list of this find was published in the White Book. We shall have occasion to return to the MIR as the principal agent of violence and of paramilitary operations later. Then it will be seen that this party tried to set up Soviets, and succeeded in establishing absolute control over wide areas of the country.

True to the law of their own nature (basically this is the same law as can be observed at work in cultures of micro-organisms), Chilean leftists divided and re-divided, producing a number of groups and factions, who at times fought each other like cats and dogs. One of the funniest of such incidents took place at the time of the split in the MAPU, which of course harboured in its bosom one wing, that led by Mr. Garreton, which was more noisily extremist than the wing led by Mr. Gazmuri. One fine day in March 1972 the latter assembled his supporters, expelled the Garretonists from the central committee and occupied the party offices, the newspaper and the MAPU radio station. When the Garretonists got wind of this violent exploit they came running, only to be received by the "moderate" wing with sticks, broken bottles, boiling oil and tear-gas bombs.

The Church gives its blessing to the Popular Front

No review of the forces in Chile that put their shoulders to the wheel and helped push it in the direction of a left-wing Leninism would be complete without mention of certain circles within the Catholic Church.

The topic is a rich one, for in Chile the weeds of Catholic Marxism sprouted vigorously in all directions and all walks of life. Those who would like to have a fuller treatment of the subject should consult Ms. Teresa Donoso Loero's remarkable book, published in 1975 by Vaitea under the title: *Los Cristianos por el Socialismo* (Christians for Socialism). In every one of its 280 pages they will find one or more examples of collusion between the Marxist movement and the so-called "modernist" party in the Church, each instance backed by dates, documents, names and photos. It is a crushing indictment, from which I can quote only a few extracts here.

The foundations were laid even before Mr. Eduardo Frei became president, during the years when Christian Democracy was growing to maturity. Progressive left-wing Jesuits, very similar to those we have in France, founded a club called the Bellarmine Centre (*Centro Belarmino*), which came to play for Catholics a similar role to that played by Freemasonry for the Jacobins in the years leading up to the 1789 revolution. Its guiding spirit was a Flemish priest, Fr. Roger Vekemans, who was in close contact with all spheres of the progressive intelligentsia throughout the world, and who soon became Mr. Eduardo Frei's *éminence grise*. To extend his influence to non-Catholic circles, Fr. Vekemans, using funds supplied by Mr. Frei as President, founded the Centre for Economic and Social Development in Latin America, a body whose real activities were purely political. At the same time one of his colleagues, Mr. Larrain, founded and ran the Jesuit review *Mensaje* (Message), which is still in existence under the Pinochet regime.

Thus manned and structured, and enjoying as it did political and moral support both nationally and internationally, left-wing progressive Catholicism made rapid inroads into the Catholic Church in Chile.

Very soon, under the name of Young Church, a group of young people inspired by a mixture of the Gospel and Marx's *Capital* was formed, and on 4 August 1967 they organized their first great public demonstration in common with the *Communist youth organization*, a march from Valparaiso to Santiago in support of the Viet Cong. It is revealing to see in the photos of this march the evident joy of these immature Christians (barely out of the catechism-class) at finally and openly being able to join hands with such daring "revolutionaries"! In a surge of emotional iconoclasm directed against their own beliefs (little did the poor wretches realize that once they had smashed their own former idols, they would embrace other and infinitely more repellent ones), our young Catholics of the Left, still carried away by the enthusiasm of the march, seized the Catholic University on 11 August 1967. This caused a national uproar, for the university was regarded as the very symbol of the highest Christain traditions. After 10 days of stormy meetings, of holding professors prisoner, of picketing the lecture theatres and the issuing of high-flown proclamations—a sort of "May 68" a year ahead of time—everyone agreed to submit the matter to the arbitration of the Archbishop of Santiago, Cardinal Raul Silva Henriquez (normally called Silva), primate of the Church in Chile.

Up till that moment no one had any idea where this ecclesiastical bigwig stood in politics. But he soon revealed his sympathies by his profuse approval of the rebels, whom he commended highly for their revolutionary theses, and by his appointment of the left-wing Catholic architect Mr. Fernando Castillo Velasco as the new Rector of the University with full powers. The latter set about filling the university with a choice selection of mischief-making agitators and revolutionary firebrands who were later, under Mr. Allende, to prove such an obstacle to the students when they tried to shake off the control of the Popular Unity front and join the democratic opposition.

A year after these events, another one took place on 11 August 1968 which profoundly shocked public opinion, namely the occupation of the venerable cathedral of Santiago by a group of 80 priests, monks, seminarists and deacons followed by 200 layfolk. Alongside the crucifix they set up two big portraits, of Comrade Che Guevara and Camilo Torres (the priest who led a Castroist guerilla band in Colombia); they led the layfolk in the playing, singing and dancing of "pop spirituals" in which Christ, returning to earth as a member of the working class, would lead strikes and say "Shit" to the bosses; they explained from the pulpit that they were protesting against three infamous crimes committed by Rome: the Pope's agreement to hold a Eucharistic Congress in Bogotá, "capital of a class-state tied to imperialism", the Vatican's ban on the contraceptive pill, and the erection of a votive sanctuary at Maipu, seen as "a symbol of primitive bigotry". The main instigator and organiser of this saturnalia, Father Luis Antonio Diaz, was a few months later to be chosen by Cardinal Silva as his personal secretary.

Two months later, pleased as punch with the furore aroused by their occupation of the cathedral, and seizing the pretext of a mild remonstrance addressed to the Movement of the Revolutionary Left (MIR) by the Frei government, the hotheads of the Young Church organized a solemn mass in favour of "the victims of repression". And so it went on. One can find examples of this sort of thing on page after page of Teresa Loero's book, which covers the period of Allende's government as well. Although I shall not begin discussing the later period until my next chapter, I will continue to deal here with the particular subject of Marxist infiltration into the Church, so as not to have to return to it later.

On 10 November 1970, a few days after Mr. Allende's accession to power, Cardinal Silva held a special press conference for the Cuban journalists who had come to attend the investiture. At this the cardinal declared: "Socialism contains enormous Christian values, and from many points of view, I find it far superior to capitalism. I pray God that Salvador Allende, a loyal, honest, clear-minded and devoted leader, may be able to bring to fruition all the benefits that he has planned for his country".

In April 1971, during a mass Congress attended by clerics from all countries, the Young Church "transsubstantiated" itself into an organization called *Cristianos por el Socialismo* (Christians for Socialism—hence the title of Teresa Loero's book) under the leadership of Mr. Gonzalo Arroyo, a Jesuit of the Bellarmine Club. During the sessions of this congress, one could hear one speaker maintaining that "the Virgin Mary fits very well into the class-struggle", and Monsignor Ariztia, bishop of Talca, assuring his listeners that "it is not enough for Christians merely to approve of the revolutionary process set in motion by the Marxists; they must join it body and soul".

On 1 May 1971 Cardinal Silva sat beside Mr. Allende on the platform at a big meeting organized by the communist trade union organization CUT, and then marched at the head of a column of Young Christian Workers as they joined noisily in the procession. On 13 November 1971 the same Cardinal Silva went personally to the airport to welcome the Communist Fidel Castro and present him with a gold-illuminated Bible. On 30 November the press published an account, with photographs, of a meeting between 80 priests and Fidel Castro. And one can see them, made up as poverty-stricken Galileans, their unkempt hair sticking out in tufts, half of them squatting on the ground, and hanging on the words of the bearded Cuban as though they came from the mouth of Christ himself.

I will end on this picture, although fellow-travelling churchmen continued to back Mr. Allende throughout his term of office. It is only fair to say, however, that such backing consistently diminished as the harmful nature of the UP became more evident. In particular, Father Vekemans very quickly dissociated himself from the new regime. He now lives in Bogotá and is busy revising all the ideas he did so much to spread in Chile.

One must also make it clear that the Catholic Church in Chile contained a considerable body of ecclesiastics who were deeply hostile to Marxism and who had the courage to enlighten their flocks along those lines. Their leader was, and still is, Monsignor Tagle, archbishop of Valparaiso, who was kind enough to grant me an interview and show me the other side of the coin. As for my question as to the relative strength of the different parties within the Church under Mr. Allende, Ms. Teresa Loero in her book answers by estimating that roughly one third of Catholics followed the Marxist line, one third opposed it, while the last third remained neutral or undecided at the outset, but moved over to the democratic opposition as it became clearer that Mr. Allende was governing in defiance of the law. One can sum up by saying that much of the Church's forces finally lent a hand in the task of Chile's restoration, although earlier many of them had played a part in its downfall.

There is nothing in this picture that need surprise us; it merely mirrors what we have already seen in not a few other democracies. This swing to an extremist left-wing position in religious circles was one of the basic factors in what I have called the "cultural revolution" that unsettled the whole western world in the 1960s, and which may well have played a decisive part in Popular Unity's accession to power in Chile. Mr. Allende put arms into men's hands; Cardinal Silva disarmed their minds.

Allende's election to the presidency

If we consider Mr. Frei's presidency as Act One of our drama, we can say that by the end of that Act all the parts had been cast in such a way that the next act could be played even further to the left. The communist, socialist and radical parties had recast their organic alliance under the name of *Unidad Popular*, UP (Popular Unity). The reader will soon get accustomed to all these initials, with the activists and irregulars of the MIR operating as their military arm, and MAPU and the Christian Left to give them a cloak of religious respectability. After a certain amount of manoeuvring, the UP reached an agreement to put up a single candidate for the presidential elections of October 1970; this candidate was the socialist doctor and Senator Salvador

Allende Gossens, a seasoned politician with three months of medical practice and 30 years of socialist-Leninist agitation behind him, and who had already made three unsuccessful bids for the presidency. The Christian Democrats, more left-wing than ever, produced from up their sleeves a certain Mr. Radomiro Tomic, an ex-ambassador almost as left-wing as Mr. Allende, just to give the UP a run for its money. The National Party, which had tried in vain to persuade the Christian Democrats to reforge a democratic coalition in opposition to the Marxist one, and had seen all their advances rejected, realized that they were now the only bulwark against the "popular" flood. In their need they turned to their one and only great man. Mr. Jorge Alessandri, hoping to cash in on his prestige. Unfortunately (and this they had not expected), his advanced years produced precisely the opposite effect, for in an age of television all the viewers could see his hands trembling as they watched him on the small screen.

Thus the Marxist forces came to the battle united and full of self-confidence, while their oppenents were divided; on one side the National Party, and on the other the Christian Democrats, who were already secretly under the spell of the challenger's views and rhetoric. The election campaign was hotly contested, since everyone realized how much was at stake. Mr. Alessandri's "nationals" won the support of all who realized the nature of the threat, including those elements of the Social Democrats who followed the former trade-union leader Mr. Arturo Ibañez, and the followers of Mr. Julio Duran among the Radical Democrats. All these trends retained a lively and sensitive feeling for democracy, and spared no effort to warn the Christian Democrats of the dangerous consequences of an alliance with the Marxists. But all to no avail; Mr. Tomic continued to equate Socialism with salvation, but insisted that the best Socialist, after Jesus Christ, was himself. Alas, this was an example of the pathetic blindness and naïvety of the weaker party, hoping to steal the thunder of the stronger, but in fact only strengthening the latter more.

The election results declared on that fateful evening of 4 September 1970 were as follows (in round figures):

Allende	1,070,000 votes	i.e. 36%
Alessandri	1,030,000 votes	,, 35%
Tomic	820,000 votes	,, 28%
Other candidates	28,000 votes	,, 1%

I earnestly recommend readers to engrave this table firmly on their memories, since it lies at the root of all that was to happen in Chile in the years to come.

The first thing that will strike the reader is that, *contrary to the idea spread throughout the world* by means of (deliberately) ambiguous news releases, the UP *was a minority party in the country, and indeed rather a small minority.* In most European countries the combined left-wing parties generally command 45 to 49 per cent of the votes. The figure in Chile fell far short of this; 64% of the citizens, i.e. practically two thirds, went on record as *against* the Marxist-Leninist coalition. The Christian Democratic electors had voted for Mr. Tomic out of sheer loyalty without in any way approving his extreme left-wing views.

The reader will also note that the election of 1970, far from marking an *upswing* for the Marxist-Leninist coalition, in fact underlined its continuing *decline*, a decline which, as we have seen, had begun as far back as 1964. You will remember that the Popular Front, from its first beginnings in 1938, continually polled a *higher* percentage than Allende's 36%, and reached the figure of 44% in 1958. And you will note, finally, that support for the Chrisian Democrats was beginning to shrink; they were paying the price of their candidate Mr. Tomic's leftist extravagances, while the right-wingers of Mr. Alessandri, despite their champion's personal drawbacks, were making a sizeable break-through as a result of their uncompromising campaign and thanks to the backing of all those of whatever political colour whose supreme concern was to save their endangered liberties. It is thus abundantly clear that the dramatic events that were to ensue were not the result of any upsurge of popular enthusiasm for Marxism, but were due to that classic error, the stupid yet tragic *disunity* of the non-Marxists.

From popular minority to parliamentary majority

What was to happen now? The Chilean constitution provides that if no candidate obtains an absolute majority of the votes, Congress (in joint session of both its chambers) decides whom to invest. Following a courtly tradition, Congress's choice has normally been given to the candidate who has won most votes. It was on this basis that three Popular Front presidents, none of whom had achieved an absolute majority, had acceded to office, Was this old rule, which had worked well among gentleman of honour, to be applied in favour of Mr. Allende, a Marxist-Leninist from such a different and more frightening background?

The rule was actually applied, though in fact it was thanks to the idiosyncratic fixation of the Christian Democrats that this happened. Mr. Allende controlled 80 votes in Congress, the Christian Democrats 75 and Mr. Alessandri 45. The latter immediately saw the danger, particularly since Mr. Tomic had hastened to pay a courtesy visit to

Mr. Allende to congratulate him on his "victory". It was rumoured that the two leaders had made a secret pact whereby each pledged his party's votes in Congress to whoever headed the poll. Mr. Alessandri therefore made a magnanimous gesture, asking the Christian Democrats to support him in the investiture vote, which would have made an imposing bloc of 120 votes against Mr. Allende's 80, in return for his guarantee to resign as soon as elected, thus leading to a new electoral campaign in which the two principal non-Marxist bodies would agree in advance to support a *single candidate* who would be certain to win hands down. Mr. Alessandri even agreed in advance that this candidate should be a Christian Democrat.

But this elegant and foolproof solution was completely rejected by the Christian Democrats. Their left-wing itch had reached such a level of virulence that "voting for the right-wing" now seemed to them as disgraceful as spitting on the cross. Mr. Frei made this crystal clear in his reply to the constant reminders from the "nationals" of the communist threat that loomed behind Mr. Allende. "Communism," he said, letting the truth out of the bag in an outburst of irritation, "is indeed an evil, but for me anti-communism is a worse evil". *In these words we have the complete key to the downfall of the Free World.* The leader of the parliamentary group of the Christian Democrats, the lawyer Mr. Aylwin, a man of great intelligence and unimpeachable integrity, confirmed this in a now famous interview on the National Columbia News Service 13 days after the Pinochet takeover, when he admitted regretfully that in the autumn of 1970 his party "felt itself far closer to a socialist-minded regime than to a capitalist one".

In the midst of this period of anxious expectancy and tense negotiation that separated the popular elections from the first meeting of Congress, Chile was shaken by a dramatic event: General Schneider, the army chief of staff, was abducted at Santiago and later found murdered in his car. The police were able to arrest two of the criminals responsible, who claimed they had merely intended to kidnap the general, but the killer himself, the principal organizer of the coup, succeeded in getting clear away. The guilty men proved to be young hotheads belonging to a small group of the extreme right. General Schneider, the very model of an ideal non-political Chilean officer, had declared that the army would not intervene in any way in the country's current problem, and would conform strictly to whatever decision Congress might make. This position was not at all to the liking of the group in question. However, it was by no means clear that the motivation of the crime stopped there. Applying the criterion of *Cui bono?*—"Who benefits from it?", some Chileans were convinced that the young men had been victims of a provocation coming from the extreme left. For in fact *Allende was the sole beneficiary of the crime,* and this in two ways: it triggered off the classic reaction of "Fascism must be resisted", and thus threw the Christian Democrats more firmly into Mr. Allende's arms; and it brought to the head of the army General Prats, unlike General Schneider no neutral in politics, but distinctly left-wing in his sympathies, a fact which was to prove of the utmost benefit to the Popular Unity government, as we shall see later.

Whatever the real facts underlying this drama may have been, its ultimate effect politically was to strengthen the left wing of the Christian Democrats, those who actively *desired* to see the Marxists come to power, by distinction from those who were merely *resigned to it*. This point is important. What we must realize is that the Christian Democratic Party as a whole voted for Mr. Allende gladly and willingly, since it expressly preferred his political coloration, and not because it was forced into it by an unfavourable tactical situation. However, it was all too obvious that the coalition it was going to bring to power included totalitarian forces, and the Christian Democrats could not afford to be seen as openly welcoming these; so, as a condition for the decisive support they were offering him, they negotiated with Mr. Allende a *Statute of Guarantees*, by which the latter pledged himself to respect the Constitution, political pluralism, the independence of the armed forces from party political allegiance, the basic freedoms of expression and organization, the separation of powers and the independence of the judiciary.

Mr. Allende signed all that was asked of him. It was obvious to the merest child that this pact was no more than a scrap of paper for him. But the Christian Democratic deputies and senators *forced themselves to believe* that he was in earnest, so keen were they to take the decisive step and prove to themselves that the Catholics had finally redeemed their conservative past record and were now true progressives capable of any political innovation however audacious. It was this gesture of the Christian Democrats that was to bring to power the open supporters of a collectivist and atheist revolution.

Thus, if on the evening of 24 October 1970 in the Chilean Congress a Western society passed legally under the control of Marxist-Leninists, it was not in any way because the Chilean people wanted this, but because a majority of the key members of a great democratic party had succumbed to a sharp attack of the "left-wing virus".

Salvador Allende

To complete our review of the actors in the drama before the curtain rises, we must pause for a moment to consider the most decisive member of the cast, the man who has just been invested as President,

Salvador Allende Gossens. There is much we can learn from such an examination.

The picture of himself that Salvador Allende projected to the outside world was that of a level-headed, responsible stateman, a reformist rather than a revolutionary, respecting the rule of law and a lover of liberty. The image he cultivated for general consumption was thus that of an experienced parliamentarian, an outspoken, straightforward man with an affable and even engaging personality; no one would ever suspect such a well-bred scion of the establishment of revolutionary extremism. But underneath this reassuring surface, the real truth was that he had adopted the official *Marxist-Leninist line* of his party and was flirting with the extreme left. In his case this did not reflect either deep conviction or a militant's devotion to a cause, for he was incapable of the one or the other. But he was well aware that he owed his position in the left-wing movement solely to the avant-garde stance he had taken care to cultivate throughout his political career. He thus projected two distinct personalities, and spoke with two very different voices: a revolutionary one for his socialist and communist comrades, and a diplomatic one for consumption in the outside world. Let us look more closely at the first Mr. Allende, the one who is speaking for the ears of his own close supporters.

In my view, the most significant event in his inner political life occurred in 1967, when he represented Chile at the Tri-Continental Conference at Havana, which brought together all the communist parties of the world, and where the decision was reached to launch worldwide all-out terrorist and guerilla action against the democracies. When he returned home, Mr. Allende organized action committees to implement the directives of this Tri-Continental Conference, the so-called OLAS (Latin-American Solidarity Organization), within which revolutionary enthusiasm was maintained at fever-pitch as each hothead strove to outdo his comrades. Photographs exist of our "gentlemanly" president lying down as he is trained to use a machine-gun by a Cuban in commando uniform. While he was president of the Senate, he offered the six survivors of the Che Guevara's terrorist group in Bolivia a refuge on Easter Island, and accompanied them there himself. He had family as well as ideological links with the extreme left. His sister Laura, a socialist member of parliament, was a fervent admirer of the hothead Mr. Altamirano. His nephew Mr. Andrés Pascal was one of the most inflammatory leaders of the MIR. His daughter Beatrice had married the Cuban Mr. Luis Fernandez de Oña, a rabid Communist who had organized Che's expedition before becoming one of the chiefs of the Cuban secret police. Fidel Castro had sent him to Mr. Allende as his personal representative, and he soon became the confidential adviser of the Chilean president and then his son-in-law.

The armed guards at his various residences, chosen personally by Mr. Allende, were drawn worldwide from all the hotbeds of guerilla terrorism, and included Cubans, Montoneros from Argentina, Uruguayan Tupamaros, etc.

His collaboration with official Communism was just as marked as with the leftists. He automatically signed any and every manifesto designed to fool the unwary and serve the cause of communist propaganda. He never condemned Stalin, but added his voice to a number of witch-hunts directed against Moscow's pet aversions, in particular Trotsky and the Chinese. A well-known incident reveals the degree to which he was dependent on the Comintern. At the period when the party line was for a struggle of "class against class", the Comintern had ordered all communists to leave free-masonry. Only card-carrying members of the Communist Party with a strong sense of discipline obeyed. Fellow-travellers in general paid no heed to the directive. Mr. Allende, to whom it was second nature to keep all his options open, chose a middle course: he remained a freemason, but in secret. And then, on 31 August 1964 the newspaper *El Mercurio* published a photograph of him entering the premises of the Grand Lodge. Mr. Allende was so furious that he completely lost his self-control and accused this hallowed organ of liberalism of . . . Nazism! All that he achieved by this was to reveal his own terror of getting into Moscow's bad books.

There is no need for us to be surprised at a Western politician of the front rank sinking to such an abject dependence on the communist machine. Such occurrences have been frequent ever since the beginnings of the Bolshevik revolution. One could make a long list of prominent figures in the Free World who showed themselves more responsive to the attractions of Communism than to those of their own society. I can quote here only a few names at random: Herriot, Benes, Soekarno, Fierlinger, Cirankievicz, Goulart, Arbenz, Fidel Castro, Edgar Wallace, Agostino Neto, Mengistu, Boumedienne, etc. Few of these politicians were in any way masters of revolutionary doctrine. They were politically ambitious, psychologically conceited and ideologically superficial men—mere mouthpieces for the ideology of progressivism, recruited by a variety of mechanisms (which I have described in detail in my book *Libertê aux Liberticides*—Freedom for the Destroyers of Freedom) into the wide and profitable network of "principal collaborators" of the Kremlin. Mr. Salvador Allende occupied a distinguished position among these. He had naïvely admitted his bias in his Concepción speech: "I am the president not of all Chileans, but only of the supporters of the Popular Unity front". Too lightweight to make a fully considered commitment to Communism, too much of an opportunist not to make full use of the levers of power that

Communism made available to him, he did no more than sing the tunes the Kremlin had written for him and his like, and repeat the slogans and directives of the Marxist creed. A single example will suffice. After his overthrow by the military, some notes he had jotted on the headed notepaper of the Central Bank, intended for a speech he was to give to economic cadres of the UP, were discovered in his safe. Here are one or two sentences from them:

"Things are good or bad according to whether they help or hinder us from seizing power ... What does the class-struggle consist of? Conquering imperialism, crushing the bourgeoisie, annihilating the capitalist class ... whatever helps to destroy the age-old exploitation, down to and including its last and tiniest traces, is moral. Whatever helps to build our new society is moral."

Just the sort of clumsy leftist text, without the slightest spark of originality, that one might expect from a rather mediocre student in the Leninist schools. But in it, one of the essential characteristics of the man stands out clearly—his duplicity. We have noted that circumstances forced the Popular Unity front to tack to and from between two lines, an extremist and a moderate one. This double-dealing called for exceptional dexterity. As chance would have it, Chile gave birth to a man who displayed this charactistic to the highest degree. Mr. Aylwin made it clear that he had always tried to believe in Mr. Allende's good faith, and had attributed his zigzigs to the pressure he was under from opposite sides, but that in the course of the "last chance" conversations he had had with him 15 days before his downfall he had been forced to realize that Mr. Allende was "intellectually dishonest". On 22 October 1970, on the steps of the presidential throne, Mr. Allende had read to the Senate the famous solemn declaration in which he said: "I understand the dispositions of the *Statute of Guarantees* which I have just signed, not only as solemn principles of a fundamental charter, but as the moral principles which will rule my conduct before my own conscience and the judgement of history"

Some time later he said to Mr. Régis Debray (who reported his words in his book *Conversations avec Allende*, 1972): "I only signed the *Statute of Guarantees* as a tactical necessity, for at the time the essential thing was to seize power ..."

The whole of Mr. Allende, all his bottomless cynicism, is enshrined in those words.

CHAPTER III

CHRONICLE OF MR. ALLENDE'S REIGN

For the world at large, the significance of the Allende phenomenon does not lie in its intrinsic interest as a slice of the history of one particular country, but in the fact that we can draw from it political lessons of general validity. This book, therefore, does not set out a straight chronological account of events in the order in which they occurred, but instead analyzes successively the major problems that characterized it. To help the reader to place these problems in their historic context, however, I add here a short summary of the events themselves.

1971: the "honeymoon", or "year of the presents"

Mr. Allende took his oath of office on 3 November 1970, and the government was formed on the 5th, with three communist ministers, four socialists, three radicals, one from the MAPU and three from various smaller groups associated with the Popular Unity front. Numerous posts such as under-secretary of state were distributed in such a way as to balance this sharing-out of ministries, so that a communist minister had a socialist under-secretary, and vice versa. The Ministry of the Interior (or Home Office) fell to a fanatical socialist, the journalist Mr. José Toha. The fields of economy and labour were dominated by the Communists, with the doctrinaire Marxist Mr. Pedro Vuskovic at their head. Left radicals were in charge of education and defence. In agriculture, a post that was to prove of key importance, Mr. Allende placed Mr. Jacques Chonchol of the MAPU, an ultra-leftist who had broken away from the Christian Democrats, and whose handling of his office led the farmers to compose the following satirical prayer addressed to the Chinese: "We beg you to send us your plague of locusts, and in exchange we will send you our Chonchol."

The new regime showed its true colours right from the outset. It amnestied the members of MIR imprisoned or prosecuted for the extortions with violence they had committed under Mr. Frei's presidency; and on 23 January 1971 there appeared a decree authorizing the establishment of People's Courts of *iletrados* (i.e. on which "neighbours" and "trade unionists" with no legal training served as judges). Seizures of farming estates and industrial properties (*las tomas*) swelled to a veritable torrent. I shall devote a later chapter to these operations, which played a political and moral role in the Allende experiment over and above their purely economic importance. It must be made clear straight away that a *toma* is a "direct" expropriation in its crudest, most savage and most *illegal* form. A band armed with clubs and rifles forces its way onto a farm, orders the whole of the owner's family to pack their bags; pushes them out onto the road; gathers together all those who work on the farm; tells them that it is their property from now on, and sets up a banner with the words: "This property has been seized by the people." The scenario is identical in the towns for the seizure of a factory, workshop, school or plot of land, except that here the former owners do not lose their family dwelling at the same time as their livelihood.

That the Allende government had its share of responsibility for these *illegal* expropriations was proved, as we shall see in the following chapter, firstly by the orders given to the carabinieri (armed police) not to intervene, and secondly by the arrival of an official *interventor* within a few hours of the seizure, proving that the authorities were "in the know" and ready for action. The *interventor*—I use the Spanish word since there is no precise equivalent in French or English—is traditionally someone appointed by a minister, provincial governor or official agency to take over the running of a business or institution in cases where the authorities or the courts consider that public order would be endangered if it were left under its previous management. The post is similar to that of a public trustee or official receiver, except that it can be used for many other reasons than bankruptcy. In normal times the appointment of an *interventor*, and his powers, are circumscribed by a number of *legal restrictions*, but the system leaves the door open to all sorts of abuses when times are troubled and the authorities are little concerned with legal niceties, as was the case under Mr. Allende. By 1 July 1971, i.e. eight months after Mr. Allende's succession, a police report noted 339 industrial seizures, 658 takeovers of rural undertakings, 218 expropriations of urban land, and 154 seizures of schools.[1]

In the spring of 1971, at a moment when the regime was not threatened by any organized opposition, Mr. Allende launched the formation of the GAP (*Grupos de Amigos Personales*, or Groups of Personal Friends), a reassuring title concealing a more sinister reality, namely brigades of hired gunmen, heavily armed and with military training and discipline, who provided an additional guard for the President and his official residences, over and above the regular units normally responsible for this. This provocative formation was officially denounced in Parliament on 3 June 1971 by the Christian Democratic

---

[1] *El Mercurio*, 4 July 1971.

group, but the only response of the government was a contemptuous "That's how it is".

Five days later, public opinion was deeply shocked by the assassination of Mr. Eduardo Frei's ex-vice-president, Mr. Edmundo Perez Zujovic, who had publicly expressed his regret that his party had brought Mr. Allende to power. On 16 June the left-wing organizer of the murder, Salazar, feeling that his arrest was imminent, committed suicide by launching a frenzied assault on police headquarters and killing three men before blowing himself up with a grenade. Feeling ran high, and affected even the ranks of the Socialists. One socialist deputy, in a violent revulsion of feeling, publicly condemned the arming of such paramilitary groups and the insolence with which they defied the law. He was heaped with abuse by the socialist press and expelled from the party.

The year 1971 saw the outbreak of the first anti-Allende strike, launched by the fishermen as a protest against the incompetent *interventor* who had been foisted on them on a trumped-up pretext, the real reason being that they had voted for the wrong candidates in the April municipal elections. A parallel phenomenon in 1971 was the homeric resistance of the great paper-mill *La Papelera* to all Mr. Allende's attempts to nationalize it, a resistance that I shall describe later, one striking feature of which was the backing it received from the entire work-force.

Despite these first harbingers of opposition, the year 1971 was on the whole a honeymoon period for the republic and Mr. Allende. Outbursts of anger aroused by the *tomas* remained localized in their remote country districts, and the expropriated owners did not manage to arouse any widespread indignation among the public as a whole. The underlying reason for this general acceptance of the new regime was this: the latter was distributing "sweeteners" right and left with careless extravagance. The workers were the most favoured, receiving pay rises that reached 50% in a year in the public services, in addition to countless bonuses. But all social classes came in for their share, big or little, in this shower of manna from heaven! Many borrowers saw their debt-burden reduced substantially. Local government authorities who had been waiting years for equipment suddenly saw it arrive, brand-new, and often bought abroad. The trade unions were moved to luxurious new premises. And so on, and so forth.

The Chileans, witty as ever, christened 1971 "the year of presents". In fact, all this largesse was financed partly by printing more money, partly by draining off financial reserves built up by previous governments. It was thus a typical case of extravagant wastefulness, born of a mixture of political demagoguery and childishly over-simplified economics, as is so common with socialist governments. These extravagances were eating into the country's substance, and in the long run would ruin it. But in the short term, or so Mr. Allende thought, they served to show what a good friend to the people he was. At the back of his mind he had one very precise calculation: if he could win enough "cupboard love" from the electorate, he would have a good chance of winning a plebiscite in favour of a constitutional reform which would free his government from the restraints imposed on it by his lack of a majority in Parliament. Mr. Allende intended to use the municipal elections due in April 1971 to sound out the public's readiness for such a move, and the UP redoubled its propaganda and poured money into the election campaign with this end in view.

But the elections were not in fact decisive. They gave the UP lists roughly 47% of the votes. This was a considerable increase when compared to the 36% they had won nine months earlier in the *presidential* elections, and showed that the flood of "presents" had not been entirely without effect. But the gain was less than Mr. Allende had hoped for; compared with the preceding *municipal* elections, the figure had increased by only 3%. The 50% threshold had not been crossed. The majority in the country was still clearly hostile to Marxism. Mr. Allende, therefore, abandoned his plan for amending the constitution.

The extremists of the UP drew the conclusion that they had nothing to gain from "the peaceful path to Socialism", and that they should bypass it by proceeding to revolutionary methods. To bring their leader round to their viewpoint, these extremists invited to Chile the Grand Panjandrum himself, the symbol and supreme architect of violent revolution in Latin America, Fidel Castro in person. The latter was not slow to respond, bringing a large suite with him, and his visit brought the "year of the presents" to a close in a display of ostentatious pageantry rare in the history of state visits.

The very length of the visit was unseemly, to start with: it lasted 25 days, from 10 November to 4 December 1971. In addition, the UP authorities displayed an excessive servility towards Castro. During most of the demonstrations that marked his visit, the national flag was noticeable by its absence—it was not even borne by the troops during military parades—and the Cuban flag alone was flown. School children had to learn the Cuban national anthem, which was often the only one to be sung, unaccompanied by the Chilean anthem. In short, although the visit was in reality on the level of, say, a tour of inspection of local bases by a commanding general, it was carried out with quite exaggerated solemnity.

Cuba had set up its embassy in a luxurious mansion in the ultra-smart Providencia neighbourhood of Santiago, which buzzed with the activities of a staff of more than 200 officials (five times that of the

French embassy in Washington). Parties and sumptuous banquets followed one another at the very moment when the country was undergoing its first period of food shortages due to the fall in agricultural production. But above all, Fidel Castro interfered in everything; handed out directives before cabinet meetings; took part in meetings of the government, and delivered inflammatory speeches on Chilean internal politics at mass meetings. Such conduct had never been seen before from a foreign head of state.

The effect was quite the opposite of the intended one. Even UP supporters were shocked. The law students had occupied their faculty building as a protest against Mr. Allende. This affront to their sensitive national pride, this affront against common decency itself, infuriated a new section of society, which now began to detest the new regime, and whose clearsightedness, militancy and courage would prove to be the great discovery of the Mr. Allende period, and an eye-opener to the whole world. I speak of the women.

2 December 1971 will remain a red-letter day in the political history of their sex. Conceiving and preparing their action in the utmost secrecy (no one in political circles had the slightest inkling of what was up), all of a sudden, like a bud that has flowered in a single night, tens of thousands of women came out onto the streets, each carrying two saucepans and clashing them together to make the point that they were empty, for, as I have just recalled, the country was for the first time suffering a food shortage due purely to political reasons. I shall return to this extraordinary event later. For the moment, my purpose is merely to give a rapid chronological summary of the events that marked the reign of the UP, and I shall report the most immediate and striking result of the "saucepan march": two days later, Fidel Castro left the country. As to its more profound consequences, these can be summed up in few words, but which are heavy as fate itself: from that day on the spell was broken. A gaping crack had yawned in the side of the regime, and this crack was to widen progressively until the whole edifice collapsed.

1972: the year of plunder

Unlike 1971, 1972 was soon to be marked by more and more frequent crises and misfortunes. In January, came the first important clash between Mr. Allende and Parliament: the latter invoked its special powers to remove three ministers from office for abuse of their authority, and Mr. Allende promptly gave them fresh portfolios. In February, the campaign against the *La Papelera* paper-mills resumed, and now became nation-wide in scale. At the beginning of March the "Cuban crates scandal" burst on the public; dropped from planes, these crates had been seized by the Customs. Mr. Allende passed them off as personal gifts for himself, but they were proved to contain arms. On 15 March the first report on copper production at Chuquicamata revealed a drop of 50% in six months. March also saw a rash of sanguinary *tomas* in the countryside, and the first appearance of that social scourge, the black market. Finally, on 29 March, as a result of the considerable drop in agricultural production, the JAP (not to be confused with the GAP to which we have already referred) were set up. These JAP (*Juntas de Abastecimientos y Precios*) set about the control of prices and the distribution of food in a highly discriminatory way, and soon became very unpopular. I shall examine in a later chapter the sinister role they played as a political police, coercing the people through their stomachs. The month of March 1972, was a real turning-point during which the whole situation in Chile darkened from grey to black. It culminated in another dramatic indication of how serious the position had become: *in one month* inflation had passed 20%.

There is a hallowed tradition in Greek tragedy according to which the more the ground gives way beneath them, the harder do the characters try to break through it. Likewise, seeing things going from bad to worse, the organisations of the UP, far from sobering down and coming to their senses, only grew more rigidly uncompromising. In April, the most radical among them met at Concepcion to create a "People's Assembly" which saw itself as taking the place of Congress, since, as they loudly proclaimed, the "deep-rooted legitimacy of class" had priority over the "purely formal legitimacy of the ballot paper". At the same time the corruption prevalent among the leading members of the UP (about which murmurs of disapproval had been circulating for months) was made public in all its flagrancy by the disclosure of incontrovertible proofs. It was revealed that Ms. Miria Contreras Bell de Ropert, nicknamed La Payita, Allende's private secretary (private indeed, since she was also his mistress!) possessed 25 cars, and that his sister had bought the super-luxury residence of Canaveral, where Mr. Allende spent his week-ends, and which La Payita was to buy from her in 1973. You can imagine the effect of this on a population whose living conditions were growing daily more difficult.

In May, came the first big anti-UP strike of the copper miners of Chuquicamata, who issued the following declaration, a totally heretical one from the viewpoint of orthodox Marxism-Leninism: "We want to take copper out of the hands of the Communists and give it back to the Chileans."

Faced with this yawning rift in the central dogma that the UP was itself the embodiment of the working class (a rift that hurt them far more than the country's worsening economic situation), the UP leaders grew alarmed, and met at Lo Curro with a view to putting a damper on the more flagrant excesses of their own extremists. These reacted by transforming the working-class suburbs and *poblaciones* (shanty-towns) around Santiago into fortified revolutionary strongholds, actual totalitarian mini-states within the national state, led by guerilla leaders who at the end of August unleashed riots in the course of which a corporal of carabineers, Aroca Cuevas, was brutally murdered. Popular feeling ran high. Public order was breaking down. The temperature was rising.

8 October 1972—the second important date in the development of popular opposition to the UP after that of the "saucepans"—saw the outbreak of the first great strike of the lorry-owners, and their example was swiftly followed by all the middle classes, artisans, shopkeepers and members of the liberal professions. This epic resistance was highlighted by the proclamation of the *Pliego de Chile* (Roll of Chile, using the word in the sense of the parchment rolls of the Middle Ages), which was to play a somewhat similar role to that of the Tennis Court Oath in France in 1789, though with the difference that instead of being directed by the people's representatives against a King, the Chilean text was aimed by representatives of the people against a government which claimed to identify itself with the people. On 24 October, as though in mourning, the whole country was but one immense unending demonstration of folded arms, in unanimous solidarity with the hundreds of thousands of men on strike.

The blow to the regime was a serious one. Shaken, Mr. Allende appealed to the army, and three generals, including the chief of staff, Major-general Prats, agreed to join the UP government on 2 November 1972, thus saving it and showing at the same time how unfounded was the charge of being "fascists" which was to be levelled against them a year later, when the country had come to the edge of the abyss and they finally toppled Mr. Allende. On the contrary, General Prats gave all the signs of being an ambitious opportunist, ready to ingratiate himself with his leftist masters. His presence in the government, however, had a calming effect, though this did not extend to the indomitable women of Chile who, on 2 December, the first anniversary of their famous march, inaugurated a new tactic, still using their saucepans. From now on they stayed at home, but in response to an agreed signal passed on at dizzying speed, all the housewives in a neighbourhood, their windows open, would begin to bang their saucepans, making a deafening din that echoed despairingly from yard to yard, street to street and from one neighbourhood to the next, as a reminder to the authorities that the children were hungry.

Despite all this, a certain calm was restored, underwritten by the military, who on 21 October 1972 insisted on the passing of a law for weapon control because of the great increase in murders and the growth of paramilitary groups. But the economic situation and the state of public confidence continued to deteriorate. On 13 December 1972 Mr. Allende, who had been to the USSR to beg them for fresh economic assistance, returned home with empty hands.

1973: The Year of Chaos

On 10 January 1973 Mr. Allende was forced to introduce rationing by the unpopular and rather absurd system of the "little people's basket", about which I shall speak later. The MAPU minister of finance brought in 12 draconian measures to tighten up the "dictatorship through people's stomachs" and to strengthen the police function of the JAPs. The second copper strike at Chuquicamata broke out on 16 January. On 10 February a resounding warning shot was fired across the UP's bows when the left-wing trade union federation CUT (a Chilean equivalent of the French CGT) suffered a stinging defeat at the hands of the miners in union elections. On 28 February a secret report of the MAPU was leaked, and proved among other things that leading activists of the UP were dividing their time between the black market and the feverish organization of paramilitary groups.

18 March 1973 saw an important trial of strength in the general election to the legislature. At first sight the result looked like a modest gain for the UP, since its share of the vote rose to 43%. However, Congress still contained a majority of 57% resolutely hostile to the UP. Moreover, an enquiry carried out by the Catholic University soon showed that the government had organized an enormous electoral fraud, the mechanics of which I will describe in detail later. All the opposition parties were indignant and challenged the results. The test was thus not very conclusive.

It proved, however, reassuring enough to the doctrinaires of the UP to embolden them to commit a really gross blunder. On 22 March Mr. Allende laid it down, by decree and without any parliamentary debate, that all schools in Chile should be merged into a single network controlled by the state, in which all pupils would receive compulsory training in Marxism. This outrageous affront to the feelings of a Catholic country, solidly attached to pluralism and free choice, soon aroused bitter resistance, initiated once again by the women but soon joined by all sections of society, young and old, bourgeois and workers, students and parents. The struggle against the ENU (*Escuela Nacional Unificada*—United National School) was to become one of the major episodes in the epic story of the Chilean people. From that moment on, the pace of events began to speed up.

On 27 March the military, scandalized by the decree on the ENU, left the government which was forced to give up the project at the beginning of June. 19 April saw the great strike of the miners of the *El Teniente* copper-mines, which kept the whole country at fever-pitch for a month, and during which the proletariat found itself facing the tanks of the very government that claimed to represent its interests. On 14 June the Supreme Court, in a solemn statement, declared the Allende government guilty of a great number of glaring breaches of legality, and that its abuses of power amounted to open violations of the Constitution, and that consequently it was now no longer legitimate.

On 26 June a preposterously absurd incident occurred that was to have unexpected repercussions. Driving past him in her car, a lady put out her tongue at General Prats, who was showing signs of renewing his flirtation with the UP government. The general replied by shooting at her car and treating her with a brutality that aroused the indignation of the public and of the general staff. The stock of the men in power fell even lower.

On 29 June Major Souper made a premature and hopeless attempt to seize the Moneda palace, the presidential residence, only to fail disastrously. In reaction, the MIR, from their strongholds in the Santiago industrial belt, unleashed bloody rioting, and from that moment onwards the streets were never free of violence, which intensified day by day.

In July, President Allende's naval aide-de-camp, Captain Ayala, was assassinated.

25 July saw the outbreak of the second big strike of the lorry-owners, who had seen Mr. Allende break, one by one, all the promises he had made in order to settle their first strike of the previous year. Chaos was spreading rapidly, and the food-shortage was growing worse, resulting from now on in the famous queues in which Chileans were obliged to stand, hour after hour, day and even night, so as to get enough to eat for the next 24 hours, an experience that was to leave an indelible mark on a whole generation. A black joke went the rounds: the queues, it was said, were a sign that the march towards Socialism would progress in Indian file.

During the first fortnight of August, the Christian Democrats tried to bring Mr. Allende to his senses by "last-chance conversations", but these failed. At the same time, and in the same hope of reaching an ultimate peaceful solution, four military leaders in General Prats' circle rejoined the government, but resigned from it once again 12 days later when, on 21 August, Congress endorsed with its own authority all the criticisms made by the Supreme Court in June, and in its turn declared the UP government to be *illegitimate*, drawing attention to the many and cynical violations of the engagements it had made in the *Statute of Guarantees* thanks to which it had been able to come to power.

Three days later, on 24 August, Mr. Allende proclaimed that he was going to establish the direct power of the people, setting this above mere legality. On 28 August the navy uncovered a plot to infiltrate its ranks and kill its officers. On 3 September the leader of the Socialist Party, Mr. Altamirano, convicted of being the author of this plot, replied by a violent and frenzied speech in which he threatened the immediate use of force to put an end to the established order and "the apes who are defending it". The capital was permanently filled with the acrid smoke of fires, tear-gas, and the explosions of plastic bombs, and echoed with the gunfire of the paramilitary groups, who now numbered 15,000 men. On 8 September, when inflation had reached the rate of 1,000% per annum, Mr. Allende announced on television that there was only three days supply of bread left. People scattered grains of corn in front of officers in the streets, as a way of telling them they were acting like chicken-hearted cowards.

On 11 September 1973, in response to the urgent and unanimous appeal of the people for them to halt the imminent collapse of the country into totalitarian Communism, economic bankruptcy and famine, the army occupied the Moneda palace, inside which Mr. Allende committed suicide.

CHAPTER IV

THE POLITICAL ROT SETS IN—LEGALITY FLOUTED

If we want to understand why the Popular Unity government flouted the law and parliament, we must bear in mind that throughout its term of office, it was a minority government. In the presidential elections of September 1970 it won only 36% of the votes; in the municipal elections of April 1971 it gained 47%, and won 44% in the parliamentary elections of March 1973.

However in addition, the percentage figures it won in 1971 and 1973 were swollen by widespread electoral malpractices, which were the subject of an investigation carried out by a body of unimpeachable authority: the Catholic University of Chile. This set up a commission composed of professors and lecturers of the Institute of Political Studies and of the School of Law, under the chairmanship of the Dean of the latter School, Mr. Jaime del Valle. In a speech broadcast on radio and television on 17 July 1973, Mr. del Valle exposed the different types of fraud that his commission had brought to light:

—Impersonation of living electors.

—Impersonation of deceased electors whose names had not been removed from the electoral register.

—Entry of the same person twice on the register, as literate and illiterate.

—Entry of the same person on the registers of more than one constituency or ward.

One could see lorries going from one polling station to another carrying electors who thus voted two, three or four times. An official of the UP had provided them with forged identity cards. A number of these were found by the investigators to bear serial numbers above the figure of eight million, whereas the official number of holders of such cards is considerably below that figure.

Moreover, at certain polling stations in districts where the majority of voters were known to be anti-Allende, it was deliberately made difficult for these to exercise their right to vote by forming long queues of Mr. Allende's supporters who had already voted. This ruse was chiefly intended to discourage the women, who had more than once made plain their hostility to the UP, and who are usually burdened by their household duties or tired out by pregnancy or a child in arms. In remote spots, polling stations were set up in the absence of any accredited representative of the opposition. Some of these malpractices could clearly not have been perpetrated without the complicity of UP officials. What is more, for the first time in Chilean history, the results were not published until the evening of the day following the election. This unwonted delay inevitably gave rise to the suspicion that some of the ballot boxes had been secretly tampered with.

In a large number of constituencies the percentage in favour of the UP had increased by 40% in two and a half years, a rather unlikely figure. Districts as unsuited to human habitation as that of the O'Higgins *Park* in Santiago had, during that same period, registered a population explosion of incredible magnitude; the electoral roll of the latter area, for example, had risen in two and a half years from 1,830 to 3,910 voters. The addresses given by the new inhabitants were checked, and it was found that several hundreds of them corresponded to avenues in the park where there were no houses—truly a striking example of enthusiasm for ecology! Other addresses proved just not to exist at all. Very many electoral registers were found to contain deletions, words over-written and other alterations that had clearly not been made by the proper officials, and whose purpose was to enable foreigners to vote in the place of a Chilean national. Identical right-hand thumb-prints were frequently found in two different polling stations.

So barefaced were these malpractices that Dean Jaime del Valle exclaimed in disgust: "Chileans, our nation has been the victim of a vile infamy". And he demanded "fresh, honest and free elections". Senator Francisco Bulnes described the fraud as "one of the most shameful things ever to have occurred in the political life of this country".

A first estimate by the commission assessed the number of fraudulent votes cast at the election of March 1973 at 200,000, or 6% of the total poll.[1] The Chamber of Deputies set up its own investigative body which gathered additional evidence of irregularities, bringing the estimated total of falsified votes to 300,000, that is, 9% of the total poll.

To these direct frauds we must add the effect of the illegal pressure brought to bear on electors by the UP through its discriminatory distribution of housing, jobs and food. The free choice of the electors was further distorted by the flood of slander, insults and damaging innuendo that the UP heaped on its political opponents, a campaign of vilification without parallel in the history of Chile. For example, a photo in the left-wing paper *Clarin* showed the leader of the Nationalist

[1] *El Mercurio* 17 July 1973.

Party, Mr. Sergio Onofre Jarpa, as a naked prostitute with the swastika around his neck. An equally despicable campaign was mounted by the Communist paper *Puro Chile* to destroy the image of ex-president Frei, making him out to be a tool of Washington, and to besmirch his Christian-Democratic Party, although it had been instrumental in bringing the UP to power, and had carried out numerous reforms prior to 1970, by dubbing it "the party of reaction".

Senator Francisco Bulnes concluded: "There is every reason to think that had it not been for this colossal fraud, the UP would not have reached a third of the parliamentary vote. And if our democratic opposition had held two thirds of the seats in parliament, we should have been in a position to remove President Allende from office".

Victory! The people, 43% of the votes; the mummies, 55%.

One wonders why the UP went to the trouble of committing all these electoral frauds since in any case, for Marxist-Leninists like them, 55% of the votes do not constitute a majority if it is the opposition that wins them. On 6 March 1973 the communist paper*Puro Chile* headlined the UP victory in these terms: "The people, 43% of the votes; the mummies, 55%, applying the contemptuous epithet "mummies" (in the sense of "hidebound reactionaries") indiscriminately to all sectors of society hostile to the UP, from the big landowners, through the anti-Marxist students to the striking lorry-owners, the miners who had "downed tools" and the shopkeepers who had put up their shutters.

The UP had been relatively successful in the 1971 municipal elections. This was because of the largesse, in the form of social advantages and increased wages, that Mr. Allende had scattered so widely at the beginning of his reign, by printing extra money and squandering all the country's monetary reserves. The people had thus been lulled into a comforting illusion of affluence. It was only after these elections that the disastrous results of this lunatic demagogeury began to be felt, and with some severity. From this moment the popularity of the UP fell sharply, and the only means Mr. Allende still had to hang on to power were those of illegality, extortion, intimidation, censorship, fraud, threats and brute force. He now brought all of these into play, using them systematically, astutely and with cool self-possession.

"Resquicios legales"—"Legal expedients"

Thanks to the expertise of his principal legal advisers, Mr. Eduardo Novoa and, especially, Mr. José Antonio Viera Gallo of the MAPU, who, as under-secretary of Justice, constituted the real inspiration, the

Machiavellian brain of that ministry behind the various titular holders of the office, Mr. Allende could always find "good" legal justifications for governing in a thoroughly illegal way. He outdid the heroes of Courteline's novels in the art of "using the law to circumvent the law".

One of the tricks his government resorted to in this travesty of legality was that of the *resquicios legales* (the term literally means "legal expedients"). These had been instituted in 1932 by a decree (no. 502) enacted during the hundred days of a short-lived socialist republic; they laid down that privately-owned enterprises whose *products* were *vital* to the nation, and *the production of which might fall dangerously low* as a result of *serious shortcomings* on the part of their management, could be *temporarily intervenidas*, that is, put under the control of a government official. I have carefully emphasized above all the restrictions governing the application of this decree, which had moreover long become a dead letter. In reviving it Mr. Allende completely ignored these restrictions. He transformed a measure intended purely as an emergency expedient into a permanent method for expropriating business enterprises and ruining their owners. Thus he declared, quite arbitrarily, that the products of the firms he wanted to nationalize were *vital* to the nation. With diabolical ruthlessness he would engineer a catastrophic fall in production in such businesses, paralyzing them by fomenting conflict between management and the trade union, or by instigating an actual takeover of the plant by a small group of agitators loyal to himself. Other methods involved cutting off supplies of raw materials (controlled, of course, by the government), or by denying such firms any financial credit, a simple matter since he had nationalized all the banks.

Mr. Allende made frequent use of the technique of unearthing, from among the 17,000 or so laws and decrees passed during the Chilean republic's 150 years of existence, obscure enactments which had lain forgotten for decades, or which were intended to apply to quite different circumstances, and applying them to the furtherance of his Leninist aims, even in cases where their application violated other, more recent laws. Another of his tricks was to enforce just those sections of a law which served the purposes of the UP while leaving the rest of its provisions in abeyance. Yet another device consisted in discriminating between supporters and opponents of the UP in the application of a law.

Nor must we forget the free rein given to the so-called "People's *Non-expert* Tribunals", i.e. improvised courts having no legal expertise, who handed down judgements without paying any attention to the laws on the statute book, on the basis of entirely new juridical principles of purely Bolshevik or Nazi inspiration, such as the one making it possible to punish any one guilty of acts hostile to "the sound feelings of the people": a principle destructive of all that has been gained in 20 centuries of legal progress.

Emergency Decrees

After a period during which stupefaction at this parody of legality inhibited any move to counter it, the courts and the *Contraloria* of the Republic reacted strongly, publicly condemning this wrongful use of "legal expedients". The *Contraloria*, or Office of the Auditor-General, had been set up in 1927, originally in order to act as a watch-dog over the state's financial transactions, but had subsequently acquired wider powers, including that of ruling as to the legality of the government's administrative acts. The distinguished holder of the office of Auditor-General under Mr. Allende, Mr. Héctor Humeres, an austere and honourable personality respected by all, made every effort to uphold the independence of his office, blocked the illegal expropriations as long as he could, and stood up to the regime with remarkable courage.

On at least 30 occasions Mr. Allende overruled the objections of the *Contraloria* by using another of his ploys—the so-called *decretos de insistencia* or emergency decrees, which had to be signed by the president and all the government ministers. Introduced by their legislator as a purely *exceptional* and *interim* measure, only to be used in *serious emergencies*, such as catastrophes, war, earthquake, etc., these decrees were converted by the UP into a regular and permanent instrument of government, enabling them to flout all checks and controls.

But it is also possible to interpret the regular use of these decrees as a tacit admission that the Marxist-Leninist revolution in fact falls into the category of "catastrophes" for which these emergency instruments were designed in the first place.

Courts and Parliament flouted

When he realized that no one was taken in any longer by his quasi-legal sharp practice, Mr. Allende's reaction was to treat with contempt the state's supreme legal institutions and just not carry out any of their rulings that ran counter to his own plans. He was thus violating both the laws themselves and the principle of the separation of powers. Like the king of beasts in an Aesop fable, the president arrogated to himself the right to decide which judgements of the courts were to be applied and which were not.

Our left-wing friends appear to think that because he gained power as a result of a free election, Mr. Allende could from then on do whatever he liked. Despite their claim to be democrats, the idea that a head of state is just as bound to respect laws as the least of his subjects is alien to their thinking or at the very least, they can conceive of it as applying to a Nixon but not to an Allende.

This is an example of pure duplicity. In left-wing thinking, law in a bourgeois regime must derive from the people, whereas in a Marxist regime it must derive from the public authorities. In fact, in both cases, the source of law turns out to be the Marxist parties; it is they who manipulate the people in a bourgeois regime, and they who have a monopoly of power in a Marxist one. Here we come up against the revealing fact that Marxists are incapable of understanding the concept of *law*. Like primitive men, they confuse this with their own will: "What I want is obvious, and hence legitimate, and hence mandatory". This is the principle underlying all dictatorships.

He treated with equal contempt the measures adopted by the national Congress to counter his constant breaches of legality as head of state. Parliament dismissed high-ranking officials and ministers for breaking the law too flagrantly. Mr. Allende immediately gave them other posts of equal or even greater importance, and thus evaded and defied the sanction built into the Constitution. For example, in 1972 Congress removed the Minister of the Interior, Mr. José Toha, from office "for taking no action against armed bands, violating peasants' rights of free assembly and discriminating against independent communications media". Mr. Allende immediately appointed him Minister of Defence. In December of the same year, by 75 votes to 42, the Chamber of Deputies dismissed the Minister of Finance, Mr. Orlando Millas, "for carrying out illegal reprisals against workers on strike" and "using methods inconsistent with our legal system". Mr. Allende straight away made him Minister for Economic Affairs.

A judge of the Court of Appeal, Mr. Enrique Paillas, declared the *Intendente* of Santiago, Mr. Alfredo Joignant, guilty of an offence under article 253 of the Penal Code, which deals with a refusal to co-operate with a properly constituted authority. Parliament voted in favour of bringing a charge of unconstitutional conduct against Mr Alfredo Joignant, and dismissed him from his post as *Intendente* (the chief representative of state authority in a province or large city, the rough equivalent of the Prefect of a French *département*). Mr. Allende retorted by appointing him head of the Criminal Investigation branch of the police—nothing less than a slap in the face for Parliament and the bench of judges.

The Chamber of Deputies dismissed from office the Minister of the Interior, Mr. Hernan del Canto, for his fraudulent action in the matter of the crates of arms from Cuba, of which I shall have more to say in a later chapter. The UP reacted by mounting a stormy mass-meeting in the square outside the central law courts and the parliament building. Until then permission had never been given for large crowds to gather in this square, out of respect for these two leading national institutions. On this occasion it was Mr. Allende himself who gave the necessary permission. The scene on 12 July 1972 was one of mindless vulgarity. Helmeted and armed bands, waving red flags, bellowed: "Traitor judges, thieving judges, bribed judges!" A speaker of the MIR, Mr. Ciro Hermosilla, cried: "We must unite to destroy the strongholds of the reactionaries (literally "mummies"), those of Parliament and bourgeois justice. We warn the swine in Parliament that they will have to answer for their acts to the people. We warn the old fossils of the Supreme Court that their days are numbered, and that they will be the first to be dragged before our People's Courts".

The Minister of the Interior who had been condemned and stripped of his office strutted in the midst of the mob, denouncing "the old gaffers of the bourgeoisie and reaction". The demonstration reached its climax when the crowd stoned the Law Courts building and marched to the Mint, where the dismissed *Intendente* of Santiago, perched on a vehicle, harangued the demonstrators in language even more loutish than that of his leader.

One now begins to understand the reason for the constant chopping and changing of ministers under Mr. Allende. Any minister who was removed from office for illegal actions was immediately rewarded by a new portfolio. But ministries also changed hands as a result of behind-the-scenes demands by the various rival groups within the UP as they jockeyed for power inside the coalition. During the three years of UP government each ministry was headed by between six and eight different ministers. This *ministerial instability*, in a Marxist-Leninist regime considered to be "tough but pure", outdid the worst examples of frequent cabinet changes in our democratic regimes—heads fell faster than coconuts at a fairground! One Minister of Agriculture, the socialist Mr. Ernesto Torrealba, held his office for precisely nine days! There was a whole cabinet that lasted for only 18 days!

These continual violations of the rule of law reached their culmination when the president *refused to promulgate*, although it was his plain constitutional duty to do so, a reform of that same Constitution approved by a joint session of the parliament and senate, namely the fundamental law of the "three sectors" in the economy, a project of paramount interest to all Chileans. Mr. Allende, who boasted so proudly of his love of democracy, had a very simple and legal means of getting this constitutional reform set aside, had he cared to use it, namely a referendum. He had merely to let the people have the last word in the matter. Of course, he took very good care not to do this, knowing full well that the people would vote against him. He preferred simply to block the reform, acting in the spirit of Louis XIV and Lenin: "The state is myself".

The media of the outside world have given a completely false picture of Mr. Allende. They have presented him, not as he really was, that is, a cunning politician, greedy for power and prepared to use anti-democratic means to hang on to it, but as a great-hearted social reformer who respected legality. Naturally, to fit in with this picture, all those who opposed him had, by definition, to be subversives, fascists, supporters of monopoly capital and the big landed estates. In reality they were plundered citizens, censored journalists, expropriated small haulage contractors, underfed housewives and miners in revolt, as we shall see in a later chapter. In short, the celebrated "Chilean democratic road to Socialism" was solely for foreign consumption. The day-to-day reality of life inside Chile was that Mr. Allende was busy adopting the practices and abuses of an embryonic communist regime.

All shades of opinion within the UP, and not just Mr. Allende, practised fraud, underhand trickery and illegality. Here is an example. The MIR, or Movement of the Revolutionary Left, a paramilitary formation whose members Mr. Allende had indulgently described as "young idealists", had forged a whole arsenal of *false official stamps*, thus enabling it to counterfeit a wide range of documents. The *White Book* reproduced photographs of a score of these, found in the offices of the MIR. Among them was the stamp of the Central Bank of Chile, enabling the group to carry out profitable financial deals; that of the Public Registrar's office, making it possible to forge false identity documents, that of the CID, thanks to which it could carry out bogus police operations, that of the Commander-in-chief, enabling it to carry out espionage in the offices of the armed forces, etc.

As for the Chilean Communist Party, it demanded that the Allende government should carry out "a massive purge of all those guilty state officials who think it is their duty to enforce bourgeois laws"[1]. A strange way indeed of following a legal path towards Socialism!

Parallel Government

It was not merely the people's elected assemblies and the courts charged with applying the laws that Mr. Allende was thus disregarding. Even inside his own government, like the good Bolshevik he had become, he acted in just as totalitarian a fashion, not informing some of his own colleagures of the measures he intended to implement. Thus the three service minister, Admiral Ismael Huerta, Generals Prats and

[1] See Juraj Domic's book, *Fundamentos de la Praxis Marxista-Leninista en Chile*, published by Vaitea, 1978.

Sepulveda, who joined his Cabinet in November 1972, were not consulted over his draconian and thoroughly unpopular rationing regulations and his creation of the JAP agencies. These three ministers learned the news the next day *through the press*, and in particular from the socialist paper *Ultima Hora*, in which the new measure was presented pictorially in a truly "democratic" manner by a cartoon in which the Minister of Finance, Mr. Fernando Flores, expressed his delight that thanks to his new rationing system "the poor will eat well, and the rich will eat shit". It can be seen that under the UP, language, even as used by, or attributed to, government ministers, had reached new heights of scatological coarseness.

One can understand the shock this was to a distinguished sailor of Admiral Huerta's calibre. He did not feel it possible to continue to hold a post of responsibility in a government which did not consult him, and which discriminated with such cynicism between two classes of citizens, offering such unsavoury fare to one of them. He, therefore, resigned. When I visited him in Valparaiso, he told me that this had not been the first time Mr. Allende had treated members of his government with such humiliating and offhanded discourtesy. The important decisions were not taken at cabinet meetings, but in an "Economic Committee" comprising only a small chosen group of ministers, and which held its meetings not at the cabinet offices but at a variety of other venues. Just as there were two classes of citizens, there were two classes of ministers, the real ones and the mere figure heads. The UP was employing here the well-known technique of the inner circle, one applied by Communists within all the movements they infiltrate: secret caucuses who make all the important decisions in closed meeting before the official meetings of the movement take place, the latter being held merely to ratify decisions already taken by the controlling clique.

Since Mr. Allende had ignored the warnings of Parliament and made a mockery of the sanctions of the courts, Chile's legislative and judicial authorities had no alternative but to proclaim solemnly *that the executive had put itself outside the laws and the Constitution.* This was indeed done, first by the Supreme Court of Justice, the highest legal institution in the land, on 26 May and 25 June 1973; then by the Office of the Auditor-General of the Republic on 2 July 1973, and finally by Parliament on 22 August. Their judgements were couched in dignified but uncompromising terms. The declaration of Congress stated that "the UP government was responsible not only for isolated violations of the law and the Constitution, but had built these violations into a permanent system of government ... with the deliberate and self-confessed aim of changing the country's structures ... without paying the slightest heed to the will of the legislature".

It is clear from all this that I have not exaggerated in calling this chapter "Legality Flouted".

CHAPTER V

VIOLATIONS OF FREEDOM OF EXPRESSION

IN ALL DEMOCRATIC COUNTRIES, freedom of expression is a fundamental right, guaranteed to all citizens by the constitution itself. In Mr. Allende's Chile, this right was backed in fact by three safeguards: the Chilean Constitution which the UP inherited, the programme of the UP, which specifically guaranteed to all Chileans "the freedoms of conscience, speech, press and assembly, the right to form organizations, the inviolability of private dwellings, etc.", and the *Statute of Guarantees*, in which Mr. Allende solemnly promised in Congress on 22 October 1970 "to respect this freedom of expression . . . as morally binding, a duty I owe to my own conscience and to history itself".

In this chapter, we shall see what Mr. Allende's conscience and the history of the UP made of an oath so movingly expressed.

The Statute of Guarantees violated

One clause of this Statute laid it down that all political parties should have free access to all communications media controlled by the government of the UP (article 9.4.). This did not prevent the UP from devoting channel 7 of state TV almost exclusively to Marxist propaganda, and in August 1972 suppressing the sole programme on that channel 7, *A Tres Brandas*, which once a week gave the opposition—a representative either of the National or Christian Democratic Party—an opportunity to debate on current political questions with a representative of the UP. Finally, on 30 August 1972, the Chamber of Deputies was forced to make a strong protest against the high-handed action of the President of the Republic.

The Statute of Guarantees assured the right of reply to anyone who had been criticized in the press, on radio or TV. Yet ex-president Frei and the rector of the University of Chile, Mr. Edgardo Boeninger, were constantly denied the possibility of replying to the vicious attacks made on them by state TV.

The same Statute also guarantees the freedom to broadcast radio programmes without prior censorship (article 10.3.). Despite this, during the strike wave of October 1972, all non-government radio stations were forced to transmit, solely and interminably, the broadcasts put out by the official agency OIR (*Oficina de Informaciones y Radiodifusion de la Presidencia de la Republica*, or Presidential News and Radio Office).

Also guaranteed by the Statute was the free importation and sale of paper, spare parts and other equipment necessary for the communications media (art. 10.3.). This clause, like all the others, was trampled on. The CORFO (*Corporación de Fomento de la Producción*, or Industrial Development Agency, a nationalized body) created an import and distribution monopoly in broadcasting equipment and spare parts. And the state-controlled Central Bank refused the TV channel 13, belonging to the Catholic University, the foreign currency it needed to buy materials essential for its broadcasts.

In the last analysis, we should not be surprised at all at these violations of freedom of expression by the UP. It is, after all, in the very nature of Marxism-Leninism to gag all opposition. What is surprising is the total gullibility of the Christian Democrats, who had managed to persuade themselves that once the UP was in power it would respect the right of others to criticize its actions. Clearly the Christian Democrats had learned nothing from the experience of the USSR, Cuba and a score of other regimes of the same type; had read nothing of Marx and Lenin, and had heard and seen nothing of how "Socialism" had been brought in by united fronts of Socialists and Communists. One wonders in what century and on what planet they had been living.

Yet, only a few months after being brought to power by the naïvety of the Christian Democrat deputies, the Chilean Socialists and Communists gave a public demonstration of what freedom of the press meant to them. During the Meeting of Left-wing Journalists held in Santiago as early as April 1971, the chairman of the organizing committee, Mr. Manuel Cabieses, director of the extremist review *Punto Final*, stated that "the journalist's fundamental duty is to commit himself to the class-struggle". The final resolution—passed unanimously, as was only proper—declared that "*objectivity in journalism does not exist* ... for a journalist, objectivity consists in identifying himself with the revolutionary historical process". Whereupon the Communist Party, applying a tried and proven tactic, launched an uninterrupted campaign against the opposition media, accusing them of being "fascist" and demanding that the government take steps against them. One communist leader even went so far as to proclaim on 12 June 1973, "We shall invade Santiago. We shall mobilize all the workers to demand the closing down of all the mass media still in the hands of the right".[1]

An authoritative and detailed breakdown of the innumerable violations of freedom of expression by the UP was made by the Chamber of Deputies in number 10 of its official journal *Acuerdo* on 22 August

---

[1] *Chile Hoy*, 15 June 1973, p. 6.

1973, and this material was reproduced *in extenso* in the White Book. The same ground was covered by the lawyer and professor Mr. Tomas MacHale in three extremely well-documented studies (*La Libertad de Expresiôn en Chile*, published by Ed. Portada, 1972 and 1973). I draw on these sources for the examples that follow.

Attacks on radio and television

To stifle the voice of the opposition on radio, the UP's first move, beginning in November 1970, was to acquire gradually a score of radio stations. In areas where the proprietors refused to sell, the UP adopted the expedient of granting itself concessions to start new stations—about half a dozen. But the listeners set little store by these new stations, and stayed tuned in to the old ones, which did not churn out a constant stream of vapid Marxist-Leninist pap, and so the UP, like all dictatorships, decided to use the "right of the stronger", and proceeded to *occupy illegally* a dozen radio stations. Groups of members of MIR Socialists or Communists, broke into the premises; ejected the owners; suppressed their programmes and substituted their own merchandise. Thus on 6 June 1971 Radio Riquelme, in Coquimbo, was occupied at the instigation of a communist woman deputy, Ms. Amanda Altamirano. On 4 November 1971 Radio Presidente Balmaceda was similarly closed down at the insistence of the under-secretary of the ministry of the Interior, the communist Mr. Vergara, backed by Mr. Allende, who had constantly attacked the positions adopted by the station, which belonged to the Christian Democratic Party. A Marxist trade union organization took over its wavelength. The Christian Democratic Party, unable to conceal their shocked amazement, described the seizure as "an attack against freedom of opinion and a violation of the constitutional guarantees which Mr. Allende had solemnly given his word to observe".

There were 10 or so violent attacks on radio stations whose line did not please the UP. On 12 December 1971 Radio Alonso de Ercilla was wrecked and its transmitter and aerial destroyed. The mayor of the district of Illapel, a Socialist, had given the station's manager six days to change his political line! Radio Arica was attacked three times. UP extremists cut its power supply and hurled stink-bombs to punish it for criticizing the communist senator Luis Valente Rossi in one of its programmes.

Radio Agricultura in Santiago and its subsidiary transmitters in Valparaiso and Los Angeles exercised a great influence over public opinion, and its denunciations of the illegal expropriations and inhuman treatment meted out to opponents in the countryside by the UP were a considerable nuisance to the party in power. The solution was a simple one: on 21 August 1972 the main station in the capital was closed by order of the governor of Santiago, Mr. Julio Stuardo, on a charge of "broadcasting biased news-bulletins"! The Communist Party wanted to buy its Los Angeles subsidiary, but the owners had refused to sell it to them. Again the solution was simple; the station was just closed down, on 24 August, on the orders of the local representative of the government, Mr. Federico Wolff, of the Socialist Party.

Radio journalists too were the victims of violence. Radio Cooperativa was a thorn in the side of the UP. The costly equipment at its headquarters in Valdivia were destroyed on 20 October 1972 by a commando raid. On the 25th of the previous September, the commentator of this company's Temuco subsidiary, Mr. Eduardo Diaz, had been beaten up by the communist *Ramona Parra* brigade, suffering bruising and concussion. On 15 January 1973 a band of eleven members of the MIR at a loose end attacked Radio El Carbón at Lota and struck the commentator, Mr. Alfonso Montoya Rivas, because he refused to read over the air their proclamation demanding the handing-over of the station to the workers, that is, to themselves.

Of course, the UP also found economic strangulation an effective weapon to apply in this connexion. Senator Juan Hamilton asserted in January 1971 that "all the important radio stations had been brought under the control of the UP through pressure, arbitrary misuse of power, by denying them the right to advertize in the state media, by putting obstacles in the way of their renewing worn-out equipment, by sabotaging their electricity supply, or by astronomical increases in their electricity or telephone charges".

The UP used the same methods to take over all the TV stations, to the point where the journalists' section of the Christian Democrats denounced "the mounting attack against freedom of information on TV . . . and the almost total control of broadcasting by the government".[1] The director and some of the staff of channel 5 were held prisoner and *flogged* (yes, you have not misread the word).[2]

Channel 9, run by the University of Chile, was subjected to particularly grave attacks. At the outset of the Allende government, the rector of this university was a leftist, and Channel 9 reflected his political ideas. It was thus left in peace. But in April 1972, he lost in the rectoral elections organized within the university, and an opponent of the Allende regime, Mr. Boeninger, replaced him as rector. The UP journalists who had produced the broadcasts on channel 9 up till then refused to recognize the new authority democratically elected by the teachers and students, and occupied the station premises. The Univer-

---

[1] *El Mercurio*, 16 September 1971.
[2] *El Mercurio*, 29 March, 3 April 1973.

sity of Chile appealed to the courts. The latter issued an injunction ordering the occupiers of channel 9 to leave the premises, but this was never carried out. Unable to dislodge the intruders from channel 9 because they were protected by armed pickets, the University of Chile set up a new transmitter, channel 6. But two days after its first broadcast, on 19 June 1973, a detachment of the civil police burst into the station without any authorization from the courts, sub-machine-guns in hand, completely wrecked all the equipment and arrested 31 students and journalists. The UP had perpetrated the most serious violation of university independence ever committed in Chile. The order for this assault had been given by the governor of Santiago of the time, the socialist Mr. Julio Stuardo.

Freedom of expression was equally denied to the cinema. *El Mercurio* of 29 March 1973 reported: "From documents supplied us by members of parliament, it emerges that the Marxist state has in the last 30 months strengthened its hold over all the distribution networks and screening facilities of the cinema, either by usurpation, by installing its nominees on their governing boards, by hiring, or by outright seizure of the companies concerned ... Its aim is to brainwash the people through this powerful medium, reducing them to complete intellectual servitude". More than half of the films screened were Soviet, a sign of the UP regime's collusion with Moscow. As a result, during the 1972 Chile Films, the state agency which dictated what films Chileans had or had not the right to see, made a loss of 216 million escudos, the Marxist government making good this deficit as it occurred by the simple expedient of printing fresh bank-notes. The reason for Chile Films' bankruptcy was that the public no longer went to the cinema, finding the fare inflicted on it—blue films, violence and Marxist propaganda—repellent and of poor quality.

The Marxists were the first to realize that propaganda is the key to winning power. What they did not realize was that propaganda is of no use for holding on to power. Faced with empty shops, the public soon regurgitated what they had absorbed in crowded meetings. Visions may indeed motivate a conversion, but life can only be sustained by a diet of reality. Once the bankruptcy of the Marxist system becomes evident, the make-believe world of propaganda loses its hold over the public, who are aware of it merely as a wearisome reiteration of lies and sickening nonsense.

Muzzling the press and publishers

To reduce publishing houses and the opposition to silence, the UP brought into play all the illegal means at its disposal, using both force and a cunning worthy of Machiavelli.

Let us deal with force first. Wherever it could, the UP resorted to the straightforward closing down of such enterprises, without any further ceremony. Thus, on 15 September 1971, President Allende announced the closure of the Chilean branch of the United Press International news agency, on the grounds that it had "lowered the country's prestige in its news reports". Faced by the unfavourable effect this caused abroad, the measure was rescinded ten days later, but the manager of UPI's Chilean office was forced to resign. The Secretary-General of the government, Mr. Hernan del Canto, threatened foreign correspondents with expulsion for the unfavourable reports they filed on the UP regime.

The Chilean opposition press and its journalists were frequently subjected to brutal maltreatment. On 18 August 1971, *La Tribuna*, organ of the National Party, was attacked by Mirists led by the chief of the *Pobladores*, or shanty-town dwellers, Mr. Alejandro Villalobos, from their armed camp of Nueva La Habana, where People's Courts were operating. They demanded the publication of a Marxist pamphlet; struck Mr. Mario Arnello, a parliamentary deputy and the political editor Mr. Daniel Galleguillos, and even tried to throw them out of a second-floor window. On 7 June 1972 the paper was sent a dynamite cartridge through the post.

Illegal occupations of newspapers were still being carried out. On 21 August 1971 a band from the MIR seized *La Mañana* of Talca, a newspaper respected for its defence of democracy. The tactics used were as follows: first of all a trade union dispute was fomented; then the Minister of Labour appointed an official *interventor*, ostensibly to settle the dispute, but in reality to operate a political takeover of the paper. The *interventor*, in this case the socialist Mr. Francisco Reyes, gave the paper a revolutionary line quite uncharacteristic of it. The provincial court ruled that the paper must be handed back to its owner, but the UP authorities refused to carry out this judgement. Consequently the matter was referred to the Supreme Court, which on 27 September 1972 confirmed that "the placing of *La Mañana* under an *interventor* is unconstitutional". Indeed, article 10 of the Constitution lays it down that: "Any individual or corporate entity, and especially universities and political parties, will have the right to found and direct newspapers, magazines, radio stations . . . The conditions of ownership and operation of such communications media can only be modified *by the law*, and such modification has to be approved, in each Chamber, by a majority of its duly-constituted members".

The Supreme Court, therefore, ordered the expulsion of the illegal occupiers of *La Mañana* to be carried out on 15 October. The local prefect of the UP government, and thus the properly constituted authority over the *carabineros* (armed police), received his instructions from the Criminal Court of Talca, but refused to carry out the court's order. The disobedience was so flagrant that on 30 October the Supreme Court declared that "this refusal to carry out a judicial order is a deliberate expression of the contempt with which the government treats the legal norms of the Republic". The Talca paper was finally restored to its owner, but it had been looted of machinery, furniture and ten tons of newsprint. And the socialist *interventor*, Mr. Francisco Reyes, was later appointed by Mr. Allende as Intendant of Talca!

The Graham Agency was already nationalized, but this did not prevent its offices from being occupied on 22 February 1973 by Mirists, led by two hotheads from the Lo Hermida shanty-town glorying in the pseudonyms of "Commandant Raoul" and "Commandant Mickey". It is almost comic to see all these apostles of "equality" awarding themselves gold braid and resounding titles, but it is proof too that their dearest desire was to replace one hierarchy by another, but this time a lawless one. The armed Mirists ejected the manager of the Graham Agency, Mr. Julio Stuardo, as being too easy-going for their taste, and installed in his place a more committed extremist, Mr. Sergio Juarez. They camped in the Agency's offices, issuing civil war communiqués calling for the expropriation of just about everybody, even down to the humblest owners of newspaper kiosks; these were obviously "fascists", since they also stocked and sold "right-wing" publications.

These occupations of premises were often accompanied by acts of violence against their managers and staff. Let me quote, from all those reported by Mr. Tomas MacHale, the assaults on Mr. Pedro Oportot Vera, director of *La Prensa* of Osorno, and one of his reporters, on 1 December 1971. The aggressor here was no less a person than the General Secretary of the Socialist Party in Osorno. Then there was the knifing of the director of the *Sepa* review on 24 November 1971, for a speech in which he opposed the city authorities of Santiago paying public homage to Fidel Castro.

Mr. Maximiano Errazuriz, a lawyer and the director of the Santa Cruz paper *El Condor*, was subjected to physical maltreatment for having dared to draw up, with the approval of the Senate, a constitutional accusation against Mr. Juan Codelia, governor of the province of Colchagua and a member of MAPU. In this he charged the governor will illegally setting up a Peoples' Court which carried out sentences, and with carrying out a search of a private house without a court order. On 16 September 1971 Mr. Maximiano Errazuriz was kidnapped by three members of the MIR, who handcuffed him, tied him down to a railway track and beat him until he signed a "spontaneous" statement. On 25 October 1971, during Fidel Castro's visit to Chile, Mr. Errazuriz was once again seized and held in detention without any legal authority by officials of the investigative branch of the police. He was again imprisoned on 18 December 1971, receiving blows, this time at the instigation of the mayor, Mr. Carlos Lira Moscoso, a member of the MAPU.

But the UP had other and more underhand means at its disposal, those that can only be characterized as Machiavellian. These varied, but were all designed to ruin the opposition press. The nationalized Central Bank of Chile put all sorts of obstacles in the way of opposition printers, publishing houses and the press importing the equipment and materials they needed. Then the state invented two new weapons for discriminating between "well-disposed" and "heretical" press organs: it requisitioned, illegally, the Ceresita paint concern, which produces printing ink, and it also took over, equally illegally, the Santiago Gas Company, which produces a gas fuel for linotype machines.

Another very effective method for ruining the opposition press was for the state to refuse to advertise in it. In this connection, the tribulations of *El Sur* were particularly instructive. The director of this paper, Mr. Ivan Cienfuegos, had on 16 October 1972 refused to publish two defamatory and alarmist communiqués. As a result, some of the paper's more extremist staff, in concert with the local political committee of the university neighbourhood, which was at the time dominated by the MIR and the UP, seized the building that housed *El Sur* as well as the evening paper *La Cronica.* In their place, they brought out a left-wing sheet, the *Surazo.* The National Council of the College of Journalists issued a strong protest, and the judge in Concepción ordered *Surazo* to cease publication. But the expropriators did not care a brass farthing for the judge's injunction, and continued to bring out their incendiary rag until 9 November, when they were ejected from the premises.

Whereupon *El Sur* felt the full force of official reprisals. The Customs Tribunal moved in to make an on-the-spot investigation into an alleged fraud in respect of machines that had been in operation since 1968. Officials of the Industrial Development Agency (CORFO) demanded immediate settlement of a debt although the paper, prevented from publishing for months, had no more funds, and forbade it to sell off machines to raise the money it owed. MIR members attacked newsvendors selling *El Sur*, and burned whole bundles of the paper, thus further increasing the paper's financial difficulties. The state-controlled bank in Concepción, directed by a socialist, refused its request for credit, while granting a loan of 300,000 escudos to the striking employees so that they could continue their action against the paper. It was at this point that Chileans became aware of the existence of a famous telex message which had been intercepted, and in which one could read: "The Popular Unity front has reached an agreement to place no advertising in *El Sur* and *La Cronica* of Concepción ... so that they will be unable to pay their debts and thus pass into the hands of the working class"[1]. It was signed Mr. Alvaro Rojas Aguayo.

Another means of bringing the hostile press to its knees was to provoke constant labour strikes and excessive wage demands among its work-force. *Ediciones Zig Zag*, a publishing house belonging to the Christian Democrats, was a well-managed and profitable enterprise. Its only fault was that it published books and periodicals that did not defend Marxist-Leninist theses. So the unified trade union organized a strike in support of exorbitant wage claims. An arbitration tribunal, chaired by a communist lawyer acting on the orders of the Labour minister, a communist himself, made an order on 11 January 1971 that *Zig Zag* should increase wages and salaries by 67% which was double the rise in the cost of living for the year 1970. Next, the UP withdrew all bank loans granted to the publishers. The aim of this financial suffocation was quite simply to bring about the demise of *Zig Zag*. And its demise did in fact take place on 12 February 1971, the very day that had been set aside by the regime as "Press Day". Through the intermediary of the CORFO agency, the UP state was able to buy up the workshops, machinery and some of the magazines of *Zig Zag* for a mere song. By this means it was able to set up at extremely low cost the *Empresa Nacional Quimantu* (Quimantu National Press), which it used as an instrument for massive Marxist-Leninist brainwashing. Among the flood of propaganda publications it poured out we find such titles as: *Marx and Engels*, *Principles of Communism*, *The Bolshevik Programme*, *What is Historical Materialism*, the complete works of Lenin, all those of Marx and Engels, 40,000 copies of a popular educational handbook on communist sociology, thousands of copies of works on the class struggle, a volume entitled *Fidel* (i.e. Castro) *in Chile*, 50,000 copies of each of the 21 volumes of the Marxist collection *We the Chileans*, and so on.

Who footed the bill for this one-sided Marxist-Leninist-materialist-dialectical-revolutionary brainwashing? You may well ask. In fact, it was the Chilean taxpayer, for the enterprise squandered a great deal of money. The losses admitted by its own management, and which the state made good, amounted to 160 million escudos by 14 June 1972, that is, after a year and four months of Allende management.

The bitterest campaign fought by Mr. Allende to ruin a press organ and take it over was that directed against *El Mercurio*. Bitter in the first place since this independent newspaper, founded by the Edwards family in Valparaiso on 12 September 1827, and today the longest-established Spanish-language newspaper in the world, was the most

---

[1] See *El Mercurio* of 5 January 1972.

respected and influential journal in Chile; and secondly because, thanks to the vast popular support it enjoyed, it was able to fight back against all the hostile manoeuvres and pressures brought to bear on it.

The media supporting the UP began by making despicable attacks on the probity of its director, Mr. Agustín Edwards, accusing him of tax frauds and illegally accepting a foreign loan, etc. All these charges were investigated by special Commissions, and proved completely unfounded. This did not prevent President Allende from slandering the director of his country's most prestigious newspaper before a congress of the Association of Latin-American Industries, i.e. before a gathering of distinguished foreigners. *El Mercurio* replied by an editorial of 27 March 1972 entitled "The Right to Honour".

Insults and slander were followed by intimidation, originating from more than one sector of the Marxist alliance. Staff and contributors received anonymous letters or 'phone calls warning them that their car would be set on fire, or that they would be arrested and tried on charges of tax evasion. There was even a threat to execute Mr. Agustín Edwards on the parade ground of Santiago if the paper continued to attack Mr. Allende and the Communist Party. Threats were soon followed by actual violence. Several branches of the paper were stoned. On 5 June there were two successive attempts to burn the Valparaiso building of *El Mercurio* with inflammable liquids. On 22 October 1972, socialists fired shots from a van at its correspondent in Concepción.

During the same period, the UP was doing its best to run the paper by the underhand Machiavellian tactics to which we have already drawn attention, and in particular by its discriminatory refusal to advertize in *El Mercurio.* As private undertakings were nationalized one after the other, private advertizing, the indispensable life-blood of any independent newspaper, was drying up in its turn. Three months after Mr. Allende's accession, the paper's advertizing revenue was down by 40 per cent. All credit being state-controlled since the nationalization of the banks, *El Mercurio* was now unable to raise loans. Lacking foreign currency, it was unable to import equipment from abroad. And finally the UP attempted to stir up labour trouble among the 14,000 employees; in this it had the support of Ms. Sonia Edwards, the sister of the paper's biggest shareholder, but a close friend of the socialist leader Mr. Altamirano. But here the UP ran up against a difficulty. To save their paper, the workers and staff, who had refused to join a government-controlled Marxist trade union, accepted a 20% salary cut, and this at a moment when prices were rocketing. This must surely be unique in the history of organized labour; we shall return to it in our chapter on Popular Opposition.

There remained one ultimate weapon for the total silencing of the opposition press, and that was control by the state of all newsprint supplies. To achieve this goal, the UP government brought its heaviest artillery into play.

In Chile a single great enterprise, *La Papelera*, was the sole supplier of newsprint to all the papers and publishing houses, whatever their political coloration. It did not discriminate against anyone, and even supplied organs that violently attacked the National Party and its presidential candidate Mr. Alessandri, the majority shareholder in the firm. The UP government decided it must at all costs win control over *La Papelera* so as to assure itself of a subservient press, and this despite the fact that the *Statute of Guarantees*, in its article 10, forbade any "discrimination between privately-owned publishing houses, newspapers, periodicals and reviews as regards sale and paper supply".

Mr. Allende's first move was to offer to buy the company's shares through the intermediary of the Industrial Development Agency, at a price four times that of its stock exchange quotation. *La Papelera* and the general public reacted by setting up a Freedom Fund. Although it only offered the quoted market price to stockholders who wanted to sell, the Freedom Fund soaked up more shares than did CORFO, which never managed to acquire more than 7.7 per cent. This was a galling setback for the UP.

The UP government's next move in its attempt to ruin *La Papelera* was to try to bring production to a halt in its plants by means of strike pickets, and to hold up on the roads the lorries delivering timber supplies. This provoked a heated protest from Mr. Fernando Sanhueza, president of the Chamber of Deputies, in a telegram he sent on 3 December 1971 to the Intendant of Concepción, a member of the Communist Party who had himself been prominent in sabotaging the free passage of the delivery lorries. The authorities even went to the length of illegally requisitioning the wood-pulp industry at Cholguan, in the province of Nuble, and expropriating the owners of softwood plantations supplying cellulose to *La Papelera*. Then the government price-control agency, DIRINCO, refused to allow *La Papelera* to raise the price of its paper, although such a rise was indispensable in view of the general increase in prices, and despite the fact that the government had already sanctioned increases for all its nationalized public service enterprises. As a result, by June 1972 *La Papelera* had already a cumulative deficit of 230 million escudos, and was now losing three million escudos a day.

This was used by CORFO, the Industrial Development Agency, as a pretext for accusing the company of inefficient management and for insisting that it should be administered by a state *interventor*. In fact, from 1956 to 1970 *La Papelera* had been managed with impeccable efficiency. It had invested 130 million dollars in the country, increased its average annual exports by almost 100% and increased production by 700%.

Each of these attacks could well have proved the death-blow; and yet *La Papelera* survived them all, thanks to the surprising degree of support it received from its own work-force and the Chilean people as a whole, a support that gave rise to a veritable heroic legend which we shall speak of later in our chapter Popular Opposition. As far as *El Mercurio* and *La Papelera* were concerned, the UP's stratagems failed because of the deep-rooted love of freedom shown by the people of Chile. But the fact remains that the Allende government did not relax its merciless war against all the opposition organs of mass communication, calculating that the economic and moral resources essential to the continued existence of the independent media were bound to be exhausted sooner or later.

CHAPTER VI

REGIMENTATION OF THE PEOPLE

THE SUPREME GOAL of the UP in Chile, and one it shared with all Marxist-Leninist parties, was to absorb and control the whole population, from cradle to grave, and to direct and channel all its activities, in the family, in productive life, sport, culture and in the trade unions. As such absorption and control became tighter and more all-embracing, it aimed and hoped to achieve a total control of men's minds, a universal brain-washing that would produce a unanimity of opinion, a total enslavement of men's souls and a complete regimentation of their bodies. Pamphlets entitled *We must all lend a hand* were distributed urging Chileans to enrol in a number of the many organisations that had been set up to cater for neighbourhoods, families, cultural, sporting and productive activities, and of which I will give an incomplete list here.

The Neighbourhood: Neighbourhood juntas, consumer co-operatives, tenants' associations, health brigades, the ominous JAPs, about which I shall have more to say later, and the even more sinister vigilance committees, whose members' task was to spy on their neighbours.

The Family: Centres for mothers, centres for fathers and legal guardians, youth organizations, children's groups.

Sports and Culture: Sports clubs, cultural and artistic centres, choir-groups.

The world of work: Trade unions, assemblies of workers in a given company, plant or workshop assemblies, production committees, committees for administering communally-owned property, workers' co-ordinating committees within a firm (All this made rather a lot of committees for rather little work), more vigilance committees, whose duty was to inform on their fellows to the proper authorities, and whose vigilance was far more concerned with the ideology of the workers than with the level of production.

Communal groupings: "Industrial cordons" the role of which I will explain presently, communal co-ordinating commandos, yet more vigilance committees, peasants' councils at communal, provincial and national levels, though the "counsel" they gave had more to do with the seizure of land than with its effective cultivation.

All these committees, groups, juntas, centres, clubs, assemblies, councils and commandos were, for the Marxist-Leninists, just so many heaven-sent opportunities to extend their control over the population, penetrating and colonizing the various bodies, infiltrating their own men into key positions within them, and thus mobilizing and indoctrinating the members and turning them into fanatical leftists, so that they became blind followers of their respective parties and trade unions. All these bodies were integrated into their respective communal co-ordinating commandos, which claimed to represent the "power of the people" within the boundaries of the locality or commune, and which had all set up local vigilance committees. These commandos had three objectives: firstly to build up, alongside the legally-elected democratic assemblies, a set of alternative bodies which would gradually take their place; secondly, to organize their own parallel police force alongside the legal one; and, finally, to prepare for an armed revolution.

This idea of a so-called "people's power", existing at first clandestinely alongside the country's legal institutions, and then later coming into the full light of day, its goal being to prepare for a civil war, this idea which is basic to the Bolshevik revolution throughout the world, was initiated in Chile by the MIR, and then adopted by the UP as a whole. So much so that in his message to Congress of 21 May 1973, Mr. Allende demanded that "people's power" *should be built into the Constitution.*

The "industrial cordons" were set up during the critical days of October 1972, following an appeal from the CUT, the "unified" trade union organization, and their purpose was, not to disperse bourgeois demonstrations but, ironically, to break the flood of strikes called by the *workers* in transport, commerce, the mines, etc., workers protesting against Marxist regimentation, and whom the UP included in their blanket condemnation of all the opposition as "right-wing fascist counter-revolutionaries". These "industrial cordons" defined their own nature and function as follows: "organisms for class-defence, embodying the power and force of the workers and facilitating their mobilization in an organized way". The word "mobilization" gave the game away: they were in fact an additional way of regimenting the working class, but one that clearly looked forward to a coming civil war. On several occasions, Mr. Allende threatened the opponents of his regime that he would put himself at the head of these "industrial cordons", especially those in the suburbs of Santiago where business and factories had been nationalized and the workers were living under the total domination of revolutionary terrorist movements.

The *poblaciones* or shanty towns, agglomerations of wooden huts lacking even the most rudimentary services such as water, gas or electricity, were subjected in their turn to drastic regimentation. The best-known of these, Lo Hermida, outside Santiago, was chosen by the Marxists as their principal bastion. By the end of Mr. Allende's reign this neighbourhood still had no water, electricity or gas, nor any permanent housing; all that the Marxists had brought it were revolutionary speeches. Lo Hermida offers us a typical example of poverty-stricken but free citizens being reduced to the status of cowed subjects, still poverty-stricken but now enslaved in addition. This under-privileged neighbourhood was swollen by a huge camp of the MIR, whose chiefs, Mr. Alejandro Villalobos, called "Commander Mickey", and his colleague "Commander Raoul", imposed a reign of terror on the destitute inhabitants. Armed bands came and went as masters in Lo Hermida, spreading alarm wherever they went; forcing their way without warning into the shanties and carrying out illegal searches with the excuse that they were looking for class-enemies or hidden weapons. A poor old woman, still trembling with fright at the mere memory of those old days under the jackboots of a "brutal and licentious soldiery", said to me: "They ransacked everywhere, and turned everything upside down in my hut. And we hadn't even got any bread; how did they think we could have afforded to buy weapons?" The Mirists incited the shantytown-dwellers to furious resentment against the "reactionaries", the "mummies" (to use their own word) and the rich, in short, against all opponents of the UP, so that Chileans from outside no longer dared to venture into the shanty towns. The Mirists were successful in turning the heads of the young people, who were glad of the chance to become activists; bear arms and lord it over others even less privileged than themselves. These young swashbucklers were feared and hated by the poor housewives, who saw them only as trouble-makers, leading their own sons astray into armed brawls, absenteeism from work and participation in violent demonstrations where their lives were at risk. I have visited a number of these shanty towns. In all of them the mothers of families look back to the Allende period as a nightmare, during which there was no bread in the larder, but lots of shouting in the backyards and lots of rifles in the streets.

The People's Courts

Another means for reducing the Chileans to a state of total obedience to the regime was that of the "People's Courts", of sad notoriety. These were set up by decree on 23 January 1971, and were "lay" or "non-specialist" courts, in the sense that their "judges" had not the slightest knowledge of or training in the law. These "judges" were elected in each district by the inhabitants, the "neighbours", (which sounded reassuring enough), but the candidates were in fact put forward by the professional and political associations into which the people of the locality had been organized (which is somewhat less reassuring), and the elections were supervised by the Prefect of the administrative area.

With such "elections" the People's Courts had a heavy political bias, and became in fact institutions, not for guaranteeing justice to ordinary people, but for repressing them in the interests of the parties that made up the UP.

At the camp of Nueva La Habana, at La Florida, 15 kilometres from Santiago, where "Commander Mickey" had imposed his own violent rule with the aid of his fellow-hotheads of the MIR, he forbade the police to enter the area to carry out the sentences of the regular institutions of the law on the pretext that the camp had its own "People's courts" to carry out "its own justice".[1] "Commander Mickey" explained as follows how justice was meted out in his territory: "Our vigilance committees investigate the crimes denounced to them, and bring the accused before a public assembly. This assembly applies physical sanctions to the accused, such as cleaning the public baths and lavatories, or moral sanctions such as being exposed publicly to the whole camp ..." He forgot to mention certain more expeditious penalties.

One of the authorities in judicial matters in this camp was Mr. Juan Marchant Berrios, called El Shandu, a member of the paramilitary VOP organization, who had already been indicted for more than one case of assault, manslaughter, theft and other offences.[2] "Judge Mickey" too could hardly set himself up as an example to follow when he presided over his courts of justice. Not only was he guilty of a number of lesser offences, but he had committed manslaughter through negligence. Driving a smart car while drunk, he had hit an obstacle, causing the death of his companion, an architect and fellow-member of the MIR.

The vague definitions of the crimes these "People's Courts" were intended to punish left the door wide open to quite arbitrary judgements and the working-out of personal grudges or political persecution. For example, they had to pronounce on "crimes against the healthy co-existence of the community", and to punish any act contrary to "sound public feeling". Turning their backs on a fundamental principle which it had taken civilized society centuries to work out, these tribunals did not lay down precise penalties for precise offences, and this opened the door to all the abuses consequent on prejudice, persecution and fanaticism. The defendant was not allowed to have a lawyer. He could be sentenced to humiliating punishments, such as compulsory work on holidays, or a public admission of guilt broadcast on radio or television. The decree setting up these courts, gaily signed by the "likeable" Mr. Allende three months after his accession to power, aroused so much

[1] *El Mercurio*, 1 May 1972.
[2] *El Mercurio*, 2 May 1972.

public indignation that it was not even possible to submit it to parliament for ratification. But this did not prevent it being put into immediate effect in some areas, and thus providing an outlet for the political venom of some of the more hot-headed local UP bosses.

The prevailing atmosphere of spy-fever throughout the country made it even easier to bring the citizens to heel. I quote: "In every bourgeois household a servant is employed who comes from the working class or the peasantry, and who is familiar with the life of her employers and the irregularities they engage in. DIRINCO (the Directorate of Industry and Commerce) has made contact with these companions, and we are studying practical ways in which they can collaborate with us, for example, by denouncing householders who are secretly hoarding goods destined for the black market in their cellars". The author of this quotation was Mr. Patricio Palma, National Director of the Ministry of Industry and Commerce, and he was advocating this system of household denunciation at a meeting of a Commission of his own (communist) party.[1]

The screw was further tightened by the practical impossibility for Chileans to leave the country after 1972. Yet one of the fundamental rights of all men, enshrined in the United Nations Charter, is that of the right to travel outside one's own country and to settle abroad. Under the rule of the "democratic" Mr. Allende this right, like so many others, was denied not so much by a formal legal interdict but, as one would expect from such a man, indirectly by a hypocritical erection of obstacles. Any Chilean family wanting to leave the country had to find a third person willing to stand as surety for all the family's taxes and other obligations, present or future. This condition in itself, plus the fact that those leaving were not allowed to take with them either money or property, made any journey abroad, let alone emigration, impossible. This makes a striking contrast with the present Pinochet regime, which not only allows its opponents to leave the country, but even pays them abroad the pensions or superannuations they are entitled to. Yes, comrade Corvalan in Moscow receives each month a pension paid by the Pinochet government!

The unified national school system, or ENU

Mr. Anibal Palma Fourcade, a Minister of Education under Mr. Allende, was the sponsor of the decree of March 1973 which announced the entry into force on 1 June of the Unified National School system, or ENU. This project was not the result of a serious study on the part of teachers, students and parents of pupils. It was a purely partisan

[1] See *El Mercurio*, 2 October 1972.

initiative, decided behind closed doors in the Ministry of Education, without any debate in parliament. The system proposed was copied from that in practice in the communist People's Republic of East Germany, from which a Chilean delegation had just returned. Its introduction showed the urgency with which the Marxist-Leninist parties making up the UP regarded the need to "create a new man", a need that had figured prominently in their speeches and publications.

The official report on the ENU confirmed this, emphasizing as it did that one of its objectives was "to develop in the pupils concepts, habits, opinions, attitudes and values favourable to *collective work*". Statements made by highly-placed officials in the Ministry of Education left no doubt as to the total Communisation which the UP intended to impose on the whole of education. Mr. Lautaro Videla, co-author of the report, stated that the ENU constituted "the definitive entry of the class struggle into education". All its details were so designed as to inculcate a Marxist-Leninist attitude to life into all Chileans from their tenderest childhood up; in other words, to regiment the people through their brains just as the JAPs were regimenting them through their stomachs.

Despite its obviously sectarian and egalitarian nature, the ENU was presented as a "democratic reform" whose aim was to give greater prestige to "socially useful labour", and to replace an education based on scientific humanism by one with a technico-political character. In it the school pupil was urged to be more open to the "real life of the country" through his contacts with industry, agricultural enterprises and public utility services. As the journalist Mr. Juraj Domic perceptively remarked, the ENU, far from making education more democratic, would in fact have made it aristocratic. It would have provided the poorer pupils with a valueless sub-technical diploma, closing the doors of the universities to them, and taking them directly from primary school into the factories, in the cities, or to those "open-air factories" which the collectivized lands in the countryside were gradually becoming. In such a system, as in Soviet education, the most under-privileged pupils would have been the children of workers and peasants, for all that they were demagogically presented as "new men", while the sons of Marxist-Leninist apparatchiks belonging to the old families would have been able to enter higher education thanks to influence, which in a bureaucratic society constitutes a class-privilege even more one-sided than does money in a capitalist society.

Mr. Allende's minister had taken good care not to make his decree public until after the municipal elections of March 1973, suspecting that it would arouse a storm of indignation. It did in fact provoke a violent reaction from the church, the opposition parties, the army, parents, teachers, the "women's power" movement, and even from the students. We shall return to these later. The point to emphasize here is that in introducing the ENU Mr. Allende was violating yet another of the constitutional guarantees he had promised to respect in return for being elected President, namely that he would maintain a pluralist and democratic educational system.

The rationing and price-control agencies, or JAPs

A resolution of the Directorate of Commerce and Industry (DIRINCO) dated 29 March 1972 and published in the official gazette on 4 April set up the *Juntas de Abastecimientos y Precios* (Juntas for Food Supply and Prices), the famous JAPs (not to be confused with the GAP, Mr. Allende's personal bodyguard). In the beginning these were purely state agencies. But the Communists soon realized the political advantage to be gained from a "dictatorship through the stomach", and took over control of as many of these agencies as they could.

The new Finance Minister, Mr. Fernando Flores, of the MAPU, took 12 measures to establish this dictatorship of the UP through men's stomachs.

Articles 2, 7, 9, 10 and 11 were essentially concerned with police responsibilities—control, supervision, denunciations—while the other clauses created a state monopoly over the distribution of the most essential food and domestic products.

It took a considerable amount of shopping time to obtain the so-called *canasta popular* or "people's basket", a personal ration of the most essential foodstuffs at fixed and reasonable prices, and all the Chilean women I met remember it as an exhausting and humiliating chore. They spoke to me of having had to queue from six in the morning until noon. Others had to spend their night queuing out of doors on a straw mattress so as to be issued with their *canasta* early in the morning before going to work. Even the poverty-stricken womenfolk of the shanty towns, who ought to have been delighted with these hand-outs of the "people's basket", did not like them. They complained that they were obliged to buy a packet of soap-powder or rice for which they had no immediate use, and thus hadn't enough money left to buy the butter or sugar which they urgently needed that very week. They also complained about the system used by the UP to impose political controls. To qualify for a *canasta* at Lo Hermida, they had to produce their voter's cards. One could thus check whether they had voted or not. Worse still, certain local JAPs had imposed a further condition, namely that any adult male who wanted to qualify for the *canasta* had to take his turn at mounting guard outside the official shops for several hours a week.

The parallel police formations, urged to take drastic action by the finance minister, ransacked shops that defied the JAPs, and especially the small businesses because these had no means of defending themselves. This reached the point where the chairman of the Retail Traders' Confederation, Mr. Rafael Cumsille, was driven to attack "the despicable action being carried out by JAP agitators in the poorer quarters". And he continued indignantly: "Everyone knows that the proprietresses of small shops are usually widows, or women whose husbands are disabled or retired. Despite this they have to suffer attack and harassment". The mob looted what little goods they had on show, so as to teach them a lesson in Marxism. Some of them were even driven to the point of suicide. The British writer Mr. Robert Moss relates in his book *Chile's Marxist Experiment* two cases of physical brutality he knew of in Lo Hermida. Two woman shopkeepers each had an arm broken for daring to criticise the local JAP.

Another serious consequence of the JAPs was that they directly encouraged the black market to spread its myriad tentacles throughout society. The regime's supporters among the smart set systematically received much more provisions and consumer durables (cars, motorcycles, sewing-machines, electrical appliances, TV and radios) than they needed, and re-sold these on the black market. They were enriching themselves at the expense of the general penury.

It is not surprising that the JAPs gave rise to nothing but violence, injustice and the black market, once one realizes that they were modelled on similar bodies set up in the USSR on 25 October 1917, following the Bolshevik coup d'état. Mr. Juraj Domic, in a remarkable series of articles, pointed out that the Chilean JAPs were copied from the system worked out by Lenin towards the end of 1917, from which emerged the decree of the People's Commissariat for Food setting up those Food Supply Committees which were the Soviet equivalent of the later Chilean JAPs. The Soviet decree called for the following provisions to be made (*Izvestia*, 19 January 1918):

1. All citizens must be affiliated to a local consumers' association (at village, street or rural district level, etc.).

2. A minimum of two thirds of the families in each consumers' association must belong to the poor classes (workers, peasants), employing no paid labour.

3. Consumers' associations, as well as small shops, are to be nationalized.

4. The transportation, purchase and sale of goods without permission of the Food Supply Committee will be punished by the confiscation of all the guilty person's possessions, together with a prison sentence of more than six months, or forced labour.

5. Food supply committees will fall under the authority of the local Soviets. (Just as the Chilean JAPs were to come under the authority of the Popular Unity Committees, or CUPs).

Lenin emphasized the imperative necessity for the Food Supply Committees to wage relentless war against the enemies of soviet Socialism and to exercise rigorous control over the distribution of food products. Entering into closer detail, he continued: "We must work out, in the towns and in the countryside, practical methods for controlling and repressing the rich, the parasites and petty criminals, our goal being to free the soil of Russia from all the harmful insects, fleas and bugs that infest it . . . In one place we shall imprison a dozen rich men, a dozen petty thieves, half a dozen of those shameless idlers who are too lazy to work, like certain Petrograd printers. In another they will be compelled to clean out lavatories. In a third, they will be given yellow identity cards so that the whole population can keep a watch over their activities, treating them as anti-social outcasts . . . In yet another spot one parasite in ten will be shot in the act . . . Nothing must be distributed or sold to class-enemies . . ."

This memorandum of Lenin's, frightening enough to send a cold shiver down one's spine, was published by the Chilean Communist Party after Mr. Allende took power, for the political education of its militants. The terror carried out by the Soviet food supply committees was offered to Chile's Communists as a model to be followed by the JAPs soon to be set up.[1]

A document of the Chilean Communist Party entitled "First National Plan for 1500 JAPs" summed up the objectives as follows: "To mobilize a great number of people, especially women, who are in general unwilling to engage in politics. To carry out a skilful political action among retail traders. To arouse an ideological struggle over problems of food supply . . . We must use this plan in such a way as to bring to the forefront the *political task* implicit in our handling of the problems raised by the psychosis of poverty".[2] If the masses wanted to have access to essential foodstuffs, they would have to submit to the control of the Communist Party. At a moment when the UP government had not yet put ration cards into circulation, the Communists, who controlled most of the JAPs, had their own ration cards printed, each bearing the words: "This card is issued by.......base" (the blank space would be filled by the name of the local cell). This gave them an immense power to control the life of local communities, and even that of each neighbourhood, each house and even each individual family. There was nothing to prevent them from entering houses, searching

---

[1] See *Leaflets of the Chilean Communist Party*, Santiago, 1971, pp. 51–61.
[2] *El Mercurio*, 5 April 1972.

through larders and carrying out all sorts of intimidation by threatening to cut off rations.

There were cases in some remote areas where communities unsympathetic to the UP and exasperated by the shortages set up their own JAPs. But these were not recognized by the Ministry of Economic Affairs, and received no supplies.

In the Minister of Finance's plan it is laid down that anyone refusing to enrol in a (state-controlled) JAP would receive no food supplies, and that the peasants—the very persons who in fact produce all the food that the land provides—would receive provisions only through the intermediary of the rural centres (once again, state-controlled). This plan was every bit as draconian as that of Lenin. Unfortunately for the UP, the poor too ended up by eating badly, and made it perfectly clear to their Marxist bosses through their strikes that this did not please them at all, in fact it did not please them one little bit.

Public opinion was under no illusion as to the totalitarian nature of the JAPs. *Ultimas Noticias* presented these agencies as "a death-blow dealt Chile by the UP."; *El Mercurio* saw them as "the shadow of dictatorship", and ex-President Frei stigmatized them "as a permanent step towards a totalitarian control of the nation".

CHAPTER VII

DESPOILING THE CITIZENS

Expropriations in the countryside

IN HIS SPEECH OF 5 JANUARY 1971 at Valparaiso, Mr. Allende declared: "I went to Cautin to warn landowners whose land has been seized that they must in no case try to take justice into their own hands nor use force . . . Those who seize land illegally will receive a light punishment, but those who try to recover it by force will be sentenced to a very heavy penalty". It is not usual for a head of State to issue such a warning, laying down one law for his friends and another for his opponents, especially when the law's lightest sanctions are reserved for those who break it most flagrantly, as in this case. The consequences were not long in showing themselves. Between 1 November 1970 and 5 April 1972, that is, in a period of 17 months, 1,767 agricultural holdings were seized by armed bands of the UP.[1]

The chairman of the MIR, Mr. Nelson Gutierrez, in a speech to the University of Concepcion in May 1971 at which the presence of the head of state constituted an endorsement of the legality of his proposals, made a call for "armed revolution", insisting on the necessity of occupying all factories and all farms. Mr. Allende's guarantee that the expropriators would not be punished, in fact, encouraged even more illegal dispossessions. Many of these, indeed, were carried out by the intervention of official state bodies such as CORA (the Agrarian Reform Corporation) or INDAP (the Institute for the Development of Agriculture and Stock-breeding).

The Minister of Agriculture, Mr. Jacques Chonchol, was vice-chairman of the INDAP, whose officials were paid to carry out agitation in the countryside and stir up the agricultural workers against the landowners. Mr. Chonchol was an expert in this field, for, as a technician for the United Nations Food and Agriculture Organisation, he had taken part in dispossessing Cuban farmers. He was thus not at all averse to seeing bands of Cuban terrorists and Uruguayan Tupamaros acting as advisers on expropriation to the Chilean Mirists and their rural offshoot, the MCR (Movement of Revolutionary Peasants). There were even salaried land-expropriators, carried on the pay-roll of the Metropolitan Park. In one area, the Cerro, a leader known as Pedro

[1] See report of the H.Q. of the Carabineros (armed police), quoted in the official gazette of the sessions of the Senate, 31 May 1972.

issued orders for the day's seizures each morning at 9 a.m., using the telephone of the local administrative offices.

The *tomas* or seizures began in force in the southern provinces of Cautin, Malleco and Nuble. The brutal methods of the MCR commandos aroused the hatred of the farmers. Small and medium farmers very soon made common cause with the bigger landowners, for it must be said that most of the expropriators drove a coach and horses through the limitations laid down in Mr. Frei's agrarian reform law, according to which only holdings of more than 80 "basic" hectares (roughly 32 acres), or land left uncultivated, could be expropriated. The "birds of prey", however, often struck at very modest rural properties, such as that of Mr. Amador Medina Martinez at Carampangue, in Arauco province, which was seized on 31 March 1972, and was only 25 hectares (ten acres). Mr. Onofre Lillo Bezanilla's farm at San Bernardo, in Santiago province, which was seized on 23 March 1972, was even smaller, measuring only 15 hectares[1] (six acres).

Faced with a united front of opposition by the Chilean farmers, the MCR found it served their purpose better to focus the majority of their agitation on the Indians. There are still about 400,000 of these in Chile, known as the Mapuches, and 180,000 of them are concentrated in Cautin province, out of a total rural population of 250,000. It was thus easy to set these Indians against the whites in a province where the latter were in the minority. The agitators had no difficulty in painting them as robbers of the tribal lands of the Indians' ancestors. At the beginning of 1972 it was estimated that there were 1,200 MCR activists in Cautin province. Their bands gathered the Mapuches together, whipped them up into a fury and launched them on a *battue* in which the quarry was not bulls but landowners. Just in the four months following Mr. Allende's accession to power there were 57 of these human *battues* or man-hunts. During the year 1971, there were 400 violent expropriations of land in Cautin province alone. They were carried out by bands of about 15 MCR ringleaders backed by 50 or so Mapuches who had been given alcohol, and were often in a state of drunkenness during the *toma*.

However the lands thus seized were not later shared out among the Indians. The socialist state is not noted for its generosity. It preferred to keep the deeds of ownership itself and directed the Indians into so-called "socialist communities" where the land was worked collectively. These collective farms had the added advantage that the Indians could be pumped full of a "class-conscious" political education, and could be trained to take their place in the armed militias. As a result the orderly estates in question quickly reverted

---

[1] See Hernan Millas, *Anatomy of a Clash*, pub. Zig Zag.

to a wilderness, and the Mapuches were soon disenchanted by the seizures.

When the farmers of Cautin, Osorno and Linares began to react and form groups for self-defence, the expropriators shifted their activities further north, to Nuble. Here the MCR found allies in the "Isabel Riquelme" and "Pedro Aguirre Cerda" peasant federations, with a membership of 22,000 peasants, and whose leader, the extreme socialist "Commander" Nelson Ugarte (once again, the military rank was self-attributed) demanded that Mr. Allende authorize the expropriation of all owners or managers of agricultural holdings without any compensation and without allowing them to keep even the tiniest patch of land for their own families. This was what was known as "retaliatory agrarian reform". Within a period of three months 100 farms were expropriated under this system.

Then the MCR switched their activities even further north into Santiago province. During the month of May, they occupied 147 farms, including some of quite modest size, like that of Millahuin, near Melipilla, seized by armed professionals most of whom were strangers to the district. It was later retaken by its owner with the help of armed neighbours. The case is even reported of a poultry farmer, Mr. Carlos Montes, whose property was seized although it only covered three hectares (just over an acre).

Mr. Allende gave the MCR—and its inspiration and motive-force, the MIR—a free hand to acquire the necessary manpower, money and weapons so that it could keep up a permanent guerilla campaign in the countryside. For more than a year, the area around Lake Panguipulli, in the south, was ruled as though it were a private fief by "Commander" Pepe (another self-awarded title), a man of 30 whose real name was Mr. Jose Liendo Vera. In November 1970, he organized with ruthless efficiency his first expropriation, of the farming estate of Carranco. By the end of 1971 this "egalitarian" with 120 armed retainers on his payroll had unleashed his hordes against 160 farms, and had become a veritable warlord and the unchallenged master of 140,000 acres of the best timber-producing land in Chile. He could never have carried out his depradations on such a scale if he had not enjoyed support among those in high places. One of these backers was, in fact, Mr. Jacques Chonchol, the Minister of Agriculture himself. Pepe was never arrested, although three detention orders had been taken out against him by the judicial authorities for personal assault. The police charged with carrying out these court orders were simply refused entrance by his sentries armed with machine-guns. Worse still, in a news film of 1972 one can see Pepe, at the time subject to a summons to appear before the court, saying farewell to the Minister of Agriculture amid repeated handshakes. Pepe finally left for Cuba in May 1972.

Mr. Allende made the following declaration one day to his bureaucrats: "Just imagine the distress of a man who has spent 40 or 50 years of his life as a farmer, who owns nothing but his field and the bread he wins from it to feed his children, his field that the law gives him the right to keep, and who sees the arrival of officials who do not enforce that law! Why should we not have human feelings?" In this tear-jerking manner, with the duplicity characteristic of the man, Mr. Allende was admitting that his followers were guilty of illegal exactions, but by his tearful snivelling he was at the same time attempting to deny his own responsibility for their actions. He snivelled, but he took no action. In the same week during which he made this declaration, with his hand on his heart, a hundred or so farms were being illegally occupied by his companions in power. One of these, Mr. Miguel Enriquez, one of the leaders of the MIR, was exclaiming: "Our feeling for bourgeois legality should be one of revulsion. We must dissolve Parliament, and take over all industrial and agricultural properties without any compensation". Mr. Allende allowed him to speak thus and to act on it. "Act", in this context, implied the shedding of blood, for most of the expropriations involved violence, and some of them were accompanied by atrocities.

The whole of Chile was shocked by the death of the farmer Mr. Jorge Baraona Puelma. For 40 years he had worked hard on his ranch of Nihuahe with his sons, two of whom were disabled. They were threatened with "revolutionary justice" if they did not leave, abandoning all their possessions. Mr. Joel Marambio, a parliamentary deputy, and Mr. Juan Codelia, the local Prefect, both of them Socialists, forced the Baraona brothers to face a "people's court" for *30 hours*. For several months the family took refuge in a tiny hut on what had been their land. This could not be tolerated. Officials of CORA (the Agrarian Reform Corporation) turned up one morning in February 1971, surrounded by armed and threatening extremists, and ordered the family to leave. As the old man was walking away, carrying some family portraits under his arm, he was struck down by a heart attack. At Bulnes another peasant, Mr. Pablo Urrutia Prieto, also died of a heart attack when he found himself dispossessed without notice. Yet another, Mr. Domitilia Palma, terrified by the bursts of sub-machine gun fire that accompanied the seizure of his estate of Brasil Sur at Lautaro in April 1971, fell dead of a cardiac embolism. There were farmers who committed suicide when they found themselves robbed of the fruits of a lifetime's work. Thus the elderly peasant Ms. Antonieta Maachell took her own life after being held prisoner by the occupiers of her farm. It proved possible to record the heart-rending act of seizure on film, and one can thus see Ms. Antonieta as she was just before she committed suicide. In the Traigen district an Italian widow whose property had been confiscated and her husband murdered, was raped, and took her own life out of shame and despair.

However most of the farmers who died when their land was seized were killed by their attackers. Let me quote just a few examples from this long, sad list. In April 1971 the young farmer Mr. Rolando Matus Castillo was shot down by MCR bands while attempting to resist the expropriation of his little five acre farm, Caren, in the Pucon district. Mr. Gilberto Gonzales was shot down by Mirists in July 1971 at La Vina Santa Blanca, in Rancagua. The bailiff of the El Cardal estate, at Colchagua, was killed in October 1971 while trying to break through the lines of occupiers to get to his house, where his wife was in childbirth at the time. In the same month the nephew of the owner of the Chesque property, at Loncoche, was seriously wounded, and Mr. Moises Huentelaf, a farm worker, was killed by armed MCR bands, who then sacked the farmhouse. The farmer's wife was forced to flee with her mentally sick son. In Traigen province my informants the brothers Andre and Albert Levi quoted to me, in addition to the case of the Italian widow, that of Mr. Raul Vasquez of Osorno, who had dared to resist the seizure of his property and was burned alive in his house.

In January 1972 Mr. Raul Quezada died tragically after being beaten with sticks by the expropriators of his farm La Rinconada at Curico. Farm workers Mr. Luis Hernan Rivas, Mr. Roberto Almonacid and Mr. Juan Manuel Rivas died in the fighting that took place at Paraguay-Centinela in the commune of Frutillar in August 1972. Mr. German Gonzales and Mr. Sergio Vergara, Christian Democrats, were killed in March 1973 while guarding a small patch of land at La Reina threatened with seizure by officials of CORA. In June 1973, a Christian Democratic farmer at Osorno, Mr. Jorge Mena, was beaten to death with sticks and iron bars. And the list goes on.[1]

Lawlessness was rife in the countryside; roads were blocked; phones and electricity were cut and the untended fields sadly displayed their unwonted bareness beneath the sky. The fanatics of the MCR spread their intimidation to those in public authority who attempted to enforce respect for the law, and even employed it against those who seemed too lukewarm in violating the law. They blocked the roads, and thus forced the resignation of the governor, Mr. Nelly Iribarra. His crime was to have sent armed police to free the two sons of a farmer who were being illegally held by the MCR! At Bulnes, 200 extremists demanding the dismissal of the local chief of the CORA, Mr. German Acevedo "for sticking too closely to bourgeois legality", occupied his offices until he was removed from his post.

---

[1] See the White Book, Santiago 1973.

Some terrorists did not even flinch from the murder of authorities who did not suit them. At Concepcion in August 1972 the chief of the carabineros (armed police), Mr. Exequiel Aroca Cuevas, was killed by a shot fired from the Socialist Party headquarters by the socialist Mr. Enrique Figueroa. Mr. Figueroa was fully identified as the author of the deed, but was never arrested while Mr. Allende was in power. An INDAP official, Mr. Hector Castillo, chairman of the regional Council for Agricultural Techniques, died at Chillan in December 1972 at the hands of a group of UP demonstrators. MCR fanatics even attacked the medical profession, normally the object of universal affection and respect. At Fresia they occupied the hospital and beat and kicked two doctors, one of them the medical director, to force them to alter an autopsy certificate in which the doctors had declared that the victim of an expropriation had died from a cranial injury. The authors of this act of violence were demanding a certificate of natural death. This contemptible attack was carried out in the presence of the subdelegate of the government.

Here is another example, equally despicable. At Melipilla a young farmer, Mr. Ramon Arrau, the owner of a small plot of land, all that was left to him after he had been expropriated, was severely beaten by 30 "agents of Marxist justice" who tied him up with wire; shut him up in a cellar and thrashed him from his head to his feet. They threatened that they would kill him if the judge at Melipilla sent carabineros to rescue him. They sharpened a sickle, telling him it was to cut his throat. The security forces arrived, rescued him and took him to hospital. He was only 30, but his hair had gone completely white. The judge in Melipilla had 41 of the terrorists arrested; found them guilty of wrongfully seizing land with violence, and imprisoned them. To teach the judge a lesson, 200 furious MCR members armed with pitchforks and cudgels occupied the courthouse; took the magistrate and six court officials hostage; heaped abuse on them and threatened to hang them if they did not release the prisoners immediately. When the Governor was about to send carabineros to the help of the judge, the MCR bands occupied the Governor's official premises. Then the highest authority in the Santiago province, the socialist Prefect Mr. Alfredo Joignant ordered the carabineros not to intervene in defence of the legal functionaries who were themselves the victims of violence. He came personally to Melipilla and made it clear to the judge and the governor that if the expropriators were sentenced to imprisonment by "bourgeois justice", comrade Allende himself would immediately pardon them. An official who had accompanied the prefect, Mr. Viera Gallo, shouted at the judge to be careful never again to arrest anyone for seizing land or forcibly detaining persons, even if he considered such acts illegal. This was the first time in Chilean history that the authorities themselves had treated a judge so outrageously.

Expropriations in the towns

Illegal occupations of houses and building sites in the big towns, carried out by the MPR *(Movimiento de los Pobladores Revolucionarios—Movement of the Revolutionary Shantytown-dwellers)*, another front for the MIR, were tolerated by the socialist Prefect of the capital, Mr. Alfredo Joignant. The MPR's leader, Mr. Victor Toro, a member of the central committee of the MIR, urged his troops to seize empty plots of land around Santiago, and the first camps were set up, and named "Lenin" and "26th of January". Gradually a chain of such revolutionary camps, each with its force of armed men, spread right round the capital. Then the expropriators switched their operations to the well-to-do districts within the city itself, such as Las Condes.

The seizures had by now become a business for professionals, who preferred to take advantage of the hours of darkness, when the neighbours were asleep, to seize other people's property. The assault squad would arrive in the evening with its arms and equipment, transported in municipal lorries lent them by UP town officials and followed by a bulldozer. They would surround the confiscated land with barbed wire; erect wooden prefabricated houses and hurriedly lay out a few paths. By morning the camp was ready, with its barbed wire, its propaganda posters, its flag, its guards armed with machine pistols, and a notice-board bearing its name: Camp Fidel Ernesto in the case of Las Condes. The leaders of these camps did not accept all the poor who wanted to move in. Thus, the Che Guevara camp on the outskirts of Santiago was initially occupied by 1,200 poor families. But more than 800 of these were expelled later, as the camp's vice-chairman, comrade Nathalia explained, for "breaches of discipline" or "political errors".

It was the UP's intention to establish state control over the whole of the Chilean economy. Its goal in so doing was to make the consumer entirely dependent on the state, so as to bring all Chileans under totalitarian (that is, both political and economic) control. For this, it was first necessary to seize command of the country's financial structures. Initially Mr. Allende had wanted to pass a law nationalizing all the banks that remained in private hands. However he foresaw the strong objections that would be raised, and never laid this bill before parliament. He preferred either to requisition the banks; to put them under the management of an official *interventor*; to ruin them or to buy them up, using methods bordering on sharp practice. For this purpose he set up the Industrial Development Corporation, or CORFO, which had authority to acquire stock in banks and other businesses. His method was quite a simple one: a rumour would be started that the government was about to nationalize such and such a bank; the prices of its shares would drop dramatically, and then no longer be quoted on the stock exchange. The CORFO could then move in and buy them at rock-bottom prices. It was in this not strikingly honest way that the UP won control of all credit, and thus decisive power over all production and distribution in the country.

Industrial and commercial firms also became subject to illegal seizures by varying degrees of violence, though here the word used was "nationalization". In these seizures, the UP was playing to mob-prejudice rather than considering the country's real interest. This becomes clear once one realizes that when Mr. Allende came to power, Chile was already one of the most socialized countries in Latin America, with practically 40 per cent of the gross national product controlled by the state. The big banks and insurance companies, external trade, key industries such as electricity, the railways and oil, all these had belonged to the Chilean state long before the UP Marxists took a hand. All the latter did was to ruin the country's economy by extending nationalization down to the medium-sized and small cells of the social organism (the ones that have an essential need for the oxygen of free enterprise) to the point where they died of asphyxia.

During the Christian Democratic government of Mr. Eduardo Frei the state had a majority interest of 51% of the shares in the copper, iodine, coal and saltpetre mines. It was anticipated that the state would take over 100% ownership of the Chuquicamata copper mines in 1982, which would have given the Chilean technicians time to acquire the necessary know-how to enable them to run mines that American engineers had just modernized so that they now represented the last word in mining progress. But this did not satisfy Allende, who wanted to speed up the whole process by the immediate and hundred-per-cent nationalization of the mines. In this he was unanimously supported by all the senators and deputies, who were afraid that any temporizing on their part would call their patriotism into question.

Mr. Allende had given an assurance that, of the tens of thousands of private businesses in Chile, he would *only* intervene in the case of the 150 that had a monopoly of the market. Of these, 45 would be nationalized, and the remainder would become mixed undertakings having both state and private capital. After two years of Mr. Allende's rule 75% of the agricultural land and 80% of industrial production was controlled by the UP state. In July 1973, the Minister of Labour, the communist Mr. Jorge Godoy, admitted that thousands of businesses, including craftsmen's workshops, had either been occupied; seized; placed under an official *interventor* or requisitioned. CORFO, the

Industrial Development Corporation, had taken 535 businesses under its control.

The *Contralor General* of the Republic, the official responsible for watching over the constitutional correctness of the executive's administrative acts, at this time Mr. Hector Humeres, was frequently forced to point out the illegality of these requisitions and nationalizations to President Allende. The UP press had in any case stopped using the term "requisition", replacing it by "appropriations for the benefit of the community". But whenever the *Contralor* rejected a requisition or nationalization as unconstitutional, a mob would gather opposite the building where his department had its offices and abuse him in such choice language as: "Mummy, fascist, traitor, in the pay of the bosses!" In the end Mr. Allende no longer notified the *Contraloria* of his requisition decrees, passing them off as just the workers themselves spontaneously taking over the businesses in question.

In April 1972, a document known as the *Vuskovic Papers* came to the knowledge of the chairman of the Fomento Fabril company, a document of 170 pages on the headed paper of the CORFO (the state Industrial Development Corporation, of which Mr. Vuskovic was vice-chairman). It set out the whole illegal strategy intended to put an end once and for all to any private enterprise in the economic field: decrees of requisition, special emergency decrees, the fomenting of labour troubles, wage increases of up to 700%, orders to the police not to prevent the seizure of businesses and not to evict the expropriators, even when they had a court order to do so, but to intervene to prevent the persons expropriated from regaining possession of their property. Violence was not excluded from this strategy. A businessman on the management of the San Bernardo refrigeration works, Mr. Enrique Nunez, died after being shot by bands occupying the works in May 1972.

Nor were the shopkeepers spared. Wholesale trade was gradually ruined as the state took over more and more of the distribution networks. Retail trade suffered from the economic segregation of one district from another. Unlike the poor quarters, rich districts, and even those of the middle classes found themselves no longer receiving essential goods and foodstuffs. A shopkeeper who had nothing left to sell naturally faced ruin. If he protested, he was maltreated by the armed bands. In April 1971, Mr. Paul Mendez, a small shopkeeper, was killed in his Santiago premises by a militant of the VOP.

On 14 October 1972, the government ordered the takeover of all commercial establishments in which the unions had voted to stop work in sympathy with the striking lorry-operators. This requisition was a direct denial of the right to strike, which had been recognized in Chile for more than a century. Worse still, the head of state went so far as to threaten that any foreign traders who joined the strike would be immediately expelled from the country. The local JAP commander sent his troops from street to street to force the shopkeepers to reopen their establishments. Those who had Chilean nationality found the courage to resist this pressure, but the Italian and Arab traders, who had settled in the country for many years, were afraid they would driven out of Chile and lose their businesses. The presidents of both the Senate and the Chamber of Deputies declared this action to be illegal, since the Constitution grants equal rights in law to all residents in the country, whether nationals or foreigners. The chairman of the Confederation of Production and Trade attacked "these serious infringements of our Constitution and of the Human Rights Charter". The threat to expel a foreigner from the country just for going on strike is a characteristic of dictatorial regimes.

Expropriations were also useful for providing the expropriators with the funds they needed in order to maintain their staff and a whole host of obedient activists. The undertakings seized in the name of the state—farmlands, banks, factories and trading concerns—were in fact shared out, after hard bargaining, between the various UP parties and their parallel organisations: the socialist and communist parties, the MAPU, the MIR, VOP, JAP, CORA etc. I have had access to a document setting out in detail the undertakings that each of these bodies managed to absorb. "Enjoy your meal, gentlemen, O upright Marxists", one might say, echoing the irony of Hugo's "Ruy Blas".

The consequent, and deliberate inflation, which grew to alarming proportions from 1972 on, had another purpose: that of destroying the currency, which is an instrument for payment, but also a guarantee of the freedom and power of the individual citizen. Once the price regulator runs wild, it becomes possible for the state to control distribution by a rationing system of which it alone holds the reins. By ruining the middle classes, inflation contributes to the political enslavement of the people. Inflation and nationalization undermine the economic power of one's opponents, and hence their political power. At the same time, the independent press saw the resources it derived from private advertising melting away. In addition, all-out nationalization of private property, by making all workers state employees, struck at the roots of their organizational independence, and thus made it easier to force them all into a single trade union federation, the CUT, whose president was a Communist, and who took his orders from the Minister of Labour, himself a Communist.

One could see the totalitarian forge at work, hammering out its monolithic dictatorship.

CHAPTER VIII

THE VIOLENT PATH TO SOCIALISM

I WONDER, DEAR READER, what impression you had in your mind when you read in the world press during the Allende period, that Chile was the stage for a unique experiment, a peaceful and legal progression to Socialism, especially when you were told that the leader of this experiment had taken an oath to respect scrupulously all the rights of citizens, as set out in a *Statute of Guarantees* that he had solemnly signed.

I am sure that the picture in your mind was of a country that had set itself the task of achieving an inspiring social objective in an atmosphere of civic peace, in which problems were studied objectively; plans were freely debated and reforms were put into effect peacefully once a consensus had been reached. This, at any rate, was the impression it was hoped to create in your mind when you were told of the miracle of a new page in social history being written without any blood being shed. How could you be expected to imagine that the authors of these reforms were achieving their ends through aggression, insult, intimidation, theft, arson, bombs, blows and murder? Yet it was these criminal acts that made up the background to political life throughout the period when the UP formed the government. This is the reality that has been hidden from you, and of which I must now speak.

Paramilitary bands

One of the first acts taken by Mr. Allende as president was to publish a decree amnestying 43 young leftists charged with criminal acts. It was this decree that restored freedom to a number of leaders of the MIR (or Movement of the Revolutionary Left), including a nephew of Mr. Allende, and a comrade Arturo Rivera Calderon, destined to become the leader of a movement even more violent than the MIR namely the VOP (*Vanguardia Organizada del Pueblo*—Organized Vanguard of the People), which bore among its "battle honours" the assassination of the former vice-president of the Republic, the Christian Democrat Mr. Perez Zujovic, who had been Minister of the Interior under President Frei. Mr. Zujovic had been struck down by a hail of sub-machine-gun bullets fired through the window of his car, before the horrified eyes of his young daughter, who was sitting next to him.

The men freed by this amnesty had committed not only political crimes but offences against the ordinary criminal law. Some of them had taken part in hold-ups in supermarkets, banks and petrol stations, and thanks to Mr. Allende they were now able to take their place at the head of organizations whose paramilitary character was to become more and more obvious as events progressed.

The VOP

Led by the brothers Ronald and Arturo Rivera Calderon, the members of this "vanguard" launched a mounting series of six particularly ferocious criminal attacks under the high-sounding banner of "revolutionary justice". They murdered the proprietor of a confectionery shop, Mr. Raul Mendez Espinoza, and desecrated his body. In May 1971, while they were stealing 41,000 escudos from a supermarket, they were caught in the act by a carabinero, Mr. Thomas Arnold Gutierrez Urrutia. They killed him in cold blood, and then appropriated his machine pistol. A quarter of an hour later the bandits' get-away van was found. It was full of VOP propaganda. This included a eulogy of the guerilla commando Francisco Ismael Villegas Pacheco, and a justification of the murder of the confectioner Mr. Raul Mendez Espinoza, described as an "exploiter and degenerate", this apparently giving them the right to liquidate him. The justification ended with the following warning: "This was the first application of popular justice, but there will be others. Our black lists contain, in addition to those of the bosses, the names of all those who help to support a system of exploitation . . . politicians, journalists, police and prison warders; they'll all be executed in our revolutionary war."

We recall that one of the leaders of the VOP, Mr. Heriberto Salazar, considered with Mr. Rivera Calderon as one of the assassins of Vice-President Perez Zujovic, attempted in June 1971 to storm the headquarters of the CID (*Policia de Investigación*) commanded by General Mackenna, he shot down three policemen and committed suicide by exploding a dynamite cartridge he was carrying under his clothes.

Most of their top crimes went unpunished. Indeed, the vice-chairman of the Christian Democratic Party accused the director of the investigation department of the police, Mr. Eduardo (nicknamed Coco) Paredes, of intentionally hampering the search for those guilty of crimes, of using his department's vehicles to help them to get away, and of issuing no order for the arrest of Ronald Rivera, who took part in the murder of Mr. Perez Zujovic, although he knew him to be guilty of two earlier crimes.[1]

[1] *El Mercurio*, 11 November 1971.

The MIR

We have already introduced this body, a half political party and half military organization, organized into regional committees heading networks of cells, each of five men, these last being action groups, not forums for discussing policy. The MIR concentrated on five main types of activity: agitational literature, violent street-demonstrations, the *tomas* or expropriations that we have already discussed, espionage and guerilla warfare.

The clandestine literature it put out was spiced with "exercises for knowing the enemy". Its *Manual of Urban Training* contained advice on spying on public employees, the armed forces, the political parties, and even on the Supreme Council of National Security. Its military training manuals covered all the weapons in use in the Chilean army and gave detailed plans of the deployment of the coastal forces of the navy. Other secret documents on *How to prepare for civil war* contained instructions on how to organize safe telephonic communications on making contacts in the army and the ministries, and on the four sorts of places of refuge: permanent safe houses, temporary hideouts, caches in which to manufacture explosives, and cellars in which to stock food supplies, propaganda leaflets and weapons.

From theory, the MIR passed to practice, and this despite the fact that the law, as in all other civilized countries, forbade any paramilitary organizations. The Mirists would parade through the streets booted, helmeted and armed, bearing red and black banners and chanting their battle-cry: "People, awareness, rifle, MIR, MIR, MIR!" Their banners flew from the tops of very long hardwood lances, at whose other end was a steel point. These were the famous *linchacos* that the Korean guerillas had used in the war of 1950. Two sticks, joined at one end by a leather thong, and called *garrotes*, served them quite literally to garrot or strangle their opponents. They also wielded *laques de goma*, lengths of rubber tube filled with lead shot, to be used as coshes. Later they showed no hesitation in using firearms. They thus spread terror in the streets and turned the main boulevards into battlefields.

A photo taken by a reporter of *El Mercurio* became for Chileans a symbol of the way the law was being flouted. In it one can see a carabinero, bent over like a child being beaten by a grown-up, protecting his face and chest as he passively allows himself to be beaten with truncheons by a helmeted member of the MIR. I advisedly write "truncheons" in the plural, for the Mirist had one in each hand. The carabineros, members of the armed police, had been ordered not to interfere with the demonstrators, and did not want to lose their jobs by disobeying. This sort of thing merely encouraged the Mirists to further crime. One of them killed a carabinero, Mr. Jorge Cortes, at Concepción in June 1971. After the elections of March 1973, armed Mirists in a lorry ran over and killed a motor-cycle policeman who was trying to arrest them.

In one of his speeches, President Allende called them "the young idealists", thus bestowing an apostle's halo on these young thugs.

The MIR was reinforced by the members of two other paramilitary brigades. One of these, the 'Ramona Parra' Brigade, was made up of young Communists, and had won its laurels by the murder of a Mirist student at the university of Concepción in December 1970. The other, the 'Elmo Catalan' Brigade, was a socialist formation, named in memory of a former secretary of Mr. Altamirano who had been killed as a guerilla in Bolivia. These shock troops were especially active in the Chuquicamata mines; the communist management of the mines gave them vehicles, and premises in which to store weapons. One of their missions was to destroy vital installations at the mines in the event of the UP being driven from power.

The French philosopher Mr. Régis Debray summed up the position when he wrote: "The most awakened elements within the Popular Unity Front armed themselves right from the very beginning of the regime. Their aim was to carry out a revolution within the revolution" i.e. to stir up trouble and commit acts of violence. Note that Mr. Debray admits that they "armed themselves right from the very beginning", that is, at a moment when no opposition to the UP had as yet shown itself.

Then the MIR decided to dig itself in in wide areas of the towns and the countryside by creating and fortifying the famous camps. Around Santiago the best known of these were the 'Che Guevara', 'Pablo Neruda' and 'La Nueva Habana' camps. In the Nahentué mountains of Cautin province, Colonel Pablo Iturra discovered a MIR camp; his troops took 28 of the guerillas prisoner and the rest fled into the mountains. The soldiers discovered a quantity of anti-tank bombs, detonators, gunpowder, rifles, Molotov cocktails, hand-grenades, a high-powered transmitter, and communist literature. Other MIR camps of the same kind were discovered far up in the Andes chain.

The MIR made no secret of the fact that these camps were politico-military bases for stirring up civil war. The leader of the 'La Nueva Habana' camp, Mr. Alejandro Villalobos (who called himself "Commander Mickey" for each local boss had awarded himself a military rank), made a speech demanding "the reinforcement of the popular militias with a view to preparing for a coming civil war."[1] The camps and the "industrial cordons" were intended as liberated zones, strongholds from which violent revolution could be spread.

---

[1] *La Prensa*, 1 September 1971.

"Industrial cordons" was the name given to the belt of factories and working-class suburbs around Santiago. In some factories in this zone the young workers were given military training and arms. They were being paid not to produce goods but to learn how to use pistols, and even sub-machineguns. These apprentice guerillas took part in the raids carried out by the MIR on bourgeois neighbourhoods to scare the "mummies" (reactionaries); on the city centre so as to intimidate the judges and members of parliament who had their official premises there, and against strikers (lorry-owners or miners) so as to break their strikes. Yes, these Marxist-Leninist militias acted as strike-breakers, a role that brought little honour to their banners. I have already told the story of how "Commander Pepe", after forcibly seizing control of 160 agricultural holdings with his band of 120 armed men, established a reign of terror over a whole region of southern Chile. This pseudo-Commander had set up in his fief a school for guerillas and an operational base similar to that of Mao Tse Tung in Yenan. The much-vaunted "agrarian reform", with its accompaniment of committees, expropriators, nocturnal operations, informers and abandoned farms had become an ideal pretext for paramilitary activities. From 1971 on, police investigations led to the discovery of hoards of arms (rifles, grenades, Molotov cocktails, and dynamite stolen from the mining centres and the security forces) in expropriated farms such as Casas Viejas, near Loncoche, and Santa Delia and El Eucaliptus near Parral. Two leaders of the Young Socialists were injured as a result of an accident to their van. Inside this the police found weapons, ammunition and explosives. The van proved to belong to the Agrarian Reform Corporation, a government agency. The two Socialists were officially employed in the work of agrarian reform. In their pockets were found lists of people to whom weapons were to be delivered, as well as instructions for commando actions. One of the delivery notes listed 150 Mauser pistols, 150 hand-grenades, 300 Molotov cocktails and six machine-guns of Czechoslovak origin.[1]

We can see now the real purpose of the great agrarian reform movement!

Communal commandos and operations centres

The communal commandos were a sort of parallel police force set up by the local authorities controlled by the UP and manned by volunteers. Their members had to be ready to drop everything at a moment's notice so as to take part in the various operations in which their commandos played a dominant role. In February 1973, these communal

[1] *El Mercurio*, 8 July 1973.

commandos were placed under the direction of a central committee, which immediately distinguished itself by raising the movement's targets to a wildly unrealistic level, calling for the expropriation of all medium-sized and small businesses, direct workers' control, the lowering of the threshold for farm seizures from 80 to 40 hectares, etc.

The operations centres were paramilitary operational bases. A secret report of the MAPU, the party formed as a leftist break-away from the Christian Democratic Party, lists a considerable number of operations centres, with the names of their detachments, their leaders, their missions and specific weaponry.[1]

The communal commandos, operations centres and industrial cordons were all part of the process of the mobilisation of a power machine intended to overawe the opposition. This military force was presented as the power of "the people"; in fact it represented merely the power of the Marxist-Leninist militias that made it up. It constituted a semi-clandestine parallel force or dual power to that of the state, which although itself avowedly Marxist-Leninist too, was considered as not sufficiently thorough-going, or which set certain limits on its official action, though the state was very willing to allow these marginal groupings to overstep them.

It is not surprising that, faced with this plethora of paramilitary formations on the extreme left, the extreme right wing of the opposition should have decided to arm in its turn. Two groups were thus founded, the 'Rolando Matus' Brigade, named in memory of a young farmer murdered by the Marxists, and the 'Patria y Libertad' movement. These right-wing groups lent valuable support to the unarmed but angry opposition mass movements of the women, students and workers. The clashes grew even more bloody. Mr. Mario Aguilar, of the 'Patria y Liberta' movement, died from a bullet fired by a demonstrator of the extreme left in Huerfana street in Santiago in May 1973.

The GAP or Group of Personal Friends

It should be noted that the paramilitary spirit and its methods, as well as the atmosphere of war fever, were not restricted to the extremist groups, but infected the supposedly "responsible" main parties of the UP. After the military coup, the army discovered in Mr. Altamirano's strong-box a report of December 1972 from the military commission of the Socialist Party to its Central Committee, a document of nine pages in which the objectives, tasks and means of a small group of militants organized as a military formation are studied exactly as they would be

---

[1] *El Mercurio*, 28 June 1973. This secret report appears in extenso in the White Book, pub. Lord Cochrane, Santiago 1973.

by a colonel for the benefit of his staff. Among the topics reviewed were: places and establishments to be laid siege to, the manpower needed and the most suitable weapons to use in each operation, the communications problem (radio, telephone, dispatch-rider), bases, supplies, hideouts and safe havens, different types of action (sabotage, raids, street-fighting) etc. The whole was followed by six pages of considerations on the possibilities of infiltrating the army.

There is nothing here to be surprised at. Surely only the mentally handicapped can now still be unaware that violence and bloodshed are an integral part of any consistent Marxist-Leninist policy. Later we shall be looking at similar dealings within the Communist Party. For the moment, let us turn our attention to what was, in fact, the finest flower of paramilitarism under the UP, the GAP, or 'Group of Personal Friends' (not to be confused with the JAP, or Rationing and Price-control Committees).

The GAP (*Grupo de los Amigos Personales*—"personal friends" of President Allende), was, in fact, his personal praetorian guard. Mr. Max Joel Marambio, who had done his training in Cuba under the pseudonym of Fontanarosa, organized the group, using strong-arm men from the MIR, the VOP and the Socialist Party. They made a strange circle of friends for a head of state who claimed to be committed to the legal road to Socialism. These armed, helmeted and jackbooted thugs were limbs of the law, some of whom had criminal records and one of whom, Mr. Bruno, had been implicated in the assassination in July 1973 of the president's naval aide-de-camp, Captain Arturo Araya. They drove through the city at all hours of the day and night at illegal speeds. With Mr. Allende behind them, they were privileged; immune from punishment, and answerable to no higher authority. A militant of the Young Socialists, Mr. Alfonso Cortes Soto, after leaving the GAP, said: "They were just hoodlums, and behaved like hired gunmen." A lad of 17 who worked as a gardener at one of Mr. Allende's residences, Mr. El Canaveral, was murdered by one of them.

Until Mr. Allende's accession to power, the protection of Chilean presidents had been carried out by members of the regular police force organized into a special presidential service, an investigative section in plain clothes and carabineros in uniform. The Chileans were shocked, therefore, at the sight of a "democratic" President moving about surrounded by armed bullies who did not belong to any regular service. The "Personal Friends" were illegally equipped with a fleet of Fiat 125 Vehicles, silenced pistols, automatic rifles and sub-machine-guns. Their instructors, imported from Cuba, North Korea and North Vietnam, were all staunch Communists and experts in urban and rural guerilla warfare.

GAP members did their training in the nearby mountain area, and in Mr. Allende's numerous personal or official residences, where shooting-ranges and hutted barracks for 200 of them had been built. El Canaveral, his week-end residence outside Santiago, had a guerilla training camp, which I was able to inspect, and a stock of arms from the USSR and Czechoslovakia, Members of the MIR would attend there for training in the use of arms and manufacture of projectiles. The "Personal Friends" also received marksmanship training in his presidential residence at Santiago, 'Tomas Moro', which he had had fortified. The White Book reproduces a military training programme in use for its garrison. Among the subjects taught were: the operational group, the offensive squad inside towns, and general considerations on urban warfare. A note specifies that classes, of six hours per day, should be conducted in as practical a manner as possible.

In addition to the GAP, 'Tomas Moro' also harboured between 120 and 180 activists recruited in the camps and shantytowns of Chile. They were given three to six months of military training. Among their instructors were two Cubans. The cultural level of these activists was particularly low. They moved around the property permanently armed like professional killers, threatening with their sub-machine guns any motorist who came too near the residence.

Although Mr. Allende claimed he had the people's backing, he moved nowhere without his GAP and armed guards. His conduct in this was strikingly different from that of General Pinochet, whom I saw in September 1978 in front of the porch of his modest family house, in close personal contact with the crowds who had come to see him, and who is not afraid to sit with his wife and children outside a café on the Cerro San Cristobal, the equivalent of London's Hampstead Heath.

Distribution of arms

Although the Carmona law, passed by Parliament under Mr. Allende's presidency, entrusted to the country's armed forces—and to them alone—the responsibility for the control of weapons, and forbade any citizen, however important he might be, to possess arms, Mr. Allende himself hid tons of them in all his public and private residences. After his overthrow on 11 September 1973, arms were discovered in the presidential palace of the Moneda, in his adminstrative offices and in his private apartments. 'Tomas Moro' was found to contain an arsenal, including recoil-less guns and mortars, sufficient to equip ten battalions of troops. At the villa of El Canaveral, in addition to tons of arms, an explosives factory was found, and in the vast park sloping down to the River Mapocho, notices issued the warning: Minefields. Mr. Allende did not stop at illegally storing great quantities of arms, but himself took part in building up arsenals and distributing these arms to his supporters. *El Mecurio* of 3 February 1974 published incontestable proof of this in the shape of a document discovered in the president's personal safe, placed between his bedroom and bathroom in the Moneda palace. It is a confidential report from comrade Jose Rivera, the president's security assessor, to comrade Allende, giving him details of his arms deliveries to the MIR and its leader, mentioned by Mr. Rivera under the code name of Miguel Enriquez. In the list figure 57mm. cannon guns, .30 calibre machine-guns with double magazines, sub-machine-guns, folding carbines, etc.

This comrade Jose Rivera, who accompanied comrade Fidel Castro during the latter's visit to Chile, also supervised the guerilla training given to the MIR at 'Tomas Moro' and El Canaveral. In the White Book one can see reproductions of the exercise-books used by these trainee guerillas, with the marks they were awarded for markmanship and combat. Here, for example, is the report made on a trainee of the name of Eduardo, who passed out first of his class from the guerilla school of the presidential household after a two-months course: "Explosives, 60—Military Tactics, 55—Weapons and Marksmanship, 54—Security, 63—Conduct, 55—Discipline, 55. Average, 59%—Position, 1st.—Remarks: Has done all that was expected of him, is fit to carry out the tasks that will be assigned to him."

Mr. Allende personally took part in some of these classes in order to learn how to handle weapons, as a number of photographs attest. In one of these the President of Chile can be seen lying on the ground firing a machine-gun. In another, an R15 machine pistol in his hands, he is taking a lesson in shooting under the direction of Mr. Coco Paredes.

Thus, despite a permanent law forbidding paramilitary militias, despite the law of 21 October 1972 restricting the control of weapons to the regular armed forces alone, despite the *Statute of Guarantees* in which Mr. Allende had made a solemn commitment before Parliament not to authorize any paramilitary formations, despite the virtuous indignation he simulated when he was accused of being personally involved in the murderous exactions carried out by the MIR and the VOP, Mr. Allende was himself providing arms for the private armies who were shedding Chilean blood.

In comrade Jose Rivera's report we have proof that in April 1971, on Mr. Allende's express orders, arms were delivered to Mr. Coco Paredes (under the latter's code-name of Escarte), the organizer of Mr. Allende's "Group of Personal Friends", so that he could distribute them to his thugs. So, only four months after coming to power, while the honeymoon between the UP and the citizens of Chile still lasted and he was threatened by no opposition, Mr. Allende was already busy arming private armies and breaking his promises. Fully aware of what he was doing, he was violating the *Statute of Guarantees* that he had signed with such solemnity.

Thefts of arms

What is more, Mr. Allende closed his eyes to the constant thefts of weapons and explosives from army depots and mine or factory storehouses. A notorious example, in 1972, was the case of the Curimon van, lent to the MIR by members of the president's bodyguard, and used to transport weapons stolen from the army (this was the van, an accident to which revealed that it belonged to la Payita). Another proof of his complicity was the armed robbery of a large quantity of explosives from the Oscar Spichiquer powder store on 3 March 1973, 20 kilometres from San Antonio, by 12 members of President Allende's own party, their ringleader being Mr. O'Higgins Palma.

One incident caused a considerable stir. On 31 March 1972, as a result of a fortuitous road accident just outside San Felipe, two men, Mr. Fernando Amaya and Mr. Pardo, were detained by soldiers. The van in which they were travelling proved to contain weapons and explosives stolen from the armed forces, as well as plans of military installations in the area. Now the van in question belonged to the Social Security Department, and Mr. Amaya was the holder of a letter of authorization from GAP. In order to whitewash Mr. Amaya and Mr. Pardo in the eyes of justice, an official of the same Allende administration, Mr. Nelson Martin, drew up the text of a *set of lies* that the two accused men were to tell under oath in court. This text was found in Mr. Allende's safe after the coup of 11 September. Mr. Amaya was instructed to make the following replies:

To question 6—I know nothing about the weapons, cartridges and grenades that Pardo was carrying.

To question 14—The letters of authorization I have shown date back to the time when I belonged to the GAP. I no longer belong to it.

To question 15—I was merely the driver of the van.

Mr. Pardo had to learn by heart a score of similar lies, such as:

> To question 7—I do not belong to the GAP.
>
> To question 10a—As to the false identity card, I bought it on the "underground" market. They took my photo and stuck it on this card, which already had someone else's name and personal details entered on it.

> To question 10b—I bought the plan of the military installations at the Army Geographical Institute, and I made notes on it because I thought an opponent of Mr Allende's was prowling suspiciously around them.

This was how justice was set at nought even within the presidential palace of the Moneda itself during Mr. Allende's term of office. But the outside world preferred to wax indignant over the relatively trifling Watergate affair.

Arms smuggling

To cap it all, the Popular Unity government went in for intensive smuggling of arms from abroad.

For a time, until the end of 1971, unscheduled flights arrived from Cuba at Pudahuel airport on Saturday nights, and their cargoes were transferred into big lorries that did not pass through customs. When the scandal broke in the press, these flights were suspended, and the smuggling was operated through Lan Chile, the nationalized Chilean airlines. Top officials, among them Mr. Abraham Ortega, organized secret imports of arms, mainly from Cuba. A special commission was set up to investigate this traffic.

Once Congress had adopted the Carmona law making weapons control a responsibility of the armed forces, the UP's paramilitary organizations had no other means of obtaining arms apart from smuggling them in. To prevent the smuggled arms from being discovered in the course of official searches, President Allende simply had them hidden in one or other of his residences, as can be seen from the affair of the "Cuban packing-cases".

This affair caused quite a scandal. On 11 March 1972 the head of the Criminal Investigation Department of the police, Mr. Coco Paredes, returned from one of his frequent trips to Cuba in a plane of *Cuba Aviaciôn*. Among his luggage were 13 very big crates weighing more than a ton; these, together with five suitcases, he declared to be "personal effects". When customs officials wanted to check the crates, Mr. Coco Paredes opposed this sharply, shocked that a police chief should be treated like the man in the street. The customs officers insisted on carrying out their duties, so Mr. Coco Paredes declared that the packing cases contained presents—objets d'art, liqueurs and cigars—that the Cuban government was graciously sending to President Allende. Note that this police chief, a socialist to boot, was in no way shocked by the president of a "democratic" country taking advantage of his position to avoid paying duty on objets d'art, liqueurs and cigars. He adopted a hectoring tone, and threatened the humble servants of the state that he would get them dismissed from their jobs.

As the customs officers continued to hold the crates despite everything, Mr. Coco telephoned to the Minister of the Interior, Mr. Hernan del Canto, another Socialist, who immediately rushed to the airport. He peremptorily told the customs officers that the 13 crates would be forcibly taken away by a police patrol he had brought with him without passing through customs. The customs men, powerless in the face of the armed police, allowed the packing-cases to pass. And these were transported to the presidential residence of 'Tomas Moro'.

Mr. Allende flouted in this way every customs regulation. He was, moreover, setting at nought a tradition whereby every president of the Chilean Republic should obtain congressional approval for the importing of any gift made to him by a foreigner. Thus president Alessandri, for example, had asked permission before importing a car offered to him by the President of Brazil.

It goes without saying that the arbitrary exercise of power on this scale daily cast further discredit on the UP government and aroused public indignation against it. This public feeling led the *Contraloria* to investigate the matter, and a commission of the Chamber of Deputies summoned the Minister of the Interior and the chief of police to make a statement in the chamber. Whereupon Mr. Daniel Vergara, undersecretary to the Minister of the Interior and a Communist, declared to reporters: "The crates contain liqueurs, cigars and objects of craftsmanship given by Fidel Castro to comrade President", and this declaration was reproduced by the communist paper *Puro Chile*. At Concepción, Mr. Allende went even further, saying: "What a fuss people are making about a few Cuban packing-cases not opened at the customs! Well, I'll tell you what they contain: jellied mangoes and presents sent by the heroic socialist mothers of Cuba to those of Chile."

However the mothers of Chile did not see hide nor hair of these presents. If that was all the cases contained, why this obstinate refusal to let the customs look inside them? The *Contraloria* could not insist on inspecting the contents of 13 crates stored at President Allende's residence, since the law had made no provision for the case of a President of the Republic keeping smuggled goods in a residence that he had turned into a fortress. But Congress relieved the Minister of the Interior, Mr. del Canto, of his office for "offences against the criminal law", and suspended the police chief Mr. Coco Paredes for "a serious offence".

After the coup of 11 September a detailed inventory of the contents of each of the 13 crates was found in Mr. Coco Paredes' flat, no. 213 in Block no. 98 of the Residencia San Borja. Here is the list for crate no. 1 weighing 79 kilos in the original Spanish: 10 pist. amet. MP40 calibre 9 mm; 40 depositos pist amet MP 40 calib 9 mm; 10 porta depositos de lona; etc. (i.e. 10 MP 40 9 mm. machine pistols; 40

magazines for MP 40 9 mm. machine pistols; 10 canvas magazine holders). Other crates were listed as containing six anti-tank rockets, 12 heavy machine-guns, ammunition and spare parts, etc. In short, these 13 crates did indeed contain a *complete arsenal* for the illegal private armies, just as everyone had rightly suspected.

To illustrate by an anecdote the stream of smuggled arms secretly negotiated between Chile's UP and foreign communist powers, one may quote an episode that made all Chile laugh in March 1972. A worthy housewife of Concepión managed, to her great delight, to buy a big bag of sugar on the black market. She took it home, but when she opened it all she found inside, to her keen disappointment, was a number of Soviet pistols concealed in a white powder! No use at all for making cakes. It appears that a quantity of similar disguised sacks had been unloaded from a Soviet ship. Some negligent accomplice of the UP must have forgotten this particular bag on the quayside, where it was picked up by a docker who thought it contained sugar as its label announced, and routed it onto the black market.

An atmosphere of violence

The present chapter, devoted to paramilitary groups, is not the only one in the book in which violence constantly crops up. We have already seen this on a grand scale in the chapters describing the plundering and regimentation of the people. This violence did not occur merely as an accompaniment to the carrying out of the main planks in the UP's programme; to this we must add an all-pervasive, endemic violence, constantly being sparked off for any number of smaller reasons of all types, ideological or religious disagreement, party rivalry, municipal intrigue or the settling of political scores. This endemic violence was directed not only against the bourgeoisie, but *against the workers too*, and this by a state which claimed to be proletarian.

It is difficult to establish precisely its full extent, since many of the individual clashes never appeared in any official report. If one merely counts up the political murders officially recorded as such, they number 122 for the three years of the UP government. This list, with names quoted and a short summary of the circumstances in each case, can be found in the *White Book*. I quote here a few examples of murders of workers other than those I have already mentioned in other chapters devoted to the chief aspects of the UP's programme:

—Mr. Orlando Silva and Mr. Sergio Olivares, lorry-owners, Mr. Fernando Carrera, soldier, and Mr. Jose Urra, worker, shot dead in one of the clashes during the great strike of October 1972.

—Mr. Luis Bravo Morales, miner, one of the El Teniente strikers, shot dead in May 1973 at Rancagua.

—Mr. Manuel Garrido, worker at Panos Continental, shot dead during a clash with the MIR in July 1973.

—Mr. Manuel Gonzalez, worker at the Lanera Austral in Punta Arenas, killed while resisting a search in July 1973.

—Mr. Robinson Gutierrez, railway worker, shot dead in August 1973 while resisting an MIR attack on a rail depot.

—Mr. Jose Navarro, worker, shot dead on 26 July 1972 for bumping into a car carrying three socialist leaders!

—Mr. Juan Millalonco, militant in the Young Christian Democrats, killed at Aisen by a socialist brigade in August 1971.

—A child, Master Oscar Pineda, aged 13, killed by a bullet in the head during an attack by a UP commando on the National Party in February 1973.

To these known dead must be added those who died in countless other obscure clashes, and whose deaths have not been recorded. Weighing up the *total* picture, one comes to the conclusion that in three years of the "legal road" to Socialism, the UP, to impose its political line, must have committed around *one act of bloodshed every two days.*

This figure is admittedly tiny compared with the millions of innocent lives sacrificed by communist regimes over a comparable period, and thus one is not justified in saying that the UP brought in a "reign of terror". It was preparing to do just this when it was overthrown. The figure is nevertheless striking if one compares it with the impression of an atmosphere of peaceful democracy purveyed by the world press. Nor is that all. A climate of violence cannot be measured merely by the numbers of persons whose blood was shed. One must take into account also the psychological halo that surrounded this relatively small core of victims, a halo of threats, intimidation, harassment, ill-treatment and hate-filled insults.

For the UP in power did not openly thrash out its disagreements with the lawcourts, the Supreme Court, the *Contraloria*, Parliament or the press in dignified and serious discussions. As soon as one left Mr. Allende's personal office, where one was treated to a recital of insincere regrets and excuses, but which were at least couched in decent language, all one heard in answer to one's objections from the leaders and militants of the UP were insults, lies and bloodcurdling threats.

Punto Final, the MIR newspaper, and *Clarin*, a fighting paper controlled by Socialists of the Altamirano tendency (i.e. the majority Socialists), both strove to reproduce the intentionally coarse snarling tone of the *Père Duchêne* of the French Revolution. They never referred to the democratic opponents of the UP other than as "stinking mummies" or "filthy monkeys". The *barrio alto* ("upper quarter"), the popular name for Santiago's smart district, was always called that of the *culos bajos* (low arses). Their opponents' womenfolk were, naturally, "whores", or at the best, "hysterical". A well-known song of the UP activists ran as follows: "*Los momios al paredôn, y las momias en el colchôn*"—i.e. "The male mummies (reactionaries) to the wall (to be shot), and the female ones to our bed". One day when *Clarin* had urged the masses to go and set fire to the *barrio alto*, a democratic newspaper published a complicated plan of the devious route the arsonists would have to follow if they were to avoid including in their conflagration the 150 super-de-luxe villas that housed all the UP chiefs, President Allende himself and the embassies of the communist countries.

It will be remembered that when Congress sacked the Minister of the Interior, Mr. del Canto, for abuse of his powers in the "Cuban crates" scandal, a yelling mob gathered in front of the Parliament building, and high-ranking militants, including Mr. del Canto himself, called the members of parliament "scoundrels", "swine", "hired traitors whom we'll get even with". Similarly, when the judge at Melipilla condemned a UP raid against the opposition TV channel, those guilty of the raid gathered in front of his house and burned the judge in effigy, calling him a "bastard".

Intimidation was the Allendists' favourite weapon. All their opponents, lower middle-class as well as upper-class, craftsmen, non-conforming workers, judges, lawyers and journalists were continually being threatened with death or maltreatment. When one of the women who had organized and led the "saucepan march" (and who had had her arm cut by a flying potato with a razor blade in it) had to face a band of shouting revolutionaries who had come to her house to arrest her, and asked them to show her the arrest warrant, the leader of the band pointed his sub-machine-gun at her breast and replied, "This is my warrant." Opponents received anonymous telephone calls or letters threatening them with terrible punishments—their car or their house would be burned, or they would be beaten up—and some were warned that a certain child of theirs would be kidnapped.

Whom can we accuse of leanings towards fascism—those who create and maintain such an atmosphere, or those who seek to escape from it?

Who, within the UP, was responsible for the violence?

It must be said that violence was not restricted to attacks by the UP against its opponents. A certain number of outbreaks occurred also *between* the different factions making up the UP. These we must examine if we hope to find the answer to an important question that the reader will certainly have asked himself: who, within the UP, was responsible for the violence? Was it the UP as a whole, or just one of its component parties?

The incident of the fratricidal struggle within the MAPU which I recounted earlier is only one of a number marking the chronic quarrels between the different champions of Popular Unity. There were plenty of others. Thus the Mirist student Mr. Arnoldo Rios was struck down by a communist commando. At Concepción, the MIR asked the CUT (the communist-dominated trade union federation) to organize on its premises a funeral vigil for Mr. Luciano Cruz, a MIR leader who had died in unusual circumstances. The communist chairman of the CUT Mr. Figueroa, refused, and the result was a bloody clash between the two camps. At the time of the assassination of the Christian Democrat Mr. Vuskovic, the communist chief of police Mr. Coco Paredes, instead of hushing up the guilt of his leftist murderers, gave it full publicity and forced those responsible to come out into the open, and this lead to their leader Mr. Salazar committing suicide. On 4 August 1972 the same Mr. Coco Paredes organized a raid on the shantytown of Lo Hermida in search of those members of a leftist group called "16th of July" who had committed a number of sensational acts of aggression. This operation cost one Mirist worker killed and 11 wounded. Feelings ran high, and the leftists went as far as to call the communist leaders murderers. Mr. Allende had to come to the locality in person to calm things down.

As a background to these violent confrontations, there were obvious differences on tactics between the different parties making up the UP, hingeing in the main on whether one adopted the "radical" or the "moderate" position. The "radical" line, supported by Mr. Altamirano, the General Secretary of the Socialist Party, consisted in a continual acceleration and extension of the movement, using the power and "armed strength of the people" (in other words, private armies) to crush all resistance to the Marxist-Leninist revolution, without worrying about winning support or votes among the population at large, and accepting all the bloodshed, tears and destruction that this implied. According to the so-called "moderate" position, championed, it was said, by the Communist Party and the left-wing radicals, the UP should on the contrary strive to widen its popular support to take in the liberal and Christian Democratic sections of the population, remain to some extent within the bounds of constitutional legality, nationalizing of course, but only within the limits of what was financially possible, and replacing "old regime" civil servants very gradually, without harassing them too much at the outset.

Most writers on the subject attach considerable importance to these dissensions within the UP. They draw two conclusions: on the one hand they see them as explaining Mr. Allende' constant vacillations between the hard and soft lines; on the other, they try to explain the chaos and violence Chile suffered under the UP as due not to the "reasonable' Communist Party but to the irresponsible folly of the extreme left and Mr. Altamirano.

I have examined this thesis with all the objectivity called for when dealing with such a question. My conclusion is that it does not hold water, for several, in my view, very good reasons.

My first reason is that, for all the apparent divergence of tactics, the two camps, the "reasonable" and the "extremist", were basically in agreement on essentials. They were all working towards one and the same goal, the complete elimination of the free enterprise system and the building of a totally collectivist society. They were all in agreement, too, on the necessity, sooner or later, of a real revolution to destroy—physically—the human and legal framework of "the past". Finally, all of them and this is the central point recognized Lenin as their supreme master. Now, what in fact was Lenin's own specific contribution to Marxist theory? It was a single idea, but a fundamental one, and one which changed the whole aspect and emphasis of the movement—the idea that the seizure of power takes precedence over everything else, and that power can only be seized and held *by the use of force and terror*, leaving all one's scruples behind one in the cloakroom. The Chilean sociologist Mr. Juraj Domic has carried out a brilliant campaign to enlighten the public on this point; it is on him that I am drawing for the following pertinent reminders.

To begin with, Lenin took care, repeatedly, to make clear precisely what one should understand by dictatorship: that is, "a power established and maintained purely by force, imposing its will without paying heed to any law or to public opinion". In his pamphlet on *The military programme of the proletarian revolution*, Lenin wrote: "If one accepts the class struggle, one is bound at the same time to accept *civil war* . . . An oppressed class that is not ready to learn to handle arms and provide itself with as complete and active a military force as possible deserves to be treated as no more than a slave class . . . When the hour strikes, anyone who is afraid to shed the blood of the class-enemy is a traitor . . . the police and the army must be totally destroyed and replaced by the people's armed militias, acting without weakness under the direction of the Communist Party." Lenin, a practical man par excellence, was not just theorizing here; he carried out his own recommendations implacably right to the end. Mr. Juraj Domic went to the trouble of retracing the history of the terror set up by Lenin *as soon as* he seized power, and drew up a balance sheet of his victims; he arrived at the terrifying figure, confirmed since by all the specialists, of a million and a half deaths during the six years of Lenin's absolute rule. This is proof enough that massacres, torture and Gulags were not innovations brought in under the monster Stalin, but were an integral part of Communism right from its first days under the leadership of the "great man", Lenin.

This "great man" was an object of worship to all the members of the UP. They all swore by his gospel. As this was essentially a gospel of *action* and not of *belief*, it was precisely in action, on the field of battle, facing the enemy and the ramparts of the system they were attacking, that all their hearts beat as one. Unlike a more doctrinal type of Marxism, which by this very fact is more open to different interpretations, Leninism is a rigid cord that binds whoever grasps it. It is less a *teaching* than a *manual of military training. Leninism is the rifle of Marxism.* One does not quarrel over the different ways of pulling the trigger of a rifle.

The above constitutes, if you like, a philosophical reason for not lending credence to the view that there were any really fundamental differences of opinion between the two wings of Chile's UP. Another reason, drawn this time from reality is that, had it wanted to force Mr. Allende to break with the "extravagances" of the leftists, the Communist Party had all the means at its disposal to do so. Mr. Allende himself too could have put an end to them without risk to himself. All the forces of law and order, the carabineros, the urban police, the army and the law courts were impatiently chafing at the restraint imposed on them by Mr. Allende's official passivity in the face of the violence and exactions of the left. The government had to exert an intense, constant and quite improper pressure to prevent these regular forces from intervening against the exactions and violence. Given the fact that the leftist groups were numerically small, and that public opinion was deeply hostile to them, it would have been an easy task to bring them to heel. But neither Mr. Allende nor the Communist Party made the slightest concrete move in this direction. Indeed, the only acts of theirs I have seen recorded have been such as to give concealed support to the hotheads and to cover up for them. My preceeding chapters are studded with examples showing clearly that in reality the head of state approved all these excesses, with only a few insignificant exceptions.

A third reason, in my view decisive in itself, for rejecting the picture of a Popular Unity front swept along against its will into "excesses" by an "immoderate" wing, is the fact that the "immoderate wing" *was in fact armed by the "moderate wing".* The Communist Party did not even need to pass through the intermediary of President Allende to restrain the leftists. It had the power to intervene directly, had it wanted to. For apart from a few weapons stolen from the army, all the leftist groups and paramilitary formations received their arms—not to speak of military instructors and all the money they had not stolen personally—from whom? You have guessed it: from Cuba. Cuba was strictly dependent on whom? On Moscow, as you know. And it was Moscow that unilaterally determined the line followed by the Chilean party. If the line or the party had really been opposed to violence, all they would have needed to do was to turn off the tap, halting the supply of arms and money, and the violence would simply have stopped. Conversely, if the hard-liners, totally dependent as they were on Cuban supplies, never slackened the intensity of their campaign, this was because the communist high command did not want such a slackening. One can state it as a general rule, in fact, that if you find Czech or Soviet arms in the hands of any given group—and this was so for practically *all* the arms found on Chilean leftists during and after the military coup d'état—you can be certain that these groups are working in the direction wanted by the Kremlin, and hence by the national Communist Party. Moscow does not provide machine-guns for people who do not serve its policies.

Finally, we have a fourth reason for rejecting the hypothesis which, to clear the Communists of all blame, credits them with relying on a sober forecast of future historical development, and shifts all responsibility for the excesses on to the leftists. This is that we possess *direct written evidence to the contrary*, found in the secret drawers of the party after the coup of 11 September 1973, and published in the White Book. Out of a considerable number of such documents, I have room only to reproduce one particularly revealing one: a note from the Santiago federation of the Communist Party to its cell leaders, dated 30 June 1973. Here is the complete text:

OBLIGATIONS for all party militants:

(a) To provide themselves with firearms.

(b) To obtain and tranport to the house of all militants on the following list glass bottles, paraffin and drinking-water.

(c) In the event of an armed clash, never to shoot at carabineros in uniform before checking that they do not belong to teams of communist militants dressed in these uniforms on our orders.

(d) In the case of a general action, our militants must evacuate the *barrio alto* (the well-to-do district) on the very first day, since we shall be using heavy bombs to destroy whole blocks of buildings, and the list of these may vary.

(e) You are reminded that all Communist Party equipment is marked with the letters Ej followed by a number. On the equipment of other UP parties there will be a capital letter between these letters and the number.

(f) Opposition leaders must be physically liquidated by specially trained groups; our militants must assist these groups whenever required to do so, and must maintain absolute secrecy.

(g) It is essential to hold stocks of candles, matches, provisions, soap, water, paraffin, etc., because we shall need to blow up waterworks, power-stations, etc.

I do not think I need to draw the reader's attention—you will surely have noticed it for yourself—to those details showing the care and the icy determination with which this supposedly "gradualist' party prepared its men, weapons, bases, logistics, strategies, demolitions, assassinations and explosions with a view to imposing Leninist Socialism through force and bloodshed.

On the basis of these observations, my conclusion is that everything that happened in Chile under the aegis of the Popular Unity front formed in the main part of the communist plan. This plan—it is an old story—could include a number of variants, alternatives and different emphases, to be brought into play either simultaneously or in turn, and which might even at times seem to clash with one another. In the Chilean drama a "legalist" approach was unavoidable, for the basic reason that there was considerable popular opposition to what the UP was doing, so that any attempt to impose the final objectives of the Communists could only have been achieved at the cost of a full-scale bloodbath; this would have dissipated at one blow the whole myth of a "democratic road to Socialism", cultivated in the outside world by a widespread propaganda campaign, and which paid handsome dividends, especially in France in 1978–9 at the period of the Common Programme of the Left. But to reduce this inevitable temporary delay to a minimum, it was useful to have *at the same time*, a body of impatient hotheads dealing body blows at the social order to knock it off balance and weaken its resistance.

The UP prepared *the decrees*, the MIR prepared *the demolitions*. One undermined the fabric of society while the other attacked it openly. By this effective division of labour, the two together prepared the way for an ultimate communist coup d'état.

CHAPTER IX

ECONOMIC DISASTER

I WONDER IF PEOPLE STILL remember that when Socialism first appeared on the historical stage, it defined itself as *a more efficient economic system*. The basic thesis of Karl Marx, the one which for more than a century was used to justify Socialism's claim to take the place of capitalism in society's progress towards a higher form of civilization, was that the drive for profit of each individual entrepreneur would lead not only to the exploitation of the workers, but also to economic anarchy and waste, and would intensify the internal contradictions of capitalism to the point where the productive forces themselves would slow down. Then along would come Socialism to liberate these forces, and bring them to full development by collectivizing the means of production and distribution, and planning the economy more efficiently.

This was the classic scheme that has nourished the hopes and dreams of the left for 150 years: on the one hand capitalism, selfish and irrational, sounding the death-knell of production, and on the other Socialism, its generous and scientific saviour. After 60 years of experience in 20 countries this generalization has been stood on its head, since it is state Socialism that has brought ruin and free enterprise capitalism prosperity.

To this constant downward slant of Socialism towards economic bankruptcy, the Popular Unity in Chile added its own distinctive steep dive, thus nullifying its own avowed goal. The Allende government devastated the country's economy just as a plague of locusts lays waste the fields. I do not intend to give here a detailed account of this catastrophe, since it is now a matter of general agreement. I shall, however, content myself with setting out the most significant results and elucidating their causes.

I must first recall to the reader's mind a number of facts already set down in earlier chapters, and which show how far the nationalization of industry and business was carried by the UP. When Mr. Allende came to power in the autumn of 1970, 40% of Chile's industrial gross national product came from the nationalized sector (energy, transport, communications, etc.). To this sector were added the copper mines, a process which began during Mr. Frei's presidency and was completed as soon as the UP took over. All the rest, that is roughly 50% of the

GNP, was produced by private enterprise. In three years of UP government, 535 private undertakings, responsible for 65% of the private sector, were nationalized. Thus the state sector finally accounted for 80% of the country's total production.

A similar takeover had taken place in agriculture, and 75% of it had passed into the hands, not of small peasant proprietors, but of a whole growth of new para-political groupings which for simplicity's sake can be lumped together under the title, soon to become standard, of "Agrarian Reform Centres" in effect collective farms. These were all-powerful local organizations for management and agitprop, staffed by inexperienced rural bureaucrats appointed by the regime, falling under the authoritarian direction of the CORA (*Corporaciôn de la Reforma Agraria*—Agricultural Reform Corporation) and the INDAP (*Instituto de Desarollo Agrario y Pecuario*—Institute for the Development of Agriculture and Livestock), two state agencies centred in Santiago and operating under the control of the hotheaded extremist Minister of Agriculture, Mr. Chonchol and his young enthusiasts, who were apter in the wielding of arms than the sewing of seed. I think that one can say fairly, therefore, without distorting the facts, that the majority of Chilean agriculture, like the greater part of industry and large-scale trade, was to all intents and purposes in the hands of the state.

If this is so, we are perfectly justified in blaming the Allende government for all that happened to the national economy during his reign. Even in countries where the bulk of the economy remains within the private sector, it has become customary to hold the public authorities responsible for its wellbeing, since they have at their command a number of levers for determining its progress. We have an even stronger right, and even a duty to do so in the case of a government that had assumed direct control over more than two thirds of the productive forces and which, moreover, had loudly asserted its right to direct them on the grounds, as it claimed, that it knew how to do far better than the industrial and land-owning bourgeoisie, degenerate bloodsuckers that these were.

Having established this point, let us review the major indices of Chile's economic collapse under Mr. Allende.

One of my principal sources here is the remarkable document drawn up in March 1974 by the Business School of the Valparaiso Chamber of Commerce under the title: *Chile's Economy under the Popular Unity Government.* My other sources, Mr. Baltra Cortes *Gestiôn Economica del Gobierno de la Unidad Popular* (Economic Administration of the Popular Unity Government), the other studies I have consulted, as well as my personal interviews with leading economic figures, such as the chairmen of the employers' association, the chambers of agriculture and the Central Bank, together with trade-union leaders, all either agree with my primary source or paint an even blacker picture.

The balance sheet

The sources show that between 1970 and 1973, during the three years of Marxist-Leninist rule in Chile:

—Industrial production declined by 12%;

—Agricultural production declined by 30%;

—Livestock production declined by 20%

—Copper production declined by 2%

—Prices, *if one includes the black market*, increased by 1,000%, that is ten times;

—Fiduciary issues (that is, the circulation of paper money) increased by 2,000%, or 20 times;

—Foreign currency reserves fell from 400 million dollars at the end of Mr. Frei's term of office to zero;

—The balance of payments had dropped from a surplus of 90 million dollars to a deficit of 325 million dollars;

—The budget, from a state of balance, had swung to a deficit equivalent to 53% of its total amount;

—The escudo (the legal currency) was devalued four times: in December 1971, August 1972, May 1973 and August 1973.

Not a bad achievement for a "more efficient economic system"! But let us look more closely at the reality hidden behind these figures, the declining vitality of the country's economic life.

Let us begin with the least discouraging, those for copper. Unfortunately, the figures here look more favourable than they really are, for they conceal the fact that two new mines, Exotica and Andina, came into production in 1972. If we look at the facts mine by mine, the decline in the production of copper per worker employed is as follows: at Chuquicamata, from an average of 39 metric tonnes per annum under Mr. Frei to a new average of 29 tonnes per annum under Mr. Allende; at El Teniente, from 21 tonnes to 17. Again, the drop at Chuquicamata from 39 to 29 is an average over the three years. At the beginning it was much higher, and I have mentioned the exasperation of the miners at the lunatic and irrelevant intrusion of political issues by the new bosses, leading to their first strike to "take copper away from the Communists and give it back to the Chilean people". This strike sounded a warning note for the authorities, forcing them to take at least some steps to restore the position, and thus stabilizing the fall in production per miner at around 20 per cent.

Turning to agriculture, we find a drop in production of 30%, or nearly a third of the harvests! To fully understand the enormity of this figure, we must see it as corresponding to a drop of 23 per cent in the area cultivated. To find as much land uncultivated in Chile as there was at the end of Mr. Allende's reign we should have to go *40 years back* in the history of the country, to a period when the population was only half as large.

It must be added that the fall in production for wheat, the most important crop, exceeded the average and was of the order of 40%, and thus only 42% of the national requirement could be met internally, whereas under Mr. Frei 85% of the nation's wheat needs had been grown in the country. This drop in self-sufficiency increased seriously for other farm products too. For rice, the percentage internally produced dropped from 69 to 46, for beef from 93 to 57, and for milk from 83 to 55. Chile was consequently forced to make a considerable increase—of 55%—in her food imports, thus depleting her currency reserves and causing a deficit in her balance of payments without any corresponding rise in productivity. An enormous and uncontrollable boost was given to the black market. Lastly and most importantly, this led to a serious food shortage which necessitated the unpopular rationing that was introduced in January 1973, a shortage which was on the point of becoming a famine at the moment of Mr. Allende's fall: just prior to this the President had announced on TV there was only a few days supply of wheat left.

The *black market* swelled to fantastic proportions from the middle of 1972 onwards, and deserves a volume to itself. Mr. Allende had celebrated his accession to power by scattering largesse on a joyful people: he had emptied the treasury chests; worn out the printing blocks producing money and greatly expanded consumption, and, not unnaturally, prices began to shoot up. As they shot up, the only expedient Mr. Allende could find was to fix them by decree. But his decrees fixed them at quite unrealistic levels, and so everyone started going in for "backdoor barter" at astronomic prices. As, thanks to nationalization, the majority of goods were in the hands of *the UP bureaucrats, these became the principal suppliers of the black market and its chief beneficiaries.*

The black market fed on itself, spreading and growing like a bush fire. An ordinary burlap sack, empty, sold for more on the black market than the official price of the maize it would contain when full. For a packet of cigarettes one could buy three cinema seats. A chicken, at the price set by Mr. Allende's agencies, could be exchanged for three eggs at the price obtained by the producer. And so on. Some of the situations this led to were quite crazy. Once the food shortage had grown to the point where it gave rise to the interminable queueing I have mentioned elsewhere, all sorts of side-effects cropped up. One of these was a new profession, that of *colero* (from the Spanish *cola*, queue). The most honest of these professional queuers just made a charge for keeping their client's place in the queue, or rented makeshift braziers or folding stools to those who got tired or cold queueing all night. The less scrupulous of these *coleros* would fill whole queues with their own clan, wife, children, uncles, cousins and friends, and carry off, at the low official price, a whole assortment of goods which they would then re-sell straightaway for ten times their price in the next street. And the UP bureaucrats had no interest in cleaning up this abuse, since they were the first to profit by it. As always happens in times of scarcity, price control was accompanied by a system of quotas. It is not hard to imagine that everyone who, for whatever reason, was in a position to help someone to get hold of a voucher entitling the latter to buy some article at the official price, would have a firm unofficial arrangement with that someone to share the resultant profit when the article was re-sold on the black market.

The worst chaos of all was naturally to be found in the import business. From the spring of 1973 there were seven different exchange rates for seven different categories of goods, ranging from 25 to 1,300 escudos to the dollar, and averaging, on a fair estimate, at 50 escudos to the dollar, whereas on the black market one could pay up to 2,500 escudos, or 50 times as much! In any transaction involving several of this wide range of exchange rates there was thus room for any number of speculations to "equalize" or "average out" the rates, making possible a multitude of "juicy" (i.e. profitable, as they expressed it in their dignified jargon) deals for the speculator. One of the most remarkable discoveries of the period was the following type of "chain-transaction". Mr. Pedro Gonzales, having acquired some attractive import vouchers, buys a quantity of product X abroad for, say, 10,000 dollars at the official rate for its category, say 50 escudos to the dollar; in other words, he obtains these dollars from the Central Bank against a payment of 500,000 escudos. He re-sells product X for 1,000 dollars to Mr. John Smith, a foreign resident in Chile who possesses dollars. But these 1,000 dollars, when he changes them back into escudos on the black market, bring Mr. Gonzales in 2,500,000 escudos. Thus without doing anything, he has made a profit of two million escudos. As for Mr. John Smith (wait for it!), with the help of an official to whom he has given a bribe of 1,000 dollars, and has obligingly passed him some other official vouchers, he re-exports product X at two thirds of the price it would normally command abroad (this, we saw at the outset, was 10,000 dollars). He has therefore paid out 1,000 dollars in buying product X from Mr. Pedro Gonzales, and another 1,000 in bribing a UP bureaucrat, and has received 6,500 in re-selling product X abroad. Mr. John Smith's profit is thus 4,500 dollars.

Let us be duly grateful to Marxism-Leninism for introducing such a rational and profit-free economic system!

The nationalized factories were all running at a loss. In 1972, according to a study made by the Economics faculty of the University of Chile, their total deficit was 22 milliard escudos (at a time when the budgetary deficit was 27 milliards). These systematic losses were covered up by the nationalized banks, and thus ultimately by the inflationary printing of more bank-notes. What we cannot establish precisely is what proportion of these industrial losses was due to a real drop in production and what proportion was due to products being diverted onto the black market. But we can be sure we are dealing with a true fall in production in the case of products that are not objects of individual exchange, such as railway lines, postal buses, electric pylons, etc. Various studies have shown that the losses made by the nationalized enterprises investigated were in general more than the sums they would have paid to the state in taxes on profits if they had been functioning normally! Their nationalization, therefore, was doubly absurd: not only did it suppress a source of gain—the profits tax—but it also created a source of loss—the sums necessary to restore the finances of the companies concerned. Hence a well-known joke of the period: "Let me explain to you what nationalization means for the state: it stops collecting ten thousand millions and starts paying out 20 thousand millions."

One sector that could not be brought into the black market, but which impinged heavily on people's daily lives—that of house-building—and which ought therefore to have been treated with special tenderness by the UP, was the hardest hit of all. By 1973 its output had sunk to *less than half* the average of the pre-1970 period. The state railways were totally neglected, and were in such a sorry state that they are still not back to normal even today. Another pointer to the absolute collapse of industry—by "absolute" I mean, quite apart from any diversion of production into the black market—is the fact that during three years of UP government there was *no productive investment in the economy:* not a single new factory was opened, no new product launched, no new public-service installation opened, apart from two copper mines and a port, the plans for all three of these having been drawn up by the previous government so that the UP merely had to let them go ahead. Here we have proof of that sclerosis of the UP's socialist economics, that unadapting rigidity which is even more serious than the other pathological signs we have noted.

Bad excuses

To escape their own crushing responsibility for the economic collapse of the country, the UP leaders, obligingly backed up by the left-wing media of the outside world, put out a number of "explanations" so lame that they served merely to reveal their own bad consciences.

Thus Mr. Allende himself claimed that the shortages were not due to people producing less, but to the fact that they were richer now, thanks to him, and so were eating and spending far more. Whereas, five years after the fall of the UP, I have often seen ordinary women whom I was interviewing in the shantytowns, shops and markets burst out into violent recriminations merely at the thought of the suffering they had lived through as a result of the shortages.

Other excuses, at first sight less ridiculous, were based on the classic accusation of sabotage and conspiracy that all unsuccessful revolutionaries tend to level at their opponents of the previous regime. Before examining this charge, it would be as well to emphasize that if it was justified in the mouth of a Cromwell or a Robespierre, it is quite incongruous when uttered by Marxists who heap such derision on what they call "the conspiracy theory of history". We all know how they jeer at any suggestion that a Communist break-through in some area or milieu that one would normally expect to be hostile to their creed may be due not to deep-seated socio-historical reasons but to the underground manoeuvres of Marxist subversives. Yet as soon as Communism scores a blatant failure, the blame is never attributed to the faulty infrastructure of its system but always to subterranean plots hatched against it by wicked capitalists. In the present case, the blame for Chile's economic disaster was to be laid at the door of the big landowners for sabotaging land reform, the CIA for undermining the UP's road to success, and world capitalism for strangling Mr. Allende's efforts by refusing him loans.

Now the big landowners had been eliminated from the theatre of operations, firstly by Mr. Frei's land reform measures, and finally by the brutal seizures I have described. They had all been ejected, and were living far away from their lands. How could they have sabotaged the work of the new leaders, and especially if this had been well-directed and had been supported by the peasants? What possibility had they had to stop the wheat from growing, the hens from laying and the cows from calving? No, the real guilty men here were the communist would-be reformers, who alienated a whole people by their violence and incompetence. In Chile, as in all the countries where Communism has seized power, the land, the hens and the cows became neglected and therefore food shortages occurred.

In the Soviet Union, it is more than half a century since the landowners, small and great, have been shot and opposition parties eliminated, and I am not aware that the CIA has had much opportunity of getting into the country. Yet agriculture continues to be the "yawning failure" of the regime, to quote Khruschev's own words. In 1979, 1980 and 1981 the USSR, which used to be a world exporter of wheat, had to buy millions of tons of it from the USA, Canada and Australia. Its national livestock herd is lower per head of the population than it was under the tsars, again, according to official Soviet figures! Cuba, once the world's biggest sugar exporter, and which has expelled all its sugar-cane plantation owners, has had to introduce ration cards for this commodity. China, where even the ghosts of its former landowners have long disappeared, suffered a serious rice famine in 1960–1962.

Contrary to the allegations of a "plot by the old gang" put out by the hard-pressed defenders of the UP, the climate in Chile at the beginning of the regime, both within parliament and in people's minds, was quite favourable to reform. Nobody, for example, had protested against the breaking-up of the large estates, or even against the amendment introduced by Mr. Allende to the law making the copper mines one hundred per cent Chilean. Public opinion was ready, too, to accept widespread nationalization provided this was carried out with wisdom and justice. In short, the UP had received from its fairy godmother a selection of very favourable gifts in its cradle, and it had to work quite hard, and contribute a large share of its own characteristic lunacy and fanaticism in order to turn these gifts into their opposites.

As for the CIA plot, the idea is too ludicrous to be worth our spending much time in refuting it. Can we seriously believe that the CIA had on its secret payroll the hundreds of thousands of workers, foremen, engineers, accountants, agricultural experts, millers, shepherds and tractor-drivers that would have been needed to disorganize or halt the country's 35,000 industrial firms and 60,000 agricultural holdings? Can we believe it could order hundreds of thousands of hauliers, doctors, lawyers, architects, shopkeepers and artisans to go on strike just when it wanted them to? Did it control the million women banging on their empty saucepans? Did it have the ability to put Mr. Allende's budget in deficit; cause the unforgettable queues for food, and organize the vast black market? Medieval superstition did not credit even the Devil himself with such wide powers. Let us pass on; the idea is just too ridiculous.

We have still not dealt with the charge that international capitalism "intentionally strangled" the Chilean economy during the UP period. Marxists delight in spreading the legend that the regimes they set up are maliciously boycotted; starved and suffocated by the "forces of money" plotting away in their executive jets as they shuttle between

Wall Street, the City of London and the Paris Bourse. To be harried thus devilishly, these Marxists clearly think, is patent proof that they are on the side of the angels.

The accusation is, of course, a complete myth. Anyone who has bothered to keep himself informed, even cursorily, about world affairs knows that international capitalism is quite incapable of carrying out any large-scale anti-Marxist strategy; it has swallowed the bluff put out by left-wing intellectuals, and has poured out, on the USSR and then on the other communist states, a constant and considerable flood of credit, economic assistance, transfusions of technological know-how, food supplies and complete factories ready to use. All the world knows that this aid has more than once saved the very lives of these regimes, always in a state of bankruptcy as they are. The rule has naturally been confirmed in the case of Chile's UP, which found effective friends ready to back it with hard cash in the sanctuaries of the World Bank (this being a subsidiary of the United Nations, and as leftist in its leanings as the latter; its chairman Mr. McNamara had considerable sympathy for Mr. Allende), as well as in the inner sanctums of the International Monetary Fund, whose director, Mr. Jacques Bernouin, a socialist, gave the UP overdraft facilities, and in a number of powerful groups of financiers. I have before my eyes the *Quarterly Report* of the Economist Intelligence Unit in London for 1 March 1973 setting out the credits granted to Mr. Allende just for the 15 months from November 1970 to February 1972. From this it can be seen that short-term loans amounted to 387 million dollars, coming from 12 capitalist countries, including the United States, while long-term loans, again from capitalist countries, came to 70 millions, the whole totalling 457 million dollars. To this we must add short-term loans of 105 million dollar's worth from the USSR. During its three years of office, the UP received credits of 823 million dollars, a figure *exceeding* the average of foreign loans received by Chile prior to the Allende regime. In addition, the Club of Paris, sympathetic to the financial difficulties with which the Allende government was grappling, granted him a moratorium on very advantageous terms. Mr. Allende did not even honour this moratorium and so the responsibility for repayment has fallen to the Pinochet government. Finally, it is not true that the UP was hamstrung by financial penalties from the outside world. The opposite is true, in fact, and particularly during its last year of office, there was a considerable rise in the world price of copper, which finally reached 37%.

There remains one last argument, in some sense a philosophical one. It is often said that a collectivist organization of the economy is so new by comparison with the usual capitalist one that regimes trying to introduce it will understandably be working by trial and error, and so are bound to make mistakes. Those who advance this argument ignore a basic principle of Karl Marx, according to which "the only problems history poses are those to which it has already provided the solutions". According to this principle, one of the most essential in the Marxist canon, a new class only takes over the controls after it has built up its own socio-economic forms within the old regime, as the bourgeoisie did during the last two centuries of decaying feudalism. A moment is reached when the old superstructures, obsolete now by relation to the new infrastructures, but still trying to prolong their dominance, are destroyed by a revolution, from which the new regime emerges already fully mature. It is, in fact, this very maturity which constitutes for Marx the justification for the revolution.

However if collectivism has not reached this stage, if it is incapable of running society without a long, costly and sanguinary period of apprenticeship after taking power, then it stands condemned as impractical and utopian even in terms of its own supporters' philosophical theory. It has even less excuse for its unpreparedness when one remembers that it has now had half a century to learn the techniques and develop its muscles, as government planning and control of the economy have increased in our modern states. It is noteworthy, moreover, that in advocating collectivization, the Marxist parties never warn us that they will need a period of difficult and costly experimentation before they can master the economic process. They never say to their peoples: "Pass us the controls, and after 20 years of waste, disorder and famine, you'll see what you'll see." Quite the opposite: it is the present managers of society whom they accuse of incompetence, and they represent themselves as superior alternatives, fully prepared to take over at a moment's notice, having up their sleeves far more effective, intelligent and generous plans that will speedily put an end to our present ills. Thus, *before* taking power they justify their claims by representing themselves as masters of economic science, and *once in power* they excuse their failure by the fact that they are beginners. In both cases they are charlatans.

The real causes of the disaster

It is thus quite clear, finally, that none of the excuses for the ruining of Chile's economy by the UP has a leg to stand on. It is obvious that the ruin stems from the very nature of the UP and from Marxist-Leninist doctrine itself. The Chilean drama, coming with that of Portugal, Vietnam and Kampuchea, and after that of the Soviet Union and all its bankrupt European socialist satellites such as Poland, once again proves this point with a sinister veracity.

Basically, the phenomenon can be explained in the following sentence: *the Marxists' main concern is not that everyone should eat properly, but that everyone should be controlled to think properly* (i.e. think along Marxist lines). The economic plans they plead as their reason for seeking power are merely a pretext, for show only; all that really interests them is the chance to wield an *absolute ideological power*. Their object in nationalizing the whole economy is to achieve this power, and has nothing to do with planning and improving the productivity of the economy. In every factory "handed back to the people" by Communism from 1917 to the present day, from Moscow to Santiago, passing by Peking, Prague, Budapest, Havana, Hanoi and Pnom Penh . . . in every one without exception we have seen the same picture, and one which sums up the futility of the whole exercise: the former managers are dismissed, and replaced by swarms of servile bureaucrats appointed for their political views and not for their competence. The atmosphere inside the enterprise, from being productive, becomes discursive and work is replaced by talk. There is an immediate glut of directors, planners, agitators, animators, draughtsmen, educators, inspectors and speakers. Thus in Chile under the UP there were on average 25% more pen-pushers and passers-on of orders and slogans than under Mr. Frei—a crushing burden on the economy. The El Teniente mine had functioned remarkably well with 8,000 workers and salaried staff; it now took on a further 4,000, including 2,000 in its offices. The industrial group SUMAR had previously worked very prosperously with 200 clerks in its offices, but had 800 of these by the end of the UP regime. The Ministry of Public Works, in full activity under Mr. Frei with a staff of 30,000, had practically ceased operating by the end of 1973, but then had a staff numbering 38,000. The Water Service increased from 183 to 1,464 employees, the *Corporación de Obras Municipales* (Municipal Works Corporation) from 200 to 12,000! The Ministry of Justice was swollen by several hundred Marxist-Leninist militants whose sole occupation was to spy on and intimidate the magistrates. Air traffic dropped by 25%, while airport personnel rose from 300 to 500. And so it went on.

If capitalism periodically gives rise to crises of over-production, Marxist regimes live in a continual crisis of over-management, a much more irrational phenomenon, and much more costly to those who live under it.

It was not only that the bureaucrats of the state, party and the Marxist-Leninist trade unions were unproductive in themselves, they forced the workers to be so too. The useful work of the latter was constantly being broken off so that they could vote for resolutions; sign petitions; listen to speeches; take part in union, party, workshop or factory meetings or join in demonstrations, processions and public meetings. All this was organized without any possibility of making their own views known, their role being merely to applaud their leaders and ratify decisions already taken. At the Chuquicamata copper mine it was reckoned that a quarter of the working hours were thus wasted in "carnival fun and games", as a disillusioned ex-trade union leader told me. In some sections, he assured me, only 80 days were worked per year.

The incompetence of the Marxist-Leninist managers and executives gave rise to countless bitter jokes, such as that of the workers in the Eperva fishing enterprise at Arica, who made it known on 6 August 1971[1] that they could no longer work under the direction of the socialist *interventor* sent to them as "he didn't know the difference between a sardine and a shark".

While on the subject of fisheries, I may be permitted a slight digression concerning Soviet aid in this field. Mr. Allende had been very impressed by what he had heard about the marvellous Soviet invention of "mechanized fishing", and had asked his "big brothers" to send a whole flotilla from the USSR to lend a hand to Chilean fishermen and show them how to go about it. The result, after eight months, was a communiqué from Mr. Miguel Lucero, general secretary of the trade union and a supporter of the UP, containing the following complaint: "The Soviet fishermen are paid in dollars to ruin our jobs. Their boats make a clean sweep of all types of fish in the fishing-grounds near our coasts; they unload tons of mackerel without bothering whether there is any room for them in the cold stores; they cut off the heads and tails, to the great dissatisfaction of Chilean housewives, who are used to buying the whole fish." A similar fate befell all the other Soviet aid operations (reminding one of the famous snowploughs that Moscow sent to the Ivory Coast). In Chile, the Soviet stone-crushers were useless after three months, their furnaces were scaled up in a year, their cranes squeaked, their drills sawed and their saws drilled, etc.

Leaving this digression, I return to the Chilean Marxist-Leninists' frenzied intrusion of politics into the economy. Over and above the direct loss of countless millions of man-hours, this led to a massive brain-drain, not only in the liberal professions but also among engineers. The latters' professional body put out on 28 May 1973,[2] a statement, based on very detailed research, to show that during the 2½ years of UP government up to that date, the number of technicians who emigrated, exasperated by the follies of the new managers and the constant frustrations they had to put up with, reached a quarter of

[1] See *El Mercurio* 7 August 1971.
[2] See *El Mercurio* 29 May 1973.

their total number! It was of course the best who left first. In most cases, I was told by the secretary of their professional body when I met him, the engineers were replaced by stooges of the UP, and one can imagine the effect this had on production and efficiency.

In the countryside the picture was an even more distressing one. Mr. Hernan Millas' and Mr. Emilio Filippi's book *Crônica de una Experiencia* (Chronicle of an Experiment) is full of heart-breaking examples. Dr. Cristobal Saenz and his son-in-law Patricio Phillips (I have met the latter) had in 20 years of hard work transformed their land at Malleco into a model estate which people came to visit from far and wide; they had introduced selected seed; planted magnificent woods; imported breeding-stock; set up an automated dairy and built dwellings for the peasants on the model of English cottages. The estate-workers had pleaded that the estate should not be expropriated. In view of its reputation, it had been honoured by a visit from the agriculture minister, Mr. Jacques Chonchol in person. Two weeks later, MCR bands came to seize it by force. Mr. Patricio Phillips asked them at least to entrust the estate to one of the universities. They laughed in his face, paid him 500 dollars as total compensation and forced him to leave within 24 hours. The following year, the estate's wheat production, which had reached a level of 35,000 quintals, had dropped to 3,200 quintals (that is, from 3,500 to 320 metric tonnes), and milk production had dropped from 800,000 litres to 260,000. The peasants, none of whom had received title-deeds to any of the land, were reduced to cutting wood at night to sell on the black market (this had indeed become common practice in the Chilean countryside, making serious inroads into the country's timber reserves).

Another example from the countryside is that of the much smaller but admirably well managed vineyards of the novelist Mr. Baltazar Castro, a great admirer of his Cuban namesake. This did not prevent him from being robbed of his land, after desperate battles involving bloodshed between his peasants and the invaders. Six months later the vineyards, the pride of the district, were unrecognizable, and Mr. Baltazar Castro wrote a pamphlet, *Chile destroyed by Allende*, in which he said of the President that he had "soiled and befouled (in Spanish *emporco*, i.e. turned into a pigstye) parliament, freemasonry, the left wing, the factories and the fields".

Invited by friends who wanted to show me the Chilean countryside, I myself visited an area of mountain pastures near Traigen which had been expropriated and handed over to some Mapuche Indians to work. Minister Chonchol's representative, not wanting to give them the title-deeds they were hoping for, told them that only personal cultivation can entitle one to valid ownership. As a result of this advice, the Mapuches wore themselves out tearing up the herbage and ploughing.

But the land handed to them was not arable, but pasture, an elementary distinction too difficult for the UP bureaucrat to understand. The result was that in a few months rain and wind had caused such erosion that the whole zone will be useless for years to come. In the same region, the workers on an estate that had been seized told me that the CORA agitators, to get on the right side of them, organized football matches for them, but these were often at times when the cows had to be milked. If it wasn't games it was, as in the factories, political meetings instead of seed-sowing. These last, when they were finally decided on, were made with "political seed", bought, that is, not as previously from wherever the best seed was grown, but from "friendly countries" like Mexico or the USSR, quite regardless of the fact that such seed was quite unsuitable to the Chilean soil. The harvests were disastrous. Fear, insecurity, the constant meddling of CORA, INDAR and the paramilitary bands paralyzed the initiative of those farmers who had been lucky enough to keep their land. Investment dried up. Plans were changed two, three or four times a year.

Underlying all these disorders, Chile's agricultural disaster was typical of the agricultural disasters that strike all communist countries without exception, and it had precisely the same basic cause: namely that the famous "agrarian reform" (of which the Communists claim to be the sole possible champions), is nothing but an enormous confidence trick. Far from fulfilling the peasants' dream of becoming small landowners, it ended in a collectivization of the land, de jure or de facto, that reduced the peasants to the status of agricultural workers paid on the basis of the work-units arbitrarily allotted to them by a Marxist-Leninist bureaucracy, the collective farms being merely open-air factories. Under such conditions no peasant, be he Chilean, Russian or Chinese, will put his heart into his work. All one can expect is slackness, waste, "fiddling" and total neglect. The USSR has never managed to emerge from this, and it never will. Now as early as 31 December 1970, the vice-chairman of CORA, Mr. David Baytelman had naïvely admitted in a press conference: "In the UP's thinking, there should be no individual ownership of land".[1] After that there was no need to say any more.

To sum up, whether on the farms or in the factories, and whether we look at the USSR, Bulgaria, Cuba, Vietnam, Kampuchea or Chile, collectivism breeds both material poverty and political slavery. It has only one watchword wherever and whenever it is applied: *plates empty and prisons full.*

The studies on which I have based the preceding picture of the economic breakdown organized by the UP are thorough and objective

[1] *El Mercurio*, 1 January 1971.

ones. They could, nevertheless, be called into question on the grounds that their authors were hostile to the UP. Such an objection would, however, be unjustified; despite the hypocritical denials and grotesque excuses of UP propaganda, the facts themselves were so evident and so conclusive that they were sometimes admitted by the very men responsible for bringing them about.

In a document on agriculture produced for internal circulation within the Socialist Party, and published by its organ *Punto Final* on 26 August 1972, one can read the following: "The whole of this period has been characterized by improvisation and inefficiency in the management of the expropriated sector; delays in getting expropriated estates under cultivation; fragmentation of estates; their paralysis; paralysis of production and dissatisfaction of peasants with the CORA. All this results in a dramatic reality: more than 50% of the land expropriated is unproductive."

Where industry is concerned, we possess another confession, coming this time from the workers and middle management of the oil refineries (*Empresa Nacional del Petroleo*), who at the beginning were active and firm supporters of the UP. In a statement of May 1973 they declared: "The oil industry, which could have ensured the country's independence in energy, is in marked decline. The blame for this does not lie with the workers, who have worked wholeheartedly. The blame lies in a political incapacity to ensure normal output."

I must also draw attention to the fact that in his third annual message, read before Congress on 20 May 1973, President Allende himself admitted that "up till now we have not been successful in creating an economic leadership . . . and I cannot help but foresee some very difficult moments ahead for the material life of Chileans".

Finally, we have the famous internal and confidential report of the MAPU which I have already quoted, and in which, after drawing the same black picture of the economic situation as I have done, the authors unequivocally state: *"This whole collapse, despite the assertions of UP demagogues, is the fault of the regime, and is not due to any hostile activities of its internal or external enemies."*

After that, nothing further remains to be said. The case has been heard.

CHAPTER X

MORAL ROT

THE GENERAL PUBLIC CHERISHES a belief that, however tough Marxist-Leninist regimes may be, they are at least honest and uncorrupted. In the case of regimes that have been in power for a considerable time, this is just not true. El Campesino, the communist ex-leader of the Spanish revolution, who fled to the USSR and was there arrested as a "deviationist", put paid to the whole idea when he told the story of how he was able to get away from the concentration camp into which he had been thrown by a "fraternal" regime and cross the USSR to Iran, and all of this thanks to the gold he had hidden in his boots, with which he had been able to bribe numerous Bolshevik officials of various ranks, all of them tough and all of them corrupt. Solzhenitsyn has confirmed how widespread corruption is in all walks of life in the Soviet Union, even in the labour camps.

However, this image of the "upright revolutionary", still so widespread in people's minds, did correspond to a reality during the initial period when revolutionaries still had a hard struggle ahead of them in which their very lives were at stake. At this stage of his career, a revolutionary belonging to one of the various branches of the socialist movement was generally a devoted and serious person, respectable, and often austere in his morality. Such a person would only turn into a pleasure-seeker some years after he had come to power, when the ruler in him had had time to replace the militant. The homosexual parties in dachas around Moscow described by Miss Svetlana Stalin did not start until after Lenin's death, and the vulgar corruption recounted by Solzhenitsyn and El Campesino was also slow to develop. By contrast, many of the Chilean leaders of the left proved to be corrupt or depraved from the very start. This is what we are about to demonstrate.

Corruption

Mr. Allende was fond of boasting of his high moral standards. He more than once said: "My hands are pure of blood and embezzlement." The first half of this piece of self-praise was not far from the truth, (what, after all, are 122 opponents murdered under the UP compared with the million and a half massacred by Lenin in a comparable lapse of time?), but the second half was a lie. Lenin was a murderer, but an honest one, while Mr. Allende was merciful but corrupt.

After the coup of 11 September 1973, very large sums of money were found on the persons and in the residences of a number of UP leaders, sums which neither their official salaries nor their personal fortunes could justify. Mr. Allende's 'Tomas Moro' residence was found to contain five million escudos and 8,000 dollars in notes. In his week-end villa of El Canaveral there were 40,000 dollars in ready money as well as statements for money held in foreign bank accounts. The ex-minister of Education, Mr. Edgardo Enriquez, father of two Mirist leaders, Miguel and Edgardo was found in possession of 50,000 dollars in notes. At the residence of the ex-minister of the Economy and ex-vice-chairman of CORFO, Mr Pedro Vuskovic, were found three cheques made out to his name amounting to a total of 60 million escudos. The list is a long one, and I can only quote it in part.

These discoveries give added weight to the declarations made by Admiral Toribio Merino Castro, in which he stated: "Chile was ruined economically because everything it produced was pillaged and robbed by thieves." Revealing that in the Valparaiso house of the communist ex-deputy Mr. Luis Guastavino, 145,000 dollars were found in the suitcase of this "son of the people", who was then preparing to make his get-away, the admiral added: "I suppose I count as a member of the bourgeoisie, but I haven't even got 15,000 escudos (15 dollars) in my current account, and all I have is a three-year-old car and quite a small detached house. Anyone who manages to put by a nest-egg of 145,000 dollars in just three years of office in a poor country like Chile must have the morals of a gangster, at least as we servicemen see it."

On the same day a leading Christian progressive, Mr. Roberto Sapiain Rodriguez, arrested while trying to flee, was found to have with him seven million escudos and 80,000 dollars. He had made his pile as director of CORFO in Valparaiso and Aconcagua. In addition, his house was found to contain hidden stocks of expensive liqueurs, record-players, radios and electric toys to a value of ten million escudos, which he was intending to sell on the black market.

The black market

Many of the leaders of the UP and its sympathizers had made fortunes out of the black market, i.e. out of the people's poverty. The CORFO had taken over control of 535 undertakings; it is reckoned that half the production of these businesses slipped through the meshes of the official market. The various constituent parties making up the UP, after hard bargaining, had shared these seized undertakings out among themselves, and then proceeded to divert about half their production onto the black market. These so-called "nationalized" industries, (a better word would be "Popular-Unitized") were compelled to sell their goods at prices well below their manufacturing costs; they thus could not help making heavy losses, though the political groups that had seized the firms made substantial profits.

For example, the MADEMSA at Santiago, a firm that manufactured electrical kitchen equipment, was put in the hands of a state *interventor*, Mr. Beca by name, who held prices down to their lowest 1970 level at a time when inflation was climbing to 100, and even 200%. Supply was lagging far behind demand, and so he reserved the cookers and refrigerators he manufactured for the top brass of the UP who re-sold them on the black market at five or ten times what they had paid for them. As another example, the *Estanco Automotriz,* a nationalized company manufacturing cars, kept its ordinary customers waiting interminably for delivery of the cars they had ordered while 2,500 specially privileged UP officials received immediate delivery, and at the official price. Some of them even bought their cars ten at a time. They re-sold them at ten times the official price on the black market. In fact the MAPU financed its election campaign by getting the *Estanco Automotriz* to sell it 100 cars at the official price.

According to a Christian Democrat deputy, Mr. Luis Pareto, the UP government had acquired 1,000 vehicles during the year 1972, many of which never took their places among those used on official business, an acquisition that Mr. Pareto stigmatized as "wasteful and immoral".[1] On 24 June 1973 the same deputy stated publicly that UP functionaries were obtaining far more rationed goods than they needed, so as to turn the surplus into cash on the black market. And *El Mercurio* of 1 December 1972 carried the allegation: "Socialist policy has led to a really scandalous number of cases of abuse of authority and shady transactions. The black market has reached proportions never before witnessed in Chile."

The drug traffic

Another source of funds adopted by some UP activists was the drug traffic. It is probable that only a tiny handful of them were "in the know", and the great majority were not even aware of the scandal, but we now have ample documented proof of its existence. In the Allende period Chile became the leading Latin-American country for the distribution of cocaine, the most dangerous of all drugs. The value of the cocaine discovered in the country after the military coup was equivalent in value to three months of Chile's external debt! Secret laboratories for processing the opium were discovered in the north and the Andes, as well as elsewhere. It emerged also that the UP's

[1] *El Mercurio*, 14 March 1972.

paramilitary groups had linked up with international drug traffickers as a way of paying for the very costly arsenal of Cuban, Czechoslovak and Soviet arms they were importing. This use of the drug trade for political purposes was unmasked through the confession made by a pilot of Chile National Airline, Mr. Oscar Squella Avendano, when he was arrested in the United States while carrying several kilos of cocaine worth two million dollars. Mr. Oscar had been one of Mr. Allende's most active election agents ever since 1958; it is thus hardly surprising if 50,000 dollars came floating down from the heights of the presidential throne to pay the bail for Mr. Allende's devoted pilot and propagandist.

A network of drug peddlers was set up in Chile, based on restaurants which enjoyed the discreet undercover protection of the police chief Mr. Coco Paredes.[1] Drugtaking spread through the universities and schools, and the scandal became so flagrant that the opposition attacked the traffic openly in Parliament. In his defence, the minister challenged claimed that cocaine found on Chilean drug traffickers arrested at New York and in Mexico was in fact intended for the personal use of President Allende and his family, and had been recommended by his doctors and dentists. The same defence was made by UP officials in reply to the Mexican government when on 10 March 1971 it arrested the brother of the director of the Communist Party's paper *Puro Chile*, Mr. Ivan Papic Pastenes, who was carrying ten kilos of cocaine. The same unlikely excuse was given to the Argentinian authorities at Buenos Aires who had stopped and searched the yacht 'Carmen', whose owner, Mr. Osorio, was conveying drugs destined for the "underground" laboratories at San Jose, Maipo, Algarrobo and Limache. The president and his family must have had awfully bad toothache!

Moral licence

Some left-wing intellectuals went in for eroticism and pornography in all its forms, in theory and even in practice, seeing this as proof of their emancipation from the puritanical inhibitions of a "reactionary" older morality. I have already told how even during Mr. Frei's regime some "progressive" circles had gone in for this particular form of avant-garde behaviour. Once the UP came to power the last barriers fell. Public opinion, as one can imagine in a country as Catholic as Chile, was outraged by the sexual licence and debauchery that went on, and the easy life and good food enjoyed by leading figures of the regime at a time when mothers were having to queue for hours to get milk and

[1] See *The Theory and Practice of Communism*, 15 November 1973, Washington.

bread for their children. One television programme that particularly shocked Chileans was that showing Fidel Castro and the numerous suite he had brought from Cuba enjoying a gargantuan feast, with choice liqueurs and sheep roasted whole in the open air in the magnificent grounds of El Canaveral, at a time when such foods had disappeared from the shops. Six years later, when I was travelling through Chile, I found the women still full of indignation at the memory.

Another scandal that could still revive their disgust retrospectively involved the state *interventor* placed in control of the nationalized MADEMSA undertaking, the socialist Mr. Enrique Fornes. He disappeared on the day of the military coup, taking with him the seven million escudos earmarked as a special bonus to be distributed to the 2,000 workers in this concern on the occasion of the national Commemoration Day. He did not have time to remove the various articles of intimate under-clothing and the passionate love-letters of his secretaries (as is confirmed in the book of the Christian Democrat by Mr. Hernan Millas *Anatomía de un Fracaso* (Analysis of a Failure), pub. ZigZag, Santiago). Stealing the money of the workers so as to lead a life of debauchery with girls of easy virtue was surely the worst depravity to be expected of the bourgeois bosses. But now in Chile, nouveaux-riches socialist politicians shamelessly flaunted a luxury and an immorality that old-style socialists would have indignantly rejected as sins typical of the class-enemy.

Mr. Allende set the example. I should have preferred not to touch on this side of his life for it gives me no pleasure to pry into the inner labyrinths of the private lives of prominent men. But to keep to this rule in Mr. Allende's case would distort my story, for his behaviour—or rather his misbehaviour—certainly influenced events, as well as having a general significance which it is important to bring out. Let us therefore examine the shady side of his private life.

In June 1972 a van with a drunken driver crashed near Curimon, on the international highway leading to Argentina. It was discovered that those in the van were UP activists, and that it was carrying arms stolen from the army. The van's registration card was made out in the name of Ms. Maria Contreras Bell, who was quickly identified as La Payita, Mr. Allende's private secretary and mistress. She admitted before a special commission of the Chamber that the van did belong to her. At the same time it became known that she owned 25 other vehicles.[1] It also emerged that her sister had bought the luxury estate of El Canaveral, which she was later to sell to La Payita in 1973. As the investigation probed deeper into the personal fortune of this little

[1] *El Mercurio*, 20 June 1972.

secretary who had been penniless until recently, its total amount went up by leaps and bounds. How and where had a hard-up working girl managed to lay her hands on so much money?

I have visited El Canaveral. It is a sort of rustic Trianon of 15 rooms, with monumental fireplaces, luxurious bathrooms, Renaissance beams, cellars and kitchens worthy of a castle, and set in a vast wooded park of nearly 250 acres with green hills, through which runs the turbulent river Mapocho, a little jewel, the sort of setting in which the Shah of Iran would have liked to spend his last days. The interior was enriched by deep carpets, old masters, tapestries and period furniture, little of which now remains, for nowadays the residence is used as a home for Chile's orphan children. In these surroundings of "luxury, calm and sensuous pleasure" (to use Baudelaire's words), Mr. Allende used to spend his weekends with his mistress, whose husband Ropert, an engineer, far from objecting to his wife sharing her bed between himself and her royal socialist paramour, in fact saw all sorts of advantages accruing to himself from this arrangement. La Payita's young daughter had her own separate small house nearby.

El Mercurio of 24 May 1972 carried the following report: "The famous Canaveral mansion, recently furnished with a luxury that is nothing less than a studied affront to all the poor of Chile, was bought by Senora Lina Contreras Bell for 350,000 escudos . . . Its value as declared to the tax authorities was very considerably reduced." Indeed, 250 acres of land at only 15 minutes distance from the capital are worth a fortune. The value of the property had been under-estimated so as to pay less transfer tax. This one short paragraph sums up all the immorality of the upstarts of the Chilean extreme left: tax evasion, corruption, theft of state funds, nepotism and ostentatious luxury. Only two important traits are missing: contempt for the common herd, and lust. We are coming to these.

At the bottom of the beautiful park, the lover and his mistress, as the "great friends of the people" that they were, had had wooden huts built where a hundred or so armed men, members of the GAP (Group of Personal Friends) responsible for the safety of the sovereign were crammed together eight to a cell on tiers of camp-beds that soldiers in the barracks of our capitalist countries would have turned their noses up at. The huge kitchens, like those of the château of Chambord, occupied a separate building. There La Payita gave her instructions for epicurean banquets for the Marxist-Leninist top brass, and bean soup for the large body of menials and the praetorian guard. We may note, in passing, that preparations for the meal of that day, a meal that was never eaten, were found at the Moneda palace on 11 September 1973. The small fry—lesser officials and the GAP bodyguard—would have eaten the classic beans so well-known to all French conscripts, but the menu for the higher echelons—not that they had any chance to enjoy it either—included chicken, small mushrooms, dates and pineapples.

But to return to El Canaveral: in vast underground storerooms were discovered freezers full of enormous joints of meat, as well as large stocks of the provisions that had long vanished from the shops in Santiago, where every night one could hear the dismal clashing of empty saucepans. In the cellars were thousands of bottles of wine, spirits and de luxe liqueurs, and the inevitable 4-litre magnums of the best whisky, Chivas Regal, President Allende's favourite drink.

While we are on this subject, it must be stated that Mr. Allende's drinking bouts were a matter of common knowledge; these magnums of whisky, in varying stages of emptiness, could be found in every room or office he used; he had even been seen half-drunk on TV one day during a state ceremony. To be fair to him, I must add that the chairman of the lorry-drivers' union, Mr. Villarin, who played such a big part in Mr. Allende's downfall, told me that he had known Mr. Allende well during his youth, and that at the beginning of his career he had been a sober man. Mr. Villarin leaned towards the theory that Marxists in his entourage had encouraged him to drink so as to make it possible for them one day, if need be, to launch a campaign against him on grounds of "bourgeois decadence". Whatever the truth of this, what is certain is that all these plentiful stocks of the best the world has to offer, found in his various palaces, had been acquired by misappropriating the money of undernourished taxpayers, and that he did not even share them with the rank and file of his own servants or bodyguards, thus exhibiting a cynical contempt for the egalitarianism with which he was so fond of larding his speeches.

We now come to eroticism. For much else was discovered at El Canaveral. We have already mentioned a veritable arsenal of weapons and a military training camp. There was also a small theatre-cum-cinema staging naked dancing-girls and couples copulating, plus a whole series of pornographic films, as well as a collection of erotic gadgets such as one finds in sex-shops, all of which were meticulously listed later by a solicitor. Thus, in addition to their corruption, these top officials of the UP displayed a degree of loose living quite foreign to the behaviour of the Bolsheviks of the heroic period. Yet for Marxist-Leninists this was indeed their "heroic age", the period in which they were "building Socialism". But this did not prevent some of their chiefs from leading the sort of life of debauchery normally considered more typical of "decadent bourgeois" or the later Merovingian "sluggard-kings".

This country "folly" of El Canaveral was not the only one, moreover, to which Mr. Allende treated himself. Shortly after his inauguration, not satisfied like his "bourgeois" predecessors with the Palace of La

Moneda in the centre of Santiago, he had persuaded the state (i.e. the taxpayers) to buy him as an official residence the luxurious villa and estate of 'Tomas Moro', which he had fortified, and in which the same mixture of objects of pleasure and military equipment were found as at El Canaveral. The military equipment here was far more plentiful than at El Canaveral: there was enough to fully equip 12 battalions, as well as a whole network of armoured bunkers. The unparalleled, scandalous and even immoral character of these fortifications is the point that strikes one most forcefully here. Can one imagine the President of the French Republic at the Elysée, the Queen of England at Buckingham Palace or the President of the United States at the White House surrounding themselves with hundreds of private bodyguards armed to the teeth, building bunkers in their grounds, and themselves undergoing marksmanship training like some robber baron in his medieval keep? Such feudal behaviour, an insolent snub to the Constitution and a provocation to the citizens, is enough in itself to discount all Mr. Allende's claims to be governing within the law.

As for the high living at 'Tomas Moro', it made a striking contrast with the traditional simplicity characteristic of Chile's earlier great men. All of these had resided in the old government palace of La Moneda or in their own homes. This is still the case today for General Pinochet, who lives in a very ordinary house that he is buying with a mortgage out of his general's pay. The country's founder, General Bernardo O'Higgins, temporarily exiled after three years at the head of the country, found himself in Peru without a peso to his name, and the Lima government had to make him a present of the modest residence of Montalban and allow him a small civil list. Mr. Diego Portales, the man who established the rule of law and constitutional government in Chile, was sometimes short of money to pay for his cigars (his only pleasure), and often had to pay his servants' wages out of his minister's salary. Mr. Alessandri, although he had a considerable private fortune, had spent his whole term of office as president with just eight suits, while Mr. Allende ordered them ten at a time, and of the best English cloth. The tailor who had made his last 20 suits is congratulating himself now that he received payment for them the very day before the military coup.

It has always been a difficult question to decide what moral standards are permissible for political leaders. The answer, here as elsewhere, lies somewhere between the two extremes. It would be ridiculous and excessive to expect them to be angels or hermits and to deny them the normal pleasures of human life. What is more, asceticism has never been a guarantee of sound political sense, far from it: the great puritan Savonarola was one of the most narrow-minded and pernicious despots of all time. Rulers have a right to enjoy life as much as anyone else, although in times of shortage and poverty like those that the Chilean people were then going through, their subjects have a right to expect a certain restraint from them. But their conduct becomes scandalous if they indulge in excessive luxury, arbitrary misuse of authority and unbridled immorality. The reason for this quite simply is that they are dissipating their powers, and do not have enough time or mental energy left to work hard for the common good, which was what they were elected to do. In my view such restraint should be more binding on socialist leaders than on those of other parties; they have after all won their votes by claiming to be more generous than the others, more egalitarian, more concerned with the needs of the people and the appeals of the poor. Even kings who feasted while their subjects fasted used to be condemned. It is even more scandalous for socialist ministers to behave in this way.

Summing up, we have seen in earlier chapters how the Popular Unity coalition had plunged Chile into the worst economic breakdown of its history. This could have been the result of unintended political miscalculations or utopian schemes, without any suggestion of positive evil intentions on the part of the politicians concerned. A number of revolutions in the past have been as disastrous as the Chilean one, and yet those who led them behaved with a certain decency and some degree of disinterestedness. This, unfortunately, was not so in the case of Chile. Far too many of those who made up the Popular Unity coalition were extravagant demagogues and hypocrites, corrupt and debauched. Not only did the Chileans have to suffer from their actions, but also they had no alternative but to despise them. It is sad that this should be so, but it is, alas, true.

CHAPTER XI

POPULAR OPPOSITION

THIS IS THE MOST IMPORTANT chapter in my book: the events it reveals are the most remarkable I have ever met. They arouse an emotion in me that I have never felt before. In all the 30 years that I have been writing about Communism, I have hitherto had nothing to report but the spectacle of a blind, cowardly world retreating in the face of Marxist expansionism. True, this expansion has sometimes been halted as in Indonesia, the Sudan, Greece, Brazil and Guatemala; but this was by military intervention. The people's hatred only burst out afterwards. In Chile, it was the reverse. It was the people who began the resistance, challenging, cursing and wearing down the communist government, and it was only afterwards that the army joined in and dealt the final blow. It was the people alone, the whole people in all its variety, the people with its bare hands, that took the initiative and bore the brunt of the struggle. The case is, I think, unique in contemporary history.

Why did it happen on that occasion, and why in that country? It is possible to find circumstantial reasons for this. But I cannot help thinking that, on a deeper level, resistance to Communism was so strong in Chile because of the Chileans, just as it has flared up now in Afghanistan because of the Afghans. I had been in the habit of bringing my analyses on the impersonal plane of doctrines, parties and combinations of circumstances. Then in burst the ordinary people, speaking louder than all the theories and the party machines, citizens of all opinions and walks of life, passing directly from their everyday occupations in kitchen or at workbench straight into the pages of history. After all, when one says that the wind of history is blowing, that surely means that one is hearing those voices raised that have so far been silent.

I have known these generous, dignified, brave and clear-sighted people on their home ground beyond the Andes, and I have loved and admired them for showing us that, in our century, men can still stand up to and defeat the communist steamroller. In the last analysis, it is their courage that has saved us as well as themselves. Before describing their heroic exploits, I want to express my extreme gratitude to them from the bottom of my heart.

The women of Chile

I have just spoken of the astonishment one cannot help feeling for this first great example of a direct, spontaneous and victorious resistance of a whole people to collectivism, and I have asked why it happened in Chile. In the midst of this astonishment, an even greater cause for astonishment strikes me, why the women? For Chile's heroic political epic possesses another considerable new feature: for the first time in history it was the women who launched the people's resistance, and it was they who kept it going. To be sure, we had seen women showing political initiative in Venezuela, and in Brazil against the fellow-travelling Mr. Goulart. But in Chile they displayed a very much higher degree of militancy, aggressiveness and clearsightedness.

I have already mentioned the resounding overture to this resistance, the famous saucepan march of 2 December 1971. I was fortunate enough to meet one of its chief organizers, Ms. Maria Correa Morande, a person whose confident charm and beautiful yet resolute tone of voice made her an ideal embodiment of the adventure she lived through, as she has told it in a fascinating book entitled: *La Guerra de las Mujeres* (The Women's War), throbbing in every line with that rare combination of civic responsibility and human anguish that inspired the women of Chile.

It was the end of the "year of presents", during which many people had felt that the UP was all set on a course that would lead to a happier future. Many, that is, except for the women, who with their practical intuition and their inborn distrust of fine speeches, suspected that a heavy price would have to be paid for all these "presents" before very long. In addition, they were outraged by the coarseness of the Mirists and Fidel Castro's insolent meddling in the country's affairs during his visit. They felt instinctively that their difficulties in obtaining food supplies were likely to grow worse. It is not surprising that one or another of them should have had the idea of expressing their discontent by forming processions in which they walked along banging two empty saucepans together; Chileans have a lively, amusing imagination and can always think up original ways of demonstrating. What is surprising is that this idea spread so fast amongst the women, with the speed and force of a seismic shock-wave. None of the organized parties had any hand in it. No newspaper or radio station mentioned it. It was all organized by telephone or by word of mouth in shops, markets, day-nurseries and offices, and all with such efficiency that on the day and at the hour agreed the main thoroughfares fixed for the procession filled up with several tens of thousands of women, each carrying the empty saucepans that proved their case.

A glance at the photographs is enough to show that, contrary to the false report immediately put out by the UP, all classes of society and not just the bourgeoisie, were massively represented. The noise of the saucepans took a little time to reach its full volume, but soon it was resounding through the city like metallic thunder, stopping as though by magic to give place to anti-collectivist slogans rhythmically and enthusiastically chanted, and then starting again. Once the first amazement had been overcome, the city began to join in. Men joined the ranks. Chilean flags appeared in the windows. Groups of young folk appeared from nowhere to act as marshals. Passers-by applauded. Florists threw flowers. Fresh contingents of women hesitated, then joined the demonstrators; "Merely to see them marching with such brave faces gave fresh heart to the most frightened", as Mr. Corneille put it in his *Le Cid*.

Then, all of a sudden, towards six o'clock in the evening, the paramilitary groups moved in. Armed with clubs, bicycle-chains and rubber truncheons, they began beating up the peaceful, unarmed women. Some, from the cover of nearby buildings threw potatoes studded with razor blades at them. I have seen the scars on the arm of one of the women. After a moment of panic, the demonstrators recovered themselves and, despite the fear they admitted feeling, they remained in the ranks. They had successfully undergone their baptism of fire—and it had been real fire, for they had been shot at by men with pistols. Despite the bloodshed, and the wailing of sirens as ambulances picked up the wounded, the women continued to march; bang their saucepans and demonstrate. They only dispersed when police began a wholesale bombardment with tear-gas bombs. But late into the night, small groups were still moving about the city and shouting their slogans, and in their homes people were re-living the details of the day, expressing their sense of shock, and reflecting.

The democratic opposition which until then had merely been muttering in a corner felt its courage returning, revived by indignation, and the very next day it began to speak out in parliament and the press and demand a reckoning. Fidel Castro fled like a rat two days later. The first big crack had appeared in the Marxist-Leninist power-structure. As the poet Valéry might have said, it now knew that it was mortal. It had gained its position through promises, programmes, verbal trickery and conjuring up enchanting visions in people's minds. The saucepans served notice on it that a much more powerful force was working against it, namely, a people's feelings. The notice was served by the most decisive section of the people where feelings are concerned, the women.

They never demobilized after this first outburst. They created their own organization, distinct from and cutting across all party allegiances, and which was spontaneously named "Women's Power". This was quite loosely and informally organized; it had no statutes, membership-cards or congress, and it passed no resolutions. It operated on a personal woman-to-woman basis, and one joined it simply by taking part in its activities, moved by a gut-reaction of instinctive distaste for collectivism, by a powerful will and by superabundant energy. Its members constantly dreamed up new propaganda gimmicks and ways of slyly poking fun at the government, a propaganda campaign that was symbolic and allusive, hinting more than it stated. Examples were the handkerchiefs tied to stakes around official buildings, and which were mysteriously replaced each morning, the popular songs adapted into anti-Allende choruses, the cookery lessons given on TV in which the carrots all had Mr. Altamirano's face, the radios permanently but quietly switched on, and then turned louder and the windows flung open whenever an item of anti-Allende news came on. Courses in self-expression were laid on for the less articulate wives to help them win over their husbands and neighbours and parry the slanted arguments of Socialists and Communists. Courses in how to organize action groups were given too, and even courses in karate, thus increasing the fighting effectiveness of the most active members in no small measure.

From that great day on, the women of Chile were always to be found at the centre and in the forefront of popular opposition to the Marxist-Leninist regime. We shall encounter them at each turn of the struggle. On 2 December 1972, the anniversary of their first demonstration, they decided to let the saucepans speak again, but this time without a procession through the streets, so as to avoid bloodshed. The new tactic was to bang them together at home, but to keep one's windows wide open, and to concentrate the noise in each different neighbourhood in turn, so that it moved gradually around the city. All the Chileans I have met assured me that the effect was quite thrilling. For Mr. Allende, listening to it from inside one of his palaces, the sound was nothing less than a death knell. This death knell rapidly became a standard tactic. Whenever a local or national event called for the protests of free citizens, the women passed the word from house to house, and in two hours the city would become the stage for a strident saucepan concert.

It is a fact that the principal organizers of this movement—I have met them—belonged to that former "aristocratic bourgeoisie" whose decisive role in Chile's history I have already referred to. Any social movement needs educated minds at its head. But these educated minds were enthusiastically backed up, and very often indeed urged on by the vast mass of women of the middle and lower classes, from caretakers to schoolmistresses, and ranging through shopkeepers, nurses, working-girls, housewives and ordinary mothers of families. Without their support and keen participation, without the sounding-board they provided, "Women's Power" would have been just one more committee.

As there were millions of them, it came to have the significance of a major force in history.

The battle of La Papelera

We have seen how relentlessly the UP pursued its aim of nationalizing or destroying the great paper-producing firm La Papelera, the control of which by a totalitarian regime would have enabled them to gag the whole free press. I have already described the various illegal manoeuvres planned by the government so as to give them control of this bastion. I shall now show how these plans were foiled by the people and the workers themselves.

Right at the beginning, you will remember, the government gave CORFO (the Industrial Development Agency) the job of buying up the bulk of the shares in La Papelera, offering up to four times their stock market value, and they made 840 million escudos (diverted, in fact, from industrial development) available to finance the operation. There were 16,500 small shareholders, which shows how firmly La Papelera was rooted in the life of the nation. They owned a sizeable share of the capital, although the majority was still in the hands of Mr. Jorge Alessandri. In response to these tempting offers, the opposition set up a Freedom Fund, and asked shareholders who wanted to sell to do so to the fund rather than to CORFO. It offered only the proper market price. "Women's Power" was mobilized. Groups of women went round collecting money for the Freedom Fund, and got together 300 million escudos in 20 days. Other women visited shareholders and begged them not to yield to the siren-songs of the Marxists. They had built up a solid body of convincing arguments, seasoned by a whole collection of striking formulas and parables, as for example: "You'll get 10,000 pesos today and 10,000 strokes with a stick tomorrow."—"Judas too sold you know who, and afterwards he hanged himself in remorse. Make up your own mind, we are leaving you this rope."—"Which do you prefer: freedom for Chile, or a pile of cash for yourself?", etc. At the end of six months the CORFO had with great difficulty managed to buy 7.7% of the shares. It was beaten, and did not bother to go on.

Mr. Allende then tried to nominate a state *interventor* to take charge of the company. Immediately, the firm's 17 trade unions organized a vote of all employees, and 82% of these (with only 12% against and 6% of abstentions) rejected any form of state intervention and made common cause with the management. When one remembers that four-fifths of these 5,000 employees were rank-and-file workers, one can see what a resounding slap in the face this was for a UP government that claimed to be "popular". The highest percentage against state intervention 88.5% was at the El Laya works, traditionally a trade union stronghold. Later the workers of La Papelera issued a defiant declaration in which, after stating that the UP "has a totally artificial view of how workers' minds work", they went on, more specifically: "We do not understand why the UP continually urges us to win the battle of production; we have been fighting this battle for 50 years, three shifts a day and 365 days a year, without absenteeism or political conflicts . . . It is thanks to the spirit and competence of the paper workers that this enterprise has become the pride of Chile."

Can one believe one's ears? There actually were, then, somewhere in the world, workers proud of their work and their country and mistrustful of state ownership!

When, after all these setbacks, the UP government, not willing to admit defeat, tried to cut the ground from under La Papelera's feet by sabotaging deliveries of wood and blocking the roads, the lorry-drivers took matters into their own hands, and managed to supply the factories by indirect routes. At the same time the women, once again, spread out like ants through the homes and shops of Chile from north to south, collecting used paper and passing it to the mills with the help of sympathetic drivers. In a few days they had collected a sufficient tonnage for two weeks' production and, more important, they had mobilized the minds of the people against the regime. At the same time they brought food, records and the support of their presence to the defensive pickets they had helped to organize to prevent the factories being seized. In the end Mr. Allende gave in, and all newspapers, whatever their opinions, continued to receive their supplies of newsprint until the end of the UP's reign.

Workers' hostility to the UP

The battle of La Papelera was not the only one to prove an object lesson as to the real mood of a considerable part of the proletariat, and a bitter lesson indeed for those who claimed to be the champions of the proletariat but whose real aim was in fact to tame and subdue it. The history of the UP is full of incidents that teach the same fundamental lesson.

The astonishing phenomenon of workers solidarity with their capitalist masters against the Marxist government was also exemplified when the regime was attempting to bring the important newspaper *El Mercurio* to heel. The UP had only managed to win over 23 out of its 1,470 workers and staff. At the beginning of September 1972, the five leaders who headed these 23, and who made up the paper's CUP (Popular Unity Committee), accused the management of "tax evasion", and made the salaries of the directors public. Five days later, on 10

September 1972, at a mass meeting where *all* the staff were present, these voted unanimously (with the exception of the 23 UP supporters) to expel the five ringleaders from the firm. Immediately the College of Left-wing Journalists mounted violent demonstrations in front of the newspaper building, and on 15 September Mr. Allende himself took up the cause of the five trouble-makers and accused *El Mercurio* of tax frauds, a charge which was exposed as a baseless slander by an ad hoc committee of enquiry. Mr. Allende stepped up his advertizing boycott, and cancelled all advertisements given to the paper by public bodies. To this the employees replied by a most amazing move; they offered the paper a 20% cut in their wages! *El Mercurio* was thus saved to continue its masterly job as a vehicle of healthy objective reporting in Chilean politics.

On 30 October 1971 the 1,500 workers of the El Canelo drinking-water undertaking, who were on strike, demanded "the expulsion of the gunmen belonging to the Ecuador Socialist Party, engaged by the state *interventor* solely as leftist activists and professional political 'insulters' ".

On 7 May 1972 Mr. Agunto Apablaza, the communist *interventor* in charge of the Helvetia factory, was removed from control by a unanimous vote of the workers. He then called in 20 gunmen from outside, armed himself with a sub-machine gun, retook possession of the premises; forced the workers to sign a document of submission to himself and removed the chairman of the firm's trade union, Mr. Victor Caceres, as a hostage.

The Chilean Telephone Company, intended as something of a show-case for the UP, since before nationalization it had belonged to the reviled American company, ITT, had for this purpose been entrusted to the socialist *interventor* Mr. Jaime Schatz, a man whose professional competence was highly regarded. On 1 December 1972 the workers came out on strike when this "great friend of the people" decided to reduce by a third the end-of-year bonus which had been normal practice under the hated exploiters of the ITT. They passed the following resolution: "We shall fight steadfastly to the end against the bureaucrats and agitators of the UP who claim that we have to obey unconditionally just because we are managed by a government *interventor*."

I have already spoken of the strike in which the Chuquicamata copper workers decided that it was becoming urgent to "take copper away from the Communists and give it back to the people of Chile". Another sentence from the same resolution passed by the men ran: "Never has any single individual done so much harm to Chile as the communist Mr. David Silberman, appointed general manager of the mine." On 16 January 1973 these same Chuquicamata miners came out on strike once again to mark their rejection of ration cards, which, as they said, "have never been of any use in mitigating the effects of the food shortage; all they have done is to foster envy among workmates owing to the unfair way supplies are shared out". On 9 February 1973, in the elections for trade union leaders, the Marxists, who had dominated the mine for 30 years, won only three places on the executive against seven for the democratic opposition. This was greeted by all Chileans as a historic victory, and the Santiago union leader Mr. Manuel Rodriquez told *El Mercurio* on 10 February 1973: "We hope to begin a programme of national reconstruction, which means removing the corrupt members of the UP government, the unprincipled politicians who have misled and betrayed the workers, the Figueroas, Millas and Altamiranos who have turned the revolution into a profitable business, all those who have traded on the black market and thrown the country into complete chaos."

One of the main reasons for the workers' growing disillusionment with the UP was made clear to me during an enthralling interview I had in September 1978 with leaders of the CEPCh. (*Confederaciôn de Empleados Particulares de Chile*), an organization grouping several hundred unions of white-collar workers in industry and commerce, a highly respected body whose trade union tradition goes back to the beginning of the century. These leaders, expressing themselves quite openly, even when criticizing General Pinochet, pointed out to me that in Mr. Allende's time many workers resented the UP works committees because they tried to *take the place of the unions*; controlled and policed union meetings; persecuted the "disruptive elements" who dared to critize the UP, and insisted on introducing an exhausting system of competitive work-targets. This veiled opposition of many of the workers to the UP turned to open hostility when in October 1972 the government signed an agreement with the CUT (the Unitary Workers' Federation) making this the sole representative of workers' interests. The old unions, accustomed to conducting their own negotiations with management, and many of which, led by old Social Democrat friends of Mr. Arturo Ibanez, had shown themselves resistant to communist infiltration, thus found themselves deprived of their right to represent the workers.

This was of course the precise intention behind the agreement.

The El Teniente strike

By a lucky combination of circumstances, the spirit of independent trade unionism that had been developed by Mr. Ibanez's Social Democrats was still a live force in eight of the nine unions operating in the big El Teniente copper mine. I have visited this mine (except the underground workings: faithful to an old superstition, the miners refuse to let women enter these, believing that their presence in the bowels of the earth brings bad luck). It is a remarkable technical achievement. It occupies a magnificent site 1,800 metres up in the Cordillera to the south-east of Santiago. No one lives there any more, for Pinochet has rehoused the 8,500 miners and their families in neat houses with all modern conveniences in the town of Rancagua down in the plain, where the children can easily get to good schools; the sick can be more easily cared for in good hospitals, and where the housewives enjoy far more comfortable conditions. The miners and other staff are driven to and from the mine each day by coach. Mr. Allende, for all his claim to be concerned with social conditions, had kept everyone living in old huts without running water, gas or electricity, clinging to the slopes around the mine itself.

In March 1973, the UP government granted a nationwide readjustment of wages as partial compensation for the rise in the cost of living since October 1972. But the El Teniente miners had already negotiated an upward adjustment within their own enterprise in December 1972. The UP government announced that it intended to deduct the whole of this increase, and in fact awarded a rise *41% lower than was due.* After unsuccessful negotiations the chairman of the El Teniente trades council, Mr. Guillermo Medina, declared: "If we accept the proposal of the Executive we shall be brushing aside with our own hands everything we have won with so much sweat, tears and blood." On 14 April 1973, eight out of the nine unions at the mine declared a strike which was called at first "the 41% strike".

It immediately became a total walk-out, supported even by the members of the ninth union which, led by a Communist, had not been a party to the strike decision. It was by far the biggest withdrawal of working-class support that the UP had experienced since it came to power, and the most resounding denial of its claim to represent the people and fulfil its aspirations. The local and national UP leaders felt more confusion, secret shame and fury than they had over the saucepan march. They immediately showed their true colours as the tyrannical little barons they were, by launching against the striking miners a campaign in which hatred and lies attained levels unknown for many years in our capitalist democracies.

First, following well-tried communist practice, the UP used the weapon of slander. It claimed that a fascist minority had forced the majority to strike "against its own class-interests", that these agitators were in the pay of the CIA, that they employed bully-boys armed with clubs who got drunk at night. Then followed manoeuvres that union tradition has always considered as utterly contemptible: the UP authorities tried to hire strike-breaking blacklegs from among the agricultural workers and Mapuche Indians in the country around Rancagua, and sent them to work in the mine under police protection. But their production was abysmally low, and they tended to desert when the miners' wives spat in their faces, and so the government was forced to give up recruiting them. Next the UP tried to intimidate the strikers by starving them out, putting all sorts of obstacles in the way of supplies reaching Rancagua. But the women of the area found dozens of ways of getting round this. The tension continued to escalate. On 23 May, when the strike had been going on for 40 days, a procession of strikers marched past the Rancagua offices of the Socialist Party when heavy firing from the building caused the death of the son of one of the union leaders and seriously wounded 12 other miners. The whole region rose immediately as one man; the 30 trade unions covering all the ancillary enterprises, shopkeepers, craftsmen, municipal workers, etc., declared a general strike and organized an immense march past, which was once again attacked by UP forces. The battle resulted in 15 men being wounded, and went on until three armoured vehicles filled with soldiers separated the combatants.

Once again the women took a hand, the miners' wives, backed up by hundreds of others sent in by "Women's Power". One evening they seized the local radio station in a commando raid, handed it over to the miners, and organized self-defence groups and identity checks for them so efficiently that they kept control of it right to the end. On 13 June the station broadcast repeated appeals urging the miners to march on Santiago to seek satisfaction for their claims.

Out of 8,000 miners, 5,600 set out, some in lorries, some in cars, others on horseback or bicycle, and many on foot. The UP government was astounded by their numbers, their determination and the support they received all along the route. On the 14th at noon they reached the bridge over the Maipu, just outside the capital. What did they find facing them on the other bank? The city governor himself, the socialist Mr. Julio Stuardo, at the head of the force of three tanks and 12 bulldozers, and backed by carabineros armed to the teeth! The socialst comrade mayor asked the workers to turn back, as the socialist comrade President had just forbidden them to enter the capital. As the miners obstinately refused to go away, the socialist mayor ordered his machines forward onto the bridge and showered the strikers with tear-gas bombs. A perfect example of "class-savagery"—the marxist "baron" class against the working class—and quite in the tradition of Kronstadt in the Soviet Union, where Russian sailors who had revolted against the stifling dictatorship of the Bolshevik leaders had been massacred in 1921.

The miners had no alternative but to withdraw, shouting catcalls the while. Night fell. Mr. Allende though he had won the game. The next day the 5,600 miners were inside the city, unshaven and dirty, but nevertheless there. They had forded the river; cut through wire fences; climbed up and down the hills surrounding Santiago; slipped along the unlit streets of the outskirts, and crossed empty lots. On the morning of the 15th they were milling around in the capital.

Here began the third act of the epic, with the miners and the police confronting each other right inside the city. The Catholic University opened its doors to the strikers and put them up in its halls, lecture theatres and individual buildings. Despite this warming gesture of solidarity, the miners' movement would have foundered in despair had it not been for the women, who once again saved the day. In the first instance it was the women of Santiago who, from the very first evening, came in their thousands with camp beds, mattresses, blankets, soap, razors and medicines for the strikers. They even managed, goodness knows how in a period of shortage, to collect some provisions. Then they began stirring up the city, with saucepans, processions, banners, flags at the windows, loudspeaker-cars, leaflets, constant lobbying of Parliament, the town hall and the CODELCO (the Copper Combine). This went on for ten days. On 25 June at 5 o'clock in the morning 3,000 miners' wives who had stayed at Rancagua also set out, led by "Women's Power" delegates. Through their radio station they declared: "This is the first time miners' wives have demonstrated in the streets. But equally, it is the first time we have had a government like this one in Chile." They reached the capital in the afternoon, and were greeted by an enormous popular demonstration. The crowds had been building up for 24 hours. This time there was no question of using force; the general indignation was too great. Mr. Allende agreed to receive a delegation of miners' wives, and gave way on their principal demands. At 6 o'clock in the evening the miners left the Catholic University in a moving ceremony, their wives on their arms and the UP regime's surrender in their pocket. It is in honour of them that I have put a picture of a miner tapping molten copper on the cover of this book.

Resistance of the peasants

In the countryside too, resistance to Marxist policy sprang from the grass-roots, mobilizing hundreds of thousands of peasants. Numerous heart-rending examples bear witness to this. Thousands of commandos formed spontaneously, armed with the traditional peasant weapons: pitchforks, scythes and shotguns, to bar the way of those carying out land seizures or to recover property illegally confiscated. There are few provinces in Chile where tales are not told of cases of vengeance organized by plundered farmers against their plunderers. The age-old reaction of countrymen to the powers that impoverish or coerce them took the form I have already described: a decline in cultivation, fields lying fallow, peasants with folded arms refusing to work; and its first consequence was a food shortage in the towns.

This reluctance to work turned in August 1972 into a wave of strikes, this time showing some rudimentary organization, using watch-words and mounting demonstrations. One of these last was filmed by a reporter. It contained shots which moved me deeply. One shows a column of typical peasants, with granite faces, thick shoes, walking heavily and without any visible leadership, yet menacingly, along a dirt road under a big banner bearing the words: "We do not want to be slaves of the state." This heartening cry, bursting spontaneously from the lungs of these toilers of the soil, sums up better than ten heavy volumes of sociology the essential error of Marxism, and the tragic fate of peasants when they come under the yoke of a state based on this error.

The ENU starts a prairie fire

I have already told how on 26 February 1972 Mr. Allende issued a decree according to which *all* schools, private and public, were to be nationalized (the initials ENU stood for *Esceula Nacional Unificada*, or the Unified National School System), and must "adopt the same structure and teach a common curriculum, so as to form the pupils' minds" (in a Marxist-Leninist direction, it goes without saying) "from kindergarten to university, and, more generally, become, under the direct control of the masses, centres for the socialist transformation of society". Despite their two and a half years' experience of Marxist excesses, the Chileans were thunderstruck by this. For the Chilean Constitution, more advanced on this point than those of many democratic countries, lays down, in the spirit of Condorcet, in its article 10, paragraph 7, that:

"The Constitution guarantees freedom of education to all those living in the Republic.

"The organization and choice of staff of private educational establishments shall be determined by the persons setting up the establishments, who must, however, observe the legal norms.

"The education given throughout the national system shall be democratic and pluralist and will follow no official party line. It can only be changed democratically after free discussion by the competent pluralist bodies."

It is thus clear that in introducing by decree alone, without any public discussion, not even a debate in parliament, such a reversal of the status quo, and setting up precisely what the Constitution forbade, that is to say an authoritarian structure and a state-imposed orthodoxy for the educational system, Mr. Allende was knowingly violating the country's basic law, which he had solemnly sworn to observe. He scarcely bothered to justify himself: the one or two "explanations" that he deigned to make were so perfunctory and so untenable as to be positively insulting to his hearers' intelligence, as for example when he said that his decree did not impose any "party line" on education "since it did not name any party" The hypocrite! It outlined a party's sectarian doctrine. He claimed that the reform had in fact been "debated" on the grounds that a commission of civil servants in the UP Ministry of Education had looked over it.

Mr. Allende was faced with a massive wave of protest, proof of how little he understood the deep attachment of his fellow-countrymen to a soundly-based free culture. Once again the women were in the forefront, and I was lucky enough to know one of the keenest organizers, Mrs. Sarah Navas, a lawyer and magistrate and a veritable force of nature when it came to argument and militancy. At a moment's notice she dropped her professional and family obligations and threw herself into the crusade to the extent of five meetings a day, starting at nine in the morning and finishing after midnight. There were hundreds of other women doing the same work just as eagerly if not as capably. Each day the crowds cheering them grew bigger. Even in the remotest parts of the country, if the news got around that Mrs. Sarah Navas or one of her colleagues were coming, the hall would be full to bursting at five o'clock.

This time the whole of society from the highest to the humblest joined in. Class differences were forgotten, and the movement became a truly national and united front. The military were by no means the least indignant. Opposition to the ENU was particularly strong in Catholic circles; Mr. Allende tried to calm it by calling in his great ally in the Church, Cardinal Silva, archbishop of Santiago, who summoned Catholic leaders of the anti-ENU campaign several times to his presence and tried to win them round by smooth reassurances. The trick did not work, and the most fervent Catholics were not taken in, particularly since the highly respected archbishop of Valparaiso issued a strong criticism of the ENU. The students themselves rose in revolt, and on 22 March 1973 a meeting of their main associations was called on the initiative of the Federation of Santiago Secondary-school Students, whose politically neutral chairman, Mr. Miguel Salazar, warned the government that if it persisted in implementing its ENU plan, the students would strike and occupy the school buildings indefinitely.

This proved to be the coup de grâce. As in all democratic countries, the student and teaching bodies in Chile had been strongly leftist and had supplied the UP with many of the mouthpieces and operational bases it needed. But from the spring of 1972 these circles had no longer found it possible to remain immune to the general and growing distaste for Marxism-Leninism, *now that they had seen it in action.* In April 1972 the election of Mr. Boeninger as rector of the University of Chile against the candidate of the left had been greeted as a triumph by the democratic opposition. From then on the UP position in the educational world went continually downhill.

The Catholic University followed suit and outdid its sister, the University of Chile, though only after an even harder internal power struggle. It had long been controlled by its leftist rector, Mr. Castillo Velasco, who had done all he could to turn it into a UP stronghold. He had even gone as far as to offer a professorship to the hotheaded minister Mr. Jacques Chonchol, and to use university funds to publish the *Cuadernos de la Realidad Nacional* ("Notebooks on National Reality"), a periodical that had served as a rallying-point and a means of exerting pressure in favour of Mr. Allende. But Mr. Velasco had not been able to get rid of a large body of teachers resistant to Marxism, nor to completely blind the students as to the real state of the nation. The ENU affair completed their disillusionment, and brought the others over to their side. The university press made a complete about-turn and began to bring out anti-UP pamphlets. When Mr. Velasco tried to defend the UP publicly he was booed. Finally 80% of the Catholic University swung over, and it took its place in the opposition, soon becoming one of its chief assets when certain of its top academics had the courage to denounce the misdeeds of the regime in the full light of day. Its TV channel, channel 13, became the principal mouthpiece for intellectual resistance to the UP. In June 1973 it was the Catholic University which gave material support and publicity to the striking miners of El Teniente. This swing back towards reason and tolerance on the part of an institution that everyone had considered as totally corrupted was one of the brightest pages in Chilean history.

The massive turn around of secondary school pupils to the anti-ENU campaign marked the climax of the students' disenchantment with Mr. Allende. The Marxists realized immediately how serious the loss of this key milieu was for them. They backpedalled and abandoned the project. But is was too late. The military officers, whose entry into the government had given Mr. Allende a valuable breathing-space, realized that they were merely being used as tools, and resigned. Thus the ENU project, designed by the Marxists to win over and bring into step those who were still hostile to their regime, had in the end alienated many of the regime's own supporters. Why had this happened? It became clear that certain basic values were deeper rooted and stronger in the hearts of the Chilean people than all the party loyalties or manoeuvres of those in power. By rising as one man, standing shoulder to shoulder, exposing the sophistries of UP propaganda; outfacing the state at great personal risk, only to prevent it from intellectually regimenting their children, the Chilean people performed the bravest and most farsighted action of all.

The saga of the lorry-drivers and the middle classes

I now reach the highest and most striking stage of Chilean popular resistance, a stage which twice reached boiling-point, once in October 1972 and again in July 1973.

For more than six months the UP authorities had been prowling like wild beasts round the great socio-economic bloc made up by the country's 56,000 lorries, owned as they were by thousands of small proprietors, fiercely independent, strong-willed, earthy in speech, efficient and practical and with a highly-developed esprit de corps. In a long thin country served by a single, somewhat dilapidated railway line, this guild of haulage contractors played a vital role in the economy, and Marxist-Leninists could hardly leave it uncontrolled. At the end of September 1972 they tested the animal's reactions by a preliminary pinprick in the lower flank: they set up a state-owned Transport Company in the southern district of Aisen.

Things moved fast. Six days later, on 1 October, the local hauliers' union, meeting in the small town of Coyaique, called a strike. On 4 October the chairman of their Confederation, Mr. Leon Vilarin, warned the Minister of Transport that if the state-owned Aisen Transport Company was not dissolved, the 165 lorry-drivers' unions covering the country from north to south would also come out on strike. Their condition was rejected, and so on 8 October a call for a general strike was put out. On the 9th not a single lorry moved on any road in Chile. The great trial of strength was starting.

Let us take a look first at the hauliers' leader, Mr. Leon Vilarin. I have interviewed him at length, and anyone meeting him cannot fail to be struck by his dignified strength, or the awareness and ability that emanates from him. He runs one lorry himself, and has a half-share in another with a Spanish Republican refugee. For a long while he was a militant member of the Socialist Party, and even fought several campaigns alongside Mr. Allende. The fact that the hauliers should have chosen a man of his antecedents as their chairman shows how unfair it would be to accuse them of having a "bourgeois mentality". He withdrew from the Socialist Party when it became too deeply involved in its alliance with the Communists, but made no public expression of disapproval. He devoted himself to his union work, which he carried out conscientiously and enthusiastically, meanwhile pursuing his own education until he made himself one of the country's finest thinkers.

From the very next day, 10 October 1972, a flood of bitter invective, ignoble slander and incitements to hatred against the hauliers was unleashed from every paper, committee, radio station and trade union controlled by the UP. This was the first barrage, a bombardment of mud-slinging. Dropping his reserve and bellowing in fury, Mr. Allende declared that the lorries of all the strikers would be forcibly confiscated and never returned. The drivers immediately tried to hide their precious working capital or have them guarded by pickets of strikers. Mr. Leon Vilarin and four of his colleagues in the union leadership were arrested! The president of the Chamber of Deputies and the vice-president of the Senate immediately paid them a conspicuous visit. The prison warders received them with deference, and then issued a statement saying "that they are employed to guard bandits and not trade unionists", and then turned a blind eye so effectively that Mr. Vilarin and his lieutenants were able to carry on directing the strike from their cells.

On 12 October a column of UP activists set out from the Plaza de Armas in the heart of Santiago, with bulldozers and mechanical shovels, turned on to the Pan-American international highway outside the city, discovered a lorry depot and set fire to it. When the lorry-owners ran up to save their property they were arrested and thrown into prison. This was another mistake, for the imprisonment set off an explosion of public feeling. On the 15th several thousand drivers' wives demonstrated outside the prison walls. On the 18th the union leaders were set free by a court order which this time Mr. Allende did not dare to countermand.

The imprisonment of the unionists, foreign as it was to the whole of Chile's democratic tradition, the unanimity and steadfastness of the strikers, the immediate mobilization of "Women's Power", as well as the support given by the Catholic University, steadily and successively put fresh heart into the nation as a whole. One after another in an impressive series which rapidly assumed the dimensions of a tidal wave, section after section of society came out on indefinite strike, partly out of solidarity with the hauliers, partly to achieve their own claims. Groups involved in this movement included: coach and bus drivers, taxi-drivers, train drivers, port workers, sailors of the merchant navy, municipal employees, forestry workers, the National Confederation of Small-Scale Industry and Craftsmen, the National Confederation of Commerce, the National Confederation of Production; and then, one after another, all the liberal professions: accountants, surveyors, dentists, barristers, architects, chemists, pharmacists, biochemists, odontologists, engineers, and even doctors—over 90% of the members of all these groups answered the strike call of their professional organizations.

Each decision to strike provided an opportunity for the members of the profession concerned to issue a solemn declaration, unburdening their hearts and expressing their unanimous disquiet at the threat to their freedom. I quote just a few typical passages:

From the Confederation of Small-scale Industry and Craftsmen:

> "For the vast majority of the country, there can be no doubt that we are facing an offensive whose aim is to replace the democratic system by a dictatorship ... Who in Chile will be able to enjoy freedom if in future food for the family, anxiously awaited medicines, indispensable spare parts for tools and vehicles, raw materials and basic products necessary if we are to provide employment and supplies for the country are going to depend on the will of political commissars great and small?"

From the merchant seamen:

> "If the government wants to stimulate output and restore peace, all it has to do is to leave the sea free and stop worrying Chileans by its constant campaigns of hatred and slander."

From the National Union of Associations of the Liberal Professions:

> "The arrest of the lorry-drivers' leaders is a scandalous act of anti-union repression, unique in our history, and one to which the liberal professions cannot remain insensitive unless they want to become servile professions tomorrow."

From the College of Agricultural Experts:

> "The unheard-of suppression of the lorry-drivers' right to strike arouses our anxiety over the increasing number of violations of the most elementary rights of the citizen by the government ... Several times already we have drawn public attention to the catastrophic failures the government has organized in agriculture and food supplies."

From the General Confederation of Production:

> "The lorry-drivers' strike means basically that the people want a free industry in a free country. As this too is the supreme goal of those in charge of the country's productive forces, they too have in their turn decided on an indefinite strike."

The Marxist-Leninist authorities were stupefied by this tidal wave. They decreed a state of siege over virtually the whole country. Their paramilitary bands stepped up their sabotage of lorries: tyres were burst; vehicles burned; signposts altered, etc. But their owners soon found the answer to this by concentrating their lorries in huge, well-guarded laagers reminiscent of the defensive circles of waggons formed in Western films as a defence against Indian attack. These camps were supplied with food, medicine and blankets by an uninterrupted stream of women, children and local shopkeepers.

On 18 October the UP government, panic-stricken, ordered that all radio stations should be allowed to broadcast only the slanted news bulletins put out by the official OIR agency. This *encadenamiento* ("putting in chains") aroused great indignation. The Supreme Court called the measure "cynically unconstitutional". The Chamber of Deputies, in a special session, taxed the government with once again, and in the most cynical manner, violating the freedom of expression guaranteed by article 10 para. 3 of the Constitution, and thus acting illegally. When a socialist mayor cut the electricity supply of the most active of the broadcasting stations, Radio Agricultura, which had become one of the bastions of the opposition, "Women's Power" collected within 24 hours enough petrol to run the station's emergency generator for a fortnight. One after the other, the country's radio stations refused to transmit the one-sided bulletins of the official agency and returned to free broadcasting. When Mr. Patricio Palma, director of DIRINCO, the (state) Directory of Industry and Commerce, decided to go in person, surrounded by troops and police, to open by force the shuttered fronts of shops that were on strike, passers-by rallied round and joined battle against the policemen quite spontaneously, without any prior organization.

On 24 October another idea of "Women's Power" was tried out, a day of silence, during which everyone was to stay at home with the windows closed, no one was to move about and nothing was to happen in the streets. These orders were obeyed by millions of the citizens. UP groups shouted themselves hoarse trying to break the silence, but only created a few scattered dark patches on what was otherwise a blank background.

In Spanish the word *gremio*, half-way between "guild, professional corporation" and "trade union", is used to describe associations of a trade-union type organizing middle-class professional people receiving salaries or fees rather than wages. Such associations could thus be called either *gremios* or "unions". The great movement of October 1972 was in fact a mobilization of these *gremios*. Under Mr. Vilarin's chairmanship, a Joint Command of the hundreds of striking *gremios* was set up, and its committee, meeting in an atmosphere reminiscent of that of the Jacobin Club in 1789, decided to issue in the name of all the constituent associations a joint proclamation making their demands public. This manifesto became famous as the *Pliego de Chile* (using the word *pliego* in the sense of a roll of parchment with seals on which important communications were written in the Middle Ages). This unparalleled document, concerned as it was with the underlying causes of the present chaos, inevitably dealt more with politics than strictly trade union matters; it contained seven main heads and a supplement. Its demands were as follows:

—The respect of the freedoms and rights of the *gremios*, the reinstatement of all workers dismissed for striking, the restitution of all property confiscated or placed under the control of a state *interventor* since 21 August 1972, and an end to the intimidation of independent judges;

—The immediate and total restoration to all radio stations of freedom of expression and access to information by ending their obligation to use exclusively the syndicated news bulletins issued by the OIR, the reopening of Radio Agricultura and other suspended stations, and an end to the unjust and illegal attempts to put La Papelera out of business;

—The implementation of the constitutional amendment known as that of "the 3 sectors" passed by Parliament, which clearly defined the economic spheres pertaining to the public sector, the private sector and the mixed sector respectively, together with an end to the nationalization of banks, to political controls on credit and foreign trade; the limitation of public intervention in agriculture to what had been laid down in the Frei agrarian reform; strict adherence to and compliance with the decisions of the lawcourts;

—Consultation with the professional bodies when economic plans were being drawn up;

—The restoration of personal security in places of work, the elimination of violence, the drastic suppression of paramilitary groups and the immediate expulsion of armed foreign extremists;

—The restoration to Chileans of the right to enter and leave the country freely;

—The dissolution of the JAPs (rationing and price-control committees), the CUPs (local UP committees) and all committees wielding quasi-police powers and exercising political control over citizens.

The supplement listed the particular demands of each *gremio*.

It can be seen that it is no exaggeration to consider this text as an equivalent to the *cahiers de doléances*, the lists of grievances drawn up in the kingdom of France and presented to the State-General in 1789. It listed all the wrongs committed by the UP, and gave voice to the muted anger of the people, and consequently the government did all it could to smother it. I have already described how, in order to extricate himself from this terrible crisis, Mr. Allende had no alternative but to ask the military to join his government. These insisted on him meeting the particular demands of the various *gremios* at least, if not the whole of the *Pliego de Chile*. Mr. Allende gave this promise. What is more, he countermanded the muzzling of the radio stations. Within a few days, the strike orders were lifted—they had been obeyed by more than 90% of the members—and the great eruption calmed down. Popular Unity continued in power, but now with one more gaping wound in its side.

Of course, Mr. Allende did not keep his promises. In the road haulage field particularly, he did not respect the agreed price structures; would not agree to lorries being sold directly to the hauliers; maintained a strict embargo on tyres; inflicted even worse harassments and restrictions on the manufacture of accessories and on repair facilities, to such an extent that seven months later Mr. Vilarin grew tired of finding himself swindled on every point, and on 25 July 1973 he declared another general strike of his association. It was a sort of repetition of the strike of October 1972, but with an even higher level of tension and violence. There were desperate attempts by the government to set up a parallel system of road haulage, the sabotage of lorries by both sides, and pitched battles between people on their way to deliver supplies to the lorry-drivers' laagers and armed bands of Marxists. On 16 August the strike committee heard that they were going to be arrested at night. They escaped across the roof-tops at two o'clock in the morning. All this took place against the now much more serious background of a country that was sinking into ruin. The stoppage of road transport had seriously worsened the food shortage, and thus antagonism between the people and the government was rapidly approaching breaking-point.

Mr. Allende had reached his Waterloo, and Mr. Vilarin was his Blücher.

Now that you have read through the main episodes that marked the Chilean people's opposition to the Marxist government, you will agree, I am sure, that I was not exaggerating when I said at the beginning that you were about to read an epic story. One, moreover, with a heroism all its own, in which the knights did not bear lances or blow on horns, but were just ordinary people handling saucepans, steering-wheels and pneumatic drills. But the basic force that drove them on was the same, an unshakeable determination to assert and maintain their *human dignity and freedom*. That this motive force should have remained intact in the hearts of a people already subjected to a Marxist-Leninist regime, and who lived in a remote country far from the main stream of events, on the edge of the world, that is the real miracle.

CHAPTER XII

THE POLITICAL OPPOSITION

Overcoming the old Adam

FROM THE MOMENT that the Christian Democratic vice-president Mr. Zujovic was assassinated on 8 June 1971 by a left-wing VOP group, it became evident to the more clear-sighted elements among the Christian Democrats that their party had made a historic mistake in bringing Mr. Allende to power eight months before, and that it was urgent to create a parliamentary opposition to the new regime. But this regime was only a minority in Congress when faced with united action by the two non-Marxist parties, Mr. Alessandri's National Party and the Christian Democrats of Mr. Eduardo Frei. A rapprochement between the Christian Democrats and the National Party was, therefore, essential, and that is just what the Christian Democrats found most difficult. Suffering from a heavy dose of the "left-wing virus", they had declared Mr. Alessandri anathema, in line with the famous fallacy: "when you win with the right wing, it's the right wing that wins." How many Christian Democrats in June 1971 still thought that a win for the totalitarian Marxists was less abhorrent than a win for the liberal right? To find out how many, Mr. Eduardo Frei, who was coming round to the need for an agonizing reappraisal, tabled a resolution condemning Mr. Allende's government's "exclusivist and totalitarian spirit" before a national council of the party soon after the assassination of Mr. Perez Zujovic. The resolution was passed, but the left wing reacted by breaking away, as I have already described, and forming the MAPU.

The majority of the Christian Democrats, once rid of their extremists, were then in a position where they could speak out more clearly against the UP, but could not yet openly call for an alliance with the right for their activists had been too thoroughly drilled into regarding themselves as "men of the left". The General Secretary, Mr. Renan Fuentealba, began the task of neutralizing gradually the virus by emphasizing Mr. Allende's continual breaches of the *Statute of Guarantees* that he had signed with them, a sore point with the Christian Democrats, who on the strength of this text had set themselves up as the guardians of democracy. The UP made this slow return of the Christian Democrats to objective reality easier by stepping up its cheap attacks on Mr. Frei and the persecutions of Christian Democratic media that I have already described.

In October 1971, driven more by its electoral supporters than by its militants, the Christian Democratic leadership forged itself another anti-Allende weapon. Faced with an avalanche of violent confiscations, Mr. Fuentealba and another member of parliament, Mr. Juan Hamilton, laid before Congress a constitutional amendment, known as that of the "3 sectors", which defined precisely which economic areas were to remain under private enterprise, which could be nationalized and which should have mixed status, as well as the legal and financial conditions to be observed in the case of nationalizations, including especially the necessity for each case to be approved by a law passed by Parliament; the circumstances under which state intervention was permissible, and the limits to the powers of the *interventores*. Congress approved this constitutional amendment by a large majority, *but Mr. Allende vetoed it*, and, until the end of the UP's reign, the amendment became the main bone of contention, judicially, politically and philosophically, between the UP regime and its parliamentary opponents. The *Pliego de Chile*, as we have seen, devoted a good deal of space to it.

The amendment offered numerous tactical advantages. The people's hostility to the confiscations, seizures, interventions and nationalizations was intense and deeply-felt, but until then it had lacked any alternative plan around which to crystallize. The amendment acted as a focus for this popular discontent, and at the same time provided a simple solution. From then on, any action Mr. Allende took in this field was bound to be illegal and unconstitutional, and would be stigmatized as such by popular opinion. Above all, this amendment accelerated the slow and difficult period of gestation needed to give birth to a patriotic anti-Allende alliance between the Christian Democrats and the National Party. The Christian Democrats had in fact realised that the sky had not fallen on their heads when they defended and voted for this text with the full agreement of the Nationalists, that on the contrary, the country was grateful to them for doing so. They realised vaguely that on the highest and most sensitive plane, namely that of the form society should take and the nature of the political system, they belonged on the same side of the barricades as the Nationalists, whether conservative or liberal ones, whereas the totalitarian Marxist-Collectivists were on the other side. The veneer of leftist attitudes which had formed a crust over their true nature was finally beginning to crack.

It cracked very noticeably after the march of the saucepans, which showed everyone where the people stood, and proved that the time for political niceties ("*I* am on the left, Senor Alessandri, do not touch me") was over. On 15 December 1971, when the country was still echoing to the sound of the saucepans, Mr. Fuentealba forced his party to make a bold change of direction by calling a large public meeting at which several hundred thousand people were present. There he made a passionate speech that he knew would be enthusiastically applauded, so that his Christian Democrats would not dare to disown him. He was in fact testing to what extent the people were ready for a break between the Christian Democrats and the UP, and as a corollary, how far they would rally to an oppositional front uniting the centre and the right.

Let me quote, from his speech, some of the inspired and unambiguous phrases that made such an impression on his hearers: "The Chilean people rejects the plans and manoeuvres hatched by the UP minority now in power to bring in, against the will of the people, a form of Socialism which has nothing in common with the free, pluralist and democratic form to which we gave our support . . . The dishonest and not very original rulers we are afflicted with are just trying to copy that totalitarian, inefficient and terrorist Socialism which has been imposed on you know which unfortunate countries."

From then on, the understanding between the two great democratic opposition forces made rapid strides. This showed itself in a number of by-elections where joint candidates were put up and scored considerable success, and in a whole series of joint actions in Parliament, such as the removal of particularly dishonest UP ministers, and the forcing of a law, the Carmona measure, on the government which gave the armed forces the responsibility for controlling the carrying of arms by individuals and civilian groups, a law which slowed down—even if it did not stop—the spread of paramilitary groups. Those elements among the Christian Democrats who still hankered nostalgically after the "swing to the left", refusing to look facts in the face, succeeded in persuading the party to try further conversations with Mr. Allende with a view to reaching some reasonable compromise agreement. But Mr. Allende himself cut the ground from under any such approach; he was ready enough to give soothing assurances in private, but followed each of these by a hard-line no compromise speech in public. The great general strike in October 1972, in which the Christian Democrats and National Party supporters fought side by side, finally melted any remaining coolness and, at the end of December 1972 the three main components of the opposition at last formally set up under the name of CODE, or Democratic Confederation, a coalition which would present a united front in the legislative elections of March 1973.

I say three components because, in addition to the two larger ones, the Christian Democrats and the National Party, there was also Mr. Julio Duran's small Radical Democrat Party. I did not mention it before in order to simplify the picture, but this active and lucid group, which enjoyed considerable prestige under Mr. Duran's leadership, had always worked to bridge the gap between the two big parties which had cost Chile so dear in that terrible drama of the legal accession of the Marxist-Leninists to power.

Indeed, as the reader has seen—and this is not to diminish Mr. Julio Duran's worth in any way—the real leaven of the patriotic alliance between the democratic parties had been supplied by the people; they had instinctively understood the danger of Communism *well before the political establishment*, and had shown the latter how it could be faced. It was a classic example of awareness of the realities of the situation moving in the opposite direction to the usual one—from the grass-roots upwards. "Drop your quibbles and grand gestures over right and left wing", this is what the demonstrators seemed to be saying to the leaders; "we have here children hungry; citizens robbed; fields laid waste, and there is the cause of the evil, in front of us, installed in the Moneda (i.e. the presidential palace). That is what we must eradicate before anything else. The only doctrine that matters is to be found not in your theories but in our difficulties", this is what the people seemed to be shouting at the politicians. The people shook the politicians so hard and so well that their theories fell from them like dead scales, and their limbs suddenly felt free.

I emphasize that this metaphor refers only to the Christian Democrats; Mr. Alessandri's National Party had never had any illusions and had, from the very outset, totally rejected Marxism-Leninism. It had shown considerable lucidity in its criticism of the UP and public-spirited unselfishness in combatting it. Men such as Mr. Mario Guzman with whom I had as long conversation, and whose anti-government TV reports on Channel 13 had the highest listening figures showed an understanding of Marxism and an urgency in their warnings against it which have few parallels that I am aware of in Europe. It was, moreover, principally the younger members of the National Party who, with indomitable energy, gave of their best in the organizing and marshalling of popular demonstrations and the provision of the logistic support these called for. Many of the women who led the "Women's Power" movement came from this party, although, as we have seen, they never acted in its name. I am not going to let myself be intimidated by the intellectual fashion among political commentators of deprecating any resistance, even a necessary and beneficial one, if it comes from the right wing. Mr. Alessandri's party was undoubtedly on the right wing, and yet it must be admitted in all honesty that it played an outstanding role in the defeat of Communism in Chile, constantly showing a clear-sightedness, sense of civic responsibility and firmness which must be admired by anyone who loves freedom and truth. In the end, it is true, the Christian Democrats joined them; all honour to them. But before that, they had deserted them, and for this they must expect to be blamed.

Another factor that led the Christian Democrats to see the light and turn against Mr. Allende was Mr. Allende himself who, instead of mending his ways, hardened in his extremism. This is, moreover, only what we would expect; in terms of its own doctrine, a revolution that puts on the brakes is not learning sensibly from experience, but denying its very nature. Adjusting or moderating one's programme is no way to be recognized as a Marxist-Leninist. Let me remind you that right up to the last moment, at the end of August 1973 when, with the final catastrophe almost upon them, the Christian Democrats made one last effort to prevent a total breakdown with their famous "last chance dialogue", Mr. Allende still side-stepped any attempt at compromise and continued his mad gallop towards the abyss.

Illegitimacy of the Allende government

The unification of the political, intellectual and parliamentary opposition naturally encouraged the grass-roots opposition of the people, and the two poles of resistance could support one another, since each initiative taken by Congress was translated into a hundred acts of resistance at the popular level. Another important sector of Chilean public life drew fresh courage from the new unity: the highest watchdog organs of the state, the Supreme Court, whose responsibility it was to ensure that the government did not overstep its legal powers in political matters, and the *Contraloria General*, whose job it was to ensure that it did not overstep them in financial and administrative matters.

To tell the truth the *Contraloria*, under the direction of Mr. Hector Humeres, a man of the highest quality, a fine example of the Chilean patrician jurists I mentioned earlier, had from the very beginning issued firm, clear public protests against the principal abuses committed by the UP government. He became a rallying-point for the opposition and a bête noire to the UP, but his prestige was such that even the most rabid leftists did not dare assault him personally. They made do with heaping invective on him.

As for the Supreme Court, it intervened more rarely, but since these interventions came from Olympus, they had the force of thunderbolts. I will sum up here the last six important texts, some from the Supreme Court, others from Mr. Eduardo Frei and the Bar Association, since they mark the final constitutional condemnation of the Marxist regime.

On 26 May 1973, after a Rancagua court had ruled that some land which had been taken over by force should be returned to its rightful owner, the UP Executive ordered the chief of the local carabineros not to evict the illegal occupants, and to drive away the rightful owner if he appeared. The Supreme Court made public a special note sent to Mr. Allende, in which it pointed out that this was "the umpteenth time that he had interfered in an act of justice", that this time he had not been content with preventing a sentence from being carried out, but had enforced the implementation of its direct opposite, that this was in the highest degree illegal and that the chief of the carabineros who had obeyed Mr. Allende was going to be brought before a court-martial (the carabineros in Chile, like the French *gardes mobiles*, are part of the armed forces) for failing in his duty and misuse of force.

On 12 June 1973 Mr. Allende replied disdainfully both with a sarcastic note to the Supreme Court and in a public speech, "that in a period of revolution, the political power has the right to decide in the last resort whether or not the decisions of the judiciary fit in with the lofty aims and historic needs of the transformation of society, which must take absolute precedence over all other considerations; consequently, it is the Executive's right to decide whether or not to carry out the sentences of the judiciary". This was the classic argument of the supremacy of "class justice" over "formal justice"; it needed all the left's gullibility to believe that the Marxists would not put it into practice when they came to power.

On 26 June 1973 the Supreme Court retorted with an even more severe note to the effect "that the fact of subordinating the decisions of the courts to the government's political options is the very definition of the *abuse of power* ... that if these were the standards the President intended to follow, he should have made this clear when he took power, and not sworn, as he had done, to observe the Constitution ... that so long as the judicial authority is not physically erased from the country's life, it will never abdicate its independence ... and that in Chile this judicial authority never has been subordinate to the executive and that it certainly does not intend to accept such subordination now that the executive has itself chosen to follow a line of total subservience to a pack of partisan activists".

On 8 July 1973 ex-president Mr. Frei, as president of the Senate, and Mr. Luis Pareto, president of the House, put out a resounding joint statement, from which I quote a few extracts:

> "In deep anxiety ... Chile is going through ... the most serious political, economic and social crisis in its history, thanks to a minority that is trying to impose a system rejected by the majority ... The country is being drained of its human capital, for the best of its professional men are emigrating in search of normal living and working conditions ... The UP government and its henchmen are shamelessly falsifying the facts and hurling cheap abuse at those who do not agree with them, so as to encourage and incite extremist groups for reasons which are all the more obvious for their handing out arms to them and transforming the industrial belts into strongholds to encircle and besiege the capital ... The authorities no

longer bother to hide their intention of establishing what they call a popular power, based on a parallel army containing many foreign terrorists— this is especially intolerable— . . . The forces supporting the government do not in any way represent this country, and only call themselves the people in order to pull the wool over their own eyes and those of others when, in fact, they are only concerned with subjugating the real people, which is hostile to them, through the action of an increasing number of paramilitary groups . . . We are not in principle opposed to major socio-economic innovations, but we categorically reject them when they are imposed by violence and lead to a totalitarian regime; the Fuentealba-Hamilton constitutional amendment (the "3 sectors") sets up an adequate framework for such changes, and it is scandalous that the UP government still refuses to adopt and apply it, *when it has been approved by a large majority in Congress* and when the *Contraloria General* and the Supreme Court have confirmed that it is perfectly constitutional. The government has only to conform to this amendment for the country to return to civil peace and normal productive life . . . We make this solemn appeal before the nation and the judgement of history, solely in order to maintain liberty, justice and peace among the citizens of Chile."

On 8 August 1973 the Bar Association, a highly prestigious organization which only seldom expresses an opinion on the general situation in the Republic, declared that "the Allende government had transformed the country's entire judicial order into a pile of rubble".

On 22 August 1973 the country woke up in dismay at the news that a group of students who had come to help the stewards at a demonstration by the wives of the striking lorry-drivers had been fired on with machine-guns the day before. In indignation, the Chamber of Deputies met in the afternoon in a stormy sitting that went on without a break until late at night, and passed by 87 votes to 47 a resolution declaring Mr. Allende's government *illegal* because it had repeatedly and knowingly violated the Constitution, the country's whole judicial order and the *Statute of Guarantees* which Mr. Allende had signed with great ceremony three years previously so as to get the votes which had brought him to power. Because of this text's importance, the high-mindedness of the thoughts it expresses, its weight and precision, and because it sums up everything described in the preceding pages, I am going to quote word for word some lengthy extracts.

"1. An essential precondition for the existence of a state based on the rule of law is that the public authorities . . . should exercise their power and confine their actions within the framework laid down by the constitution and the laws, and that all inhabitants should be able to enjoy the guarantees and fundamental rights assured them in these texts;"

"2. The juridical nature of the Chilean state is the birthright of the people who forged it over the years and made it the basis of the consensus, so that any attack on it not only harms the cultural and moral foundations of the nation, but also makes all democratic life practically impossible;"

"3. Article 2 of our Charter states that sovereignty lies in the nation, *and that the authorities cannot exercise more powers than the nation gives them*, and article 3 states that a government which oversteps this principle is subversive;"

"4. The present President of the Republic was elected by Congress on the basis of a *Statute of Guarantees*, which was afterwards incorporated into the Constitution, its object being to make sure that he observed the basic rules on each point;"

"5. It is blatantly obvious that the UP government's only objective, from the outset, has been to subject the people to *totalitarian* political and economic controls which are utterly contrary to the representative democratic system set up by the Constitution;"

"6. To achieve this end, the UP government has violated the Constitution and the laws in all sorts of ways, not occasionally, but repeatedly, knowingly and methodically. It has, for the same reason, attacked all the other regular authorities in the state and connived at the creation of parallel and illegal authorities which act by force and represent a most serious threat to the nation;"

"7. The UP government has usurped the legislative functions of Congress by taking a series of measures of far-reaching implications for society which should have been enacted through legislation, by holding up to ridicule the parliamentary censure of several ministers, and above all by refusing to adopt the constitutional amendment of the three sectors passed by Parliament;"

"8. The UP government has attacked the judicial authority by encouraging campaigns of slander and insults, by protecting convicted criminals among its own supporters, and by refusing to carry out sentences which it did not approve of, going so far as to claim the right for itself to decide whether or not a court had made the right judgement;"

"9. The UP government has systematically violated the resolutions of the *Contraloria General*;"

"10. In particular, the UP government has trampled underfoot people's rights and their freedom of expression in the following

> instances, cited, from among dozens of others, for their outstanding gravity;"

A long list follows of the most scandalous extortions, the particularly illegal confiscations, the machinations against La Papelera, the violent assaults on newspapers and journalists, the radio stations forced to close or to broadcast only material issued by the Presidential Broadcasting Agency (OIR), the channel 9 affair and the persecution of channel 13, the violations of the right to strike and to hold public meetings, the repression of the El Teniente miners, the attempt to impose Marxism in the schools, the "police control on stomachs" by the JAPs, the flogging of arrested opponents, the anti-constitutional limits on the right to leave the country, etc.

> "11. The rule of law in Chile is made to look particularly ridiculous by the creation of a series of parallel and subversive authorities, inspired by and under the protection of the UP, and intended to set up a totalitarian dictatorship from below, including such bodies as the communal commandos, the UP Committees, the Peasants' Councils, the neighbourhood Vigilance Committees, the JAPs etc;"

> "12. The most serious threat in this connection is that of the shameless development, under the government's own wing, of numerous paramilitary formations, which are plunging the country into permanent, arbitrary violence, and which threaten to prove beyond the capacity of the army itself to control."

If any readers doubt any of the facts that I have reported, let them re-read this authoritative text and their doubts will disappear. For in just two pages the people's elected representatives, the persons best placed to know the facts, and two-thirds of whom had voted Mr. Allende into power, sum up and confirm on each point all the extortions, all the illegalities, all the abuses and all the violence that I have described in the preceding chapters. This condemnation of the Allende era by Chile's most authentic representatives seems to me to be beyond doubt.

CHAPTER XIII

THE FINAL ABYSS

A country in its death throes

I HAVE FIXED 22 AUGUST 1973 as the beginning of the death throes of the Marxist regime in Chile because it was on that day that Parliament issued its historic statement proclaiming *the Allende government's illegality*. Indeed, during the 20 days that separated this first stroke of the passing bell from the final collapse on 11 September 1973, the hitherto steady pace at which the drama was unfolding began to accelerate hour by hour, like that of a body in free fall.

However, in the final analysis, the process of absolute polarization, which now left no choice other than the death of the Marxist regime or the death of Chilean democracy, had begun as early as 1 July, the day after Colonel Souper's failed coup, which came to be called the *tancazo* because it was carried out with the use of the dozen tanks of the armoured regiment which the colonel commanded. Let us rapidly review events between 1 July and 22 August, that is, the build-up to the death throes, before taking up the story of the final agony itself between 22 August and 11 September.

During the *tancazo* of 30 June, Mr. Allende, panicking, broadcast pathetic radio appeals "to the people" and "to the workers", especially those of the industrial belts, calling on them to come out immediately on to the streets and proceed to the Moneda Palace, the town hall and the UP committees, where they would be given arms. *No one moved.* It was only later, when Colonel Souper's men had been surrounded and disarmed by other battalions of the regular army under the command of General Prats, and the danger had been averted, that the leftists controlling the belts organized protest risings there. These were marked by the breaking of windows; setting fire to cars and the hunting down of militants of the democratic opposition.

On 12 July the lorry-drivers began their second national strike and, as I have reported, the climate immediately proved a good deal tenser and more violent than in October 1972. Assaults, beatings-up and sabotage of lorries followed one another without interruption. Shortages increased; the shops emptied and queues became positive nightmares. On 27 July, the Christian Democrats made one final effort to renew a dialogue with Mr. Allende and make him see reason. These "last chance talks" failed on 3 August. On 7 August, a plot was discovered in the navy: UP commandos aimed to take over the two largest battle cruisers; kill the officers and then force the port of Valparaiso into submission by threatening to shell its inhabitants from the two captured vessels. The arrested sailors denounced the Secretary General of the Socialist Party, Mr. Altamirano, and Mr. Garreton of the MAPU as the leaders of the operation, and these two, far from denying the fact, boasted about it. Since they were parliamentary deputies, they could not be prosecuted until their parliamentary immunity had been lifted. The navy demanded this, and it was due to come up for discussion in Parliament on 11 September 1973.

On 10 August, the communist mayor of Santiago, Mr. Faivovitch, followed by armed gangs, tried to storm a laager of 500 lorries set up by the striking hauliers in a suburb of Santiago. But the strikers had been warned; had removed the essential mechanisms from their vehicles and bogged them down in the mud. After a pitched battle which caused numerous casualties, Comrade Faivovitch, by way of revenge, forced the drivers to spend the whole night outside in jackets or windcheaters—in August, Chile is still in the middle of winter—and in the morning he tried to force them to get the lorries out of the mud at gunpoint. The drivers refused to move. Then Mr. Faivovitch heard that the city had learned about the raid and was in an uproar; a massive column was advancing on the laager. He withdrew, having achieved only one thing: from midday, shocked at his action, the craft *gremios* decided one after another to go on strike as well. The nightmare of October 1972 was happening all over again. When on 21 August the government fired a hail of bullets at the young people who had come to support a demonstration by hauliers' wives, and the next day, 22 August, an indignant Parliament passed a resolution "outlawing" the government, there was once again a total halt to all those economic activities which had remained in the private sector, this time including the liberal professions.

This brings us again to the critical date of 22 August. Before reporting the main episodes in the death-struggle which began then, I would like to try to sketch in for you the backcloth against which they occurred, and which I think I can reconstruct, first of all, thanks to the many available texts describing it, and then from personal accounts, all agreeing on the essentials, which I have collected from over a hundred witnesses from all walks of life whose memories of the events of that time of Greek tragedy six years previously are still as vivid as a nightmare from which one has only just woken up.

There was hunger in every home, for there were no savings left to spend on the black market. In the hospitals, patients were hungry and lacked medicines, alcohol for disinfectant, bandages, and even soap. More than one patient had to lie in other people's soiled sheets. One doctor had seen a skeletal diabetic die due to "shortage", because he had not been able to give him the necessary dose of sugar. Everyone's nerves were on edge; people were only sleeping for three or four hours a day, and were spending eight to ten hours a day including nights queuing for supplies, looking like a crowd of refugees, unwashed, their clothes crumpled, cheeks sunken and eyes red-rimmed.

To get to work in the centre of Santiago, they took more and more tortuous routes, for the main thoroughfares were permanently filled with rioting gangs. Some carried gas masks to get through the thick clouds of tear-gas or smoke from fires. I have some striking photographs of newspaper-stall holders wearing gas masks so as to carry on their business. Judge Sarah Navas had to make a detour of a mile in order to get to the law courts where her office was, and when paramilitary gangs massed in front of it, hurling abuse at the magistrates, she could only get in by a small rear door. When cars ran out of petrol, they had to be pushed for hours to get to the increasingly rare pumps where they would be given three litres to get them home. Offices, workshops, trains, the mails no longer worked to a timetable. Buses might stop anywhere and make you get off. Two out of three people needed for a job were not there when one rang them because they were out queueing.

The newspapers were full of war photographs and communiqués: the wounded dragged onto the pavement in the midst of clouds of gas, a body covered with a coat, or just with newspapers, helmets and sub-machine-guns, faces filled with hate. Here are the headlines for just one day, 31 August 1973, which I jotted down in the national library: Allende's terrorism is laying Chile waste ... Clashes and conflicts at Chillan ... State of emergency for shopkeepers ... The Supreme Court asks for guarantees to enable it to sit in safety ... Murder of Second-lieutenant Hector Lacrampette ... Christian Democrat student seriously wounded at Quillota ... CUT's office at (such-and-such a place) burned down ... The armed forces intervene to drive off Mirists at Concepción ... Five seriously wounded at Antofagasta ... Hauliers' president kidnapped at Coyaique ... 20 terrorist attacks in the capital during the night ... Bomb at a warehouse in La Serena ... Stones thrown at Valdivia town hall ... Dynamite found in the homes of five teachers ..., etc.

Such is the gloomy chorus that accompanied the final cracklings of the Allende regime.

Between 27 and 29 August, the three military ministers, who had come back into the government for a second time, saw that the latter was paying no attention to the resolution passed by Parliament and resigned. It is at this point that an incident took place which Admiral Montero later disclosed and which convinced him that the UP was preparing to make a very serious move. He had gone to see President

Allende at midnight to announce his resignation; he had found him half drunk and heard him say: "What's happening now, however much you complain about it, is only a trifle compared with what the MIR and the Communists are getting ready to do." This admission was soon public knowledge, and aroused great anxiety.

By July, the most determined of the Marxist-Leninist leaders were saying more or less openly that there was only one solution left to them: an "auto-coup", the word "coup" qualified by "auto" because it was to come from the state itself. It was known that intensive preparations were being made for this. It was known, too, that Mr. Allende had written to Mr. Corvalan, the communist leader, after the resignations of the officers from the government, saying "We have touched rock-bottom". Finally, it was known that the government was up against the wall because of its obligation to adjust salaries on 1 October to take account of the rise in the cost of living since 1 July; this stood at 350%, but the public coffers were empty. According to the most alarmist rumours, the UP's armed groups were to kill all the heads of the armed forces and the principal democratic leaders; take over all the media and close Parliament. But all this might be nothing more than the sort of rumour which starts spontaneously and spreads quickly in periods of extreme tension, when everyone feels that a volcano is forming under his feet, and wonders when and how violently it is going to erupt. The Carmona law on the control of arms, at the same time as it gave the authorities powers to close the hide-outs and arms caches of the paramilitary groups, revealed how impressive their numbers and armaments were.

On 2 September the socialist extremist Mr. Altamirano confirmed everyone's fear in an inflammatory speech in which he plainly announced to the "reactionaries" that the "people", in response to the UP's call, would "put them, once and for all, out of all possibility of doing any further harm", and was actively getting ready "for the decisive battle to take over total and exclusive control of society by means of its own army".

On 4 September, Mr. Allende returned to the charge, on a barely less strident tone, at a public meeting called to celebrate the third anniversary of his election, and attended by 25,000 of his supporters; he declared that the time for shilly-shallying was past, and that he was going to establish "the full power of the people" over and above the "outworn institutions" of the bourgeois state.

The next day, Wednesday, 5 September, the women organized the biggest political demonstration in Chile's history. This time, the 400,000 who assembled in front of the Catholic University no longer demanded that Mr. Allende should govern according to the law; they would be satisfied by nothing less than his complete departure, and they announced that if he had not resigned by the following Tuesday 11, they would take up position in front of all the main barracks and would not budge until the troops came out to expel this president who had put himself outside the law.

On 6 September, rumours about the preparations being made by the UP forces for the "auto-coup" were growing more intense and more precise, and the word Jakarta appeared on the walls, immediately heightening the atmosphere, since it suggested that the diabolical 1961 putsch carried out by the Communists and Mr. Soekarno's supporters in Indonesia against the generals, with all the revolting tortures that accompanied it, was about to be repeated in Chile, this time successfully.

On 7 September Mr. Allende announced over the radio that *there was now only enough wheat, and therefore bread, for three days.* An intense shudder of fear ran through the whole population.

The masses, more and more anxious, turned in despair to the military, their only possible resort, since the UP was too heavily armed to be overthrown by civilians. I have already described how women threw corn under the officers' feet to tell them that they were behaving like frightened chickens. Soldiers anxiously asked their superiors "How much longer?" Some officers' wives cold-shouldered their husbands.

It was the beginning of the end.

The putsch

On Tuesday, 11 September, at dawn, this intolerable period of waiting came to an end. Radio and TV stations announced that the armed forces had left their quarters and were marching on the public buildings "to evict the rulers, now no longer legitimate, and put an end to the chaos". The statement, repeated every 15 minutes, asked the population to have confidence in the army. I need hardly try to convey the intense jubilation with which this news was received by the majority of the population.

The operation, the fascinating details of which can be read in General Pinochet's memoirs, published in May 1980, was carried out with remarkable speed and precision. By-passing all the UP's strongholds and fortresses, the armoured vehicles drove straight towards the centre of government and the information nerve centres, the radio and TV stations, on the assumption that once the head had fallen the supporters would lose heart and give in. The calculation proved correct. By a cunning manoeuvre the UP had been prevented from making any appeals over the radio. The previous night at midnight, when their programmes stopped, the two stations of the Communist and Socialist Parties had been visited, under the Carmona law, by military detachments claiming to be investigating allegations that there were secret stocks of arms there. Those in charge of the stations could only let them search. After an hour, the soldiers apologetically withdrew. But the next morning, nothing could be broadcast, for the visitors of the previous evening had sabotaged the transmitters.

By eleven o'clock, all strategic points had been seized and the Moneda palace was surrounded, with President Allende inside. The army *repeatedly* offered to send him abroad by plane. He refused, and ordered the armed groups protecting the palace to open fire. The army replied with an aerial bombardment. Fire and smoke spread rapidly. The industrial belts upon which Mr. Allende had relied so heavily did not make a move. A truce allowed the women, among them Mr. Allende's two daughters, to leave the palace. Resistance in the city was no more than sporadic. From here on the story is taken up by Dr. A. Guijón, Mr. Allende's personal physician, who stayed with him to the end. According to the latter, "the president called together the last squad of those faithful to him and told them that they had to surrender. Someone fetched a broom and, by way of a white flag to hang from it, I got a white coat out of my bag; to do this I had to put down my gas mask. Meanwhile, Mr. Allende had told his supporters, 'Go on ahead, I'll follow you and bring up the rear.' Led by La Payita, the group went down the stairs, and I followed behind. At the bottom, I realized that the air was very thick and irritant, and went back up to fetch my gas mask. Then I saw Mr. Allende, sitting on the sofa in the Independence drawing room where we had just left him, with the rifle Castro had given him between his knees, the barrel pointing towards his throat. What followed lasted only a split second. I threw myself at him to stop him, but he had already pressed the trigger, and when I landed on him, he was already dead. I stood petrified in front of the body, and that was how the soldiers found me."

The announcement of his suicide put an end to the fighting, at least for that day. By three o'clock in the afternoon, the military were masters of the capital, and proclaimed that the commanders-in-chief of the four services, army, air force, navy and carabineros had formed a junta, deposing the Allende government and assuming full powers, with the chief-of-staff of the land army, General Augusto Pinochet Ugarte, as president. The next day the junta published its declaration of principles, recognizing that this was the first time in Chile's history that the armed forces had intervened in civic affairs, and giving five reasons to justify the taking of this extremely grave and exceptional step:

"1. The imminent threat of the nation falling irreversibly under a totalitarian communist dictatorship, with all that this implied in terms of bloodshed and future suffering;"

"2. The widespread chaos and the prospect of famine;"

"3. Parliament's resolution of 22 August declaring the Allende government no longer legitimate, and Mr. Allende's decision to ignore this resolution;"

"4. The impossibility of removing the government except by force thanks to the heavily-armed paramilitary groups it had raised;"

"5. The appeal for help, ever more widespread and urgent, addressed by the people to the armed forces, and the fact that the supreme duty of those forces is indeed to protect the people from mortal dangers, wherever these may come from."

In this statement, the junta made it clear, too, that it would only remain in power for as long as it took to re-establish Chile's normal democratic regime, which must never again, however, allow itself to be exploited and used by forces bent on totalitarianism. I shall return later to this important promise.

A few thoughts about the coup

The Marxist-Leninist parties had thus lost the prey they had thought was within their grasp, but they were able to console themselves by unleashing a formidable worldwide campaign of hatred against the new power, exploiting to the utmost its tainted origin in a military coup d'état. I shall come back to this. For the moment, I will just make the following remarks.

The failed *tancazo* of 30 June and the successful coup of 11 September prove without a shadow of a doubt that the working classes, even if they went on voting for the UP, were by no means prepared to die for it. However, it must not be taken from that that no one fought on the side of the Marxists. In fact, the day after the coup, when they had recovered from their surprise and dismay at Mr. Allende's death, the paramilitary groups pulled themselves together and began a vigorous resistance. The fighting lasted several months, was heroic on both sides at times, and caused several thousand deaths.

To be successful, the coup needed more than its leaders' steadiness and technical ability, together with the people's support. It had, in addition, to be able to relieve quickly the extreme tension which the country was living through. The soldiers had foreseen this, and had already tracked down stocks of victuals accumulated for the black market. The day after the coup the army requisitioned these stocks and began to distribute them among the population. It was essential that the country should quickly feel in its very vitals that it had escaped not only from fear but from famine as well. Later on, this emergency relief was to be supplemented by massive shipments of grain from Argentina.

Plan Z

The military coup led to the discovery of a whole host of secret documents which glaringly spotlighted and furnished irrefutable evidence on the Marxist leaders' real machinations, plans and motives. With the Prussian concern for order, precision and adherence to the rules which had always been instilled into the Chilean army, General Pinochet's men noted down the exact time and place of each discovery; had each document legally recorded and photographed, and published everything at the beginning of 1974 in a *White Book*. No denial of any of these documents was ever made by the UP leaders. I am now coming to the most important of these discoveries.

I have referred several times to the rumours going around among the public during the last weeks of the regime, according to which the UP were shortly going to mount an "auto-coup", of a savagery summed up in the word Jakarta, and which was to be the final solution for the Marxists in the sense that Hitler used these words when speaking of the Jews. Was it morbid imagination or a terrible reality? Well, on 13 September at five o'clock in the afternoon a group of soldiers opened the safe belonging to the former under-secretary of state for the Interior, the communist Mr. Daniel Vergara, now on the run, and found there the *proof*. This was a small folder of typewritten pages, bound in a white cover on which was written by hand in large letters with a felt-tipped pen:

"Plan Z"

I have a photocopy of this page in front of me as I write, with its tense, twisted, evil Z, and even eight years after the event I cannot help shivering. For I know what the contents are. Here is an analysis of them.

At the top lefthand side of the first page, written by hand:

From P 4

To AGP, Santiago

Date: 25.8.73

(My note: It has not been possible to establish for certain who P 4 and AGP were).

Then the heading, in underlined capitals:

PLAN OF MOBILIZATION AND OPERATIONS FOR COUP D'ETAT

Then, on a separate line to the left:

Code name: PLAN ZETA

Then:

1. **Circumstances under which plan will be put into operation:**

"Z.A.: The launching of a Coup D'Etat to seize TOTAL POWER and impose the DICTATORSHIP OF THE PROLETARIAT against the action of part or the whole of the Armed Forces supported by civilian groups."

(Capitals and underlinings are in the text).

2. **Popular Forces**

The groupings loyal to the UP that can be relied on are listed.

3. **Basic principles for the execution of the plan**

The known rules for an urban uprising, here supported by the government itself, are summarized.

4. **Objectives of the plan**

"4A. Eliminate the commanders of the Armed Forces."

"4B. Confine to quarters those units whose commanders have been killed."

"4C. Strict control of all road, rail and air access to Santiago, Valparaiso, Concepción and Antofagasta."

"4D. Occupation and defence of strategic centres."

"4E. Surrounding and liquidation of centres of sedition, and arrest of the seditious."

(My note: Mr. Allende's supporters used the term "seditious" for their democratic opponents).

"4F. Security of the channels of communication between government and people and between the politico-military commanders of the auto-coup and the fighting armed forces of the people."

"4G. Ensuring the safety of Mr. Allende and the other political leaders of the UP."

4. (continued). On the realization of objectives.

Introduction

It will be essential to eliminate *physically* the General Staffs and Commanding Officers of units, so as to weaken and demoralize the disloyal reactionaries. To this end, advantage will be taken of the national festivities (Author's note: this refers to 18 September, the National Day commemorating the Declaration of Independence in 1810) so as to carry out full-scale co-ordinated action in all the principal towns at the same time.

"A1. The Regional Commander (of the "auto-coup") will deploy the special corps, NPE, in the principal town of his particular area, to shoot the officers leading the military parade on 18 September."

"A2. At the same time the GAP (the personal bodyguards) at the Moneda palace and those appointed to the provincial governments *will execute the generals, admirals and other officials gathered for the official banquets.*"

"A3. The military units whose commanders have been killed will be taken in hand rapidly by the loyal elements which we have been able to infiltrate into the army. As we have not been able to do this for the marines, they will have to be neutralized as soon as possible by other military units then under our control".

"A4. The sentries at barracks will be *physically* eliminated at the outset by the special NPE—3 Z groups."

And so on. Every detail is catered for. It is emphasized that after the military chiefs have been killed, the first priority will be to take over the media, radio, TV, newspapers, and the principal propaganda themes to be broadcast are specified. In connection with the most important strategic operations, the forces and special plans prepared for them are mentioned by their code names: NPE, AGP, L6, G0, GSA, etc. It thus became clear that the network of paramilitary groups was a great deal more extensive and more highly-organized than had been thought.

However the most spine-chilling revelation is surely the preparations for a *Marxist Massacre of St. Bartholomew*; I mean that night of the long knives which was to coincide with the official receptions of the National Day. In the mind's eye, one can see the dignitaries invited, talking in all good faith to President Allende or to each other, and then being invited by the waiters to move on into the next room, or staying in the main room which the host has left on some pretext, and then having their throats cut, or being stabbed, or shot then and there, or tied up and taken down to the cellars to be executed there.

So it was true. The rumours about the auto-coup were justified. Moreover, an eminent member of Military Security, with whom I have spoken, told me that his service got wind at the end of August of a plan to kill all the principal military leaders, and that analysts had concluded that the most likely date would be the night of 18–19 September during the festivities of the National Day. It was this blood-bath, then, that Mr. Allende was thinking about when under the influence of alcohol, he let slip to Admiral Montero that all the exactions the admiral was complaining about were mere trifles compared with "what the MIR and the Communists are getting ready to do".

Note, the Communists. That is another piece of political information which can be culled from Plan Z. Remember that it was found in the safe of a communist minister. It is another proof, and a sizeable one, that the whole legend of "communist moderation and prudence", a legend that was spread knowingly, naïvely absorbed, and complacently repeated by left-wing commentators the world over, was a colossal bluff. Yes, this reassuring myth which maintained that the UPs "excesses" were perpetrated only by irresponsible left-wing extremists, whereas the Communist Party, scientific, disciplined, taking the long historical view, was only working towards a rapid development of the infra-structures in a perfectly legal manner, this whole story was no more than a fairy tale for children.

The proof was there that the Communist Party always had two irons in the fire at the same time, that of "natural", non-violent progress, and that of "forced" progress, running through the whole gamut of violent means up to and including the murder of men and the destruction of institutions by coup d'état. When is the world finally going to understand that Communism has any number of strings to its bow, and has no moral scruples whatever in using, in turn or even concurrently, whichever of these, however base, will serve its turn, provided it leads to the only thing that interests it, namely power, absolute power?

To sum up, we have shown beyond any possible doubt that at the time that the Chilean military intervened, the country, already sinking into total economic chaos thanks to the activities of the UP, was on the brink of being plunged by the same UP by means of a bloody coup d'état, into complete totalitarian dictatorship. *It was the eleventh hour*, from every point of view. It is also clear that, given the massive armament and organization of the UP's paramilitary groups, there was no other conceivable way of preventing the nation from falling bloodily and irreversibly under the yoke of tyranny than intervention by the army.

Was the pronunciamento really wanted by the people?

I have stated that a large majority of the Chilean people wanted—ardently even—the army to intervene to overturn Mr. Allende by force, at least in the final phase of chaos, shortages, violence and hatred. This is obviously a crucial point; one's assessment of the drama in Chile depends radically on whether it is true or false. Do I have evidence to prove it? I think that I have, and that it is both plentiful and overwhelming.

1. First of all there were the many explosions of popular hostility which I have recounted. They were common knowledge and no one has ever denied either their magnitude or their violence. Remember especially that at the time of the putsch, the country was in the midst of a general strike of all the *gremios*. Moreover, there is no need to twist the facts to deduce that a nation is going to object violently to a government which tells it there is only enough bread left for three days.

2. During my visit to Chile in September 1978, I questioned over 150 people from all classes and of all opinions, in Santiago and the provinces. Many admitted quite candidly to me that, at the beginning, they had followed Mr. Allende. Others were still anti-Pinochet, at that time. Not one, and I mean *not a single one*, denied that in September 1973 the vast majority of Chileans had eagerly wanted to see Mr. Allende go. Even those who, as they told me, would have preferred him to retire without being forced to by tanks, added that once he refused, there was no entirely civilian body of opinion in a position to force him to do so, given the large forces of armed militia he had at his disposal. Moreover, the revulsion in popular feeling could not have gone further than it had done, and Mr. Allende, instead of listening to it, had made up his mind to stifle it finally with his "auto-coup", introducing a reign of terror. The mere idea that it was still possible to find some legal means of setting aside a regime with such a record of the most shameless illegalities seemed quite unrealistic to everyone, just about as unlikely as abolishing Mount Aconcagua by voting against it.

3. Even those sections of the population which had remained Marxist made no reaction to the coup, as I have stressed. The fighting that took place over the next few months was waged exclusively by professional armed groups. There was not a single walk-out in a single factory, not the slightest rising in any of the suburbs or industrial belts, not one student demonstration, not even a Committee of Public Safety, even in those remote small towns which were controlled by the UP and where no troops were based. On the other hand, in every city and in all areas of the countryside, thousands of spontaneous gatherings and processions took place expressing the heart-felt relief of a whole nation.

4. The scathing denunciation of Mr. Allende's illegality and illegitimacy made by Congress, the Supreme Court, the College of Barristers and the *Contraloria General* clearly implied that these institutions wished to see the government eliminated as soon as possible. As their members had noted to their cost that this was impossible using civilian pressure, the obvious conclusion is that they were calling for military intervention. Then again, no one denied that these august corporate bodies accurately reflected the views of the majority of the country. The pure unvarnished truth is that, once these institutions had issued their solemn condemnations, it was Mr. Allende's government which had lost its right to remain in office; *it was maintaining itself in power purely by force*. As the French *Declaration of the Rights of Man* of 1791 says: "When a government becomes despotic and oppressive, revolt becomes the most sacred duty . . ."

5. It was not only indirectly that the legitimate representatives of the majority of the people expressed their hope of cutting the Gordian

knot. We have the written proof that this was their most urgent desire. This proof is the extraordinary interview given by ex-president Eduardo Frei on 10 October to the Spanish newspaper *ABC*. Despite the author's unrivalled political and moral authority, this interview was suppressed by most of the world's press so as not to introduce a jarring note into the countless variations of the general chorus of abuse of "the infamous conduct of Pinochet's fascist soldiery" in overturning Mr. Allende's pure new-born democracy by force.

Mr. Eduardo Frei began his interview with a long, barely controlled cry of anger at the "*unbelievable lies*"—his words—put about on the subject of the events in Chile. I quote: "Why has the world been told these lies, leaving it in ignorance of the fact that Mr. Allende had led the Chilean economy into disaster? Why has it not been pointed out that all these nationalizations—banks, industries, mines and agriculture—were carried out illegally? Why was the world not told that the Marxist bureaucrats were only interested in two things: the black market and the paramilitary groups? . . . No, no, *there was no land reform under Allende* . . . Armed guerillas violently seized lands and then neither handed them over to the poor peasants nor cultivated themselves . . . Production collapsed . . . We had nothing left to eat, no more spare parts . . . Violence predominated.

"Mr. Allende had no scruples in destroying the country in order to carry out his Leninist programme, a programme intended to annihilate all opposition . . . People in Europe can have no idea what it was like! They have been blinded by the great illusion that it was worth trying to set up a democratic form of Communism. But such an attempt is not possible. *It is a contradiction in terms.* (Italicised in the text.) It is not true, it is not true. *The whole world has contributed to the destruction of my country; the only way out for it now is military rule.*" (My emphasis.)

So much for his cry from the heart. The rest of the passage adds nothing to what I have already said of the ruin caused by the UP, although such a strong confirmation, coming from such an eminent man, who had helped to bring Mr. Allende to power, leaves no room for further doubt. What is important for our purpose here is that the man has blurted out the great truth which it was hoped had been buried for ever. Mr. Frei is emphatic: "What the world does not know is that the Chilean Marxists had at their disposal a supply of arms, stored in thousands of different hiding-places, that was superior in quantity, and sometimes in quality, to that of the nation's army . . . *The army saved Chile.*" (Italicised in the text.)

Such an assertion, with all that it implies for the history of our times, and coming as it does from the most liberal, the most progressive and the most responsible of the Christian Democrat leaders, is well worth dwelling on for a moment—"THE ARMY SAVED CHILE."

He said it at a moment when the whole outside world was vilifying those same soldiers for allegedly "violating Chilean democracy", although, as Mr. Frei shows, this had been violated long since, in the most shameless manner, by Mr. Allende, the Marxist-Leninist. Ex-president Frei continued to insist, ramming home his point as though he were a fugitive from hell trying to bring home its horrors to listeners who were blind.

"The civil war was consummately planned by the Marxists, and the world either does not know this or doesn't want to know it . . . *the soldiers were called on by the nation, and the task they accomplished was a legal one* (his italics), for the legislative and judicial authorities, Congress and the Supreme Court, had publicly denounced Mr. Allende's presidency and regime, charging them with respecting neither the Constitution, the laws passed by Parliament, the *Statute of Guarantees* signed by Mr. Allende himself, nor the opinions handed down by judges who were totally independent politically. *Mr. Allende came to power in order to establish Communism by violent and undemocratic means* (his italics) . . . The arms that had been seized thanks to the Carmona law proved that Mr. Allende had been preparing for civil war *from the moment he became president* (my emphasis) . . . Those arms were Russian . . . Since when has Chile officially possessed Russian arms?"

At this point, the interviewer interrupted ex-president Frei to ask him whether it was true that these arms came from Fidel Castro, complete with instructors, guerillas, irregular troops and experts in armed subversion.

"That is so," replied Mr. Frei.

Why, then, was the world told such lies? Why was such a man, even more untrustworthy in politics than he was in his private morals, so idolized in Europe, where he was so little known?

Why was the world told such lies? Alas, why did Mr. Frei lie to himself when, on that fatal October day in 1970, he handed the presidency over to this "untrustworthy" man by voting for him in Congress, doing violence to his own conscience to make himself believe that "this untrustworthy man, totally unscrupulous in his purpose of making the country communist", was going to take any notice of a mere scrap of paper such as the *Statute of Guarantees*? But let us not be too hard on ex-president Frei: here he was, now that misfortune had befallen him, picking himself up and, like a wounded bull, bellowing in his attempt to redress the balance.

Mr. Frei continued:

"I tell you that when a government like Mr. Allende's refuses to carry out laws; defies and insults the Supreme Court; takes no account of a huge majority in Congress; provokes economic chaos; *arrests and kills striking workers* (my italics); scorns and tramples on personal and political liberties; starves the people in order to hand over the country's products to the leftist and communist monopolists of the black market—when a government commits all these abuses and crimes, then REBELLION BECOMES A DUTY. (Capitals in the text.) It is a legal right that has been proclaimed by all statesmen and all liberal historians. If a people has been so weakened and so harried that it is no longer physically able to rise up against a regime that surrounds itself by gunmen, especially ones brought in from abroad, then indeed THE ARMY SHOULD LEND IT ITS STRENGTH AND CARRY OUT THE TASK FOR IT."

For us French, it is heart-warming to hear Chile's greatest democrat justifying the action of his country's generals in September 1973 by reference to the spirit of 1789 and our own *Declaration of the Rights of Man.*

To my mind, any attempt to give an honest account of the military coup and, more generally, of the whole Allende experience in Chile, should take as its *basic text* the Frei interview I have just quoted. It demonstrates, without a shadow of a doubt, and in a way which is as moving as it is dramatically clear, that the roles in the affair were the exact reverse of those generally attributed: Mr. Allende was the violent usurper and Gen. Pinochet the saviour of his country. There is nevertheless one last point left to consider: if it is admitted that Pinochet responded to the people's appeal for a champion, did he remain their champion once the coup was successful?

The question of whether Gen. Pinochet kept faith with his historic mandate, whether he managed to save Chile from communist totalitarianism without subjecting it to another, will be dealt with in a later chapter. As for the title of "saviour of the country" which he and his companions in the junta could claim at the time of the coup, it seems to me absolutely justified. An essential fact which is always forgotten confirms this: before the coup these same military chiefs had repeatedly proved their respect for the Constitution. Not only had they carried out all the UP government's orders, but some of them had even become ministers in the government. Up to the very last day, they had begged the President to return to legality, going so far as to guarantee that new elections would go without a hitch under their supervision. When, on that dramatic night, Admiral Montero went to hand in his resignation, the only demand he made, in the name of the General Staff as a whole, was the disarmament of the paramilitary groups and a return to the ballot-box in absolute freedom for everyone, including the Marxists.

Furthermore, the real putschist spirit, the sort that leads to coups d'état against democratic governments, is always visible well before the event in the fascist tendencies of the superior officers who are about to revolt. There was nothing of the sort in Chile. No one ever detected in any of the members of the coup of 11 September the slightest sign of fascist leanings. The Chilean generals had no political preconceptions, no plans for reshaping society, no ideological affiliations. May God forgive me if I am wrong, but I believe that they still do not have any. They are clearly simple—but excellent—technicians, who have grown up within the protective framework of service discipline, ill at ease with fascist or communist dogma, allergic to any sort of propaganda, who only acted at the very last minute, and then only because they were forced into action by their horror at the gulf that was yawning in front of the country, and their conviction that they were responding to the universal desire of the whole nation.

No, truly, never in history has there been a military coup d'état which was less of a plot hatched by a minority of officers and more of a rescue operation in response to the appeals of the majority of the people.

CHAPTER XIV

THE LESSONS OF THE ALLENDE EXPERIMENT

"I'M COMPLETELY LOST", I can hear my reader interjecting at this point. "You write that Chile's UP was communist, and at the same time you tell us that members of parliament, journalists and trade union groups openly opposed it from the inside. The two sides of your picture do not seem to fit together. In a communist regime there is no parliamentary opposition, there are no strikes and no saucepans banged in the streets. On the other side, you have spoken of political assassinations and of countless serious violations of human rights, thus tending to show that the UP regime was not a democracy either. So what exactly was it?"

Socialist tone but communist intention

"The key to the mystery lies in the fact that, as far as trampling on human rights is concerned, totalitarianism is much, much further away from democracy than is commonly believed. Take the case of those who are persecuted because of their political opinions. How many are there altogether in the score or so of democracies still functioning as such in the world today? It would be very surprising if they amounted to more than double figures, and even these will turn out to be victims of some malfunctioning of the system which can easily be rectified. How many such imprisoned political dissidents are there in the score or so of totalitarian communist regimes? Several millions, and even so, the figure is limited only because since the deaths of Mao and Stalin, Communism has become a little less repressive. Before that, the figure would have been nearer to several tens of millions. In totalitarian regimes, what one can call the 'rate of political delinquency' of the rulers is *a million times* higher than in democratic regimes."

"All right, let us admit that this ratio of misconduct exists. What conclusion can we draw from it?"

"That the range is so wide that there is room between its two extremes for an intermediate regime a thousand times worse than democracy and yet a thousand times less horrific than totalitarianism. That was the position of Chile's UP."

Freedom a thousand times more trampled on than in the democracies? Of course. One has only to read once again the accounts of Mr. Allende's violations of democracy as I have set them down here. Just imagine a thousandth part of these being carried out in France by Giscard d'Estaing against Mitterand, or our President refusing to ratify a constitutional amendment passed by a two-thirds majority in Parliament, and one will immediately get an idea of the huge scandal that would have arisen, and the cries of "fascism" that the left would have raised.

Freedom a thousandfold less trampled on than under a communist dictatorship? Of course, since in spite of all the persecutions, violence and acts of illegality that the UP inflicted on its opponents, they were still on the whole able to express their views in Parliament, the mass media and the streets.

However if the UP regime occupied an intermediate position between democracy and totalitarianism, a sort of geometrical mean, why have you called it "communist"? My answer is that it was communist in spirit, in outlook, in its terminology, and above all in its *grand design.* What the UP was, in fact, trying to do was to establish a collectivist regime while infringing civil liberties only up to the half-way level, as I have said, so as to break the association that is now automatically made between Marxism-Leninism and the Gulag. But in this incongruous mixture, the main constituent, as far as the UP was concerned, was collectivism, and freedom was very much a secondary one. The situation, if you like, was that of a burglar who, in order to gain possession of a hoard of wealth, will go to any extremity of crime except, so he swears to himself, that of actual murder. We know that the balance in such a situation is an unstable one, containing as it does a basic objective and a tactical concession. If the thief sees the wealth he desires slipping from his grasp, he'll end up by killing just the same. Likewise, the UP, after three years of a hybrid regime, a cross between freedom and dictatorship, saw that its basic objective was obviously not being realized, and decided to extinguish the last remaining flicker of democracy and bring in the total darkness of terror.

In short, it had become clear that on the intermediate level on which the UP had chosen to operate, *there was already too much oppression for freedom to be able to breathe, and still too much freedom for oppression to be able to last.*

To achieve Socialism, all opponents must be killed immediately

Why did the Chilean Marxists not succeed in achieving their aims while restricting themselves to this illegality without terror, a situation which nevertheless already put them in possession of rights far in excess of those they had any claim to? Was it purely a mania to dominate that drove them to overstep these limits?

The answer is no. It was not a mere gratuitous leaning towards extremism that led the men of the UP ever deeper into despotism and violence. They were forced to move in that direction by a fact, the discovery of which constitutes the major fruit of the Chilean experience, namely that *collectivist Socialism is of its very nature hateful, and thus arouses hatred.* So that whenever it steps out of the dream-world of men's imaginings and becomes a living reality through governmental enactment, the people dig in their heels in protest, and more and more constraint is needed to force Socialism through. Let us analyse this observation more closely.

What idea is one trying to implant when one hails progress towards Socialism "by legal means" as a marvellous thing? Surely it is the very idea that the Christian Democrats swallowed so uncritically, the same one that Senator Aylwin expressed so candidly in his celebrated interview, when he admitted that "We thought that the best way of guarding the country against the danger of a Marxist dictatorship was to carefully avoid, of course, any totalitarian tendencies, but at the same time to further the process of socialisation so long as this was pursued in a democratic manner". The assumption underlying this statement is that Socialism in itself is a desirable goal, and that the only reason why people have disapproved of it is because so far its protagonists have been extremists who have insisted on establishing it by violent and destructive means. All one needs is to enter the waters of Socialism step by step, and everyone will appreciate its delicious coolness.

However if the water itself is poisonous, entering it a step at a time along a rose-edged path will not increase its charm one iota. This is what the UP leaders very soon realized: as soon as they passed beyond mere verbal recommendations of the socialist medicine and actually tried to make people swallow it, the reaction of the latter was one of rejection, however gently the doses were administered. Collectivisation of the land is marvellous as a dream, but in the real world no one wants to give up his own little plot, especially when one is compensated in stage money or not at all. Planning sounds all very well at the blueprint stage, but when it is used as a pretext for those who know nothing to force the hands of those who do know, stifling all initiative, so that the end result is chaos, financial skulduggery and penury, nobody wants it. Similarly, no one is very keen on educational egalitarianism when it takes the form of forcing children to recite the Marxist catechism daily. No one will stand for the nationalized banks totally refusing one any credit if they feel that your views do not fit in with those of the authorities. And so it goes on. Each individual dish proves as unappetizing as the complete socialist menu once one actually has to eat it, and not just talk about it.

This then is the great secret.

Despite the disastrous failures that have resulted whenever its principles have been put into practice, Socialism still has prestige. The poverty-stricken totalitarian regimes to which it always and everywhere gives birth are always blamed on the excesses of fanatics or on adverse circumstances, while Socialism itself is held to have concealed virtues which will finally blossom when Socialism puts on its famous "human face". Not a bit of it. This ultimate illusion must be deflated. This infatuation for dream-world Socialism has been one of the biggest collective mistakes in human history. It can only lead to dictatorship and impoverishment, for the very good reason that all it offers is state collectivisation and planning of the means of production and exchange, and that this recipe is basically unpopular, unproductive, absurd, socially harmful and destructive of liberty, and can only give Socialism an "inhuman face". This inbuilt and unavoidable flaw becomes evident from the very moment that the first concrete measures of the socialist programme are put into practice. It is at this point that the subject peoples realize that Socialism is just as unpleasant in detail as in its totality, at its birth as when it reaches full maturity.

This is what the Chilean Marxists did not understand. They had confidence in the illusion they were peddling, and believed that a limited dose of illegality and confiscations, discreetly carried out and concealed from the outside world by their propaganda machine, would be enough to eliminate its opponents, and that the flame of Socialism would do the rest—that is, that once the first steps towards Socialism were taken, the as yet undecided sections of the population would be won over and fall into line. Hence the strategy of the geometrical mean between democracy and totalitarianism. In fact it was the precise opposite that occurred. As the socialist system emerged from the realm of ideal concepts and showed itself in its true colours, so far from attracting them, it repelled ever wider sectors of the people. The test of real life proved fatal to the credibility of Socialism. An essential lesson for all of us!

After the Portuguese people had rejected a similar attempt at collectivization, Mr. Jean-Paul Sartre had told the Portuguese Communists: "You did not kill enough people." Mr. Régis Debray, during his interview with Mr. Allende, had warned him: "If your objective really is to introduce Marxism-Leninism into Chile, you won't succeed unless you put 200,000 Chileans to death!" Mr. Debray and Mr. Sartre were right. The Chilean experience, followed by that of Portugal, leads us to the following generalization: if a government wants to establish a collectivist system, *it must kill all its potential opponents at the outset.*

Lenin had realized this long before Mr. Debray and Mr. Sartre. He had made the right choice when he set up his reign of terror immediately after seizing power.

The leftist stigma

Another reason why it is impossible to establish such an inhuman regime as collectivist Socialism in a humane way is that from now on its supporters can never again dissociate themselves from the vociferous ultra-leftists, and these last have added a number of new and most unattractive features to the face of revolution.

The first is that ostentatious display of hatred and the crudest vulgarity to which I have already drawn attention. Earlier Socialists had always taken care to make it clear that it was a system, and not men that they were attacking. Even the Leninists, who did attack individuals, did so within a political context, and not as though they were common fishwives swearing at each other. At the height of their polemic, they did indeed call their opponents "oppressors", "bloodsuckers", "bunglers" and "profiteering sharks", but they did not sink to calling them "old shitbags" or "mummified buggers" (I beg my readers' pardon for these literal quotations from the language of the UP). But from now on, leftist Socialists will treat their enemies just as anti-semites treat Jews.

Another nauseating seasoning the Chilean leftists added to the already not particularly appetizing dishes served up by the UP was that of continuous and ubiquitous violence. For traditional Socialism, violence was to be concentrated in a single revolution, and the forces of the state were its only target. Nowadays leftism strikes; breaks; mutilates; burns and blows up any old target indiscriminately in and out of season. Physical violence, the bloodstained companion of violence in speech, has become the permanent climate within which they press their demands. This has gone so far that even success seems suspect in their eyes if it is achieved through peaceful agreement.

A third new feature in the Chilean revolutionary picture is that of moral disintegration. The Socialists of earlier days had been, if anything, rather austere and moralistic, and only developed into debauchees many years after gaining power. By contrast, many leaders of the Chilean UP were corrupt libertines from the very beginning. Decency, moral standards, discipline, respect for work, and good manners they considered to be just so much "middle-class nonsense", which a truly liberated leftist owed it to himself to reject with scorn in favour of the whole gamut of immediate pleasures, carnal ecstasy, dionysiac trances, and acquisitive fingers dipped directly into every purse, public or private.

Finally, the fourth characteristic contributed by the Chilean leftists to traditional revolutionary practice was what one might call puerile idiocy. When I described some of the arbitrary illegalities committed under the aegis of the UP, the reader was probably astonished by their economic absurdity. To be sure, most of the collectivist measures inspired by Karl Marx's theories have proved to be inherently destructive and harmful. But at least the conscious revolutionaries of yesteryear were not vandals in intention or by instinct. These limits were swept aside in Chile, just as terrorism is sweeping them aside throughout the world today. In many instances, those carrying out land confiscations seemed to be acting in some ridiculous and flamboyantly theatrical stage-play before a wildly applauding audience, and assigning the seized lands to uses that went against the most obvious common sense, purely for the sake of the gesture or striking speech this enabled them to make, or to suit the setting against which they were performing. It was just the same for the seizures of workshops and urban land. One has only to consider the case of the *poblaciones*, or shantytowns, which they took under their control. The leftists amused themselves setting up a whole ritual to regulate entrances and exits, meetings, distributions of various kinds, badges and emblems and armed parades, in short, everything connected with show and pageantry, whereas they never nailed one plank on another to keep the rain out of a hut, never paved a muddy roadway, never laid a pipe for running water, never opened a new school. The poverty-stricken inhabitants, whom the leftists were swearing they had come to liberate, were in fact no more than puppets in the political show they were staging.

One can sum up as follows what I have just said about the eruption of leftism within the ranks of the revolutionaries; hitherto the chief defect of Marxism had been its effects on the political and economic planes; but now, in addition, it becomes ugly on the human plane. To its congenital defect—state control—leftist terrorism has now added the leering grin of irrational lunacy.

Now, the reader will ask, why cannot Marxist movements any longer free themselves from these unwelcome hare-brained hangers-on? The underlying reason is that these movements are gnawed by doubts about their own credibility. They have quietly lost faith in their doctrines. Why? Because when their beliefs have been put into practice, they have always ended in horror. They refuse to admit the fact and continue to swagger, claiming still to be the essential vehicles of the great drive towards liberation, but a voice within them replies that all they will ever generate is disaster. So, unwilling to give up playing at their role of righters of wrongs, they have begun to over-emphasize abuse of their opponents, artificially fomented dissension, hatred, violence, irrationality and destruction as values in themselves. Irrational

Leftism is Communism after it has gone bankrupt. This compares starkly with the triumph of the free-enterprise system which, while people were dying of hunger and terror in the communist countries, was widely dispensing freedom and material well-being in the areas where it prevailed. So this latter-day Communism, impotent yet still arrogant, adopted the instinctive reaction of all barbarians when faced with civilised communities: the flaming torch of destruction.

Verbocracy

To be more precise, since we are after all in the twentieth century, and almost everyone can read and write, the new leftist Marxist-Leninists supplemented their use of the flaming torch by a new verbal weapon, that of casuistry.

You will have been struck, as I was, by the fact that the followers of Mr. Allende among the upper bourgeoisie of Chile never spoke of themselves otherwise than as "the people". The crassest demonstration of this charade was the famous headline with which the UP newspapers announced the results of the March 1973 elections: "The people 43%, the backwoodsmen 57%." This trait is nowadays characteristic of all the world's Marxist parties, however small a minority they are, and even when they constitute only a tiny grouplet: they always hold forth as though they were the inspired interpreters of popular feeling, the sole and chosen champions of the people! This is a regression into childish egocentricity, for it is well known that every child considers himself to be the whole of humanity. The word-spinners of the UP artificially compensated for their own lack of weight by arrogating to themselves, verbally at least, the consent of the people as a whole, This is a kind of identificatory magic. Like animistic witch-doctors who believe they can call up the spirits to come and dwell within them just by chanting their names, the Allendists hoped to take over the identity of the people merely by invoking it, following the principle of "I am you, ergo you are me".

All this pitiful trickery staged by the UP in Chile merely showed that the latter was shouting its head off in a vain attempt to carve a place for itself in history, a history that plainly had no time for it. Here is another important lesson we can draw from the Chilean drama. It confirms the fact that Socialism—and I mean any Socialism, not just Communism, where the fact is already only too obvious—Marxist and leftish Socialism, which so many of our mentally retarded contemporaries still persist in seeing as a harbinger of progress, is nowadays an ageing and outworn hag, its unlovely face riddled by the wrinkles of demagogy, negligence, penury, rationing, bureaucracy, censorship, secret police and bully-boys, so outworn that it can only impose itself on the modern world by a combination of lies and coercion.

Why then do not the men of the Marxist left not finally draw the lesson of all these repeated failures, come out of their subterranean bolt-holes and take their place in modern democratic life?

The answer cannot be avoided. Since they can no longer believe in their "socialist" programme, this can only mean that its realization was not their real motive for acting. We must look elsewhere for their basic motivation, and one can only see one possible one which could explain their conduct, namely that their real purpose is to wield power and become members of a new privileged class. If they were to admit the complete bankruptcy of every system basing itself on the Marxist recipe for the last 60 years, they would *ipso facto* be forced to admit that the existing order, that of modern free enterprise, is a hundred times better and they, therefore, have no raison d'être. But in that case how could they continue to keep up their pretence of being enlightened critics, generous seekers after justice, the only oracles who could accurately forecast the march of history, a pretence, moreover, that was winning them so much prestige and so many votes! If they were to admit unreservedly, without seeking to avoid the issue, that the Soviet experiment, the total application of Marxism to government, has proved a disastrous failure, what other stock-in-trade would be left for them to sell? They would be admitting that the system, the advocacy of which gave them their sole claim to be considered as progressive innovators, is a vicious one in its very essence, productive only of oppression and misery, and they would be proved to be not so much bankrupt pedlars, with nothing in their sacks to sell, but even worse, to have only germ-infected wares to offer.

Their only way out, therefore, is to leave their so-called solution shrouded in a haze of ambiguity, and to build their career purely on words, illusions and emotional frenzy—a career, moreover, motivated solely by a lust for power, and totally unconcerned with the suffering that its fulfilment would entail for the nations it enslaved. What does it matter that totalitarian Communism is following in their footsteps, that tomorrow men will bleed and weep, that the lie will hold sway, so long as they, the Marxist speechifiers are raised to power and prominence by their out-of-date balloon of slogans, inflated with noxious gases? This is what I mean when I say that nowadays the Marxist left is nothing but a verbocracy.

The great deceit

It is this that explains what must have seemed to the reader the most outstanding feature of Allendism: its deceitfulness. It is quite obvious that a party based only on word-juggling cannot help being dishonest. We have just seen how they distorted the facts to support their assertion that they and they alone represented the people. Over and over again in the pages of this book, we have caught them red-handed playing a double game, involved in tortuous sophistry and the deliberate spreading of confusion in men's minds. To leave you with the taste of what was the dominant characteristic of their rule, I will give you a few particularly revealing examples of their hypocrisy.

In a speech he made in November 1970, shortly after Mr. Allende's rise to power, Mr. Luis Figueroa, leader of the Marxist unions, came out with the following outrageous statement: "True freedom of expression can only exist in a society in which all the communications media are controlled by the state. The ideal model is the Soviet Union, where news is only made public when the public is mature enough to receive it; thus, instead of being a mere merchandise, news becomes an instrument of political education."

I know of few texts in which double-talk—the use of one language when one is making demands of those in power, and of its opposite when one is in power oneself—has sunk to such a level. Or rather, I do know of some, and here is another sample from the Chilean UP, which in just three years had the doubtful honour of performing every item in the repertory of the world's left-wing. On 17 June 1973, faced with an upsurge in popular discontent, the Socialist Party brought out a leaflet for its militants to teach them the best way of answering workers complaining about shortages and destitution. Based on countless quotations from Lenin, Che Guevara and Fidel Castro, this text attempted to persuade workers that the struggle for "wage adjustments" was a feature of capitalist society (!), and that in the revolutionary phase the country was going through, everyone ought to be satisfied with what the government granted him. Workers demanding wage increases were selfish, and unworthy of being considered "new men".

This is not very different from the parody invented by the more vulgar-minded lampooners of the Socialism of the 1848 period. They imagined an agitator, rather like a fairground barker, saying to a typical proletarian: "Come and help us make a revolution, and you'll get a bigger share of the cake." Then, when the workman had fallen for the enticement, had brought his tempter to power and asked for his promised share, the agitator replied: "Aren't you ashamed to be asking for more, you vile materialist? Stay bent down where you are, or you'll be putting the revolution in danger!" Nowadays even the most reactionary satirists would no longer dare produce such a gross parody to discredit Marxism. It has taken the Marxists themselves to stage it, in full life-size.

Here is one last typical example of the duplicity of the UP. On 18 April 1971, President Allende, inaugurating the first National Congress of Left-wing Journalists, asserted: "There can be no place for objectivity in journalism . . . the left-wing journalist's supreme duty is to serve not the truth but the revolution."

The cry comes straight from the heart. Or rather, one piece of meaning is still concealed: for the word "revolution" we must read "our power". How far we have moved along the downward path since the days when Mr. Jaurès said: "Even more than that of the disinherited, Socialism is the party of truth!"

Chile's lesson for France

The sheer impossibility of finding any humane way of introducing Socialism into a modern society, (an impossibility that has become only too clear since the Chilean experiment), carries serious implications for France. For one of the factors inhibiting progress towards totalitarianism in Chile would not be present in France. This obstacle is the fact that the UP government was a minority one. Even those of its members who advocated that the UP should speed up the development of a dictatorship felt inhibited by the fact that 64 per cent of the citizens had rejected their programme at the polls.

Now in France the braking effect exercised in Chile by the markedly minority position of the Marxist parties does not exist. The Socialist-Communist coalition comes to power in France after legally winning a majority, and so it has a completely free hand. This coalition is remarkably similar to the UP in Chile in its basic characteristics and coloration: its Socialist Party is not social-democratic but Marxist, its Communist Party is firmly Stalinist, the tone of its utterances is that of the immoderate left, its climate is extremist. The same hothead Mr. Régis Debray, is once again speechifying at the presidential palace, this time in Paris, where he has been appointed an "adviser", and Mr. Allende's widow, a regular visitor to the Élysée, keeps the flame alive.

In fact, the Communist Party is considerably stronger in France than it was in Chile. Its parallel power-structure, both in the party and the trade unions, has already honeycombed the country, and its four ministers, including two of the highest importance for the life of the country (health and transport, this last able to control the movements of the armed forces) makes it possible for the Communists to penetrate the state from the top downwards from its vantage-point in the government. Faced with such power, a power that is both legal and total—total in the sense that it dominates at the same time the executive, the legislature, the unions, schools, local government and the media—resistance in France is far more defenceless than it was in

Chile. Even if a serious movement of resistance were to arise, the regime's counter-attack could well prove to be tougher than is its present carrying-out of its Allende-style programme. At such a juncture, who will there be in a position to halt the formation of the thousands of committees that will invade every walk of life, for they will be acting under the unimpeachable banner of the "popular will"? And, with the lesson of what has happened in Chile and Portugal behind them, the French Communists, who already have a vast party machine capable of controlling the country, will not be slow to unleash a torrent of Allende-type exactions, violence and illegalities. They will not leave open to French democrats the possibilities for resistance that were available to the Chileans and Portuguese. The French Marxists will not fail to learn the lessons of the failures of their brothers in Santiago and Lisbon. Hence it is vitally necessary for the anti-Marxists to learn these lessons now. They can be summed up in this maxim, a simple one, but which has world-wide application: In no circumstances should one lift a finger in support of any move that could bring the Communists or extreme left-wingers to power, either directly or in association with some other party. If this disaster should materialize, one should immediately organize all-out resistance to it.

In view of the extraordinary importance of the lessons that the Allende period has for the world as a whole, it is useful, I think, to sum up those lessons that I have already brought out in the present chapter.

What Mr. Allende proved once again is that the Marxist and collectivist left has no right at all to the halo of an "advanced ideology" that it still wears. One really has to have one's eyes firmly and wilfully closed not to see that what was destroyed in Chile was Marxist Socialism's claim that it could run society more humanely, more justly, more rationally and more efficiently than could free enterprise. Mr. Allende's was just the culmination of a long series of economic and political failures of the socialist recipe, of which the most resounding and the most tragic is that of the Soviet Union. He confirmed the rule, a rule that now permits of no exception and which must be accepted as a historical law, namely that wherever and whenever the Marxist socialist formula is introduced, we see the growth of culpable negligence, inefficiency, the canker of bureaucracy, widespread shortage, the despoiling of poor and rich alike, galloping inflation, lies, censorship and, in the end, tyranny.

The fascination that Socialism still exerts over so many well-intentioned minds nowadays is thus totally unwarranted. Marxism today is an obsolete, outdated and sterile doctrine, embodying, in very fact, all that is reactionary in our epoch. The working class is the first to suffer from it, together with the middle classes, dispossessed as they are for no reason and without benefiting anyone, and these are closely followed by the liberal professions, who discover—too late—a thick cloud of obscurantism where they foolishly expected to find the clear air of universal emancipation.

Among French politicians more closely concerned with the Chilean affair, special mention must be made of certain Christian Democratic leaders and left-wing radicals who, like their Chilean counterparts, suffer from the leftist itch. Let us hope that what has happened in Chile will cure them of their urge to woo the left, and induce them to look elsewhere for a way to make a name for themselves.

In fact, the man who ought to reflect most deeply on what has happened is Mr. Mitterand. If I did not mention him in the first place, this is because one despairs of ever getting him to think deeply. After so many and such tragic experiences, among which that of Chile can rightly say of itself: "et je meurs la dernière et la plus misérable", ("and I am the last to die, and the most wretched of all", a line from Racine's tragedy *Phèdre*. Translator's Note). Surely Mr. Mitterand must now understand that collectivist methods carry within themselves a deep organic and inherent defect: there is no other way fully to plan an economy except by using the knout.

By refusing to learn the lesson of Chile, Mr. Mitterand shows that the Socialists just do not want to learn anything. They have walled themselves inside their own fantasy-world, and this will inevitably lead them to their downfall the final and irrevocable downfall of these blinkered fanatics as they sit keeping each other awake by reciting a breviary of doctrines that once had enormous prestige, but which now have historically been overtaken by events and are inexorably stiffening into fossils. Socialism may continue to boast and swagger, but the finger of death has already touched it.

That is, unless it makes up its mind to survive by the death of others, for this is the conclusion drawn by its extremists from the events in Chile. As their own private Mephistopheles, Mr. Jean-Paul Sartre, said after the defeat of the Communists in Portugual: "They ought to have killed more people." There was one major detail that he left unspecified: how many more must be killed?

Now, from our experience of Communism in the quarter of the globe that at one time or another has been under its sway, we know what the total cost has been up to now: following the scale of J. P. Sartre it amounts to *150 million dead*. No, you have not mis-read: I have indeed written "150 million". More than twice the total number of casualties in the last two world wars. Compared to this, Robespierre was a "softy"; he clearly had not read Sartre. By comparison with the population concerned, this figure is equivalent to a holocaust of *five million Frenchmen killed*. That is the amount of innocent blood that a collectivist regime has to shed in order to maintain itself in power against human reason and human nature. Here are the only alternatives that a joint socialist-communist regime in France, led by Mr. Mitterrand and Mr. Marchais, has to offer: it will either collapse after a few years, like that of Mr. Allende, under the weight of the disasters it will itself have inflicted on the French people, or it will survive on the communist model, that is, it will still have brought about the same disasters, and in addition it will have killed thousands of Frenchman.

English speaking readers will have followed the story of developments in the Chilean left against the background of the leftward swing of the British Labour Party and the increasing take-over of its key organs and local branches by Trotskyists and other extreme left-wingers. For the moment this danger appears to be balanced and neutralised by the reassuring emergence of a more moderate Left, in particular by the alliance between the Liberals and the newly-formed Social-Democratic Party led by non-marxist ex-members of the Labour Party alarmed by its drift to the extreme Left. But this new moderate force has yet to prove that it can win wide electoral support, and it cannot be ruled out that a deepening economic crisis, with mass unemployment and growing racial tensions could bring the "new" Labour Party to power, committed to unilateral nuclear disarmament, to getting rid of American bases in Britain, to quitting the EEC and to massive nationalization.

CHAPTER XV

FOREIGN INTERVENTION IN CHILE? AGAINST WHOM? IN WHOSE INTERESTS?

A CRY OF SCANDAL went up throughout the world at the alleged intervention of industrial corporations and the American information services in their attempt to prevent a Marxist government coming to power in Chile. What are the real facts?

Intervention by ITT and the CIA under Mr. Allende

It is true that some local managers of the American International Telephone and Telegraph corporation had been alarmed by the prospect of a Marxist-Leninist government in Chile, for that meant the loss of all ITT's assets in that country—nearly a hundred million dollars. It is true that local representatives of ITT got in touch with other American companies in Chile, threatened with the same catastrophe, in order to try and collect funds to help the democratic parties. But all these moves failed miserably, proving once again that, as Karl Marx had written, "capitalists are their own gravediggers". Furthermore, these local ITT managers, in an attempt to block Mr. Allende's rise to power, made contact with certain members of the opposition with a view to starting exploratory talks; but neither President Frei nor any minister in his government ever took part in these. This move, again, was a failure. They also contacted two or three superior officers of the armed forces, but here again the ITT's action came to nothing.

As you can see, there was nothing here to warrant such an uproar. It all boiled down to nothing more than fears, even if quite natural ones, and to plans, none of which were ever realised either in money or in action. Cross-currents of this kind are characteristic of all electoral campaigns in every country in the world.

Let us add one small detail to the history of world capitalism: the ITT documents, memoranda and correspondence proving the facts I have just recounted were used by the Overseas Private Investment Corporation (an insurance company compensating private investors for any confiscations they suffered in foreign countries) as a pretext for refusing to reimburse ITT for the value of their assets seized by the Marxist-Leninist government. This is further proof that Marx was oh so right when he wrote that "the capitalists would be their own gravediggers".

As for CIA intervention, it emerges from all the evidence brought before the American Senate sub-committee investigating this affair, that it amounted to practically nothing. First, an ITT manager had offered the CIA a million dollars to help the propaganda campaign of the Chilean anti-Marxist parties. This offer was refused. Then, after the election which gave Mr. Allende a slender relative majority, a CIA official submitted to an ITT executive a plan for engineering a breakdown in the economy, designed to frighten the Christian Democrats and stop them from giving their votes to Mr. Allende. This plan was never carried out, nor even seriously discussed inside the CIA.

Mr. William Colby, for two years director of the CIA, supplied the following evidence under oath at the enquiry: "It is true that the CIA had a ten-year programme for 1963–73 to try to help Chile's centre parties—*not those of the right*—to win the elections against the Marxist parties. It is no less true that this plan was very soon abandoned. At the time of the Chilean presidential elections in 1970, Washington decided not to back any candidate. Mr. Allende's overthrow was not organized by the CIA, but by Mr. Allende himself, for it was his policy that led to the revolt, first of the people and then of the soldiers who finally brought him down. I stress that this was in no way a 'CIA coup'."

To sum up, it is undeniable that some American economic and political interests toyed with the idea of attempting to influence the presidential elections in Chile—and this is blameworthy—but it is also undeniable that these projects never took practical shape and so had no adverse effect on Mr. Allende's electoral chances. It is no less undeniable that Mr. Allende set in train generalized confiscations and started a civil war which destroyed his country's economy and created a more devastating climate of class hatred than any foreign intervention could have done. It is even less undeniable that political and economic interference was exerted, on a far more considerable scale, by Soviet Russia and Cuba in support of the UP candidates. This was carried out through the mediation of their secret services, their embassies converted into fortresses, the Chilean Communist Party—one of the most servilely submissive to the Kremlin—their fifth columnists, their subversive agents and hired killers on the spot in Chile.

But what the world at large is still totally unaware of, although it was revealed at the ITT/CIA show-down, is that these "tough but honest" Marxist-Leninist parties were getting more and more used to holding out their begging-bowl not only to the East, but to the West as well! For they had realized that in the West there were innumerable highly-placed fellow-travellers in the embassies and ministries, as well as the "diggers of their own graves" in industry and banks, and all busy buying indulgences from the Leninist parties. These parties themselves were hard at work collecting all the money they could not only from Moscow, but also from the coffers of the capitalists. Thus Mr. Edward Korry, the American ambassador in Chile, declared under oath to the American Senate sub-committee (it would be wonderful if such committees existed in the USSR, to investigate all the KGB's interventions in the affairs of the Free World): "Before the 1970 elections, representatives from *the three political camps* in Chile approached the United States embassy *to ask for financial backing.*"

The Senators were staggered. Yes, emissaries from Mr. Alessandri's National Party, Frei's Christian Democrats, but also from *the Communist and Socialist Parties* had not been afraid of crossing the threshold of the most capitalist embassy in the world to ask for electoral funds. The Marxist-Leninist parties had little justification indeed for criticizing the Americans for getting involved in Chilean affairs, since they themselves had invited them in by asking them for money.

Is it true that the capitalist countries tried to strangle the Chilean economy during Mr. Allende's term of office?

When the UP authorities' total incompetence in managing the economy had become only too evident, when there was no more bread at the bakers' shops, when there were endless queues which could no longer be hidden from the world, when the monetary reserves had dried up, when the empty saucepans were beating out their poignant appeals, then we heard *ad nauseam* the excuse that "it was the fault of the capitalist countries", who had refused credits to the heroic "people's power"; had organized an insidious boycott of Chilean trade; had disorganized production; rendered the land sterile; decimated the livestock, and dissolved the currency. In short, the capitalists were made to play, in relation to the incapable and incompetent Marxist authorities, the same role as had been assigned to the Jews as scapegoats for the disastrous results of royal policy in the days of a spendthrift and bellicose monarchy.

Now it must be made quite clear that all this is a pack of lies from beginning to end. Over the three years that his Marxist government was in office, Mr. Allende received 822.7 million dollars of credit from abroad. How can it be claimed that a government has been attacked financially when in less than three years it has pocketed 823 million dollars in new loans, *75% of which came from western countries*! (see the Finance minister's report, October 1973)? Where is the international aggression against Mr. Allende that is so constantly dinned into our ears? If the American and European banks had really wanted to overturn Mr. Allende, they would never have invested so much money in his crumbling economy. For what principally emerges from the story is the Marxist government's total incapacity to make good use of the funds so freely given to it.

When these capitalist countries came to re-negotiating the external debt of a Marxist economy that was visibly drifting onto the rocks, we can detect no sign in them of any hostile feeling, though this would have been quite justified in the circumstances. On the contrary, one is aware of *an unequalled generosity*. It is not me saying this, but comrade Orlando Millas, Finance Minister in the Allende government: "In January 1972, I obtained from private banks in the United States an agreement which included: a) the granting of three loans totalling 240 million dollars over eight years; b) funding for three years' debts . . . During 1972 and 1973 we made only one token payment of 5% of the debt; in December 1976 there will still be a balance of 55% of the debts, which will be re-financed—capital and interest—for a period of three years. To sum up, repayment of our debt will be spread over eight years. The financial success of my negotiations can be summed up by saying that it constitutes a substantial reduction in the constant drain on our foreign currency reserves; we shall no longer be obliged to honour our obligations over the years 1972–73 and 1974 . . ."[1]

The UP government was as pleased as could be with the arrangement it had squeezed out of the American private banks. So it would be foolish to take Mr. Allende seriously when he blamed the capitalist countries' "blockade" as the reason for the disasters caused by his own economic policy. This was the same Mr. Allende who boasted to Parliament: "During the years 1972 and 1973, I got them to agree that Chile should make only one token payment of 5% of our debts!"

The same benefits were obtained from the private European banks in April 1972. They granted Mr. Allende 60 million dollars over three years to fund his debt repayments, on generous terms similar to those of the American banks. Furthermore, on 19 April 1972, the members of the Club de Paris agreed to a year's postponement of the repayments due on Chile's debt for that year. Thus minister Orlando Millas was able to boast of his success in his *Report* in these words: "The financial formula can be expressed as a net saving of 65 million dollars . . . The resultant repayment plan—three years' grace, six in effect—at a mutually convenient rate of interest—accords perfectly with our expectations." The Marxist minister went on to make clear the advantages he had gained from Belgium, France, Switzerland, England, West

[1]Speech made on 15 November 1972, quoted by Alberto Baltra Cortes in his *Gestiôn econômica de la Unidad Popular*, published by Orbe, Santiago.

Germany, Holland, etc., and concluded: "To sum up, the total alleviation obtained through the re-negotiation of the balance of external payments will be of the order of 600 million dollars."

Mr. Allende's Minister of Finance was jubilant. He had every reason to be so. But where, in all this, lay the financial aggression? Where was the economic strangulation? Where was the boycott of Marxist Chile by the wicked capitalist countries? Far from it; all one can see is help, kindness, benevolence, or, to call a spade a spade, blind stupidity on the part of the capitalist countries concerned, a blindness and stupidity which continued to be evident throughout Mr. Allende's reign, even during the worst year of his economic bankruptcy.

In 34 months, Mr. Allende had gained 823 million dollars in *new credits*, to which must be added 180 millions in uncompleted agreements. (I am taking no account of investments here.) In short, Mr. Allende had put the Chileans in debt to the tune of 1,000 million dollars, that is 1 million dollars for each day of his reign. 75% of this had been generously provided by the capitalist countries.

On the other hand, the West, which had been so generous to the Marxist-Leninist Allende who despised it, proved extremely grudging towards the Pinochet regime which respected it. The capitalist states stopped all credits for Gen. Pinochet. Mr. Allende, who had fought his presidential campaign by unremitting attacks on the economic dependence of Frei's Chile on the West, thus became considerably more dependent on it than either Mr. Frei or Gen. Pinochet. No doubt he knew in his heart of hearts that dependence on these milch-cows, the Western nations, committed him to nothing, and did not prevent him either from insulting them; pulling the wool over their eyes or cheating them. These were debts that he had not the slightest intention of ever repaying.

None of this should surprise us. There is a long and abundant tradition of assistance given to Communists by international capitalism, either in the hope of some quick immediate profit, or because the bourgeois governments concerned were persuaded by their progressive intelligentsia that any other action would be "reactionary". As early as the 1920s Lenin had owed the success of his NEP, New Economic Policy, solely to the rush of loans and investments from foreign capitalists. Since then the stream of aid has never stopped flowing from Washington, London, Bonn, Sydney, Rome, Paris. For example, France lent the Kremlin 15 thousand million francs at 3 % over 15 years at a time when Frenchmen were having to pay between 10 and 15% interest on their borrowings. Loans at ridiculous rates, credits, shiploads of grain, complete factory installations ready to use were being granted to Moscow by all the capitalist governments under such advantageous conditions that they amounted virtually to subsidies. Europe's capitalist governments even granted 300 million new francs per year in economic aid to the communist authorities in Hanoi, at a time when they were perpetrating a nightmarish genocide on their own people. The Washington government, that had stopped economic aid to Gen. Pinochet's Chile because human rights were not sufficiently observed there, granted "most favoured nation status" (which, under American law, must only be bestowed on countries fulfilling all the required conditions as to individual liberties) to . . . guess whom? . . . to communist China, a country where there is no political freedom, no trade-union freedom, no religious freedom, no freedom of opposition. Without this massive aid from free enterprise countries, collectivist Communism would long since have collapsed throughout the world.

Thus, there is no myth falser than that of a world capitalist plot against the Marxist regimes. These last, following the approved Leninist tactic, carry their impudence to a very high level: on the one hand they pocket the plentiful economic aid received from the capitalist countries, and on the other they accuse these countries of strangling their economies. They are like beggars who arouse the whole street against those who have just filled their begging-bowls.

So all this fairy tale of a world plot against the UP is false. It was not international capitalism, but Mr. Allende, in fact, who, in decree after decree, plundered the small hauliers, small businessmen, farmers, industrialists, the Chilean lawyers and doctors, whose ruin provided a leaven for the opposition. It was not international capitalism which decimated Chilean livestock, it was the armed UP gangs who under the pretext of "agrarian reform" sent the breeding stock to the slaughterhouse. It was not international capitalism that kept workers' salaries lagging far behind the dizzy rise in prices, or took the land from the Chilean peasants. It was Mr. Allende!

By contrast, it is a fact that Mr. Allende was quite happy to accept *a far more stringent dependence* on Soviet Russia, from which he received several hundred million dollars worth of credits. For these credits, indeed, were not without strings; they implied political censorship—sealed lips on the subject of the "workers' fatherland"—the acceptance of Cuban and Soviet economic, political and military advisers, and the presence of Latin-American terrorists on Chilean soil.

Foreign involvement in Allende's Chile by the communist countries

"The Soviet Union is Chile's elder sister." It was Mr. Allende who made this declaration of *loyal homage* to a foreign country, a declaration that has no parallel in Chilean history. In a letter to Mr. Allende, the president of the Christian Democratic Party expressed his anxiety over the fact that most of the exporting of the country's copper was entrusted to a Russian shipping company, Baltic Steamships, and that Soviet technicians had access to Chile's industrial secrets. Chilean military intelligence received a report at the beginning of 1973 according to which 20,000 foreign military instructors, including Soviet nationals, Cubans, Czechoslovaks and East Germans, were scattered throughout the nationalized industries of the Cerillas industrial suburb, and that large quantities of Czechoslovak arms had been stockpiled there.

The "vassalization" of Mr. Allende's Chile by Soviet Russia was carried out mainly through the mediation of *Cuba*. Fidel Castro's interventions in Chile's domestic life were frequent, public, and were carried out with a quite unwonted effrontery. Soon after Mr. Allende had come to power, in November 1971, Fidel Castro landed in Chile with a large and boisterous escort for a ten days' visit, and then lengthened this to three weeks. The Chileans had to put up with the most powerful foreign security machine that they had ever encountered. Cuban helicopters, filled with uniformed strong-arm men, appeared wherever the great Teacher of Communism went. His political interference knew neither bounds nor decorum. He took the liberty of attacking the opposition; insulting it, calling it "fascist", "mummified", and "reactionary". Suppose the Prime Minister of Great Britain, Mrs. Thatcher, in the course of a visit to France, had called the socialist-communist alliance "tyrants", "fascists" and "old windbags", there would have been a general outcry throughout the world! This is what Fidel Castro called the Chilean democratic opposition, and no one overseas was put out in the slightest.

To mark Castro's departure, a meeting was organized in the National Stadium, which can hold 80,000. Not even 30,000 came. Castro used this as a pretext for a scathing criticism of the UP, using the insult to his person from the Chilean people as proof that the UP was incapable of mobilizing the people either willingly or by force. He put forward his own achievements in this direction as an example, and made the following recommendations: to mobilize the masses in a few hours, all that needs to be done is to set up *vigilance committees* in each local district, and for the leaders of these to take all the inhabitants well in hand. Further, the Marxist regime must establish complete control over jobs, all food supplies, all housing, all credit. Then it would be child's play to make the people attend all official gatherings.

Mr. Allende took this to heart. After Castro's visit, Chilean politics took a radical turn to the left, the noisy, sabre-rattling militants of the left gained the upper hand, and the sinister *vigilance committees* made their appearance. That was the first example of unmitigated interference by a foreign head of state in the affairs of the Chilean people. It was to be followed by many others on the part of Castro.

In August 1973, two high-ranking officials from the central committee of the Cuban Communist Party arrived in Chile on an unofficial visit: vice-premier Mr. Carlos Rafael Rodriguez, and the chief of the secret police, Mr. Manuel Piniero, under his assumed name of Barbarossa. They were the bearers of a letter from Fidel Castro, written in his own hand, and which was found after the military coup among Mr. Allende's papers. It was dated from Havana, 29 July 1973. It said: "I am sending you two confidential agents *under the pretext* of discussing the non-aligned countries with you. In reality I would like them to examine with you *the domestic situation* in Chile and the dangers that the putschists represent for the revolution . . . The most important thing is to warn the enemy that there are forces ready and fully armed to go into action against him . . . Let my two envoys know all the points on which we can collaborate with you." (Published in facsimile in the *White Book*.)

Besides being a shameless interference in Chilean domestic policy by Fidel Castro, it was nothing less than a call to civil war between Chileans, and what is worse, the bearded fellow launched his call from such a distance that there was no risk of the blood spilled splashing onto him.

Marxism's foreign legion in Chile

Fidel Castro did not limit himself to giving Mr. Allende straight-from-the-shoulder lessons in political dictatorship. He had left behind on the spot his bravoes and secret agents to make sure that they were carried out. His visit to Chile in 1971 was accompanied by the setting up of several so-called "eastern" networks through the agency of Mr. Fernandez de Ona, a chief of the DGI (*Dirección General de la Inteligencia*), the Cuban secret police, who had prepared Che Guevara's terrorist expedition to Bolivia. To make his position even safer in Chile, Mr. Fernandez de Ona married Mr. Allende's daughter. This Cuban did not even hesitate to take his wife's place in the office of the Chilean Presidency. He was even seen participating in person in the military training of the GAP, the personal friends of Mr. Allende.

On 3 April 1972, *El Mercurio* published the second part of the ITT confidential papers, the section concerning Cuban intervention in force in Chilean affairs, a document about which the so-called liberal press had been curiously silent. There one could read that "Allende's daughter, Beatriz, received instructions in Cuba on subversion and guerilla warfare in Chile. She brought back a portfolio containing a great deal of advice for the President: as, for example, that he should take administrative measures to prevent qualified technicians from leaving Chile . . . The most alarming sign is the presence in Santiago of members of *the Cuban political police*, trained in Moscow and led by the Cuban Mr. Luis Fernandez de Ona. It is said that his mission is to safeguard the security of the Marxist coalition. He has proposed as a model the 'Committees for the defence of the Cuban revolution' organized by the Cuban general, Alberto Boya, in 1959 . . ."

The 150 members of the swollen Cuban embassy in Santiago, plus a strong Cuban armed guard, were put under the command of Mr. Manuel Piniero, another Cuban liaison officer between the Cuban secret services, of which he was chief, and the Soviet military intelligence services in Havana, the GRU. It was their job to spy on all milieux where there was opposition to Mr. Allende. Visits of Cuban officials to Santiago followed one another at an alarming rate. Between 1 January and 31 July 1973 such visits numbered 633. Yes, you read that correctly: 633 visits in 200 days, or more than three every 24 hours. That is without counting the thousand or so underground members of Castro's army already in the capital, armed with false identity papers, many of whom had been given posts in the Chilean administration by Mr. Allende! On 11 September 1973, "eastern" agents took part in the armed resistance to the coup, and this explains why some communist legations were shelled. We have seen the vast quantities of arms sent by Cuba to Chile. Cubans also played an essential role in the training of the MIR, the Chilean Movement of the Revolutionary Left, in tactical guerilla warfare and terrorism. Yes, the Cuban Liberation Directorate, the headquarters of subversion throughout Latin America, was particularly active in Santiago under Mr. Allende. Here we are dealing with maximum foreign intervention, not just political or economic, but *military* as well.

Terrorists wanted by all the Latin-American police forces, soldiers left over from all the revolutions converged, like moths attracted by a lamp, on Marxist Chile, which soon became their promised land, for they were allowed in with no identity checks, simply on the basis of their service records in the *International of Blood*. They were immediately supplied with papers and a job as cover, and taken on, not by the Chilean forces but by the *Cubans*, who, after enrolling them, rebuilding their morale and re-training them, incorporated them in the groups of subversive activists already at work.

It was interventionism raised to the power of 2: a foreign thieves' kitchen was taking it upon itself to incorporate foreigners into the ranks of Chilean terrorism. The turmoil was maintained on Chilean soil by a directorate with its head-office in Havana, using yeasts scraped from the dustbins of world-wide terrorism. I should like to give a few examples of this.

Thus, 81 Brazilian terrorists, wanted by the Brazilian police for their kidnapping of the Swiss ambassador to Brazil, took refuge in Chile in June 1971; re-trained under Cuban direction and were then actively involved in subversion inside Chile. One of them, a student, Mr. Milton Santos da Silva, became a leader of the paramilitary movement, the MIR. He was killed in a scuffle on 15 June 1973. Another Brazilian activist was in charge of the conversion of forklift trucks into armoured vehicles in the nationalized automobile combine, MADEMSA. A third was a member of the extreme left group which, together with a Bolivian and a Venezuelan, fired on workers from a Chilean factory in July 1973, killing the union leader Mr. Manuel Garrido and wounding three workers. On 8 August, Ms. Nieves Menendez, a female "tourist" from Uruguay and a survivor from the crushing of the Tupamaros, took part in an attack on the first-aid headquarters (*Posta Central de Primeros Auxilios*) in Santiago, to capture medical supplies for a secret guerilla field hospital. Other Uruguayan ex-Tupamaros set off a terrible explosion in August 1972 when handling explosives in a militant socialist's house near Valparaiso. The commando group of the extreme left which killed second-lieutenant Hector Lacrampette on 28 August 1973 included a Mexican who had entered Chile as a "tourist" (and had immediately been given a job in a state industry), two Cubans and an Uruguayan (the last three managed to make good their escape).

One may add that in April 1971 there was a public demonstration by 80 *priests in favour of Marxism*: 65 of the demonstrators were foreigners! The 'Movement of Christians for Socialism' received its instructions from the *Mexican bishop* Mendez Arceo, who was a pupil of the communist theologian Mr. Illich, a Yugoslav living in Mexico.

So the "patriotic" Chilean Socialists and Communists found it normal and useful that bearded Cuban hired soldiery, mercenaries from Katanga, Uruguayan Tupamaros, Argentinian Montoneros and Mexican *pistoleros* should be used to keep the Chilean Marxist-Leninists permanently in power by violence!

Today, Cuba is still training Cuban and Chilean terrorists in the making and use of bombs to carry out against Gen. Pinochet's Chile the type of terrorist acts which finally put an end to South Vietnam's independence. Its field agents enter Chile illegally across the Andes mountains, armed with false passports and a large quantity of very sophisticated explosive materials. Thus the bomb that killed lieutenant Luis Carevic in April 1979 was fitted with the very latest in explosive technology. It had four independent detonating systems: a clockwork mechanism, plus a tape-recorder set off by the slightest noise, plus a plunger activated by the slightest movement, plus an instability system which set it off on impact. Three bombs were placed in 24 hours, one in a lawyer's house, the other two right in the middle of Santiago. In the first six months of 1979, a hundred attacks of various sorts were carried out using bombs, plastic explosives, etc.

All this proves that terrorism is likely to become more widespread in Gen. Pinochet's Chile, and that it is still, as it always has been, *exported by a foreign state*, for no native Chilean is capable of constructing such super-sophisticated devices. But international opinion does not seem to be moved in the slightest by such examples of foreign interference against the Pinochet government. After all, the interference is neither Yankee, capitalist or multinational in origin; it is just communist!

American intervention in the domestic affairs of Pinochet's Chile

World opinion was indignant when it heard of the manoeuvres by ITT and the CIA against Mr. Allende. But it did not turn a hair (was it even told?) at the announcement of American State Department intervention against Gen. Pinochet. Yet on 1 March 1976 the nationalist leader Mr. Pablo Rodriguez accused the American ambassador in Santiago, Mr. David H. Popper, of "shameful intervention in Chile's domestic affairs", and demanded that he be declared *persona non grata*, since his activities were leading not to closer ties between the United States and Chile and its people, but to the creation of internal divisions and the overthrow of Gen. Pinochet.

These accusations made by the Chilean nationalist leader seem all the more plausible since Mr. David H. Popper's whole past shows him as holding extreme left-wing opinions, as is evidenced by a study on him published in an American publication, the *Herald of Freedom* of 23 April 1976. Since the present government in Chile is anti-communist, it would have been logical, and in line with all diplomatic tradition for the person chosen as the U.S. ambassador to Chile to be somewhat anti-communist. Now we read in the *Herald of Freedom* that Mr. David H. Popper's name was on the famous list of "security risks and subversives", that is, subversive elements constituting a risk to the security of the USA, and which was submitted to the Secretary of State by the late Scott McLeod in 1956. We learn that Mr. David H. Popper was brought into the American Administration by the notorious Mr. Alger Hiss in 1945, and that he worked for him. Mr. Alger Hiss was sentenced to ten years' imprisonment for his subversive activities on behalf of Moscow.

Publication 4861 of the American Senate's hearing shows that Mr. David H. Popper was affiliated to the Institute of Pacific Relations (IPR), a body specializing in pro-Soviet propaganda. An IPR hearing (5193) again proves that Mr. David H. Popper was a member of the board of directors of the magazine *Amerasia*, itself cited by the Senate

Judiciary Committee as "a publication controlled by the Communists". On the same *Amerasia* board were: Frederick V. Field, identified as a Communist and Soviet spy; Philips J. Joffee (alias W.Philips), identified as a Communist and sentenced by a court for the theft of 1,500 secret documents belonging to the American government and found in the offices of *Amerasia*; and Mr. Owen Lattimore, cited by the Senate Judiciary Committee as "a conscious and articulate tool of the Soviet conspiracy".

It is not my intention to start up another witch-hunt against Ambassador Popper, or get him the sack. But according to established diplomatic ethics, he should have been sent to one of the many communist countries behind the Iron Curtain who are in harmony with his inclinations, and not to Chile, where his convictions drove him to work actively against the government to which he was accredited. Mr. David H. Popper's nomination as ambassador in Santiago under Gen. Pinochet can only be construed as deliberate provocation. It is exactly the same as if the French government had sent me, Ms. Suzanne Labin, as ambassadress to Moscow!

The AFL-CIO interventions

What are we to make of the threatening ultimatum from the AFL-CIO leader, Mr. George Meany, to President Pinochet: "If by 28 November 1978 I have not received a satisfactory reply from President Pinochet regarding trade union liberties in Chile, the AFL-CIO will be prepared to co-operate with all its brother trade unions in Latin America and the Caribbean to mount an international action against the Chilean government's repression of its workers . . ."?

This pressure from a foreign trade-union super-power capable of closing all ports to all Chilean exports merely by issuing a strike-call through its dockers' union, was this not a considerable intervention in an independent South American nation's domestic affairs?

What made it worse was that two AFL-CIO vice-presidents, Mr. Thomas Gleason and Mr. Sol Choikin, had already been received by President Pinochet; he had patiently explained to them that he had to prevent communist infiltration of the unions. Mr. Meany's envoys were given every liberty to question whomever they wanted, to go wherever they wanted, to take as much time as they wanted. In spite of this, their report to Mr. Meany was a hostile one. That is why the chairman of the *Confederaciôn Nacional de Provincias Agrarias Unidas*, Mr. Paul Orrega, protested that "Their report was based on information which was totally lacking in impartiality, for they only met union leaders who are totally divorced from the majority of our country's trade-union organisations." He added indignantly that Mr. Meany's ultimatum "clearly represents an interference in the domestic affairs of a sovereign state".

Mr. George Meany went so far as to send President Pinochet a message, accompanied by the threat of an international boycott of Chilean commerce, giving him the order to reinstate four sacked union leaders at a nationalized copper mine. Quite apart from the fact that these four activists were dismissed for organizing a political meeting during working hours, causing a general halt in production, this raises the question as to what justification an American union has for demanding that this or that measure shall be taken inside another country.

One's first thought is that even if we admit that at the time there was not much freedom for trade unions in Chile, there is even less such freedom in fifty or so countries of the Third World, and little or no trade union freedom at all in the countries behind the Iron Curtain. Now, the AFL-CIO has never sent any ultimatums to any of these countries. If Mr. George Meany thinks, like Karl Marx, that "the proletarians have no fatherland", and that, therefore, he is allowed to intervene in the workers' struggles in foreign countries, why then has he not done so at any time in the last 50 years in the case of the USSR, and in the last 30 years in China, Vietnam, Cambodia or Cuba? Why hasn't he directed his thunderbolts at all those tyrannies where the trade unions are reduced to the role of parallel state police forces, and which have never been kind enough to allow his investigators in, or to permit anyone at all to discuss union rights freely with their fettered workers?

A Ukrainian worker, Mr. Leonid Mikhailovich Sery, born in Odessa and father of seven children, wrote to Mr. George Meany two moving letters about the miserable living conditions of Ukrainian workers: safety regulations totally flouted; frequent accidents at work; totally inadequate medical services; constantly increased production targets for unchanging starvation-wages; canteen sited at an enormous distance from a place of work that had no drinking water; appalling and expensive food which hardly ever included meat, milk, butter or fruit; housing consisting of dirty, dark corners of cellars, attics and half-ruined barns. Summing up, Mr. Leonid Mikhailovich wrote: "We do not live, we rot in suffering and penury. Inspired by one of our comrades, we, the Ukrainian workers, tried to organize a union which would have seriously defended workers' rights. The authorities threw our leaders behind bars and, on 3 November 1977, the KGB wrote me a letter threatening to put me in prison for seven years, followed by five years of internal exile, if I went on complaining. So, with eight mouths to feed, I shut up. That, dear Mr. Meany, is the situation of our country's workers . . . Our working classes do not have the freedom to eat their fill, to have decent holidays, to strike, to organize their own trade unions. Isn't that slavery?".[1]

But Mr. Meany, whose haughty, principled conscience was kept awake by any attack on union rights when it happened in Chile, did not even reply to these dramatic letters from a Ukrainian worker. He did not order a boycott of Soviet ships berthing along the American coasts. He sent no ultimatum to Gierek's communist government which refused the Poles the right to organize free trade unions.

An eminent Chilean trade unionist, Mr. Bernardo Ibanez, who worked for ten years in the International Labour Office in Geneva, and then for two years in the Inter-American Institute for the Development of Free Trade Unionism in Washington, under Mr. Meany, in fact, and who therefore is someone who knows what he is talking about as regards union rights, wrote to Mr. Meany on 30 August 1978: "You ought to know how the Communists used violent means to take over the Chilean workers' organization, the CUT, that great union created by the old Social Democrats, the Christian Democrats and the old Radical Party. Once in control of the CUT, the Communists forged the same chains for the Chilean workers that Fidel Castro's followers had forged for the workers of Cuba . . . Under Mr. Allende's leadership, the Communists had transformed my country into *one more Soviet colony* . . . Dear Mr. Meany, human rights were not observed in Mr. Allende's Chile, nor were trade union liberties . . . Independent workers' action was methodically suppressed by the Communists and their shock troops, as was the case during the Sowell miners' trike and the hauliers' strike, when several of the strikers were murdered by them . . . How is it that, at the time, your great union confederation did not send Mr. Allende an ultimatum threatening to boycott him?"

All this goes to show how mistaken is the opinion that Mr. Allende was coerced or bullied in any way in his actions as head of government by any foreign power. No, any such interference was practised only *against Gen. Pinochet* and always in favour of Mr. Allende. This may be amazing, but it is true. President Carter stopped all military and economic aid to the Pinochet government. Senator Edward Kennedy exhorted the AFL-CIO to boycott Chile, not just for trade union reasons, but also for reasons which had nothing at all to do with the proper concerns of the great American labour confederation, namely that the Santiago Court of Justice had refused the extradition to the USA of three Chilean officials suspected of conspiring to murder a friend of Mr. Allende, Mr. Orlando Letelier. Now, have the United States ever demanded the extradition of the Soviet KGB officials who supplied arms to the killers of Mr. Kravchenko, Mr. Krivitsky and so

[1]Quoted in *East-West Digest*, London, December 1978.)

many other defectors from the Soviet hell who had sought asylum in the United States? Have they ever demanded the extradition of those, whether Soviet or Cuban, who supplied arms to the killer of a President of the United States, John F. Kennedy, the brother in fact of the Edward mentioned above, who seemed much more affected by the death of the Marxist-Leninist Letelier than by that of his own brother.

Even more strongly interventionist, Mr. Edward Kennedy tabled a bill prohibiting American private banks from giving credit to Pinochet's Chile. Just stopping military and economic assistance by the American state was not enough for him, for he wanted to stop all credit from non-official sources as well. That is to say that he was demanding that the United States—that bastion of free enterprise—should embark on the downward path that leads to a dictatorial planned economy, in order to teach an anti-communist government how to behave!

CHAPTER XVI

REPRESSION UNDER PINOCHET

RARELY HAS HISTORY OFFERED US the spectacle of a campaign of political hatred carried to the same pitch of intensity as that aimed against the Pinochet regime in Chile. Not a single newspaper, radio or TV station on the left in any country in the world failed to add its voice to the outcry. In this, the heaviest stress was of course laid on the appalling repression Gen. Pinochet was alleged to be carrying out against his enemies, and which rode rough-shod over all human rights.

It was a contest as to who could tell the wildest horror stories: bodies were floating through Santiago down the Rio Mapocho (the Mapocho is a glacial torrent down which it would be difficult to float a dead cat). Negroes were being lynched in the streets (I did not meet a single Negro in the whole of Chile). Opponents were tied to grids and left for the condors (a bird which is on the way to extinction; there are now only a few pairs left on the wildest peaks of the Andes). Mr. Allende's former assistant, Mr. Van Lanker, was thrown from a sixth-floor window in Brussels by one of Gen. Pinochet's killers (Mr. Van Lanker stated, when he came round after the news of his "assassination" had made the headlines, that he had fallen by accident). The agricultural colony of Dignidad is being used by the Chilean government as a cover for a huge enterprise for torture and secret burials, as is proved by the refusal of the German colonists allegedly farming it to open to visitors barns from which groans could be heard, and from the roofs of which an aerial photograph had shown foul-smelling smoke rising (the West German ambassador had the barns opened for him and found new types of grain which were being dried by a special method which the peasants wanted to keep secret). In a dramatic comminqué, Amnesty Internationl announced that eleven left-wing militants had disappeared after being tortured; all eleven were found in good health by the French journalist M. Kéraly, but no one, except the review *Itinéraires* and the *Minute* and *L'Aurore* newspapers mentioned a word about it. The press made the most of what Mrs. Gladys Diaz said about her husband having been tortured to death. But it ignored the statement made under oath on *4 January 1977* before an officer of the law by the aforementioned husband, testifying that he had never been proceeded against by the Chilean police, that he was living at such-and-such an address, where any visitor would find him in excellent health. And so on *ad infinitum*, with no limit to the acrimony of tone or the falsification of the facts!

This flood of little lies could be adduced as sufficient reason for rejecting outright the entire accusation of terrorism made against the Pinochet regime. Nevertheless I intend to investigate it objectively, leaving completely to one side the justifiable suspicion which these provenly false charges point to their accusers. The importance of the subject requires a serene and thorough approach.

The civil war

We have seen that on the very day of the pronunciamento and Mr. Allende's suicide, 11 September 1973, everything happened without any real resistance from Mr. Allende's supporters. These latter, however, once they had got over the initial shock, recovered themselves and began to fight back. One may find it surprising that the Marxists should have woken up *after* the coup had been carried out, and when the army was in control of all strategic points. But it must not be forgotten that the paramilitary organization built up by the UP was of such proportions that there was nothing inherently absurd in the idea of re-capturing power. Even if this objective had no chance of success, the UP had to put up at least some resistance to show that it was not just a worn-out garment, discarded because no one wanted it any longer. Furthermore, an armed struggle could supply a number of colourful propaganda stories which would serve to arouse world opinion against the "brutal soldiery".

For all these reasons, such a struggle was unleashed within a few days of the coup d'état. Needless to say, the masses took no part in it. On the contrary, most of the information which guided the regular troops against pockets of UP resistance came from the people. The actual fighting was carried out, though with remarkable tenacity, exclusively by *the professionals* from the paramilitary groups. Thanks to the plentiful and up-to-date weaponry these groups had at their disposal—heavy machine-guns, grenades, bazookas, field telecommunications, and even some artillery in the provinces—military engagements sometimes required a considerable effort from the army. Fighting was intense in October and November 1973, and then fell off in December, and it stopped altogether in its strictly military form from February 1974. However, armed resistance never completely died out.

How many casualties were there in this civil war? I have done some research on this point in the newspapers of the time and in official government reports. I have not been able to arrive at any exact figure. All that I can say is that the number was probably over 2,000 and under 3,000, 30% of the deaths occurring among the regular troops, including the police and 70% among the UP combatants. This puts the civil war in an intermediate position on the scale of political upheavals, higher than the "easy" military coups in Brazil and Greece, but well below the struggles between Communists and anti-Communists in Guatemala, Nicaragua, Indonesia, Iran, the Yemen and Vietnam.

One remarkable peculiarity about the Chilean fighting is worth noting: those members of the regular troops who committed excesses were punished by the military command, and nearly one hundred were demoted and imprisoned! At the time of the 1978 amnesty, there were still 30 behind bars! This fact alone, which has no precedent in the history of counter-revolutions, is a good illustration of the strong respect for law of the military junta which had taken power.

To the number of deaths, we must add arrested UP supporters. The number of these is estimated at 4,000. About 70 were tried by emergency tribunals (abolished at the end of 1975) and shot. The others were placed in various camps, but from 1975 on these camps began to empty, either because sentences were reduced or else because most of the internees had emigrated. General Pinochet had promulgated a law allowing any opponent who had been taken prisoner while under arms to opt for emigration, in which case he was handed over to the foreign embassy of his choice, provided the latter undertook to evacuate him by air to the country of his choice. By the beginning of 1976, there was not a single camp left in operation, and the prisons contained only a few hundred political detainees who had actually broken the law. When the April 1978 amnesty was declared, there were only 170 prisoners of this type left, including 30 soldiers still serving sentences for their excesses committed during the unsettled period. As of 1979, there are no longer any "political" prisoners in Chile, in the sense that no one is interned or sentenced for expressing opinions, however extreme. On the other hand, terrorist violence and incitement to break the laws are criminal offences in Chile as everywhere else, and agitators guilty of either of these find themselves liable, after due process of law, to penal conviction.

In this connection, the following anecdote seems to me significant. During my study trip to Chile I met a young woman who quite openly told me of her communist sympathies. When I told her of my visit to the Minister of Justice, who had assured me that there were no longer any political prisoners in Chile, she sharply objected: "That's not true, and the best proof of it is that I myself have been a political prisoner." "Oh," I cried, interested, "in what circumstances?" "It was on 1 May last year. I was arrested for taking part in a forbidden demonstration." "And how long did you spend locked up?" "About a day."

I could not help smiling. I explained that she was entitled to criticize the government for not allowing demonstrations on 1 May, but that once a demonstration was *prohibited*, even in the most blameless of democracies, those who defy the prohibition are taken to the police station and kept there for a few hours. The young woman looked at me with hostility. This accusation had been one of her strong cards against the regime, and I had just torn it to pieces.

Let us go back to the camps which operated until the end of 1975. A thousand horrifying stories went the rounds about them, with such copious details that I admit that I was taken in by them myself. But my enquiries give the lie to this fabricated demonology. I am not talking about the famous sports stadium belonging to the armed forces which was used for the first two months as a provisional clearing-house for those arrested before they were sorted out, and where nothing at all happened except the inevitable overcrowding, and the obligation on the officers living in the area *to give up their apartments to house the Allende leaders*. There were seven camps, the three main ones, through which 80% of internees passed, being at Chacabuco in the north, Tres Álamos 15 kilometres from Santiago, and Dawson Island, for the leaders, in the far south.

We have a report on Chacabuco from *El Mercurio* (always extremely objective in its reporting), dated 3 March 1974, written in collaboration with two foreign journalists, an American and an Austrian, who have never denied a line of it. Chacabuco had been built originally to provide lodging for the workers and technicians of the old magnesium sulphate mines, which had been abandoned 35 years previously. The little cottages had, however, remained habitable, and were used to house the prisoners. The report gives full details of how they lived, and the classic picture emerges of a strict but humane internment camp, like those, for example, organized by civilised countries at the outbreak of a war for confining the nationals of countries that had become the enemy. In fact, the French camp for German internees at Gurs, which I knew in 1940, was worse. In the camp at Chacabuco the food was adequate; the work bearable; there were workshops for voluntary craftwork, and medical facilities were satisfactory.

I gathered evidence on Dawson Island from several people who lived in the area and often visited the prisoners, who, being UP leaders, were allowed individual cells in clean, heated huts, with reading and television rooms and a sports ground. A nearby hotel had been requisitioned to put up wives visiting their husbands. I have in front of me three photos showing Mr. Luis Corvalan, well-dressed, merrily chatting behind the barbed wire, together with his wife and children. In a letter to his niece, the uncle of a Chilean friend of mine asked for some flower seedlings, as a group of internees had decided to form a horticultural team. Parcels from friends and acquaintances were distributed regularly. Obviously, none of this changed a place of enforced detention into an idyllic holiday resort, but it did make for something infinitely different from the horrific concentration camps of the Hitler regime and the communist Gulags.

As for the Tres Álamos camp, I visited it personally because it has remained intact, having been converted into a detention camp for juvenile delinquents. I took numerous photos. The whole camp is surrounded by a man-high fence topped by three rows of barbed wire, making it up to two metres in height. A single watch-tower serves the whole area of 7½ acres. Any three-man commando of political prisoners could easily have surmounted this barrier. If no one tried to escape, it was because the UP combatants knew they would be exposed to the hatred of the public once outside the camp. The detainees slept in bunk beds, four men to a room nine metres square with a big window. I have a photo of one, and also of the clean, well-lit refectory. I have a photo of the combined sports ground, catering for football, rugby and tennis and with a running track. I have a photo of the meadow, still lined with the same barbecues, where the prisoners could receive their families for a picnic on Sundays. Here too, there was nothing, truly nothing, comparable with the hellish death-camps of Hitler's Germany, Soviet Russia or the Cambodia of Pol Pot. Here, too, the evidence forced itself upon me. Bloody battles were indeed fought. There was massive repression. But the battles and repression were carried out in the way this is done in civilised societies. At no time during these Chilean engagements did the authorities attempt to exterminate, or even dehumanize, their opponents.

Moreover we have proof of the truth of this evaluation. The leader of the Chilean Communist Party, Mr. Luis Corvalán, as is well known, was exchanged by General Pinochet for the Soviet dissident Mr. Vladimir Bukovsky; when he arrived in Moscow, in perfect physical condition, he was asked about his stay on Dawson Island. Far from making a horror-story of it, as did all Soviet dissidents who had escaped from the gulags, he avoided making any precise reply, and merely side-stepped the question by saying: "Oh, it was just a camp."

Yes, a camp. But one inside which life was liveable. A thousand leagues separate it from Vorkuta or Buchenwald, and even from the Cuban gaols in which Major Hubert Matos rotted for 20 years, seven of them without seeing a single visitor, and in which he lost the use of an arm through the beatings he was subjected to.

Amongst the slanders spread about the Pinochet regime, I have mentioned the flagrant lie of an émigrée about her husband being tortured to death when in fact he was found in perfect health in Santiago. Two other instances of obvious fabrications about torture can be found in Hugues Kéraly's article in *Itinêraires*, which I shall refer to later in the context of the disappearances. The author even refers to a *Manual of torture stories*, which the MIR had prepared for use by those of its militants who might find themselves in prison for acts of terrorism. In it, imaginary situations were built up crammed with those famous physiologically plausible details "which couldn't have been made up".

If such a manual, in fact, existed, it would not seem that the English doctor, Miss Sheila Cassidy, based her own "revelations" on it. The case involving her is, in fact, the most suspect as well as the most famous of those highlighted by the leftist media. On 18 October 1975, a police assault was mounted against the Santa Eugenia district, in the Malloco suburbs, where information received had led the authorities to believe that a secret MIR cell was operating. Indeed, as soon as they came within range, the carabineros were greeted with heavy fire. After a half-hour's battle resulting in two deaths, the police were able to surround and seize the premises, and found, besides a store of arms and pamphlets, several terrorists. But their leader, Mr. Nelson Gutierrez, had managed to escape, even though wounded in the leg. He was found some days later at the convent of the nuns of Notre-Dame at 1128 Orellana Street, being tended by a doctor who gave her name as Sheila Cassidy, of English nationality, who had come to Chile, she said, to take the veil (rather a long way to go, considering that her congregation had a house in England). Although the police were forced to storm this convent too, they left the doctor unmolested, arresting only the Mirist leader. But the doctor, at whose private address MIR literature and a revolver were found, was worried, and asked the fathers of another Irish religious order to shelter her at their house at 350, Dr. Larrain-Gandarillas Street. What she did not know was that this order was being closely watched by the police because of the constant help it gave to terrorists. There was a police assault on her third hiding-place, during which the doctor herself used a rifle, seriously wounding a policeman. The caretaker of the building was killed during the firing.

The investigations into the charges against Miss Cassidy lasted two months. On 29 December 1975 she was expelled from the country with a safe-conduct. It is at this point that the noisy exploitation of the affair for propaganda purposes began. The doctor was hardly back in Britain when she claimed that she had been abominably tortured; flogged and several times subjected to the agony of electrodes applied to her vagina, leaving her with deep bruises. She said that she had had to crawl to board the aeroplane which brought her back. As one would expect, public opinion in Britain was aroused. The Chilean government issued the most categorical of denials. The doctor persisted in her allegations. The campaign snowballed to the point where Her Majesty's government recalled its ambassador to Santiago for consultation. There was one discordant fact, though no one appeared to notice it: the doctor refused—for reasons of self-respect, she said—to be examined, at the Chilean government's expense, by doctors whom Gen. Pinochet offered to pick at random from the medical academies *of three neutral countries.* The pretext was an absurd one: how could her self-respect be compromised by having it confirmed that she had been subjected to such atrocities by such a barbarian regime? Nor can one believe that a person who was a doctor, and who had told the whole world about her vagina, could have been deterred from undergoing a medical examination purely out of modesty. Imagine the terrific blow she would have dealt Gen. Pinochet if she could have produced confirmation of her charge, signed with the names of eminent doctors who were above all suspicion!

When I went to Santiago and got from Teresa Donoso the book which I have already mentioned about the collaboration of numerous churchmen with the Marxists, I found reproduced on page 264 a sort of little ode in prose composed by the auxiliary bishop of Santiago, Jorge Hourton, and published on 11 January 1976 in *Comunidad Cristiana*, a weekly supplement to the *Iglesia de Santiago*, the official magazine of the archdiocese. What did this ode say? It was entitled: 'Farewell to Dr. Sheila Cassidy'. Amongst other lyric outpourings I read: "We went with her to her plane, on the 29th, on a radiant sunlit evening. Happily, she got into the bus which was to take her to the plane. She held out her arms and broke into a joyful laugh in reply to her friends' affectionate farewells." This description is clearly incompatible with the stories of a pitiable woman, stiff-jointed and almost crippled as a result of the tortures she had undergone. I immediately became certain that Dr. Sheila Cassidy had lied.

Three further thoughts occurred to me. The date of this affair in which our pious firebrand of a doctor was implicated shows that her resistance to the military coup was not just a sudden impulse. For by the end of 1975 only the toughest and most committed elements of the MIR were still continuing the violent struggle, and it was among these that she was discovered. On the other hand, note that a text in praise of a foreigner who did not deny her ties with the terrorists of the extreme left, and who fired shots at General Pinochet's police, was free to appear in an official church magazine in Santiago without any unpleasant consequences for its author. We have only to imagine such a lyrical text written about Bukovsky (no irregular guerilla-fighter, he) on his departure from the country, and printed in a Soviet magazine; the magazine's editor would have found himself in prison. My third thought: what sudden fit of lunacy could have come over the Chilean police for them to expel from the country a woman whom they had fearsomely tortured, when there was nothing in the world to stop them from holding her?

This obviously rigged affair, together with others of the same type which I do not have space to analyse here, lead me to think that the Pinochet regime did not have recourse to torture. To be sure, one cannot rule out the possibility that during the months of violent civil disturbances, some local minor leaders may have indulged in acts of abominable cruelty towards adversaries captured arms in hand. Exactly the same thing could have happened the other way round. But systematic torture once calm was restored, no.

It is very difficult, as is well known, to prove innocence, i.e. to establish that so-and-so did not do such-and-such a thing. That is why the law puts the burden of proof onto the prosecution. Up till now, no opponent of the Pinochet regime has produced trustworthy proof that its police regularly uses torture.

The disappearances

The most virulent campaign against the Pinochet regime was the one involving the much talked-of disappearances. According to the picture repeated a thousand times by left-wing-and other-media throughout the world, opponents of the regime were taken away, without arrest warrants, in sinister raids by the political police, after which the unfortunate creatures disappeared from the land of the living without anyone knowing what had become of them. It was understood that the police had either killed them in some subterranean dungeon, or were holding them incommunicado in impenetrable oubliettes. The sorrowing families, the Church and lawyers all asked the authorities to make enquiries, but nothing ever came of it.

So one of my first tasks on landing in Santiago in September 1978 was to contact the Vicaria de la Solidaridad (Solidarity Vicariate), a service offered by the archbishopric and run by progressive religious persons who have undertaken the defence of missing persons; it publishes a magazine, *Solidaridad*, filled with violent attacks on the Pinochet regime. (Ah, what wouldn't one give to be able to interview such a Vicariate in Moscow!)

I had come ready with the latest figures for missing persons, which, as given by Mr. Rosalynn Carter, stood at 2,500, a considerably lower figure than that bandied around by the media, which averaged generally about 15,000. My first surprise came when I found that the Vicaria claims concerned only 651 cases of missing persons. Thus, right at the outset the number of missing persons had fallen from 15,000 to 651. 14,349 persons had un-disappeared!

My interlocutors at the Vicaria and I soon agreed that the reported disappearances fell into two very different categories. On the one hand there were those which had happened during the civil war, and about whom it was impossible to establish by documentary proof how, from where or when the person presumed missing had passed into the world of those having no official existence. On the other hand were those who had been officially arrested, the date and place of their imprisonment and the reason for it being known, but who had disappeared afterwards; that is to say, they had been seen in jail by visitors or by fellow-prisoners, but no news of them had been received subsequently. I shall deal separately with those people missing "from prison" later, and will concern myself first of all with the earlier category of those missing for whom no precise details exist.

My interlocutors at the Vicaria did not conceal the fact that this category was a very confused and obscure one. Disappearances dating back to the height of the civil war could obviously not be taken into account. Men are always disappearing in the chaos of the fighting, killed, in hiding, or escaping abroad. No reliance can be placed on a story told five years after the event about the exact movements of a given combatant. The same is true, more or less, of the stories spread around about secret arrests: "a black car came while I was out, some policemen got out and my husband (or father, or cousin, or friend) was taken away"; or else "the telephone rang, my husband (or father, or cousin, or friend) was asked to go to an office, we don't know which, and he never came back"; "my husband (or father, or cousin, or friend) got on the train, I saw some policemen on the platform, and I never saw him again", etc. There can be absolutely no proof that scenes of this type actually took place; they could quite easily have been made up, from beginning to end, by the propaganda co-ordinators of the Communist Party, and retold on their orders by wives, cousins or friends who also belonged to the Party. For whenever, in cases of this type, the authorities have asked for the co-operation of the family or friends in order to reconstruct the details of what happened, the latter have always side-stepped the request; this has meant that the courts, in the 23 judgements mentioned to me, have had no alternative but to reject the complaint.

If there really were any disappearances, there is absolutely nothing to show that they were not the disappearances of people who wanted to leave their homes once and for all. I telephoned the Ministry of the Interior in Paris, and discovered that there are about 6,000 missing persons a year in France! (That is, out of 19,000 cases reported to the police, only 13,000 are found.) By comparison with these 6,000 annual disappearances in France, 650 unexplained disappearances in five years in Chile are clearly insufficient grounds for accusing a whole regime of riding rough-shod over human rights.

Mr. Barboza, a Santiago barrister hostile to the Pinochet regime, and who had assembled a group of lawyers to study a democratic constitution, told me that some of the "missing persons" were quite simply husbands who had left home. He was, indeed, representing at the time a woman who knew perfectly well that her husband was in Argentina, but preferred to claim that he had "disappeared", because this would entitle her to a state pension straight away. I would add that in the case of Marxist-Leninist terrorists it was often more convenient for the family to confuse the issue and disguise the voluntary, illegal flight as a disappearance brought about by a repressive regime.

To increase the confusion even further, many Chilean followers of Mr. Allende had multiple identities, each one complete with official papers forged while their regime was in power. It is estimated that the UP offices made out 150,000 false identity cards for its Chilean or foreign supporters. Obviously, this made it possible for a person to assume a variety of aliases. For example, Mr. José Castillo, a well-known trade union leader, told me that he had been associated for a time with a certain Mr. Andrés Savella, a Socialist, who turned out in fact to be the same man as a Mr. Manuel Rojas who had been declared missing. Mr. José Castillo met him one day, clearly alive and kicking. This same man possessed a third identity under the name of Mr. Victor Domingo Silva.

It so happens that I was able to judge for myself how misleading some of the files on "missing persons" were. When I went to see her, the Minister of Justice was, in fact, right in the middle of a file on an affair which was causing quite a stir in Switzerland, and which she showed me. A man from Geneva, Mr. Jaccard by name, was travelling via Buenos Aires to Chile to visit his parents who lived there. When he did not arrive, the latter made inquiries and discovered—to use the version that we may call "the plaintiffs"—that Mr. Jaccard, had, it was alleged, been arrested at Mendoza in Argentina by the Argentinian police at the request of the Chilean police. The fact that these two police forces should both be looking for him suggests that he was connected with the world communist apparatus working against the Chilean and Argentinian presidents. What made me smile was the idea of the Argentinian police handing him over to the Chileans, for at the time, the two countries were on the point of going to war over the islands in the Beagle Straits. But let us continue.

Thereupon, according to the plaintiffs, Mr. Jaccard was transported to the border and handed over to the Chilean carabineros; and there were witnesses to the scene. Feeling that the whole weight of the accusation lay there, and that these witnesses represented the only thread by which it was possible to trace events back to their source, the Minister of Justice wrote to the plaintiffs' lawyer, asking for the names and addresses of these witnesses. What was the lawyer's reply? I'll give you three guesses. In a letter which I have read over and over again, he answered that it was with regret that he was unable to supply any of this information! "How can I possibly investigate this case?" sighed the Minister.

The person I spoke to at the Vicaria admitted finally that stories of this sort could not be used as the basis for any serious conclusion. So he fell back onto the disappearances of the second type, those assumed to have happened following the known and recorded imprisonment of the missing person, for in those cases the plaintiffs have what appears to be convincing documentation at their disposition: legally authenticated statements from identified witnesses, affirming that they had seen Mr. X in prison until a certain date, but had not seen him since, and that the authorities had refused to give any indication as to what had become of him.

Now, when I questioned Mr. Rillon, a legal expert who was in charge of the human rights section of the Ministry of Foreign Affairs, about these rather more worrying cases, he revealed to me that in all the cases submitted to the Ministry of the Interior, the sworn statements had been made by anti-Pinochet emigrés before foreign commissioners for oaths, in Holland, Sweden, East Germany, etc. Such statements have absolutely no legal value, first of all because there is no way of confronting their authors with other witnesses, nor of submitting the concrete details to analysis with a view to corroboration, as is the rule in any legal system, and also because the people who made the statements were committed militants and obviously quite prepared, in view of the impunity they enjoyed thanks to being in exile, to put their signatures to any lie capable of harming their hated enemy. Such persons, moreover, do not consider false statements made in the service of the Communist Party as in any way blameworthy. There are well-known Leninist texts making such an action binding in honour on all true revolutionaries. They are at war, and in time of war a committed soldier does not hesitate to use deception to mislead the enemy.

In most of the cases which Mr. Rillon was able to investigate, the alleged "missing person" turned out, quite simply, to have been released from prison in a perfectly normal way. To which the accusers replied that he had indeed been released from his cell, and had been taken as far as the prison gate, but that as soon as he had passed through it, another group of policemen concealed outside had seized him again and taken him away to an unknown destination. Clearly, on that basis, that is, in the absence of any possible proof, one can say anything one likes and continue to protest indefinitely. In other cases, the authorities quite simply could find no trace of the alleged imprisonment. This was perhaps because aliases were being used, or because these were cases of irregular, indiscriminate arrests made during the civil war; they may even have been pure and simple invention.

There was another odd thing. Even in the murky totalitarianism of the Soviet Union, which can make use of terror and the vastness of the Siberian wastes to hide its crimes from public knowledge, the misdeeds of the secret police are always found out in the end. The sheer impossibility of total concealment meant that it always became known, in the end, that a given prisoner had been killed by a bullet in the back of the neck, another sent to such-and-such a camp, another to a mental asylum, and yet another buried in such-and-such a spot. How is it then that in Chile the accusers have no concrete details, let alone rumours, that they can spread about the fate of people who have disappeared while in prison? If they were killed, they must have been buried or burned; in that case, wherever the grave or the crematorium is, it is just not possible that no one—a tramp, a postman, a hunter, a road-mender, some shepherd, camper or lumberjack—saw anything suspicious, which they would obviously tell to those around them; or that the undertakers themselves, even if they were policemen, never breathed a word to their friends, acquaintances or landladies. Tales of this kind, even if only whispered, would inevitably have spread through the bush telegraph. Yet nothing, emphatically nothing, has come to light over a period of years. Knowing that these hundreds of burials could not have taken place totally unnoticed, the Vacaria, in my presence, adopted the notion that *the missing persons were possibly not dead and would one day be seen again alive.* In that case they must have been locked up in hiding-places for years, and it is even more unlikely that these could have operated for so long, with so many people shut up, without anybody in the whole length and breadth of the land, ever noticing something fishy.

Thus in the end, by the time I had completed my enquiry, this second category—people missing from prison—proved as lacking in hard, provable facts as the first. One possible exception might be the following affair, though it is not one that Gen. Pinochet's opponents care to boast about. In 1976 the veteran Communist Mr. David Silberman was in prison on several charges. One day, a trio of very official-looking civilians appeared to take him away, stating that the colonel of the CID wanted to question him. They produced an authorization which was perfectly in order. The prison governor rang the number the trio gave him to check. The colonel answered the phone and confirmed the order. The prison governor let Mr. Silberman go with the three. *He was never seen again.* When checks were made, it was found that the stamps on the authorization were forged and the telephone number was that of a public call-box. The prison governor was prosecuted for negligence, and Mr. David Silberman is still on the Vicaria's list of missing persons. He has indeed disappeared, but if you want to find him again, you must make enquiries not at the Ministry of the Interior, but in the secret communist network.

An organisation considered a priori to be beyond reproach, Amnesty International, has been caught in the act of lying on this very subject of the Chilean disappearances. On page 20 of its edition of 29 March 1979, the weekly paper *Télérama* published an article by Mr. Jacques Marquis entitled: The Chilean Face of Barbarism, in which the author recalls and comments on eleven recent cases of arrest, followed by torture and disappearance, culled with all the details, from Amnesty International's so-called 'Circulars for urgent action'. One can judge the flavour of the article from its conclusion: "Now," writes M. Marquis, "imagine the most sadistic refinements possible, graft these on to the process, and you will still be far short of the truth about the journeys to the far side of horror made by thousands of men and women in Chile every day."

Now at the time this revelation appeared, and it was of course widely amplified by the media, a Catholic journalist, Mr. Hugues Kéraly, was packing his bags for a study trip to Chile. He determined to track down these eleven cases, and used most of his time in April 1978 to this purpose. He published his results in the June 1978 issue (No. 224) of the monthly review *Itinéraires*, which is directed by the famous theologian Mr. Jean Madiran, on whose moral integrity no one has ever, to my knowledge, cast doubt.

Mr. Kéraly's conclusions amazed even me, and I consider myself pretty blasé where lies favourable to Communism are concerned: *all* of the latest disappearances reported by Amnesty, all, do you hear, without a single exception, that is, eleven out of the eleven, proved to be *false*. The only true fact in the whole business was that on 16, 17 and 18 January 1978 the police did indeed raid several MIR strong-points, just as police forces throughout the world should do to all *terrorist* cells, and they did, in fact, find a large quantity of arms, ammunition and inflammatory pamphlets there; one of these operations turned into a bloody battle in which the Mirist leader Mr. German de Jesus Cortez Rodriguez met his death weapons in hand, and was not arrested only to disappear later, as Amnesty International maintains. One of the women mentioned was never arrested either, and was found to have emigrated to Havana, from where she sends back communiqués and signed letters to her friends in Chile. Five other women also mentioned by Amnesty as missing were traced by Mr. Kéraly with no difficulty, and found in good health in a women's prison run by nuns, where visits, correspondence and the attendance of doctors and lawyers are very easy to arrange. It is in connection with two of these women that Mr. Kéraly shows how totally incredible the accounts of their torture were. All these prisoners were awaiting trial, like their fellows in the Baader-Meinhoff gang in Germany, the Red Brigade in Italy, the Corsican terrorists in France and the IRA in Britain, etc. Amnesty went so far as to accuse the Chilean police of the cruel treatment of the eight-month-old baby of one of these women, cruelty which brought on pneumonia; the baby was supposed to have disappeared, too. Mr. Hugues Kéraly found him in a hospital, being given the best possible care for a congenital kidney condition. In short, I repeat, out of the eleven allegations of disappearances, all eleven were lies!

Let it not be said that this is just an exceptional combination of accidental errors. Calculation of the probabilities shows that if eleven out of eleven weighings made on a particular set of scales are inaccurate, then the probabilities are more than 100,000 to one against this being chance, and that the scales can be relied on to weigh accurately in other cases. If Amnesty claims that its good faith has been abused, then one wonders what value to attach to its famous claim that it takes particular care to investigate each of its cases. It is true that the director of its research department, centred in London, is a Dr. Roebuck, who has been exposed as a member of the *Communist* Party in Australia.

A new attack on the theme of the missing persons was launched at the end of 1978, when a charnel-house of 15 unidentified bodies was discovered in a lime quarry at Lonquen, 60 kilometres from Santiago. The Pinochet government did not react like a despotic power, but fulfilled all the requirements of the law. It insisted that a thorough inquiry should be carried out by the Supreme Court. The latter nominated Mr. Banados as the examining magistrate, and he left no stone unturned. The bodies could be seen by anyone claiming to be able to find some sign by which they could be recognised. Numerous experts were consulted. In the end, Judge Banados established in July 1979 that 11 of these 15 bodies were those of a group of extremist terrorists of the neighbourhood, whom the local lieutenant of carabineros, Lautaro Castro, had, during the fighting in the autumn of 1973, been ordered to take to the clearing-camp at the sports stadium. They never arrived. Judge Banados concluded that the eight carabineros who, under Lautaro Castro's orders, had made the arrests on 14 October 1973, had killed them on the way to the stadium and thrown their bodies into the quarry. The Pinochet government *arrested* the carabineros and their captain and stripped them of their rank. Later they benefited from the 1978 general amnesty, which had been made applicable to terrorists as well as to soldiers guilty of excesses during the civil war.

So there was indeed, in this case, an instance of "missing persons" in the sense in which the term was used by Gen. Pinochet's accusers, but in a context which fits in with the hypotheses which I have considered probable: it was a question of a settling of scores during the fiercest period of the civil war—October 1973—between local enemies, with no encouragement from higher authority. The Pinochet government, so far from hushing up the affair, did its best to throw all possible light on it, published the judge's report and took sanctions against the guilty.

Another false report: on 18 February 1980 a reporter discovered one of the 651 "official" missing persons, by the name of Mr. Juan Chacon, working in an isolated village in the south. He had been arrested three years before for theft, but because of insufficient evidence the judge had released him. Whereupon Mr. Chacon had decided to leave home. His wife did not know of his arrest but, knowing that he had previously been a militant in the UP, sincerely believed that he had been imprisoned, and the priest in whom she had confided sent his name to the Vicaria with no further investigation, and there it was entered on the "carefully documented" list. His wife then received substantial aid from an international association giving help to missing persons.

To sum up: so far no one has produced any serious proof in support of the accusation that, once peace had been restored and because the government wanted it, the Pinochet regime had political enemies arrested and made them disappear into thin air. Simple logic drives me to the conclusion that the Pinochet regime is not guilty of this crime. One merely has to ask oneself what their motives could have been for carrying out such a policy. All the missing people were unimportant nobodies; no doubt they almost all turned out to be left-wing extremists, when it has been possible to discover their political attitude, but they were very minor extremists. Now Gen. Pinochet arrested hundreds of extremist opponents who were considerably more active and more dangerous, and has since either released; pardoned or exiled them, thus allowing them to continue an effective opposition to him.

No, this story definitely does not stand up to analysis. The most credible explanation is that the people labelled "missing" by the propaganda campaign either went missing during the 1973–74 civil war, or never existed at all—since they were simply aliases—or have run away for private reasons, or again and above all, have been militants ordered by the party's parallel underground organization to become "sleepers" until given the order to join the secret terrorist networks. They have obeyed and disappeared, in fact, into the underground networks in Chile or abroad in order to fulfil the needs of the illegal struggle, often without a word to their nearest and dearest. The

Party, adept at passing the buck, takes advantage of the disappearances which it has itself contrived, to blame them on its enemy.

If this type of machination surprises you, it is because you still have a lot to learn about the Machiavellian techniques of Leninism.

The UN investigation

Numerous complaints were made against the Pinochet regime and its repressive nature to the relevant United Nations Commission, alleging that it was violating human rights. Although many of these complaints were discredited by the unworthiness of the complainants, most of whom habitually violated human rights in their own countries far more seriously than Chile did, Chile allowed representatives from this Commission to come and make enquiries on its soil. Before analysing its conclusions, it is important to emphasize that this attitude of Chile is unique in the records of the UN. So far, no important nation has ever managed thus to overcome that jealous regard for its own sovereignty which makes it jib at the mere idea of foreign eyes, any eyes at all except those of its own judges, prying into its domestic affairs. The communist regimes, so notorious for their infringements of human rights, erect such impregnable barriers around themselves that no outside body has ever dared ask them for permission to come and inspect anything, certain as it is of being rudely refused before finishing the sentence. It was quite as unthinkable in the case of Nazi Germany.

By contrast, Gen. Pinochet opened Chile's gates wide to the Commission, even though it came from the regime's declared enemies. The Senegalese chairman of the Commission of Inquiry, Mr. Abdoulaye Dieye, was honest enough to acknowledge this demonstration of good faith when expressing his gratitude to Gen. Pinochet at the end of his inquiry. He admitted that he had been able to visit all the persons and places he had wanted to without the slightest official interference. Moreover, this Commission was not the only outside body that came to investigate human rights on the spot in Chile. There was also one from Amnesty International, one from the International Association of Jurists, one from the Red Cross and one from the American AFL.-CIO.

This having been said (and it needed emphasizing), let us see what elements the UN gathered together upon which to form its judgement after the expenditure of so much hot air. The visit took place in February 1978, and it took a whole year for its five members to write their report, which appeared on 1 February 1979 with the number E/CN04/1310. I have read it from cover to cover. The whole Chilean press published very objective summaries of its findings, which, it must be said, represent no great danger to the regime, since they add up to practically nothing.

On the main subject, that of "missing persons", the report quotes numerous examples, but (and this has to be seen to be believed) all the names and addresses and most of the dates are omitted. It cannot be claimed that this discretion was necessary to protect those concerned from reprisals, since in theory they are already past caring, having long ago been snatched into the black hole of non-existence by the police. When dates are given, they are all from a long time ago; there are none later than June 1976. In the five to ten lines devoted to each case quoted, the conditions under which the disappearance took place are sketched in such an elliptical way that nothing can be understood. To my great surprise, I found very few from what I have called the second category, the only one with a basis which might possibly be valid, that of persons missing from prison.

The report's authors believed that they were making up for these deficiencies by including the dramatic letter sent to Gen. Pinochet on 9 November 1978 (i.e. *after* their visit) by ten assistant priests and the archbishop of Santiago, Msgr. Silva, the great friend of Mr. Allende and Fidel Castro. The letter too was reproduced widely in the Chilean press, (and once again I cannot help asking the reader if he can imagine the equivalent happening in Moscow . . .). In this letter, the signatories say that they enclose the list of the 651 "missing persons" which the UN report does not reproduce. Surely this letter from the eleven assistant priests provides adequate documentation for the charges?

Unfortunately it does not. As a letter, it is extremely confused. As its principle evidence it offers phrases such as . . . "public outcry", the "spontaneous agreement", and the "drama that everyone agreed had taken place". Unlike the UN report, the priests' letter does give names. In reply to the authorities' argument that they were never given the details necessary to enable them to shed light on the cases and to investigate each one fully, the letter mentions 60 cases, using the following imprecise form of words: "It should be easily possible to question X (a government servant) about the position of Z (an opponent)." Nothing more. This does at first sight seem to provide at least some factual data to work on, and so we eagerly work through the list. But we then find that the persecuted Zs are mentioned by name, whereas the persecutors, the Xs, are only referred to by the position they held, several years previously, and no name is given; 50 times out of the 60 there is no date either, which means that it is not even possible to check back to the identity of X, the government agents, for they may well have since been transferred. In the ten references to Xs "who know . . . (what has happened to Z)" where the authors do give a date, we note that it is during the spring of 1974, i.e. at the height of the civil war, when anything could have happened, in either direction, and nothing can now be proved.

On the subject of torture, the report is even less convincing. It mentions just one case, yes, just one, that of Mr. Pizarro Vallejos, and here their luck has really deserted them, for he is free, and no trace of torture has ever been found on him.

The report roundly criticizes the action of the government in disbanding some trade unions without a single line to a consideration of the reason it gave for this, which was that they were dictatorially controlled by Communists. There is not a word about those unions—and there are far more of them—which have continued to operate, albeit with limited rights; I shall come back to this later. Talking about the new leaders in some unions, who should have been elected and who were, it is true, nominated, the report analyzes in depth their origins, political stance and affiliations so as to make sure, magnifying glass in hand, whether they had any illicit ties with the regime. How one wishes the UN would carry out a similar meticulous investigation into Cuban and Soviet unions!

That is not all. Since the investigators could find nothing important to say on the subjects that formed their terms of reference—repression, torture and missing persons—well, they filled their report with snippets of scandal from any other area that occurred to them. A large number of pages are devoted to unemployment, wage/price indices and health conditions, as if, even if there were shortcomings in these fields (and what country does not have them?), this had anything to do with human rights. They even descend to discussing the lot of rural workers, and the state of the transport system and municipal budgets, which were apparently not in a very healthy condition!

Clearly they were nit-picking: any stick was good enough for them to beat Gen. Pinochet with. It takes the UN to dream up the idea of quoting broken-down buses or overspent town-halls as "violations of human rights"!

If an articled clerk in the first year of his legal apprenticeship presented such a document to his principal to use in his brief, he would immediately be sacked.

CHAPTER XVII

THE PRESENT POLITICAL SITUATION

The Referendum

In December 1977 the Pinochet Government, weary of being labelled "Fascist", and heartened by increasing prosperity, launched a referendum on the following question: "In the face of international aggression against the Government of our country, I support President Pinochet in his defence of the dignity of the country, and I reaffirm this Government's right to create new institutions for the country."

Opponents would, of course, allege immediately that Gen. Pinochet would rig the referendum. In fact, the campaign was freely conducted by both sides, to the extent that, political parties on both sides being still forbidden, expressions of opinion for and against were signed by individuals or by ad hoc groupings. Numerous proclamations appeared in the press in favour of a vote against, or advocating abstention (the position taken up by Mr. Eduardo Frei). Many appeals and interviews on radio and television also advised a vote *against*. There were even street marches *against*. There were no meetings, either *for* or *against*, because all political meetings were still banned. In a report seen on French television from a French journalist, M. Dieuleveut, Chileans picked out at random on the streets of Santiago were seen answering, without any sign of fear, that they would be voting *against*. In general it was a properly conducted campaign, giving equal chances to both sides. The electoral law itself was honoured; 150 foreign journalists, together with 100 specially invited diplomats from the Organisation of American States, monitored the processes of balloting and vote counting carefully. There was no indication of any kind of coercion or of rigging. These were the results on the evening of 4 January 1978. 11% abstentions, in fact a remarkable result in view of Frei's recommendation in favour of abstention. The votes were as follows:

4·7% of blank or invalid votes, a normal percentage

75% in favour

20% against

Which of the Communist or pro-Communist governments who accuse Gen. Pinochet could claim as much? Such countries have never offered anything other than elections with only one candidate, with no right of reply whatsoever for the opposition, and resulting in a 99·9%

poll with 99·7% in favour. How can one speak of Fascism when 20% of the population is perfectly free to vote against the government?

For myself, I consider that the result of the referendum reflected very accurately the state of mind of the Chileans at the time. Given that the military regime had saved the country from unprecedented economic disaster and political hell, given that it had restored a desperate financial situation, given that it allowed the people to live in peace and without fear, in contrast to Mr. Allende who had plunged the country into lawlessness and violence, it is not in the least surprising that 75% of the people should have expressed their confidence in Gen. Pinochet and that the whole of the opposition should only attract 20% of the population. This is a valid indication.

Liberalism

A normal dictatorial regime, finding itself thus legitimised by an undoubted popular concensus, would have profited by turning the screw and by trying to crush the opposition completely. With Gen. Pinochet, it was the reverse. Feeling himself to be more certain of his power, he launched a substantial political liberalisation. On 5 March 1978, he swept away the last remnants of the state of siege. On 4 April, he decreed a general amnesty for political prisoners. On 5 May, he granted the right, to any exile who should request it and who would undertake to renounce opposition to the government by means of joining armed subversive groups, to return to his country. Up to the present, several hundred emigrés, among them political leaders such as Mr. Jaime Castillo, Mr. Leighton, Mr. Velasco, Christian Democrats or Radicals, have asked to take advantage of this concession and have returned to this "Fascist" country. How many well known Soviet dissidents have returned to the USSR? None.

Further liberalisation measures: on 1 June, the Enrique Ortuzar Commission, was established charged with the preparation of a new constitution to include the restoration of elections, of political parties and of parliamentary activity. In July, a commission of jurists and lawyers was set up to draw up modern liberal reforms of the Penal Code and of prison conditions, which Mr. Allende had allowed to stagnate. Finally, on 8 August, DINA, the secret police which had led the repression was abolished.

On the eve of my arrival in Santiago, on 1 September 1978, the first signs of activity in the workers' movement since the military takeover had broken out in the copper mines of Chuquicamata. Calling for an increase in wages and a reduction in working hours, workers at several levels and in some workshops had occupied the canteen; refused their meals, and then stayed put without returning to work. Naturally I was much interested to see what would be the government's response; I expected it to be harsh.

I was amazed to read, the following day, in *El Mercurio*, the complete statement of the trade unions of Chuquicamata—so trade unions still existed—setting out starkly the workers' grievances and roundly reproaching the government for paying no attention to them. On Saturday 9 September, in its main daily morning news bulletin of 8–9 a.m., the radio station *Co-operativa Vitalicia* put out a broadcast so strongly hostile to the Pinochet government that after a few minutes, unable to believe my ears, I took out my pencil to write it down. Here is the text: "The workers are disgusted with the declaration of the Minister of Finance, M. de Castro, alleging that they belong to a comparatively privileged class . . . Let not the government think that it is sufficient to label the workers' actions as 'Communist' in order to stifle their voices; if the Communists can give effective assistance in the achievement of our legitimate claims, the trade unions will collaborate with them."

The reference to the government's abuse of the label "Communist" is explained by the fact that on 5 September, although up to that date the strike movement had been left alone, communist pamphlets appeared in the mine and in the village, with the consequence that eight miners, already known to be veteran Communists, and one of whom held an important administrative position, had been arrested. They were put under house arrest. The episode ended in a compromise, and by the time I left the country all the activists who had been arrested had been released without any charges being made against them. In the USSR, such an incident would have been bloodily suppressed, and those responsible would have been imprisoned in hard labour camps. The most important newspaper in the capital could never have allowed them to use its columns, as in Santiago.

It is certainly regrettable that eight striking miners should have been arrested. But in comparing Gen. Pinochet's response to the Chuquicamata strike with that of the Allende government to the strikes of October 1972, it is clear that the Socialists' repression of the workers was much more severe than that of the general. Gen. Pinochet did not dismiss a single worker, while Mr. Allende ruthlessly threw out on the street the officials who had supported the movement, among them 28 employees of the Central Bank and 70 workers in the state railways, and under Gen. Pinochet not a single striker was injured.

After my astonishment at this airing of accusations against the allegedly dictatorial Pinochet Government, I was no longer surprised by the many other examples which I saw every day of the freedom to criticise which exists in Chile. Firstly I discovered the *Vicaria de la Solidaridad*, of which I have already spoken, powerful, well organised, and very vociferous in public. Then I found the magazine *Hoy*, and brought back several issues to France. It comes out every week, with 64 profusely illustrated pages, and 30,000 copies are freely on sale through subscription and on newspaper stalls. Its criticisms of the military government are at least as sharp and detailed as those which were directed every week at the Giscard Government in France by our own *Nouvel Observateur*. Incidentally, the *Nouvel Observateur* is also freely on sale in Santiago.

After my departure, some friends sent me two issues of *Hoy* which carried two interviews—with whom?—you will never guess: one with the Marxist-Leninist Mr. Altamirano, ex-Secretary-General of the Socialist Party, condemned for high treason, and the other with Mr. Almeyda, Mr. Allende's ex-Minister of Foreign Affairs. Under the pretext of commenting on the projected constitution, these two leaders were, in fact, calling for a revolt against Gen. Pinochet. Despite the fact that the Chilean press had been allowed a large measure of freedom of expression, there was a specific decree forbidding statements by the heads of the parties which had dragged Chile towards totalitarianism. *Hoy* had, therefore, broken the law. The government suspended the weekly for two months, and immediately there were protests from all quarters.

This incident is a good illustration of the limits on the liberty of the press at present in force in Chile. These limits do exist, but they are very liberal. Here are some further examples. The Jesuit monthly, *Mensaje*, is an opposition paper which circulates freely in Chile. In the rest of the press, including *El Mercurio*, some 75% of the articles are favourable to official actions and about 25% are critical or directly hostile. As Mr. Hugues Keraly wrote: "The press is free to criticise everything, provided that personal honour is respected, and the clergy can preach to its heart's content, provided that it is not caught with weapons in its hands."

Although Communist agitation is still forbidden, books on Marxist doctrine are freely on sale. There is no literary censorship. I spoke to countless people who expressed openly, and in public places, sharp criticism of the Pinochet government. A young intellectual, who at the beginning had supported Gen. Pinochet, told me over luncheon at a restaurant that he now regarded him as a dictator as harsh as the rulers of Communist countries. I retorted that if this was true, he would not be there to tell me so in peace. I also observed that people come and go within the country and abroad in perfect freedom, whereas in Communist countries they are cut off from the world by an Iron Curtain, and require an internal passport to go from one town to another. The "heartless dictatorship" of Gen. Pinochet sends their pensions abroad to emigres who are entitled to them, including the

Secretary-General of the Chilean Communist Party, Mr. Luis Corvalan. Hello, Solzhenitsin, Bukovsky and friends—how much of your pensions and other monies due to you do you get from the Kremlin?

Trade Union Rights

Contrary to all that has been published abroad, the only trade unions to be dissolved in Chile after the pronunciamento were those completely infiltrated by the Communists. All the others, even those opposed to Gen. Pinochet, were left alone. I had a two-hour interview with the national executive of the CEPCH, Confederation of Employees in Chile, which has 300,000 members, in the course of which the majority of the trade union leaders present strongly attacked the Pinochet Government which, according to them, was reviving the economy at the expense of the workers.

The truth is that Gen. Pinochet left intact the trade union organisations which had not been taken over by the Communists, including those of Chiquicamata which had been recaptured from the Communists *during* the time of the UP government, but he imposed a series of restraints which severely limited their powers: the prohibition of general discussion meetings, the prohibition of collective bargaining, and the removal of the right to strike. When old leaders died, they were not replaced by elected successors, but by applying the rule that the most senior trade unionist, in the highest position, should automatically take their place. It was thus untrue that the trade unions had been dissolved, but true that they had been restricted.

This severe regime was in its turn abandoned on 30 June 1979. The government issued a new charter of trade union rights which henceforth authorised collective bargaining but only after the issues had been fully explained to the workers and in the strict context of the conditions of employment applicable to each sector or to each enterprise. At the same time the right of trade unions to elect their leaders in free, democratic elections was restored, provided that such leaders were not taking part in political activity. The right to strike was also restored, but subject to the agreement of the workers, to be expressed in secret ballots, and the right of non-strikers to carry on working if their numbers amounted to more than 25% of the work force. Strikes by government employees remained forbidden. According to this charter, the new trade unionism was to be a) free, b) democratic, c) self-financing, d) autonomous and apolitical.

These restrictions are neither fascist nor particularly reactionary. Before the war of 1939 they were recognised by all shades of liberal opinion anxious to prevent the abuse of trade union freedom, for example by the French Radical Party; and the right to strike was forbidden to government employees. The French trade union law of 1884 included a clause which forbids all political action by officials, and, were it not for the weakness of our rulers, the CGT, so politicised that it has become a transmission belt for the Communist Party, ought to be dissolved as illegal. Let us remember that even the Socialist Mr. Leon Blum, troubled by the savage outbreak of strikes motivated solely by political agitation and without any corporate foundation, explored the possibility of limiting the right to strike by introducing compulsory arbitration. As to the requirement for trade unions to consult the workers by secret ballot before calling a strike, this forms a part of labour legislation in a number of democratic countries such as the German Federal Republic and Austria.

The principle of freedom of association and of workers' right to strike is sacred, but it is perfectly normal to limit it, as with all other rights, so that excesses and manipulations cannot divert it from its true purpose, the defence of the interests of the wage earners, and turn it into a weapon for political intimidation of the masses. In general, apart from a few points of detail, the trade union law of June 1979 prepared by the Pinochet regime seems to me to be comparable with the true spirit of democracy, which does not consist in leaving its subjects defenceless against totalitarian subversion.

Elections of student representatives in the universities were also authorised from May 1979. The first of these resulted in a triumph for the apolitical candidates, who were able to show that they neither served nor opposed the regime. In this connection, it should be noted that Mgr. Silva, the Archbishop of Santiago, had gathered together the majority of the professors who had been excluded from the Catholic University because they had been too close to the UP—but who had neither been arrested nor exiled—and had set up with them an Academy of Christian Humanism, very left-wing and very anti-Pinochet. Despite its open ambition to transform itself into a university in competition with the official Catholic University, this academy functions freely and sponsors a periodical, *Analysis*, another anti-Pinochet organ which is freely on sale at news stands. Can anybody point to an anti-Castro periodical circulating freely in Cuba?

On 31 January 1980 the neutral weekly *Que Pasa* published the results of a wide-ranging opinion poll carried out among wage earners of all classes with a view to finding out if the new legislation would bring advantages or setbacks to the trade union defence of workers' rights. 55% of the workers questioned approved of the new legislation, 16% condemned it (a further indication of freedom of expression) and 29% said that it was too early to judge. On 1 May 1980 3,000 recently elected trade union officials laid a number of grievances before Gen. Pinochet, among other matters on social security, which in Chile, as everywhere, is in a state of crisis. In August 1980, one year after the new trade union freedoms had been promulgated, Gen. Pinochet had won his gamble. A new trade unionism has been born, depoliticised, but nonetheless militant and independent.

The present climate

Observers of good faith can no longer deny that at the present time the Chilean people enjoy personal freedoms, including those of thought and expression, in an atmosphere of peace, security and the rule of law identical with that in democratic countries. The independence of the courts of law has remained sacrosanct. Only subversive and terrorist activities are repressed. The new trade union organisation established in May 1979 has already organised several strikes which have been scrupulously respected.

However, there remains a large sector which has not been restored to normal, and it could be said to be the most important, that of the political parties, of elections and of Parliament. The government continues to function without Parliamentary control, there are no legislative elections, and political parties are still banned. This, however, with surprising impartiality; the military government forbids parties favourable to itself as well as those which are neutral or hostile. This is in striking contrast with the position under all totalitarian Communist, Fascist or Nazi regimes. Under the Pinochet rule, there is no one-system party, no official all-consuming monolithic party, no party of any kind.

Furthermore, the Pinochet government is no more publicly obtrusive than those of France, of Britain, or of the United States. Its discretion is in strong contrast with the reverberating, all-pervading, obsessive self-adulation with which all Communist regimes, foremost among them that of Fidel Castro, deafen and stupefy their subjects. No compulsory mass parades, no slogans broadcast over street loud speakers, no regimented crowds, no troops of militiamen or SS, no red, brown or black shirts, no resolutions passed with 100% approval by the workers in factories or offices, no fanatical political songs, no rhythmic marches, not even a personality cult. In every day life, there is nothing to distinguish Santiago under Gen. Pinochet from Paris under Mr. Mitterand. Gen. Pinochet himself strolls in the public parks without a body guard, and returns every evening to his middle class house in his own car, escorted by no more than two motor cyclists. There are no guards at the entrances to the factories, on the bridges, at the railway stations. There is no ban on photography. If this is Fascism, then it has certainly changed since the days of Mussolini, Hitler, Stalin, Mao and Castro.

Surprising as it may seem when Communist activities are kept firmly under control, the regime is far from practising systematic anti-Communism in the ideological field. It is true that Gen. Pinochet is one of the few living heads of state who dares to make public denunciations of Soviet imperialism, that formidable reality which preoccupies the whole world and which Mr. Hua Kuo Feng, the Chinese Communist leader, names. Gen. Pinochet dared to speak of it in his message to the nation, in 1978, on the anniversary of the 11 September 1973. But I soon discovered that in daily life, anti-Communist propaganda is very limited, and many Chileans expressed their regret at this silence.

Once again, it looks as though the Chilean military rulers are simply soldiers, who are much more preoccupied with actions and morals than with ideologies and political creeds. These soldiers are relying on just two incentives to gain the support of the Chilean people: the still vivid memory of the cruel sufferings endured under Mr. Allende, and Chilean patriotism, warm, visceral, but without political tone, and carrying with it the traditional values of order and hard work. At no level is there any organised education in the errors and failures of Marxism-Leninism.

Nevertheless, the regime has muzzled the political parties and operates without an elected Parliament. Is that not enough to brand it as totalitarian?

The reality is not so clear cut. The leaders and militants of the old left-wing, centre and right-wing parties meet at their will in small groups in each other's houses without arousing any disquiet. There flourish, in complete freedom, innumerable loose groups, generally named after the number of people who started them; the group of ten, the group of 18, the group of 24, etc. They debate unhindered and air their opinions uncensored in the press and on radio and television. They have particularly multiplied in the fields of trade union affairs and constitutional problems.

As to the views of the leading figures in the former political parties, these appear at length in all the Chilean dailies and weeklies. There are without doubt in present-day Chile more channels for the development of political life than can be found in the many one-party states which escape such severe strictures.

If the Pinochet government is unwilling that political life should gather around the old parties, this, it is claimed, is because it does not wish to re-establish, in the guise of democracy, a regime similar to that which led to the Allendist tragedy, a divisive, soft and verbose regime wide open to totalitarian subversion, a regime which Pinochet called "formal democracy", thus unwittingly applying to pro-Marxist tolerance the same epithet used by Karl Marx to describe a democracy guilty of pro-capitalist tolerance. To avoid the risk of an inevitable return to the Kerenskyist leftism which afflicted Chile in the 1960s, General Pinochet intended that the new constitution should protect Chilean democracy from corruption by Leninist totalitarianism.

The plan for such a constitution was drawn up over a period of five years by a commission of 30 constitutional jurists presided over by Mr. Alessandri's ex-Minister, Mr. Enrique Ortuzar, and graced by a sociologist of the highest distinction, Mr. Jaime Guzman, of whom I have already spoken. It provides for a presidential government, the President to be elected for an eight-year term by universal direct suffrage, and with the French proviso that if no candidate obtains an absolute majority in the first ballot, the two who got the most votes go forward for a second ballot; this should avoid the resort to arbitration by the Congress, which was what led to the Allende drama. The draft constitution provides for a legislature with two elected Chambers; a completely independent judiciary; a referendum for questions which can be answered by a yes or no, the right to call one belonging either to the President or to the Parliamentary majority; and wide powers for local governments. It provides for the neutrality of the armed forces, to whom, however, the right of "assistance to the people" is conceded should there be a grave and urgent threat of a potential irregularly armed dictatorship.

There is provision for a constitutional tribunal and for the retention of the office of Controller-General.

A Preamble recalls that "men are born free and with equal rights and dignity", a touching echo of our own French Declaration of the Rights of Man and of the American Constitution; then, going further than these, it specifies that "the state is the servant of the people", after which it lists a series of essential rights, "which are above those of the state", comprising freedom of speech, of expression, of association, equality of opportunity in the pursuit of happiness, the right to work and to health, the right to safety of person and possessions, the free exercise of all creeds and of teaching, and even rights of recent inspiration such as to an unpolluted atmosphere and to the defence of one's good name against slander.

In all this there is an irreproachable spirit in which I can find no shadow of fascist inspiration. At the worst one might regard as "right-wing" the constitution's ban on attacks upon the family and on the preaching of class struggle. This brings us to the clauses concerning the functions of political parties, to which we must pay special attention.

Parties are free to set themselves up and to function within the framework of the following obligations: they must publish their finances, which must have no foreign source, and they must prohibit any recourse to violence, which is considered a serious crime. The parties have no monopoly of political activity, which is left open to individuals. They must not meddle in matters which do not concern them, particularly those of the universities and the trade unions. Above all—and it is this article which has been falsely interpreted as a ban on "left-wing parties"—"parties must organise and conduct themselves according to democratic standards, and maintain, in their ideology, their statutes and the conduct of their members, loyalty towards democracy and the republican system of government, as well as to the principles and standards which constitute the essence of the rule of law, which excludes any theory and any programme which could favour a totalitarian regime".

Simply by studying these obligations, it is clear that it is not the left-wing parties which are anti-constitutional, but totalitarian parties. The famous principle according to which it is proper to take away the liberty of "liberticide" parties is being put into practice. I shall return to this point. For the present, I confine myself to pointing out that these obligations, too, are devoid of Fascism, since we have the equivalent in Article 4 of the French Constitution, where it is stated that "political parties are free provided that they respect the principles of democracy and of national sovereignty"; and there is another equivalent in articles 18 and 21 of the Federal German Constitution, designed to prevent a return of the Nazi parties, and of which the logical consequence, during the 20 post-war years when Germany had logical governments, was the outlawing of the Communist Party, the Nazi Party of our time.

This provision seems to me to be an admirable one, and to offer, during the period of evolution from authoritarian government, a valid democratic alternative which will be proof against the totalitarian virus. Alas, instead of rallying to it, Christian Democracy lurched back into its leftism and into its old fallacy which maintains that democracy commits suicide if it proscribes its murderer, the Communist Party. Still worse, the Christian Democratic leaders have declared that they were prepared to accept an alliance with the Communists to oust Gen. Pinochet.

They have understood nothing and they have learnt nothing. It is heartbreaking, but it explains—without justifying—Gen. Pinochet's reluctance to give them an influence in the country at present. After what Chile experienced under Mr. Allende, after what is happening in Cambodia, in Vietnam, in Afghanistan, now in Poland, in short in all the parts of the world bowed down under Communist tyranny, it is understandable that a leader who cares about the destiny of his country should hesitate to allow the return to the political arena of those elements which had already surrendered to Marxism-Leninism and were preparing to do so again. If President Frei had accepted the clauses in the Constitution which prohibited "liberticide" parties, he would have been justified in calling for the immediate return of the other parties. By rejecting them, and showing that he only aspired to a revival of the old type of democracy, a type which the makers of totalitararism can corrupt to their hearts content, he justified Gen. Pinochet in waiting until new political forces could emerge which would at least be immune from Marxist hypnosis. The Constitution obliged the Chilean parties to face up to the essential problem: *do they intend to tolerate, or to forbid, communist subversion*? From now on, it is up to them to decide. The ball is in their court, not in Gen. Pinochet's.

In fact, the Chilean opposition has tended to evade this subject, a rather delicate one for them. The campaign for "No" in the referendum took as its target a more controversial aspect of the constitution, that which provides for a "transition period" to last for eight years under Gen. Pinochet, political parties to emerge only after they have drawn up their rules, and Parliament only at the end of this period. The opposition aroused public opinion against the excessive length of this transition period, and against the unusual combination of a text of permanent legal validity with a Presidential election—a combination which disquieted even some of Gen. Pinochet's supporters. As a result, by the evening of 11 September 1980, the "Yes" vote only won by 68%, a setback of 7% in comparison with the plebiscite of 1978, with 28% "against" and 4% nil.

In all the world media, this operation swelled the flood of anathema against Gen. Pinochet. The commentators and many leaders of opinion gave full vent to their exasperation at seeing Gen. Pinochet "perpetuating himself", although they had never displayed any irritation with the endless tyrannies of Boumeddienne, Castro, Tito and their Marxist comrades, who have never announced any return of any kind to democracy, at any date in the future.

Another incongruity was the "friends of the people" who complained that Gen. Pinochet had not immediately restored the liberty of the political parties, never rejoiced that he had solved the Chilean economic problem, restoring to the people a decent standard of living, free from queues and the black market. These great-hearted democrats, who claim to be concerned above all with the material well-being of the people, are not concerned with it at all when it is a question of Chile. They have only one theme tune: "What does it matter what happens to the people, provided that the political parties prosper?" This is, in fact, the identical theme as that of the Communist regimes, if the singular is substituted for the plural—"What does it matter what happens to the people, provided that the Party prospers?"

One last observation. The campaign for the referendum of 11 September 1978 was a free one—public demonstrations of opposition, in the street and in the Chilean press, numerous signed declarations which were violently "against"—all unthinkable in a totalitarian regime. The counting of the votes, monitored by journalists from all over Latin America, was honest. Nevertheless the world media once again applied the sacrosanct law that the epithet "totalitarian" must be applied to everything which is done in Chile. But they could not resist the temptation to point out that Gen. Pinochet's position had deteriorated, as was *proved* by the fall in the number of his supporters from 75 to 68%. An obvious contradiction in terms, since if the percentage of votes is taken as an element of (or basis for) proof, that implies those votes are genuine . . .

One thing or another—either a regime is totalitarian, and there is nothing to be learnt from the votes (which in any case can only vary between 99.7 and 99.9% in favour of the government), or one can count a substantial opposition to the government, once of 20%, another time of 28%, and it has been demonstrated ipso facto that the regime is not totalitarian.

No, it is not, as is once again self-evident to all. It is only, as I have already said, authoritarian. With, henceforth, the time irrevocably fixed for a complete return to liberal democracy.

CHAPTER XVIII

THE ECONOMIC RECOVERY UNDER PINOCHET

In 1974, the Pinochet Government inherited an economy which the Marxist-Leninist Popular Unity had thrown into complete chaos and bankruptcy. Industry and agriculture were at a standstill. Inflation was galloping towards an annual 1,000%. Customs duties had reached 500%, even on goods of primary importance for the manufacturing industry. The budget deficit had reached 24%. Annual income tax had reached 70%. To this legacy of catastrophe was added, in 1974, the world energy crisis, whereby the price of oil—on which Chile depends for 80% of its energy requirements—quadrupled. To cope with this, it would have been necessary to quadruple the value of exports, whereas these had slumped after the general fall in production under Popular Unity, and a time when the world price of copper had fallen by half, from 1.10 dollars a pound under Mr. Allende in 1973 to 0.59 under Gen. Pinochet in 1975. This cost the Pinochet economy a shortfall of 1,000 million dollars to be made up each year, at the very moment when oil prices had gone up four times.

We must add to this state of collapse the enormous foreign debt—capital and interest—which Mr. Allende had incessantly negotiated and renegotiated, with no thought of settlement, and which landed on Gen. Pinochet's shoulders. Thus in 1975 the military government found itself faced with a real economic and financial catastrophe. All the prestigious economists in the world gave up the Chilean economy for lost in a very short time; even the most hopeful predicted that it would take at least a decade to emerge from this deep depression. It extricated itself in three years, and brilliantly.

This was to be called the Chilean miracle. How and why did this miracle come about?

Administrative Reforms

First of all, the Pinochet government took a series of urgent measures which could be described as "revolutionary" in comparison with the policies which had restricted and bled the economy of Chile for decades.

Above all it was necessary to stem the flood of pesos brought about by Mr. Allende's policy, based on the belief that all difficulties could be solved by printing money, but which led to galloping inflation. The Pinochet government decided to make a drastic cut in the inflationary expenditure of their predecessors, an expenditure which a gross national product on a downward slope could no longer support. Government expenditure had reached 43% of the GNP! The insane expansion of the public sector under Mr. Allende had unbalanced and paralysed the economy. Nationalised industries, which could have operated perfectly well with 500 employees, had to support 2,000. To give the illusion that the master-state was providing full employment, Mr. Allende had solved the unemployment problem by recruiting a plethora of bureaucrats and ruining the country.

To get rid of this plethora and to ensure the profitability of investments, the Pinochet government took urgent steps; extension of unemployment benefit from six to 12 months; a programme of minimum employment; cities and provinces to undertake public works and to give preference to the unemployed at a guaranteed minimum wage. These were the classic remedies.

Moreover, in order to absorb the bureaucratic surplus, Gen. Pinochet devised a much more original plan: the famous Programme of the New Business Man. Special assistance was offered to government servants who were willing to resign voluntarily and undertook to become small businessmen. They were granted loans at very low interest rates, exemption from taxes, and technical assistance; opportunities were offered in 58 different kinds of businesses. A fund of 100 million dollars was set up to finance this programme, which was aimed at the transformation of useless pen-pushers into producers of useful goods.

Furthermore, in May 1976, a national Five Year Plan was launched for the development of science and technology, with priority given to the following categories: management studies, electronics, international marketing, agricultural techniques, mining, the development of marine resources, and the food industry.

By 1977, unemployment in Santiago had fallen from 20 to 12%, although it was increasing throughout the rest of the world. It still stood at 12% in 1980.

It must be taken into account that since 1950 successive Chilean governments, all more or less interventionist, had operated in accordance with three economic principles:

1. The artificially low valuation of the dollar, aimed at making certain exports very cheap;

2. The imposition of extremely high customs duties to limit the import of luxury articles, but also affecting essential manufactured goods;

3. The arbitrary fixing of the prices of a large number of items.

Mr. Allende merely pushed these measures to the limit, which had several undesirable results:

1. The stimulation of the production in Chile of luxury goods of no value to the country;

2. The decline in the production of goods for everyday use, consequently the necessity to import them and the draining away of foreign currency without a compensating balance in productive equipment.

3. The decline in Chilean exports caused by over-valuation of the Chilean peso.

The result was a heavily subsidised economy, producing one raw material and non-essential goods, and importing articles for everyday use and food which the Chileans could very easily have produced themselves, thus saving their foreign currency. An even graver consequence was that the economic power of the state was increasingly replacing the private sector in areas where this sector was no longer attracted by the very reason of state-imposed restrictions. Lastly, another unfortunate consequence was the ceaseless search for foreign loans, which left Chile chronically in debt and increasingly dependent upon foreigners. The continual rescheduling of the national debt became a regular exercise. Forever deferring settlement, there was a refusal to face up to present economic failure, and this in turn led to a deteriorating future.

This deplorable policy was characterised by an economic growth of 1.3% a year per head of the population (at a time when in many countries it was over 8%) and by the loss of national independence. Mr. Allende's measures merely aggravated a situation leading to catastrophe.

The economic reconstruction plan of April 1975

Against this already sombre background, I must remind you that in 1975 two additional burdens were added: the price of copper exports fell by half, and the price of oil imports quadrupled. In addition to the urgent measures which I have already described, the Pinochet government decided to rescue the Chilean economy from collapse by setting in motion a market economy which was to include the most radical possible suppression of state controls. This was the April 1975 plan, which represented an 180 degree turn in relation to the Allende period. The team charged with devising and carrying out this plan consisted of a number of professors and economic experts from the Catholic University of Chile. Since most of them had obtained higher degrees from the University of Chicago in the USA, they were nicknamed the "Chicago Boys".

Denationalisation and Elimination of State Ownership

This team exploited to its limit the free market, the law of supply and demand, internal and external competition, decontrol of prices, and above all private enterprise, that best of fertilisers. To achieve this it was first necessary to denationalise hundreds of companies and banks, of which 494 under Mr. Allende's government had been annually responsible for a 700 million dollar deficit; this without taking into account the loss of revenue to the state through taxes on profits which General Pinochet now gets from business activity.

This programme of industrialisation posed problems which were even more difficult than might be thought, given the precarious conditions into which companies nationalised or partially controlled by the state had fallen. Since they were running at a loss and their capital had to some extent been dissipated, many of their former owners were unwilling to take them back. They received compensation. Some had disappeared. The CORFO sold many nationalised enterprises at a loss to Chileans or to foreigners. Those which nobody wanted were put into liquidation. Others continued to function under the CORFO consortium.

For the first time in history, a country was irrevocably denationalising key sectors of the economy. The state retained control only of some 20 companies for reasons of national security (energy) or in order to develop the country's resources (copper, coal, steel, railways, electricity, petroleum, strategic materials).

Another measure taken by the Chicago Boys, in the tradition of the Ehrhardt policy which had re-established the post-war Federal German economy, was to restore to the Chilean peso its true value. The dollar had been kept by Mr. Allende at an artificially abnormally low level, with the object of reducing the price of food imports, since Chile could no longer produce enough. The official value of the dollar under Mr. Allende was 240 pesos, while on the black market it was worth 3,000 pesos. The Pinochet government strongly devalued the peso and kept it at a floating exchange rate. This adjustment undoubtedly had an inflationary effect, but it was indispensable to the economic development of the country, since it would be extremely favourable to Chilean exports, thus to the production of Chilean goods, thus to the job market.

It was not enough to decentralise economic activity by denationalisation, it was also necessary to secure a free market economy. To achieve this, state monopolies and excessive controls had to be eliminated, arbitrary price-fixing by the state was brought to an end, and cost allowed to adjust to the far more realistic world prices. At present, the Pinochet government only controls the price of some 10 commodities, whereas the Allende government controlled 3,200!—in other words, all goods and services. As a result, the country has regained confidence and gone back to work.

Tax Reforms

Under Mr. Allende, government taxation amounted to 43% of the gross national product. The Pinochet government decided to put an end to such an exorbitant charge, which was eating up nearly half of the GNP. It was decided to put an end to the discriminatory treatment used and abused by the UP to the advantage of the nationalised enterprises, giving them scandalous privileges, such as non-payment of taxes and duties, such as the obtaining of loans at derisory interest rates, at the very time when private enterprise was being brought to bankruptcy by ever-increasing charges, by the suppression of credit, and by the impossibility of importing the machinery or the spare parts which were indispensable to their operations.

The Pinochet government decided upon a simplification and equalisation of taxes for all private and public enterprises, thus obliging the latter to use their resources, ulitmately those of the people, to better effect. In March 1975, VAT was introduced as a fairer and more equitable tax for all.

The increase and diversification of exports

Like most other developing countries, Chile had always existed on the exploitation of raw materials, concentrating on a single commodity. First this was saltpetre, which provided essential nitrates for agriculture. Then the Germans invented synthetic nitrates, and the export of saltpetre fell dramatically in the 1920s. Copper was able to replace it, but Chile was still in the dangerous position of a one-product exporter. When the price of copper fell by half in 1975, the Chicago Boys decided to launch a major effort to diversify exports in such a way as to increase their total value. To achieve this, they advocated two principal measures: devaluation of the peso to its real value, as we have seen, and freedom to export and import no matter what products. An ad hoc office was set up to advise producers who were able to supply new, original and marketable exports. They were skilfully chosen to exploit all the possibilities of the Chilean soil; to stimulate the creativity and pride of the producers, and to provide employment by favouring high value-added goods.

Thus for the first time Chile started to export all kinds of early fruit and vegetables which grow during her spring and summer, when it is still winter in the northern hemisphere and when the demand is at its greatest and the price at its highest. She also began to export timber from the immense forests of the coastal region, seeds, excellent wines, barley and oats, fish, hides, etc. These non-traditional exports, which stood at 71 million dollars in 1973, rose to 800 million dollars in 1979 and are continuing to grow fast. Today the battle has been won. Chile has finally emerged from a century and a half of dependence upon a single raw material.

For more than half a century, extremely high customs duties had condemned Chile to poor quality and very costly industrialisation, impoverishing the people. To cure this evil, the Chicago Boys established, in May 1975, various measures which at the time were considered very daring and very risky. They were to be crowned with success.

Firstly, the massive opening up of the country to foreign trade. Under Mr. Allende, a large range of goods was out of reach of the Chileans because, before they could be brought into the country, it was necessary to make an advance deposit which could be as much as 10,000%. Next, a substantial reduction in the customs duties on the import of all goods. These import taxes, which under Mr. Allende were between 50 and 550% for manufactured products, and were nil for certain agricultural commodities, were standardised and reduced, first to between 60 and 35%, then to 10% in 1979 for all imported goods with the exception of cars and some luxury items. This made it possible for industrial and agricultural concerns to import, under tolerable conditions, the machinery they needed to increase their production.

Growth of Investments

Banking reform was carried out with a view to achieving a substantial increase in savings, which had fallen to their lowest level under Mr. Allende. Decree No. 455 of 1975 was designed to reassure national capitalists and to encourage them to invest in new sources of employment. Annual interest rates, which under Mr. Allende had risen to 70%, were lowered to more realistic levels. The restoration to private ownership of a number of banks which had been nationalised, increased regionalisation of the banking system, the development of two new banks whose function was to look for highly profitable investments, brought about an increase in personal and commercial savings and, as a result, in investment.

Furthermore, the introduction of a law on foreign investment helped to attract capital from abroad, already beginning to return and to assist in Chile's economic development. Needless to say, this could only be achieved by the guarantee of a minimum profit for the investors. With this aim in view, Chile did not hesitate, in 1975, to leave the Andes Pact, which in six South American countries imposed severe tax discrimination between native and foreign investors, by preventing the latter from taking out more than 14% of their profit, and had thus discouraged them. The Pinochet government decided to increase this right to 51% of the profits, after payment of taxes. Economic good sense prevailed over parochialism.

Now let us examine the results obtained by this boldly liberal economic policy. I shall deal separately with industry and agriculture.

Growth of Industrial Production

Yes, the Chilean miracle made itself felt after three years. Copper production, which stood at 743,000 tons in 1973 (I have rounded up all the figures which follow), rose to 1,250,000 tons in 1980. That of molybdenum rose from 5,000 tons in 1973 to 13,000 tons in 1979. That of silver from 156,000 kilos in 1973 to 290,000 kilos in 1980. The gross national product per head, which was 685 dollars in 1973, rose to 937 dollars in 1977. In 1981 it exceeded 1,500 dollars. Only Venezuela (thanks to its oil) and the Argentine (thanks to the fertility of the pampas) had a GNP per head higher than that of Chile. It was half the amount in Peru, and a quarter in Bolivia.

The American journal *Business Week* of 21 May 1979 reported: "The annual rate of growth of the GNP, which was an average of 4% from 1953 to 1972, fell to its lowest level during the years 1973 to 1975, rose to 5% in 1976, and to 8.6% in 1977 .. Business which, in 1973, under Mr. Allende, enjoyed 97% state protection, were thrown into a free market. Hundreds went bankrupt. But in 1978, no Chilean enterprise made a loss, and things are even better in 1979."

In fact, the production of motor vehicles during the first quarter of 1978 rose to 3,170, that is 70% more than in the first quarter of 1977, when 1,870 were produced. Production at the Peugot-Renault group *(Automora Franco-Chilena)* was 1,400 vehicles in the first quarter of 1978 as against 770 in the first quarter of 1977.

A report by the Ezanco-Latin American Chamber of Commerce states that industrial production increased by 8.2% in the course of the first six months of 1978 in comparison with the same period in 1977, and then again by 8.5% in 1979. This level of growth is greater than in the Argentine, Venezuela, Brazil and Mexico, the richest countries of Latin America. According to the Department of Studies of the Sociedad Fomento Fabril, industrial production again increased by 15% during the year 1980 in relation to the year 1979 the biggest growth having been in the transport industry, 37% and in the construction industry, 22%.

To all this must be added the encouragement of scientific research and technical innovation. The crowning glory, in July 1980, was the opening of a marine platform for oil extraction in the Chilean section of the Straits of Magellan, entirely designed and built in Chile, and at the highest level of modern technology. It must be said alas that from the end of 1981 until the middle of 1982 difficulties have appeared.

The Pinochet Government's Agricultural Policy

Mr. Allende had expropriated 5,809 properties consisting of some 10 million hectares, in fact 58% of cultivated land. These vast expropriations, and the consequence of the land lying fallow and the complete standstill in technical improvements, had led to a catastrophic fall in agricultural production and in animal husbandry. To remedy it, the Pinochet government took the following measures:

1. Transfer of nationalised land to peasants or to private farmers, or to co-operatives free of state intervention;

2. All properties of 40 basic hectares or less, in the hands of their owners, were declared inexpropriable;

3. All properties of 40–80 basic hectares were declared inexpropriable;

4. The owners of properties of more than 80 basic hectares were invited to split them up, and to sell a part of them on the free market;

A joint study by the Catholic University of Chile and the Ministry of Agriculture shows that as a result the Pinochet government had at its disposal some 10 million hectares expropriated by Mr. Allende (here again I am rounding up the numbers to facilitate an overall view). Some three million hectares were restored to their original owners, that is approximately 40,000 families. About three million hectares were purchased from their former owners and resold to 37,000 small farmers, against repayment by them to be spread out over 30 years with the minimal interest of 6%, at a time when inflation was at 160%, and some three million hectares were sold to companies for semi-industrial exploitation, about one million hectares had been allocated by Mr. Allende to 197 co-operatives or other collectives. These collective properties—not nationalised—comprising some 10,000 families, were not interfered with by Gen. Pinochet. But out of these 197 collective farms, 185 immediately asked to be split up once again so as to escape from their suffocating collective status.

Having restored the regime of the small private proprietor in the country—no small task given the dislocation left by its predecessor—the Pinochet government tackled the even more pressing problem of prices.

For many years the rural sector had been subjected to a policy of imposed agricultural prices which had been very damaging to it. Production and investment were tailored to fit strict standards, rather than the real needs of the people. By keeping farm prices artificially low, agricultural workers had been discouraged and production had fallen, leading to ever increasing imports of foodstuffs, and the ever greater drain on foreign currency.

The Pinochet government decided to make a radical change in the policy of fixed prices. Decree No. 83 of October 1973 removes all controls from farm prices and ensures a free system of national and international exchange. Domestic prices thus drew closer to world prices, at least in countries where agriculture is not subsidised. However an agreement was drawn up between those responsible in agriculture and the authorities to protect Chilean agriculture against dumping. This agreement applied, for example, to powdered milk from the European Economic Community, which arrived in Chile subsidised at 800 dollars a ton, while the price in Europe was 2,100 dollars.

Furthermore the opening up of Chile to foreign business interests guaranteed to the farmers a substantial fall in their running costs. All agricultural implements, machines and tractors, means of transport, lorries, cars and even fertilizers can now be bought by the Chilean peasants much more advantageously than in the past.

Now let us look at the results achieved by this liberal agricultural economy.

Increase in Agricultural Production

These liberal measures brought about a revival in agriculture even more spectacular than that of industry. Agricultural production rapidly reached an annual rate of growth of 7.6%, the highest in recent decades. This is only an average rate of growth, since already by 1975, that is two years after Gen. Pinochet came to power, the rate of growth for some of the most important products was very much higher: 115% for rice; 60% for sugar beet; 100% for sunflower seed.

In 1977–78 progress was even more spectacular. Again in comparison with the years 1973–74, rice production increased by 205%; that of beans and lentils by 50%; of peas by 25%. Production of milk increased by 850 million litres in 1973, by more than a billion litres in 1977. The number of cows doubled, rising from 325,000 in 1973 to 675,000 in 1977. Meat production increased from 89,000 tons in 1973 to 173,000 tons in 1977. In the same space of time, egg production went up by 15%, that of poultry by 6%. Sugar rose from 28,400 tons in 1973 to 403,000 tons in 1977. Cellulose rose from 154,000 tons to 465,000 tons, and so on for all other Chilean agricultural products.

As to the area under cultivation, this was at an average of 16% greater during the farming year of 1977–78 than in 1972–73. For rice, the increase was 148%.

The consequence of this horn of plenty which flowed from small private properties was that the export of farm and husbandry produce, worth only 22 million dollars in 1973, rose to the remarkable level of 240 million dollars in 1980 and is still going up. At the same time, food imports fell spectacularly. Whereas they had risen to 600 million dollars in 1973, by 1976 they amounted to no more than 130 million dollars. Chile now imports practically no meat, although general consumption continues to increase.

The Chilean Economic Miracle—International Results

As a result of this remarkable revival of industry and agriculture, the general economic situation recovered at so rapid a pace that it is no exaggeration to speak of the Chilean economic miracle.

Inflation, which Mr. Allende admitted was 700% in 1973, and which was in fact 1,000% if the black market is taken into account, had been brought down by Gen. Pinochet to 30% by 1978. This is how it went: 1973: 1,000%; 1974: 376%; 1975: 340%; 1976: 174%; 1977: 64%; 1978: 30%; 1979: 30%; in 1980: 20%; in 1981 it stabilised at 8%, that is the Swiss level, and the lowest in the world. It should be noted that the Chilean peso is tending to strengthen against the American dollar.

Exports have grown from a total of 1,310 million dollars in 1973 to a total of 4,700 million dollars in 1980, with a small recession in 1981. The Central Bank states that even Chilean industry, which had never exported a great deal—90 million dollars in 1973—has begun to sell manufactured goods and machinery abroad; 625 million dollars worth as early as 1977. Diversification has proceeded at a record pace. Whereas in 1973 copper alone accounted for 82% of total exports, in 1980 it no longer made up more than 45%. In 1980, non traditional exports were 11 times higher than in 1973, having risen from 71 million dollars to 800 million dollars!

The balance of trade which Mr. Allende reduced to a deficit of 880 million dollars, was restored in 1977. It was again in deficit by 200 million dollars in 1978 because of the further fall in the price of red metal. Since then it has almost been restored to balance.

The Chilean foreign debt was renegotiated in 1975. From that date, Chile has paid up punctually. In addition, Chile has settled her debts with most European and Eastern countries, and has also made advance payments, both on interest and on debt repayment, to a number of countries, including France, in June 1979.

The balance of payments achieved for the first time, in 1977, a surplus of 18 million dollars, despite the payment of 800 million dollars in settlement of capital debts and in interest on foreign loans.

Reserves of foreign currency; the reserves of 500 million dollars, which Mr. Allende had inherited from Mr. Frei, and which he reduced to zero, had reached a billion and a half dollars under Gen. Pinochet by 1978.[1] In March 1979, Chile's gross reserves of foreign currency reached their highest level in history at two billion dollars[2] and then 2.3 billion in 1980.

Investments: the significant lowering of the level of inflation, number one priority in the Pinochet plan, was the key to the Chilean economic miracle. It made an excellent impression upon investors. The value of Chilean bonds rose in such a way as to attract a flow of foreign capital through loans or direct investment. As a result, total investment, which between 1973 and 1976 had not reached 300 million dollars—a pathetic 100 million a year—rose in 1977 to 940 million dollars and in 1981 to more than a billion and a half dollars.

An investigation into the year 1978 shows that 57% of investment was financed by foreign credits; 30% by self-financing of Chilean firms; and 13% by Chilean capital.[4] Private enterprise began to invest at levels well above those previously recorded. The average level of increase from 1976 to 1981 was an annual 18%, the highest in the world.

Yes, the success of Pinochet's economic policy has opened up the Chilean market to international capital investment. Every week new banks from countries all over the world are financing long-term investment projects, such as the construction of vast storage depots, of giant refrigeration plants, of port installations, of factories for fruit juice and tomato concentrates, for paper pulp etc.

Irrefutable Evidence

If the Pinochet experiment can be critisised in the political field, in the economic field it is unanimously regarded as a success. It has saved Chile. It deserves all the more praise when so many leftist regimes, which spend their time giving lessons in economics to everybody else, have degraded and wrecked the economic life of their own countries. Pinochet's rebuilding of the economy of Chile is today unreservedly

---

[1]*Moniteur du Commerce International* of 20 March 1978.
[2]*Economic and Financial Survey* and Central Bank of Santiago.
[3]*El Mercurio*, 24 May 1979.

acknowledged by all shades of opinion, even by those who are most hostile to him such as our own paper *Le Monde*.

The experts of the IMF have praised Gen. Pinochet's economic achievement. To quote one of their reports of 27 June 1977, it emphasises: "The very favourable results in the balance of payments in 1976 have made it possible to take measures aimed at achieving the Pinochet government's two principal objectives. the reduction of the rate of inflation and the revival and acceleration of economic activity. *Considerable progress has been made in this direction.*"[1]

This opinion, which cannot be suspected of coming from an acolyte of the Pinochet regime, removes all doubt about the remarkable recovery of the Chilean economy. All the most authoritative sources confirm this judgement. Thus, *Les Etudes Economiques of the Banque Francaise et Italienne pur l'Amerique du Sud*, in February 1978, stated that the economic recovery was undeniable and "that it is the result of the special plan decided upon by Pinochet in 1975, at a time when all the contributory factors appeared largely negative". A report by the Franco-Latin American Chamber of Commerce, Circular No. 52 of August 1978 elaborates on the same theme: "The assessment which we made in our Circular No. 83, of December 1977, was broadly confirmed, and the results in the first six months of the year 1978 indicated that this economic recovery is progressing in Chile."

Let us also quote *Business Week* of 21 May 1979, where it is said: "Chile is at present living through nothing less than a rebirth of its economy. After a chaotic decade marked by the extremes of socialist centralist planning . . . entangled in 1973 in a 1,000% inflation . . . today the economy of Chile has a surprisingly healthy appearance . . . Inflation has been reduced to 25%. Foreign investors have returned to Chile. The fundamental motivation of this revival is to be found in the new regulations favouring private investment."

Thus, in despite of its innumerable detractors abroad, Gen. Pinochet's economic team has won a game which all thought lost; it has brought to life an economy profoundly weakened by many years of excessive protectionism, and killed by the now defunct Marxist-Leninist Popular Unity. This is the Chilean miracle.

What Was The Price? Standard of Living?

It was obvious that such a recovery, starting from nothing, would require heavy sacrifices from all the population. While during 1974, 1975 and 1976 the workers and the peasants were working hard for a minimum wage, civil servants, non-commissioned officers and army

---

[1] *The Economic and Social Year*, January 1978.

officers, as I myself was able to observe, were also all living very modestly. Small craftsmen, small shopkeepers, small entrepreneurs had to struggle desperately for the survival and then the prosperity of their small enterprises, and many failed. In short, these were the years of the lean cattle. But it was still easier than in Mr. Allende's days. The black market had disappeared. Ration cards had vanished. The interminable queues were no more. Once again the shop windows were full of foodstuffs. Each year the rate of inflation went down. Progress was being made towards daylight and hope, and no longer into darkness and misery.

It was not until 1976, thanks to the significant drop in inflation, that the purchasing power of the Chilean people began to increase by an average of 15% over four years. This is confirmed in an article in *Business Week* which states: "In spite of *a real increase of 15%* in 1977 and 1978, Chilean revenue per head of the population only amounts to the annual 1,000 dollars of ten years ago." According to this source the Chilean standard of living in 1978, although better than in the years 1973–1975, had not yet risen above its level under President Frei before the arrival of Mr. Allende, but from then on, in 1979, 1980 and 1981, it has shown a very significant improvement.

I must point out that very reliable Chilean sources give a more favourable picture. The most distinguished of these is the Economic Department of the University of Chile, not to be confused with the Catholic University. Politically, it maintains a strict tradition of scientific impartiality, to which it owes it recognition and its use by the most eminent economic study centres of the world as the best source of information on the Chilean situation. It has kept this reputation for nearly 20 years, under successive Chilean regimes. This department has developed a means of calculating real salaries and incomes, independent of inflation, and taking into account the value of social benefits. According to these specialists, taking as a base the figure 100, as at 1 January 1970, the world index of the real income of wage earners was at 34 in October 1973, that is to say directly after the Allende hurricane, then reached the level of 109.7 on the 1 January 1979, and, according to the article which appeared in *El Mercurio* on 6 June 1980, the level of 120 in May 1980. The estimate for 1981 is 130 in spite of a recession beginning at the end of the year.

The University's study centre also publishes an index of consumption representing what is known as "general prosperity" in the sense that the articles listed are too widely distributed to apply only to the privileged classes. Among these figures I cite as examples that at the beginning of the Pinochet era, one million television sets and 50,000 modern cookers were sold, and that five years later these figures had risen to 2.7 million television sets and 123,000 cookers, that is to say that they had almost tripled. The *Mercurio* article shows that between May 1978 and May 1980 the working hours that an average worker had to complete in order to buy a washing machine had gone down from 165 to 120 hours. There is now a car to every 20 inhabitants, compared with the former one to a hundred. Remarkable progress.

However, I have given the average increase in the standard of living, whereas not all the population has benefited equally. There are still 10% unemployed, for the work force continues to increase at an unprecedented rate of from 4 to 6% per annum. Poverty in the streets of Santiago and Valparaiso, poverty which already existed under Mr. Frei and which was aggravated under Mr. Allende, still exists under Gen. Pinochet. It is a black mark. Undoubtedly there is no more nervous exhaustion in queues, no more humiliating ration cards, no more scandalous black market, and certainly 70% of the population sees its standard of living regularly improving, but progress is still slow for the wage earners, and there remain the 20% of the poor. It is this fact with which Gen. Pinochet is reproached.

Without doubt the return to prosperity, made up of the flourishing of business enterprise (production, commerce, services, etc.) has been achieved through, first of all, giving scope and preference to the class of town and country entrepreneurs, on whose efforts the whole experiment was founded. The base of the pyramid had remained badly off and there is no question—if we are honest—but that this meagre lot has only been accepted in silence because there has been a military regime which, until 1977, banned any organised protest. This is what critics call "the social price" of economic recovery.

From now on it is therefore necessary to reduce and then to eliminate this social price, and to direct a portion of the benefits of economic recovery downwards. The Pinochet government is well aware of this, as is shown by the restoration to the trade unions, in June 1979, of the right to collective bargaining and the right to strike. It is generally acknowledged that increased purchasing power had been achieved for some of the working population. Unemployment remains the major concern, but it is well known that this is a world wide problem, which even the most advanced democracies do not know how to solve. Perhaps the order of priority followed by Gen. Pinochet could not have been otherwise: first, to get everyone back to work, to productive, genuine and appropriate work; then to ease conditions for the fertile class of big and small entrepreneurs, by no means all of them "bourgeois", such as peasants, shopkeepers, artisans, lorry drivers; finally, to give them back the possibility of profits to be used to step up production the only true source of prosperity. Only then to loosen the belts which the wage earners had had to tighten during the first phases. The time has come to tackle the last phase with resolution. The results of the years 1980–81 show that this is making steady progress.

Gen. Pinochet's Social Policy

The left always likes to think that it has a monopoly of social concern and that the right continues to take no interest in the material and spiritual condition of the under-privileged. They are two generations out of date. For half a century, all the governments of the world, of all complexions, have given priority to these problems. For a long time past reforms have been a part of modern society, and a social conscience has ceased to be a point of difference between the "caring" left and the "selfish" right. The only remaining harshly anti-social regimes are the communist ones, where workers in towns and fields have been led back into ancient serfdom, if not to slavery in the gulags, and where they are exploited much more cruelly than they have ever been by capitalist societies. Nevertheless, there are still attempts to discredit anti-communist regimes by alleging that they do nothing in the social field. Naturally this derogatory reproach is levelled at Gen. Pinochet. An examination of the facts show it to be a false accusation, and demonstrates that in this context the Pinochet government follows the example of all civilised governments, and is even better than the average.

The social services budget of Chile in 1978 exceeded by six points the total of all other budgets (it made up 53% of all government expenditure), as in France or in Sweden, and more than in Germany, in Italy or in the United States. With the concern for getting to the root of things which is characteristic of the military approach to problems, the Pinochet government looked for the sectors of greatest deprivation, where shortages had the worst effect, and where in consequence intervention would be most rewarding in the long term. It was decided to tackle child malnutrition and children's education.

The battle against child malnutrition has in Chile a world-famous advocate, Dr. Fernando Monckeberg, who was put at the head of the National Nutrition Institute, and with whom I had a long interview. This scholar and man of action, the author of *Food and Nutrition Policy in Chile* (National Food and Nutrition Council, 1977), demonstrated that chronic malnutrition in very young children from the poorest classes is one of the most serious social evils, not only because of its distressing direct results—underdevelopment, illnesses, mortality, but also because of its indirect effects: irreversible deterioration of the mental faculties, apathy of the parents in unhealthy conditions and with alimentary, social and medical prejudices. I have said that 20% of the people of Chile belong to this poverty fringe, and that this is the reason why Chile must still be regarded as a not completely developed country. It is certainly in this class that most of the infantile malnutrition is to be found, Dr. Monckeberg proved that it also affects important sections of the peasantry and the proletariat despite their respectable incomes, and that this was due to the well known fact that primitive life styles spread contagious diseases.

Dr. Monckeberg calculated that in 1968, nearly 67% of Chilean children between nought and five years of age showed more or less serious signs of malnutrition. Mr Allende had tried to do something about this scourge; but, in the bureaucratic fashion of the UP, all he did was to distribute free milk to poor families. Unfortunately, those families did not always give the milk to their children, and by 1973 this foolishness of the adults, aggravated by the general famine, had raised the percentage of the unhappy under-nourished children to the disastrous level of 72%. It was necessary to change tactics; to make the children come to social or medical centres; to give them other foods as well as milk; to educate their mothers; in short to combine a better diet with better maternal education and better medical care; and also to extend the diet supplement beyond five years, by providing a free and substantial breakfast in schools.

From 1975, all this was carried out methodically and with enthusiasm. In 1980 there were no more than 1% of under-nourished children in Chile. Infantile mortality among babies between nought and one year old had fallen from 78 per thousand in 1970 to 27 per thousand in 1980 (the Latin-American average is 85 per thousand, in North America it is 17 per thousand); and among chldren between one and four, the rate had fallen, during the same period, from five per thousand to 1.4 per thousand (Latin-American average 6 per thousand, North American 0.8 per thousand). These figures are confirmed by international organisations.

At the UNICEF (United Nations Children's Fund) conference in Mexico in July 1979, Chile was regarded as one of the countries which had make the most progress in the fight against malnutrition and infant mortality.[1] This had been reduced practically by half in nine years, a remarkable achievement. Furthermore, a report by World Bank experts recognised that Chile is the only country in Latin America where all children without exception receive primary education.

Social action on the environment came only second. We have seen that under-development was still very considerable in the vast shanty-towns *poblaciones*, which surround Chile's town centres, and that Mr. Allende had done practically nothing to get rid of them.

In his 1975 plan, Gen. Pinochet resolved to try for a breakthrough. He decided to concentrate efforts on the replacement of some *poblaciones* by modern districts. But, in conformity with the general outlines of the plan, he only granted loans for projects where the future beneficiaries were prepared to make a partial repayment, in 20 or 30

---

[1] *El Mercurio*, 15 July 1979.

years. It was essential that they should be stimulated to earn for themselves what was needed to escape from their hovels. This strict policy at first limited progress, but there was a regular increase, and in 1978 there was a return to the average number under Mr Frei of 26,000 new state-aided dwellings each year. In addition, private enterprise also resumed building activities at a fairly rapid pace. In 1979 the rate of the Mr. Frei era had been passed and the construction sector was increasing by 25.8% (Annual Report of the University of Chile, March 1980). This development has been maintained over 1980 and 1981.

The other social services: health, care of the aged, continuous educational programmes, holidays and cultural activities, etc. benefited under Gen. Pinochet from the same degree of attention as in all developed countries. There was perhaps a distinctive feature—considerable expansion in social help given by private citizens to other private citizens. The denigrators will mock and say at once: "of course here they are, the benevolent reactionaries; this is the famous paternalism which ties the beneficiaries to their benefactors with hand-outs, this is world charity which humiliates those who receive it."

Let us reflect a little. *La Secretaria Nacional de la Mujer*, Chile, succeeded in recruiting more than 11,000 women of all ages and of all classes, who worked voluntarily and benevolently for an average of four hours a day to bring a variety of social services to particularly deprived families and individuals. In addition, 1,500 other women volunteers formed a uniformed, full-time service. A monthly magazine, packed with practical advice on health, child care, diet, the rudiments of medicine, housekeeping, etc., wise and expert advice, is distributed free of charge in an edition of a million copies. *La Secretaria Nacional de la Mujer* has also given a great deal of help to the shanty-town families in settling in to their new little houses equipped with electricity and running water, for the new tenants had to be shown how to avoid ruining them.

How can such help fetter anyone? The voluntary workers do not represent any firm, any institution, any ideology, other than to teach ignorant mothers how to feed their children better; to teach reading to adult illiterates; to encourage families with some means to leave their hovels; to find work for the elderly unemployed, etc. Furthermore, charity is not in itself shocking; it is one of the fundamental teachings of all religions. It is only questionable when it becomes an excuse for the consolidation of privilege. But when, as is the case with *La Secretaria Nacional de la Mujer*, charitable works are disinterested, on a large scale, systematic, and carried out mainly by ordinary women, they can only arouse admiration. Through this means and at this level, we fall in the category of the public sector or social protection, as carried out, for example, in France by the social services, a protection which all progressive people, all popular movements, demand and approve—so long as they do not emanate from General Pinochet.

Lessons to be learnt from the economic and social recovery under Pinochet

The first and fundamental lesson to be learned from the spectacular economic recovery brought about by Pinochet is that free enterprise had once again demonstrated its enormous superiority over collectivism. Ultimately, it is by restoring initiative to the individual entrepreneur, industrialist, businessman, artisan or peasant, and also in imposing upon him the risks inherent in tackling a free and competitive market, that Chile has pulled its economy out of the mire from the brink of bankruptcy into which it had sunk under Mr. Allende's bureaucratic Commandism. It has been proved yet again that general economic state planning is a fatal trap, for the simple reason that in economics there are no known laws which make it possible to calculate in advance, on a long-term basis, what should be done for all products and for all people. The only operative key is the continuous empirical adjustment of production in the light of actual requirements and market conditions; this is only possible by means of the internal competition between a variety of free enterprises.

Spurred on by the thirst for profit? Naturally, it must be admitted without reserve, the hope of gain is, together with creative ambition, the principal agent which stimulates business enterprise. This temptation is in no way disgraceful so long as it is accompanied by the acceptance of risk, and limited by social legislation which prevents its promoters from trying to achieve their own aims by detestable exploitation of the work-force. This is the essence of modern liberalism.

In a major interview published by *El Mercurio* on 17 June 1978, the former Minister of Economics Mr. Baraona, one of the sharpest minds in Gen. Pinochet's team, made this illuminating remark: "Socialism has never wished to understand that it is absolutely impossible to have a *wealthy society without wealthy people*. It is a foolish dream. What we want is a *rich society without poor people*. What does it matter if some people have three cars so long as everyone has one?" All the misery of workers and peasants living in Communist countries arises from the fact that their leaders prefer to have millions of poor people rather than one single rich man!

The last comment that I wish to make is connected with another passage in the Baraona interview. He says: "If the Pinochet regime were a dictatorship which wished to perpetuate itself, it would be the most foolish dictatorship in history. Why is this? Gen. Pinochet inherited from Mr. Allende enormous centralised nationalised economic power and he is voluntarily breaking it up. He could have controlled factories and land, he is giving them up. He could have controlled prices, he is abandoning this. He could have controlled foreign trade, movement of capital, the banking system, he renounces this. His would be the only dictatorship which would have deprived itself of its most important powers, which it only depended on itself to retain."

Ex-President Nixon, in his book *The Real War* published in 1980, makes a similar remark: "The disparagers concentrate solely on political repression in Chile, while ignoring the freedoms which are the result of a free economy . . . The re-establishment of economic rights could well be the forerunner of the restoration of political rights."

I made the same observation during my stay in Chile. All true dictatorships, above all in our own time, whether of the right or of the left, have concentrated above everything else on maintaining the most extensive and far-reaching control over the economy, for they are aware that, together with their police system, it provides an unequalled instrument for subjugating the whole of society. Hitler and Mussolini established a network of control. Since they were dependent upon capitalism, and thus did not dare to carry out the whole Marxist programme, they did not push nationalisation too far. But if they had found it already carried out by a previous regime, they would have rubbed their hands and taken good care to return nothing to private ownership as they did in Nazi-occupied Russia during the war. The denationalisation undertaken by Gen. Pinochet as soon as he came to power, and the return to a liberal economy very largely open to private enterprise, provide irrefutable proof that he had no totalitarian intentions.

CHAPTER XIX

THE CAMPAIGN AGAINST PINOCHET: A FALSE SYMMETRY

I HAVE GIVEN ELSEWHERE SOME EXAMPLES of the intense campaigns of hate and calumny against the Pinochet regime which has filled most of the world mass media. I shall not revert to them. I shall devote this chapter to the social and political questions which they raise.

There is no comparison between misdeeds

The principal effect of these campaigns is to establish in the mind of the public a sort of symmetry, or of equality in evil, between all dictatorships, be they communist or anti-communist. What does it matter, says the man in the street, conditioned by this propaganda, what creed is professed and what aims are pursued by such regimes, I am as much against one as the other because they are both dictatorships.

I shall show first that there is no common measure between the misdeeds of these two sorts of dictatorships. Further, that the two are not equally condemned, but that anti-Communists are condemned enormously more strongly than Communists.

It has been established today, through dozens of demographic works, that the communist regimes which have existed in the USSR for the past 65 years, and for the past 35 years in China, in Vietnam, in Cambodia and other satellites, have massacred, after coming to power, about *150 million* of their subjects, that is to say some 15% of the populations concerned—180 times more than the French terror of 1793. Still today, millions are being dumped in concentration camps and in inhuman prisons, or brutally killed. What do we find in Chile?

We have seen that the overthrow of the Marxist President Allende by General Pinochet cost two or three thousand dead, mainly during the period of the fighting. Once the military juntas was in the saddle, several thousand opponents were arrested, and some 20 were executed. The terrorists set up several pockets of resistance, but they found no support among the people and by the end of 1975 they were in full retreat. We know of the Corvalan-Bukovsky exchange in December 1975, which gave freedom to a Soviet political prisoner. The only remaining political prisoner in Chile was the former Communist

Senator Jorges Montes. It was suggested that he should be exchanged for the anti-Castro leader Mr. Huber Matos, who had been rotting in Cuban gaols for 19 years, without arousing any special concern from public opinion. The Cuban dictator refused. Nevertheless, the Communist Senator Jorge Matos was released on 18 June 1977. From that time there were no more *political* prisoners in Chile. However, the Pinochet government also decided to release the Allendists who had been tried and sentenced for crimes under the Chilean penal code. It was no longer a question of political prisoners, but of criminal law prisoners, of whom some were expiating crimes of misappropriation of funds, of tax frauds or of terrorism. Among them 33 were sentenced to life imprisonment. There remained a little over 200 prisoners in this category who would have been condemned in the courts of any country in the world. Well, even they were set free by the amnesty declared on 5 April 1978!

To this should be added the following significant comments:

1. The violence which Gen. Pinochet employed in Chile was in response to an immediate and deadly communist totalitarian threat. In contrast, in the communist dictatorships considerably more widespread and cruel violence has persisted for 60 or 30 years, and this cannot be justified by a danger of the return of the former enemy classes, which have long ago been wiped out. When the Communist powers themselves suffer traumatic shocks, as in Budapest or Prague, or are faced by guerrillas, as in Afghanistan, it is by *hundreds of thousands* that the rebels are massacred, with tanks, flame-throwers, napalm, gas, and in the lowest depths of the gulag.

2. When Gen. Pinochet effaced the Allendists, he respected certain standards. The statements published abroad by the Allendist leaders interned on the Chilean islands, and the facts which I have reported earlier, show that they received enough food, that their work routine was tolerable, that they received parcels and visits, and that they were allowed to correspond with their families. Once again, is there anything in common with the forced labour camps of Pol Pot, of Hitler and of Stalin? Those were places of concentrated horror, where men were systematically transformed by maltreatment, first into skeletons, and then into corpses, and of which Solzhenitsyn so magisterially, and after so many others, drew a picture which made the whole world shudder with indignation against the executioners. Nor, under Pinochet, was there any equivalent to Hitler's abominable gas chambers, or to the psychiatric hospitals of Brezhnev where the detainees are slowly dehumanised with nerve poisons.

3. In contrast to the Communist dictatorships, the Pinochet regime is not surrounded by an Iron Curtain, the obscene ring of barbed wire,

revolving searchlights, police dogs, mine fields and machine guns which surrounds the vast Communist prison along a 25,000 kilometer frontier, preventing the inhabitants from fleeing towards the Free World which holds such a fascination for them. In contrast, under Gen. Pinochet, the frontiers are all freely open; whoever wants to get out, can leave when he wants, without any interference from the authorities.

4. The anti-Communist dictatorships only strike at their enemies, whereas the communist dictatorships strike at everyone, including other Communists whom they have slaughtered, giving a scale of madness to their violence. In Cuba, Fidel Castro has thrown into prison or condemned to death many of the comrades in arms who helped him to power, such as Mr. Huber Matos; and members of Castro's family who disobey him are in danger of death, as his sister Juanita, who lives abroad in exile, has revealed. Stalin killed almost all of his comrades of the October Revolution. Mr. Boumedienne imprisoned his chief comrade in arms Mr. Ben Bella for 14 years, whereas after three years Gen. Pinochet released his ferocious enemy, the Communist Mr. Corvalan.

5. As with all anti-communist authoritarian governments, the Pinochet regime spares daily life. Every one can make a free choice of husband or wife, of partner, of occupation, of worship, and of a school for his children. On the contrary, in the communist regimes fear pervades every aspect of everybody's lives. No-one confides in anyone else, since everyone fears denunciation. A passport is need to travel within the country. Anyone may have to account to a communist street committee for his purchases, for his outings, for his love affairs. Death is the penalty for innumerable innocent activities which are arbitrarily attributed to plots against the regime.

6. A great human drama has demonstrated in a manner which cannot be denied that every day life is infinitely harder and more sombre under a communist dictatorship than under a strong anti-communist regime. This was the desperate flight of the Vietnamese boat people after the conquest of South Vietnam by the Communists of North Vietnam. Everyone was appalled by the sight of these poor wretches, wild-eyes or weeping, crowded like cattle on no matter what hulk, and who were risking the most appalling dangers; drowning, death from hunger or thirst, epidemics, robbery or death at the hands of pirates, abandoned in groups on a waterless beach, anything rather than endure communist tyranny.

These tragic spectacles of the Hai Hong, or of the thousands of the shipwrecked drowning in the China Sea, or of the 30,000 Cambodian refugees on the shore of death, or of the 60 Vietnamese clinging to an oil drilling platform in mid-ocean, dying there like animals because no-one would answer their SOS; these spectacles expose in a flash the immensity of the fraud which is perpetrated when an equal balance is implied between communist dictatorships and strong anti-communist regimes. It is enough to recall that there was never any Hai Hong taking desperate refugees far away from the shores of Chile. In fact, although any Chilean is free to leave with his property, very few leave the country. And of the Chilean emigrés who left during the time of the civil war, many have returned. Equal balance?

Here is another striking example which proves how false is the symmetry drawn between the misdeeds of communist and anti-communist powers. On 5 April 1980, when it was announced that they could leave their country if other governments would grant them an entry visa, 10,000 Cubans invaded the little garden—2,000 square metres—of the Peruvian Embassy in Havana. They camped out on the lawn, five to a square metre, and in the trees and on the roofs. They endured the most appalling living and sanitary conditions rather than return to Castro's yoke. Which anti-communist dictator was ever rejected by his subjects in a demonstration of despair and hatred of this magnitude?

Just think of it, at the same time as the Cubans, subjects of a regime praised or courted by the whole world, were fighting to leave their country, Chileans, opposed to a regime which the whole world condemns, were fighting from abroad to be able to return to their country. There are thousands of these candidates for return to the Pinochet regime among the very persons who accuse Gen. Pinochet of being a Fascist! But they know full well that life in Chile is in fact very tolerable, on the material, moral and political levels, since, even in the absence of political parties, it is possible without danger to voice open opposition to the regime.

Thus today we are witnessing the development of a noisy campaign which aims finally at what? To enable Gen. Pinochet's opponents to go and live under a Pinochet who is condemned, whereas in Cuba a dramatic campaign is necessary so that the allegedly pro-Castro inhabitants may go and live far away from a Castro who is admired.

This explodes two lies at the same time; that which talks of the infamy of the Pinochet regime, and that which speaks of the virtues of the Castro regime. The only equality of balance is in the equal blatancy of these two untruths.

7. Another factor illustrates the strong contrast between these two types of regimes, misrepresented as equals in guilt. Gen. Pinochet has opened all doors in Chile to a number of commissions which have come to investigate human rights in Chile such as UN, the Red Cross, Amnesty International, AFL-CIO, etc., while no single communist state has ever accepted any scrutiny. On the one hand there is openness

to investigation, on the other fierce resistance. Can it really be believed that the two regimes are equally guilty?

8. Anti-communist dictatorships do not preach outside their own frontiers. Overseas, there is no Pinochet party, any more than a Galtieri party or a Suharto party. In contrast, Fidel Castro or Moscow parties are to be found everywhere. Communist dictatorships are served, reinforced and shelterd by the most colossal propaganda and subversive machine in history, of which the pressure is continually felt on the fate of the whole world. Communist dictatorships are the carriers of a virus which poisons the world, anti-communists are not.

9. Finally, communist dictatorships are capable of diabolical excesses which equal Hitler's anti-semitic massacres. We remember, for example, Stalin's insane purges of 1936–1938, when millions of people suddenly disappeared from the land of the living, without knowing why, after a tap on the shoulder from the police, to end up in a ditch with a bullet in the neck, or in a prison cell, or in a death camp. More recently, we recall the apocalyptic genocide, unprecedently cruel and widespread, of the poor and gentle Cambodian people by their new communist masters; forcible evacuation, within 24 hours, of the three million inhabitants of Pnomh Penh, Pharaonic slavery for millions of Cambodians, the massacre of a tenth of the population in the most horrible fashion; suffocated with plastic bags; drowned with stones tied to their feet; whole families buried alive; a miserable kneeling Indian file, chained together, their throats cut with bayonets. This was done by a communist government. Alone in the world of the 1970s, unique in contemporary history, a communist government exterminated; crushed; dehumanised its peoples by such means and on such a scale. Who still dares to speak of Pinochet?

The true relationship between misdeeds

If we put together all the characteristics of the two types of dictatorships, communist and anti-communist, which I have described, so as to make an overall comparison between them, it is impossible not to conclude that the former are ten thousand times worse than the latter in regard to the trampling underfoot of human rights. From this we must deduce that these two types of regime are fundamentally different, since a social phenomenon changes its nature when the order of magnitude of its manifestations changes too much. This is a law which the general public, including Marxists, frequently disregards, but to which, however, Karl Marx attached crucial importance. Indeed he summed it up in a famous phrase; "quality is changed by quantity". This means that when an evil doubles or triples in intensity it remains in the same category, but if it is multiplied by 1,000 or 10,000, you enter a new world.

The theft of a loaf of bread and the theft of a post office van are both thefts, but the articles stolen are so different in importance that the whole century of Victor Hugo was indignant that the first offence should be punished as severely as the second. No, 5,000 unemployed do not have the same significance as three million. In the first case, there is a fault in adjustment, in the second there is a major crisis. No, a confrontation which leads to ten deaths is not the same as a guerilla campaign which causes 100,000. No, an inaccuracy once a month in a newspaper is not the same thing as ten inaccuracies in a day . . . No, no and no again, a regime which causes the death of 1,000 armed opponents has nothing in common with another which deliberately sacrifices a hundred million unarmed innocents.

In fact, the Pinochet regime in Chile does not even merit the description of "dictatorship". The appropriate designation is that of *authoritarian* government. This is how sociologists describe a government which operates without parliamentary control and does not permit organised political parties, but allows the people to live; think and criticise freely, and physically represses only illegal acts of subversive violence, such repression being contained within humanitarian limits. The classic examples have been, in the nineteenth century, those of Napoleon III in France (say, from 1858) and of Franz-Josef in Austria. In the twentieth century, Mr. Diem in Vietnam, Mrs. Gandi in India, the Greek Colonels, Mr. Suharto in Indonesia, Mr. Boumedienne in Algeria, Mr. Nyerere in Tanzania, Mr. Videla in Argentina, and Gen. Pinochet belong to this category. In contrast everything is changed due to the scope, the rigour and the cruelty of the repression practiced by Mao Tse-Tung, Fidel Castro, Ho Chi Minh, Pol Pot in Cambodia, Kim Il-Sun in North Korea, and the other communist leaders, together with Hitler, Mussolini, etc. Here we are dealing with *totalitarian* tyrannies, fascist or communist, which constitute a profoundly different phenomenon.

There is no parity in the condemnations

It is remarkable intellectual dishonesty not to take into account such great differences of degree as I have indicated between Gen. Pinochet and Brezhnev. To quote Gen. Pinochet as an example of anti-democratic violence instead of Brezhnev or Pol Pot is as if a sociologist, studying militarism in Europe in 1914, were to take Montenegro as an example instead of Prussia, or to put Montenegro in the same category as Prussia.

Furthermore, if so many people include Gen. Pinochet when they reproach Brezhnev, it is not because they really believe that the two are equal. In fact, they want to excuse their audacity in criticising a left-wing power by simultaneously criticising a right-wing power. They say to the guardian of leftist orthodoxy to which they have committed the control of their mind: you can see, I have not become a reactionary in spite of my criticism of a communist regime, since in the same breath and with as much conviction I am equally condemning the anti-communist generals.

Of course they would not admit that they are falsifying the balance of their judgement with the sole aim of giving themselves the courage to pass judgement upon Moscow. They justify themselves by an *affectation of fairness*. Their usual line of argument is as follows: what does it matter to me how many of the opposition are in prison, it shocks me quite enough if there is only one. For I, Sir, am a sensitive person who cannot bear *any* infringement of liberty. You should admire my strict morality and my impartiality; if a government violates one single right of one single man, I condemn it loudly whatever its political colour.

The trick here is that the reason for action is confused with the degree of action called for. A doctor is justified in treating a patient for as little as a cold in the head, but it would be an absurdity for him to expend as much energy in doing so as if it were a question of cholera. Thus it is certainly right to criticise a government for infringing human rights even if it does so only once a year, but it is terribly wrong to do so with as much vigour as about a government which tramples the rights of man underfoot a thousand times a day.

This trick has a double advantage for those who practice it; for their own glory, they can plead democratic hypersensitivity, at the same time as, for their own convenience, they are giving currency to a distortion of the facts which greatly favours Communism.

Favours Communism? Certainly so, and powerfully, for to judge a large crime according to the same standards as a small one is always to disguise it. It is an old trick of casuistry, making it impossible to see the wood of crime for the trees of infringements. The truth is that today the only monstrous political *system* is that of the gulag. It is so monstrous and so menacing that all available forces of sanity in the world should be mobilised to fight it. Those who, like Amnesty International, cry in the market place that they intend to fight publicly, at the same time and with the same intensity, against Communism and against all the dust thrown up by regimes which are a hundred thousand times less evil, are helping to divert public interest from the heart of evil at a time when it should be focused upon it. When the other great monster of our century, Nazism, was laying waste our world, would we not have regarded as its accomplice anyone who said: I agree that we should resist it, but let us not forget to give half our attention to the King of Nepal, who has just illegally arrested his cousin.

In reality the service rendered to Communism by the champions of "equal balance" between its tyranny and the anti-communist dictatorships is much greater. Because, as it is already untrue that the two trays of the scales are equal in weight, it is even less true that the two sides are equally accused. In fact the communist tyrannies are denounced to a much lesser degree than the authoritarian anti-communist governments.

For nearly two years, the majority of the media, overflowing with curses against Gen. Pinochet, said not a single word about the Dantesqua genocide perpetrated by the Vietnamese and Cambodian governments against their own peoples. There then appeared some restrained three-line news items on the papers' inside pages. A check which was made throughout the year 1976 on the columns of the *Washington Post* showed that this paper, prototype of the "liberal spirit", reported 58 times on violations of human rights in Chile, 24 times in South Korea, but only once on communist North Korea despite its ten concentration camps and its bloody attacks on South Korea, four times on Cuba despite its "human cages", its 20,000 political prisoners, and the countless numbers of those missing and executed, nine times on Cambodia despite the two million killed by repression, not once in South Yemen despite its 15,000 political prisoners and the number of assassinations of political opponents which take place there.

The partiality of the *New York Times* is even more striking; 66 violations of human nights reported in Chile, 61 in South Korea, three in Cuba and only four in Cambodia. As to the American television network NBC, in one year which included the genocide in Cambodia, it did *not once* mention this unprecedented violation of human rights, whilst consistently arousing public opinion about attacks upon human rights in Chile, in Argentina and in Uruguay.

Who had heard of the horrors committed by the North Vietnamese Communists in South Vietnam before they were exposed by the heart-breaking drama of the boatloads of refugees sailing towards death? Who ever speaks of Castro's loathsome prisons, filled to overflowing for the past 20 years with tens of thousands of political prisoners, regularly replaced when there are deaths from maltreatment? Who has heard of the mass hangings of the opposition in South Yemen, in pro-communist Ethiopia, in Angola and Mozambique? Who has heard speak of the Cabinda children, 3,000 deported to Cuba in 1977 because they refused to join the Angolan army? And of the further kidnapping of Cabinda children in 1979, who were sent to guerilla camps in the USSR and Cuba? Who put pro-communist Afghanistan under Taraki Amin outside the bounds of humanity for its 15,000 political prisoners, crammed into overcrowded gaols before the Soviet invasion, and of whom 3,000 were shot, and for the 48 students who were shot in front of their homes and their families because they had refused to take a course on the life of the Soviet puppet, their President? If Pinochet had committed one hundredth part of these savage acts, all the newspapers of the world, trembling with indignation, would have spread it over five columns.

To this is added hypocrisy. For in the case of Chile the role played is that of the hyper-sensitive pure democrat who abhors *any* military coup d'état. Now, in fact, there have been a number of coup d'états carried out by *Marxist soldiers*; by General Ne Win in Burma, by General Taraki in Afghanistan, by General Mengistu in Ethiopia, by Colonel Qaddafi in Libya, by Colonel Boumedienne in Algeria, by Marxist-sympathising Captains in Portugal, by Generals Barrientos, Torres and Ovando in Bolivia, by Colonel Peron in Argentina, by General Velasco Alvaredo in Peru, by a Sergeant Major who had been trained at the Soviet Lumumba University in Liberia, etc. All these Marxist pronunciamentos were *applauded* by the left!

There are very few among the Western heads of state who would dare to shake Gen. Pinochet by the hand, whereas all indulge in free and friendly exchanges with Brezhnev. And this is not because Brezhnev's power obliges them to humour him. The Marxist Mr. Sékou Touré rules over a small marginal country in Africa which France could perfectly well ignore without the least consequence to herself. He is in fact one of Africa's bloodiest tyrants; at the least sign of opposition, he subjects his people to the most abominable maltreatment, in the Cambodian fashion. For good measure, he is keeping some 20 Frenchmen in his filthy prisons. This has not prevented our former President Giscard d'Estaing from clasping him to his bosom, to the loud applause of a left-wing press touched by the "reconciliation". It was the same story when a French Minister paid a visit to the Hungarian butcher Mr. Kadar, who on the orders of the super-butchers of Moscow massacred his own people in revolt in 1956. Mao Tse-Tung, one of the cruellest and most obtuse tyrants in history, was described as "a guiding light of world thought" by President Giscard d'Estaing, who would consider that he was dirtying his mouth if he admitted any virtue in Gen. Pinochet. If Gen. Pinochet should die tomorrow, there would not even be an Embassy secretary from the Western democracies to follow his funeral procession, whereas the President of the United States, the heir to the throne of England, the French Prime Minister Barre, etc., jostled each other, competing in their eulogies, behind the coffin of Tito, the cynical dictator who denounced to the Germans the non-communist Jugoslav freedom fighters, who tortured thousands of his political opponents in prison, among them his friend Djilas, who arranged the assassination abroad of some of those who had managed to escape, and who strutted about in 14 palaces while his people, through his oppressive and imbecile bureaucracy, were living in a permanent state of under-development. In deference to the left, the American Trade Union Congress AFL-CIO decided upon a maritime boycott of Chile because Gen. Pinochet had refused to restore certain trade union rights, but it has never boycotted any of the communist or communist-oriented countries where trade unions are reduced to a police role, assisting the authorities to enslave the workers.

When French radio and TV vented their fury on Gen. Pinochet over the assassination of Mr. Letellier in the USA, no Chilean diplomat was ever given the opportunity to defend his government's point of view on the air. But when French radio and TV were appealing for assistance for the hundreds of thousands of dying Vietnamese refugees, they specified many times "that politics must be kept out of it", and there was no question of blaming the officials in Hanoi. On the contrary, communist Vietnamese diplomats were free to come and "explain" on the air the atrocities committed against the castaways by their government.

Without exaggeration it can be said that the media controlled by the left condemn Gen. Pinochet, by no means as often as Brezhnev, but a thousand times more. As we have shown that he is ten thousand times less guilty, it follows that *the index of bad faith on the left amounts to ten millions.*

This colossal bad faith is not gratuitous. It has a very precise and important purpose: in making Gen. Pinochet the greatest villain in the world, the left avoids this place being filled by Brezhnev. The left wishes passionately for the overthrow of Gen. Pinochet in Chile, although he is no threat to either the peace or the liberty of the world. It accepts philosophically the perpetuation of Brezhnev in the USSR, although his tyranny spreads wider every year, and the coming to power in our own countries of his surrogates could be as apocalyptic for our democracies and our lives as in Cambodia and Vietnam.

Yes, the left desires, and desired with hatred, the overthrow of Gen. Pinochet in Chile, of the Shah in Iran, of Mr. Mobutu in Zaire, of Mr. Diem in Vietnam, of General Park in Korea, of Mr. Begin in Israel, of Bishop Muzorewa in Rhodesia, of Mr. Somoza in Nicaragua, of General Evian in Turkey, although it is well aware that this can only lead to the establishment in these countries of communist governments, and thus to the extension of the rule of the gulag which, elsewhere, it purports to deplore. But for the masters for which it has a very soft spot, for it never calls for the overthrow of a Castro, of a Qaddafi, of a Nasser, of a Pham Van Dong, of a Kim Il Sung, of a Neto in Angola, etc., although it is perfectly aware that this would lead to tolerable regimes for their peoples.

Why?

One question remains to be clarified; it troubles all the Chileans, and will doubtless bother you too, dear reader: why this violence of the media of the left against Gen. Pinochet? Why their false analogies between communist totalitarian dictatorships and anti-communist authoritarian governments? Why this heavy bias in favour of the worse? What is the secret stimulus, the powerful venom, which, even after Solzhenitsin, forces the left to cling to Communism, at any rate in an international context?

I think that the key to this mystery lies in the unforgiveable failure of the socialist formula when applied by the communist regimes. This failure has made it impossible for those of the left, at least for the left of slogans and riots to pretend that they hold the key to a social system superior to our own. But then, *what is there left for them to offer?* We have reached the heart of the problem. To what can prophets turn when they can no longer predict a millennium? How can they keep up their fine postures of being upright accusers of the established order, of intransigent rebels, of inspired judges, which have brought them so much prestige? . . . and so many votes? Only one course was left to them so as to continue their blustering; this was to maintain a strict silence on any constructive proposition, and to throw themselves with all their might into pitiless denunciation of present conditions, constant denunciation, denunciation everywhere, denunciation for denunciation's sake.

Thus their deep-rooted complicity with Communism becomes more understandable. If the left admitted that it is the communist apparatus which foments bloody troubles all over the world, it would have to defend the regimes under attack, and then its position of absolute criticism, all that remains to it, would collapse. If on the contrary it denies that subversion is a product of Communism, and presents it as the result of genuine popular discontent, it can utilise it to enlarge its chronicle of accusations against the established order, and thus improve its own position as its enemy. You can surely see, says the left, that this world is so loathsome that everywhere the people are in revolt. Communist attacks on it support the left's own viewpoint. The logic is inescapable. The left justifies its existence henceforth no longer by offering a *programme*, but only by attacking an *enemy*—the established order—and this enemy is *the same enemy* as that of the Communists.

From this, it is obvious that Communism becomes the objective ally of the left, and it is in its interests to support it. If it cannot support its achievements, then it will support its conspiracies.

This also explains why, when a crisis occurs which obliges the established order to defend itself by installing unusually strong governments, as in Chile, this left-wing, defined by clamour and uproar, attacks with a kind of frenzy. It is rather hard to blacken the established order when this order is democratic. But if certain freedoms are temporarily suspended, and if this task is entrusted to a general, then what a feast, what an opportunity for the left to make a scandal! It throws itself into it with zest, puffs out its chest, makes a meal of it. It also easily wins a political good conduct mark, since it is enough to condemn the generals to appear virtuous. The left is proud of showing how much more inflexible it is in the "defence of great principles" than the "infamous right". Finally, it enjoys the delicious thrill of shouting in unison with the Communists. Because, to its eternal regret, it can no longer warm itself beside Brezhnev, it is more than happy to be able to join him at least in hatred of Gen. Pinochet.

CHAPTER XX

THE CRIME OF RESISTANCE

In order to make a sensible assesment of the Chilean events, we must first deal with the platitudes which are uttered about military take overs in general.

The usual pose is that of the hyper-sensitive democrat who execrates a priori any military coup d'etat. Just imagine, these officers to whom the republic has entrusted its weapons, and who take advantage of this to seize power for themselves by force, what a disgraceful betrayal of confidence! As a backdrop to this scandal which the left assiduously foments, there appear the old obsessions about brass hats, goose steppers, reactionary sabre-rattlers, inveterate Fascists. For some time past, this picture of the officer corps has become an absurd caricature.

The double standard

A major enquiry carried out by the Rand Corporation in 1965 among South American officers, Chileans in particular, had already revealed that most of them had *left wing* tendencies. Had they not joined the Allende government? Colonel Peron, who organised the coup d'etat of 1944 led his party into an alliance with a wing of the Communist Party, and his party under the leadership of some other colonels, later became the paymaster of a number of extreme left-wing groups, among them that of the Montoneros terrorists. In Columbia, the dictator Mr. Rojas Pinella followed a similar path. In Bolivia, Mr. Paz Estensoro, put in power by the army, set up a socialist regime and carried out a massive agrarian reform. In Peru, General Velasco Alvarado overthrew in a coup d'etat the civilian President Belaunde Tery, himself strongly left-wing, and established a Marxist regime. In Panama, all the forces of the left are expanding under the sway of the "putschist" General Torrijos. In Mexico, the fellow-travelling President Lazaro Gardenas, a general of his country, was mainly responsible for introducing the communist infiltration from which the country is still suffering. The final irony is that the founder of the Chilean Socialist Party in 1932, Marmaduke Grove, was an Air Force Colonel! Outside Latin America, let us not forget that the right-wing Portuguese dictator Salazar was overthrown by a military coup carried out by Marxist officers.

This break with the old prototype of right-wing military disciplinarians by a large proportion of the officer corps in Latin America and elsewhere has been established for some time, and illustrates profound sociological and ideological changes. Ambition, now is better served by assuming a "progressive" attitude than by sticking to the stereotype portrayed in Courteline's descriptions of military types. The shameful model of a Colonel Henry of the Dreyfus affair, heel clicking, medals, reactionary intrigues, has also vanished from most of the Western armies. It is wise to remember that the bourgeois officer corps in Western nations shed their blood to deliver Europe and Japan from Fascism, Nazism and Militarism. In Europe and America, the General Staffs were the arms, and often the brains, of the revival of democracy. General Patton, General McArthur and their officers did as much to restore democracy and freedom in Japan and Germany as all the socialist parties in the world.

Let us also not forget that in Nazi Germany the strongest resistance to the Fuhrer originated among the higher ranks of the armed forces, whose revolt of July 1944, smothered in blood by Hitler, is commemorated by democrats all over the world. We should remember that if this revolt by the German officers had succeeded, it would have been nothing less than a strictly military coup d'etat. Nevertheless the world would have gone mad with joy at the success of such a putsch against Hitler.

This example is made even more striking by a long list of cases which reveal the hypocrisy of the "non possumus" proferred by the left about military coups . . . only, and *only*, when they do not go in its favour. I have already recalled that there have been many which have conformed exactly to the description of the "scandalous" abuse of force: in Burma, in Afghanistan, in Iraq, in South Yemen, in Algeria, in Ethiopia, in Libya, in Portugal (Mark One), in Peru, in Equatorial Guinea, in Panama, in Salvador, in Liberia, etc. And, as I said, in regard to them the lips of the left-wing purists were suddenly sealed. But I was mistaken, their mouths were in fact filled with praises of these goose-steppers and sabre-rattlers, but leftist or Marxist ones. On Equatorial Guinea, a left-wing paper carried this astonishing headine: "At last a military coup!" This is worse than double standard. It is a standard which leads to condemnation when the military coup is carried out by certain people, and exactly the opposite standard, leading to celebration when the military coup is carried out by other people. And to which military coups does the left apply the second standard? It is enought to look at the list which I have drawn up to see that it is to pro-communist military coups d'etat.

The denouncers of the Pinochet coup d'etat fall into a further inconsistency. They belong to those left wing circles which, when Communism is condemned for the horrors which it unlooses, reply that these are only the unfortunately unavoidable means to the achievement of a splendid end; the classless society. To excuse Communism, they invoke the famous maxim that "the ends justifies the means". But if some generals pull out from the body of Chile the dagger which was causing its democracy to bleed to death, in other words if they use forcible means for ends of salvation, then straight away these same left wing circles find that they are tremendously concerned over the means, and declare, in complete contrast to their first tune, that no ends can justify the means for not being absolutely irreproachable. It is another example of the double standard.

Thank God, the Chilean people, having come so close to the grave, did not succumb to suicidal vertigo on the altar of principles, and proved, by summoning the generals to their aid, that they had not lost the will to live.

Let us also consider a counter-proof. Suppose that the Chileans had bound themselves absolutely to the sacrosanct axiom (only so when it serves the interests of the left) which forbids miliary intervention in civil conflicts. In what way would they have served democracy? In a matter of weeks, they would certainly have fallen under a full *totalitarian tyranny*, with no more parliamentary freedom, but with a thousand fold harsher political slavery and material suffering. The Pinochet regime holds out considerable possibilities for a return to complete democracy, infinitely greater than those, precisely nill, which would have been offered if Pinochet had *not* acted. For, in that case, the Chileans would inevitably have fallen under an impenetrable and irreversible communist dictatorship on Cuban lines. Who would not trade an eternity in hell for ten years of purgatory?

Ingratitude

There are some democrats who agree that it was fortunate that the pronunciamento put a stop to Chile's imminent fall into the long night of Communism. But since the price to be paid was the establishment of an authoritian government, a type of regime which they on no account wish to be seen to be approving, they prefer to conceal their inward relief. When the need arises, they even add a few notes of accompaniment to the chorus of denunciations against the "putschist" generals. They think to themselves that in this way they can simultaneously protect the country from Communism and protect their own utterances from the reproach of being "right-wing".

In deciding to write this book, I was determined not to practise this double standard ploy. I knew that I should put myself in bad odour with the proponents of liberalism, of whom the most sectarian will call me a "reactionary". Too bad. It will not be the first time that I have taken the hard, strong road. But I cannot conceive how it is possible to rejoice inwardly that you have been saved by a military force from a terrible fate, and outwardly to look askance at it. It was perfectly well known what political system Mr Allende would have set up and I have shown that this was planned, applied and ready for total implementation. Nevertheless a decision was made that a non-Communist system would be a thousand times preferable to the tyranny from which Chile would be delivered, and the help of the military was invoked. So I regard it as illogical and dishonest that what is thought in secret is not said aloud, and that is *thanks*. We have seen that ex-President Frei, an impeccable democrat, has done so in an interview in Spain which had wide repercussions. The worst form of cowardice is to be ashamed of one's friends. In order to defeat Hitler, the democratic powers permitted themselves an alliance with Stalin, that is to say with something very much more diabolical than the Chilean Army, and furthermore they thanked him profusely for his contribution.

Why is Pinochet Hanging On?

On the other hand, it is perfectly understandable, after having given credit to the Chilean military for the good which came of their intervention, to consider that at the end of a certain period of time they should withdraw and hand over to a normal civilian democratic regime. By appearing to take root for more than the time necessary to wipe out the Marxist-Leninist enemy, they can understandably be regarded as abusing their rights as deliverers. Here we are entering a more honest discussion which we have already begun and which I should now like to conclude.

The military can only instance one reason for not at once ceding power, and that is that a return to the old game of the political parties would revive the risk of a new offensive by the forces of Marxism-Leninsim. It could be argued that even if all the old parties of the UP recovered their liberty such a risk would be negligible, since these parties are profoundly discredited. Would not the still vivid memory of the sufferings they caused be a sovereign remedy against the resurgence of their old demagoguery?

Alas, this would not be a sufficient safeguard. Firstly, because such rabble-rousers can always find fresh material for demagoguery in the current situation, for example in the "social cost" argument of the economic recovery or the "conspiracy of foreign capitalists" referring to foreign investments. Secondly, because the Communist organisation could be rapidly reconstructed in all its strength. This is in no way surprising, whatever damage it suffered, because it is in fact nothing but an appendage of the soviet state which as long as it remains inviolate and powerful, retains all the means to grow new tentacles everywhere, even if the old ones have been lopped off, and with even greater ease when they have, as in Chile, been neither decapitated nor decimated. We must not forget that thanks to its inexhaustible resources, the communist machine has survived considerably longer, stronger and more severe repressions by Hitler, Mussolini and Salazar. Gen. Pinochet is a very, very long way behind.

Above all, the danger would arise from the fact that, apart from the nationalists, the old Chilean political parties, led by the Christian Democrats and followed by the left wing radicals and Socialists, are again starting to open their hearts and their country's institutions to agents or auxiliaries of Communism, without thought of the consequences. I gave proof of this in the last chapter.

Thus, if Chilean democracy recovers, there remains only one way to protect it from a repetition of the tragedy; *it is to make the return of the "liberticide" parties impossible.* I have told you that this is the path which Gen. Pinochet's new constitution advocates. But you may have thought that this method is in itself inadmissible. For the commonest idea among democrats is that their own principles preclude them from excluding any political party. I want to finish this book by trying to show you that this idea is false and dangerous.

It is legitimate to deny liberty to the "liberticide" parties

When it is said, with reason, that there is no democracy if opposition to the established government is not free to act, one implies "free to act in a democratic manner". But opposition by the Communist Party does not respect democratic norms, and this takes us at once to the heart of the argument. Liberty, says the scrupulous democrat, is above all that which I give to others to oppose me. And I reply: that is true, but on condition that those who oppose me do not intend to gag me, or, as is done more efficiently in the cellars of the KGB, to kill me, so that I shall never again be able to oppose them.

True democracy implies that a right which I grant to an adversary, such as the right to liberty, should also be guaranteed to me. That is to say that there should be an obligation of reciprocity, which has always been the basis of all agreements, and only fools let thieves get away with it. It is because this principle is so self-evident that we find this obligation of reciprocity expressed in the most striking terms by some of the best minds. Thus Karl Mannheim wrote: tolerance cannot go so far as to surrender to intolerance. Montesquieu and later Jean Jacques Rousseau proved that for a right granted to all (as in this case the right to freedom) to be truly universal and permanent, it is necessary to exclude from its benefit (Outlaw from society, Jean Jacques Rousseau would say) those who intend to destroy it. In addition no rule of conduct can be regarded as truly assimilated by a social group unless this group punishes those who infringe it. The prohibition of stealing and murder is only effective because the police arrest thieves and assassins. Likewise, the right to liberty will only become effective from the time when the forces of law and order apply sanctions on those who attack it.

It seems to me valid to regard democracy as a system favouring the organisation of political discussion on the lines of a market; the free market of ideas, which are offered to potential purchasers like articles in a shop window and in accordance with the laws of competition. Every one knows that the commercial market has only been able to function properly where controls have gradually eliminated major frauds. No-one has ever considered it damaging to the principle of free economic competition to prohibit the display of merchandise not on sale in the shop, the opening of shops which purport to be independent but are in reality branches of a monopoly, the sale of poison as a health tonic, the misuse of the trade mark and prestige of a product in order to pass off an inferior article, the ruin of rivals by slander, etc. Well, all these fraudulent practices, which no liberal regards as anti-liberal to prohibit, have their exact parallels in politics. The Communist Party displays merchandise—prosperity and liberty—which it does not intend to sell; it opens shops—the crypto-communist organisations—allegedly independent but secretly affiliated to the Party; it sells Fascism as Socialism; it uses the label and prestige of Marxism to pass off its by-product, Stalinsim; it ruins its rivals by slander.

Honest competition can only operate when unfair competition is eliminated. Without an impressive collection of prohibitions and the state machinery to enforce them, the commercial market would be nothing but a jungle. Thus to consider it an abuse to ban the Communist Party amounts to saying that it is all right for the law to impose a minimum standard of honesty on the trade in plums, but disgraceful that it should do so on the trade in ideas, a trade where integrity ought to be more important to us. It is to proclaim that the jungle can rule in politics. To allow a party which has no respect for the rules of democracy into a free society is as ridiculous, in the political realm, as to allow false measures in commerce.

Heresy Yes, Conspiracy No

Every one knows that the totalitarian parties, such as the Communist Parties, are instruments for the depersonalisation of their members. The fragmentation into small cells which do not offer a broad enough framework for worthwhile discussions and which are nothing but commando units to enable the Communist Party to gain control of the levers of society, the stifling intellectual orthodoxy, the plethora of professional activists, the absolute pre-eminence of the apparat over the rank and file, the rigged congresses which elect by a 100% majority leaders who have been pre-selected, the omnipotence of the leaders, compliance obtained through intimidation and dissidence suffocated by fear, the systematic use of factions meeting in secret in order later to circumvent plenary assemblies, all this aims at alienating the personalities of the members of the Communist Party. Whereas the domocratic parties are meeting places for ideas, totalitarian parties constitute prisons for ideas. The armed political terrorists of today are the certain forerunners of the crushed citizens of tomorrow. Democracy aims to make of each citizen a source of choice. This aim is frustrated if it allows its citizens, gathered together in hundreds of thousands in totalitarian parties, to be turned into gramophone records relaying the slogans issued by the ruling bodies of such parties.

To this profound fossilisation of its inner life, the Communist Party adds the permanent falsification of its external actions. Everything it says to the public about its intentions is a lie. The programme, the doctrine, the final aim are nothing but disguises for its only, concealed objective; the achievement of *absolute power*. The Party makes use of a vast network of parallel organisations, in particular in the trade unions, which have been secretly penetrated. It deploys unlimited calumny, deception, and intimidation. It spreads its influence in the state by infiltrating its agents or accomplices. It saps institutions and undermines the economy. In short, it extends its empire not by the democratic process of *conviction* obtained in the full light of day, but by the totalitarian means of servile *obedience* controlled in the darkeness of fear. An illuminating example was to be seen under Mr Allende. Although the Chilean Communist Party formed part of the government and enjoyed all the facilties conferred by office, it did not cease to maintain a vast clandestine apparatus of which the tentacles reached into the wheels of the administration, into other political parties, and even to the parties allied in the UP. What has been said can be summed up in an illuminating phrase: the Communist Party is not a *political movement*, but an *apparatus of conspiracy*. And that is one of the essential reasons why it should be banned by a democracy worthy of the name.

Thus we arrive at a fundamental idea. When it is proposed that their Party should be made illegal, the Communists shout, and their deputies repeat, that this is being done in order to stifle their subversive ideas, and to prevent, by police action, the dissemination of the great ideas of Marx and Lenin about the evils of the capitalist regime. This argument is nothing but a great confidence trick. It is perfectly true that democracy, if it wants to avoid sclerosis, is obliged to allow everything to be said on all matters, whatever one is defending, God or the Devil, money or work, internationalism or the native land, struggle or collaboration between classes, the family or free love. It is perfectly true that no political movement should be harassed because of the content of its ideas. The one essential condition which democracy has the right to impose on all political or ideological movements is that they should conduct the trade of ideas honestly, and that none should threaten the freedom of others to carry on this trade. This is what is done by the Communist Parties. It has been very well understood by Professor Sidney Hook in the title of his book, which concludes as I do: *Heresy Yes, Conspiracy No.*

This is what is not understood by those who allow themselves to be led astray by cetain well-known and very badly digested catch-phrases. For example this one, which they regard as irrefutable (albeit cynical) and which a Communist is supposed to say to a democrat: "When you are in power you owe me freedom in the name of your principles; when I am in power I take it from you in the name of mine". A mere dirty trick, of which the evil lies in this, that the Communist never says before coming to power, that his principle will be the suppression of freedom. Thus he lies, and conceals himself behind a conspiracy. He plays the game but has no intention of obeying the rules.

Similarly, many purist liberals admire a phrase which the French attribute to Voltaire and the English to John Stuart Mill, and believe that this phrase obliges them to tolerate totalitarian parties: "I disagree absolutely with what you say, but I will defend to the death your right to say it". The misinterpretation is that it presumes your opponent is acting in good faith. The Communists have never acted in good faith and despise such a concept. There would be considerably less enthusiasm for a statement like this, which neither Voltaire nor John Stuart Mill would ever have dreamed of making: "I am in complete disagreement with the lie you are telling, but I will defend to the death your right to tell lies". Democracy is obliged to ensure to everyone the freedom to express their opinions, but by no means the freedom to disguise them. Thus in giving complete freedom to the Communist Party to operate legally the serious error committeed lies in the confusion of these two freedoms:—*the freedom of opinion and argument*, honourable and, in fact, unassailable, and the *freedom of deceit and conspiracy*, seditious and unacceptable.

One-Way Tolerance

Furthermore, those democrats who maintain that the prohibition of the Communist Party would be a disgrace because it would trample on the sacred obligations of tolerance, are not at all worried about calling for the prohibition of fascist organisations and opinions. Their tolerance of the left knows no bounds, their tolerance of the right is nil. After the war, these one-way liberals organised the worst *witch hunt* in history in order to uncover the former members of Hitler's party in Germany; and without any pangs of conscience, having made up their minds that Germany could never return to true democracy until the last Nazi had been unmasked and placed beyond the bounds of humanity. But when it is suggested that similar (but much less savage) measures should be taken against the present-day Nazis, the Communist apparatchiks, the leftist purists get on their high horse and shout that tolerance is being betrayed.

Thus they show a repulsive partiality. When it is proposed that totalitarian parties should be banned, they pretend to act upon a principle, but in fact are acting out of speciousness, since they support the ban for fascist parties and oppose it if it applies to communist parties. In fact, there pseudo-liberals object because damage would be done, not to liberty, but to the Communist Party. They make a great parade in lip-service to liberty, but they have no real love for liberty since they admit that its very rituals kill it. When the communist murderers of liberty appear on the ground, they do not have the instinctive reaction of genuine devotion which consists in covering with one's own body that which is threatened, while crying, despite any flag displayed by the attackers, "Stop—You Shall Not Pass". They are to liberty like the false mother whom Solomon exposed when she was prepared to let the child be cut in two rather than renounce her claim. One who allows liberty to be stabbed rather than to defend it is indeed a false democrat.

It is high time that true democrats learn not to confuse *tolerance* with *surrender,* and not to believe that democracy, unlike a woman, is only virtuous when it abandons itself to anyone who wants to ravish it. It is high time to teach true democrats to mock the fallacy according to which, alone among all regimes, democracy, because it is founded on liberty, cannot defend itself without contradicting itself. This fallacy is an excellent means of making liberty unattractive to the significant number of people who do not fancy suicide. Some will refuse to support a system which refuses to defend itself and them.

Some people have a practical objection. Given that a democracy should have the right to ban totalitarian parties, how can this be put into practice? How can it be proved that a certain party has "liberticide" designs without falling into a hateful intellectual inquisition? This disquiet is really astonishing. What! the crime of totalitarianism today oppresses the world. Its nauseous vapours rise up to heaven and stifle the century. And it is alleged that it cannot be ojectively identified and calmly checked! Come now! It is much easier to define, to recognise and to proscribe the crime of totalitarianism among political forces than to detect, prosecute and punish the innumerable offences under the law which people may commit in civil or economic life. Nevertheless, at the urgent demand of the leaders of society, this has been achieved in all civilised communities. To do as much to counter the crime of totalitarianism, an equally strong determination would be needed, but a great deal less detailed labour. I have drawn up a Code of Citizenship of only several dozens of articles, (while the Civil Code contains 2,500), which would permit the effective pursuit of the crime of totalitarianism without doing the least injury to the principles of tolerance and liberty. The new Chilean Constitution contains a similar provision In fact the difficulty lies not in detecting but in ignoring the totalitarian nature of the Communist Parties. The democrats tie themselves into knots in order to make believe that the communist parties are "no different from any others" and to dress them up as embodiments of social aspirations in order not to have to deal rigorously with them as enterprises of totalitarianism.

After the suffering of the Chilean people during the Allende years, no wonder Gen. Pinochet says "Never again".

In ending these pages, I want to clear up any misunderstanding about my own position.

I have defended the Pinochet regime firstly because it has saved the Chile I love from the limitless and irrevocable tragedy which would have ensued from its fall to totalitarian Communism, and secondly because the regime is the victim of a worldwide campaign of exceptionally vicious slander which only benefits that very Communism. In other words, I have above everything wished to honour the true facts and to restore a true perspective. But I have not defended General Pinochet through love of military regimes. Despite the verbosity, the weakness, the mediocrity, the compromises with which, alas, it drenches us daily, democracy still seems to me to be the least bad of all the political systems.

This means that the regime which to me still seems the most desirable is that which is headed, not by a general riding on his tanks, but by a president elected by his people, even if the general should have the virtues of a Pinochet and the president the failings of a Carter. What seems best to me is a regime which respects personal dignity and freedom of thought; a regime which inlcudes a permanent public debate, several responsible political parties bringing together like-minded people and competing *fairly* for politcal power, a parliament elected by universal suffrage to pass the laws, a government limited by a legal constitution, an independent judiciary, encouragement for free enterprise together with a competitive market and active social solidarity, the safety of legitimate property and of personal integrity. A regime which, of course, also imposes duties: work, defense, of honety of non-violence, of legality. That is how I would wish all nations to live. It follows that Communism, which today is practising with implacable ferocity the exact opposite of all that I desire, is to me the greatest evil and the supreme menace of our times.

Consequently in my opinion a democracy which does *not* resist this threat, and which even opens its gates to its cohorts, is not worthy of the name it bears. It deserves to vanish, as all forms of life vanish when, instead of defending themselves against the agents of destruction which attack them, they give them a friendly welcome. In particular, the present-day Western Democracies, which are usually held up as examples, but which on the whole are endlessly complaisant about Communism and even pride themselves on this complaisance, take it as proof of the authenticity of democracy that it should permit free circulation of the communist poison in their veins, these democracies are imbecile and suicidal. For me, it is exactly the contrary which proves the health of a democracy; that its body be kept closed to the totalitarian virus. It is only then that it becomes a superior system worthy of defending. Otherwise, it is no more than a fun fair where the barkers attract the crowds with promises of freedom only to deliver them inside to the janissaries of the gulag.

The refusal to lose body and soul in such a charade was Chile's greatness. Faced with urgency in September 1973, it could only save itself by the *sword*. It had a perfect right to unsheathe it. Today, it is preparing a better defence; *the law.*

For all the democracies of the world which do not intend to die of the blackmail which the "liberticide" parties practise in the name of liberalism, for all those who do not consider it a crime to resist Communism and who understand that this poison of totalitarianism must be eliminated from public life, there is no other choice; if they do not want to have to wipe it out in hot blood with the sword, they must wipe it out in cold blood with the law.

This, in my view, is the great lesson which Chile is teaching us, us the free men who are faced by the forces which are plotting our destruction:

WE HAVE THE RIGHT TO RESIST THEM.

AND WE HAVE THE MEANS.

Postscript

While I was working on this book, what was my surprise in hearing one morning the radio announcer reporting the following comments from our most reputable leaders and newspapers:— "A military putsch has at last taken place to save the country . . . bled white by a disguised civil war, torn to pieces by irresponsible political parties, ruined by a stagnant economy, it was sliding towards the abyss . . . The army was the only remaining effective and respected institution . . . in carrying out its task through a putsch, it was only doing its duty, which is to protect the people against mortal dangers. . ."

I could not believe my ears. So there could be redemptive pronunciamentos? Unworthy democrats and worthy generals? Conditions to be respected by political parties? It was, then, legitimate to dissolve Parliament and to suspend freedoms where they were giving birth to violence, gravedigger of all freedoms? Was I dreaming? At last I was hearing described in truthful terms the tyranny-generating chaos into which Mr. Allende had plunged Chile, I was hearing, oh miracle, justification of Gen. Pinochet for having rescued her. Had the world suddenly understood? Was I writing this book in vain?

It was not long before I realised my mistake. The broadcast was not about Gen. Pinochet, but about General Evren, who at the head of his tanks had just seized power in Turkey. As he had overthrown a government of the right and not a Marxist President, everything was in order, and respectable people could without dishonour applaud his great feat of arms.

INDEX

ABC, 167
AFL-C10, 195-198, 214, 251, 257
Abarzua, Carlos Morales, 16
Academy of Christian Humanism, 222
Acevedo, German, 76
Acuerdo, 51
administrative reforms, 229-231
Agrarian Reform Corporation (CORA), 72, 75, 76, 81, 86, 103 115, 116
Agriculture
  policy, 236-237
  production, 104, 105, 109, 237-238
Agriculture, Ministry of, 236
Aguayo, Alvaro Rojas, 58
Aguilar, Mario, 87
Ahumada, Hermes, 16
Aisen Transport Company, 140
Alessandri, President Arturo, 2, 3
Alessandri, President Jorge, 6, 23, 24, 25, 60, 93, 124, 130, 146, 149, 186, 225
Allende, Andrés Pascal, 18, 27
Allende, Laura, 18, 27
Allende, Salvador, ix, 6, 8, 13, 14, 17, 20, 22, 26-29, 64, 65, 215, 218, 224, 226, 229 *et seq.*, 260 *et seq.*
  advent of, vii, 21, 22 *et seq.*
  chronicle of reign of, 30-39
  economic disaster under, 102 *et seq.*
  end of regime, 155 *et seq.*
  expropriations in the countryside under, 72 *et seq.*
  fall of, vi
  foreign intervention in government of, 184 *et seq.*
  illegal storage of arms by, 89 *et seq.*
  illegality of government of, 152-154, 155, 161, 166
  intervention by ITT and the CIA under, 184-186
  legality flouted by, 40 *et seq.*
  lessons of the experiment, 171 *et seq.*
  moral standards, 117 *et seq.*
  people's power, on, 63
  political opposition to, 146 *et seq.*
  popular opposition to, 129 *et seq.*
  suicide of, 160, 200
  violations of freedom of expression under, 50-61
  violence under, 82 *et seq.*
Almeyda, Mr., 220
Almonacid, Roberto, 76
Altamirano, Amanda, 52
Altamirano, General, 3
Altamirano, Mr., 13-15, 17, 27, 39, 59, 87, 97, 98, 129, 156, 158, 220
Alvaredo, General Velasco, 256, 260
Amaya, Fernando, 91
Amerasia, 194-195
American State Department, 194
amnesty for political prisoners, 218
Amnesty International, 199, 211, 212, 214, 251, 254
Ampuero, Mr., 5, 12
Analysis, 222
Apablaza, Agunto, 132
Araucanos. *See* Mapuches
Araya, Captain Arturo, 88
Arbenz, Mr., 28
Arceo, Mendez, 193
Ariztia, Monsignor, 21
arms,
  distribution, 89-91
  smuggling, 92-94
  thefts, 91-92
Arnello, Mario, 55
Arran, Ramon, 77
Arroyo, Gonzalo, 21
Auditor-General, Office of, 44, 48, 150, 152, 153, 166
L'Aurore, 199
Avendano, Oscar Squella, 120
Ayala, Captain, 38
Aylwin, Senator, 25, 29, 173

Baader-Meinhoff gang, 212
balance of payments, 239
Balfro, Mr., 17
Balmaceda, President, 2-3
Baltic Steamships, 190
Banados, Judge, 212
Bar Association, 150, 152
Baraona, Mr., 246
Barbarossa. *See* Piniero, Manuel
Barboza, Mr., 208
Barre, Prime Minister, 256
Barrientos, General, 256
Baytelman, David, 115
Beca, Mr., 119
Begin, Mr., 257
Bell, Maria Contreras. *See* de Ropert, Maria Contreras Bell
Bella, Ben, 250
Bellarmine Centre, 19
Benes, Dr. E., 28
Bernouin, Jacques, 110
Berrios, Juan Marchant, 65
Bezanilla, Onofre Lillo, 73
black market, 105-106, 118-119
Blum, Leon, 222
Boeninger, Edgardo, 50, 53, 139
Boumedienne, Colonel Houari, 28, 227, 250, 253, 256
Boya, Alberto, 192
Brezhnev, L. I., 11, 249, 253-254, 256, 257, 259
Bruno, Mr., 88
Bukovsky, Vladimir, 10, 203, 205, 248
Bulnes, President, 2
Bulnes, Senator Francisco, 41, 42
Business Week, 235, 240, 241

CEPCh. *See* Confederation of Employees in Chile
CGT, 222
CIA, 108, 109, 134, 185, 194
CID, 83
CODE, *See* Democratic Confederation
CODELCO, 136
CORA. *See* Agrarian Reform Corporation
CORFO. *See* Industrial Development Agency
CUT. *See* Unitary Workers' Federation
Cabieses, Manuel, 51
Caceres, Victor, 132
Calderon, Arturo Rivera, 82, 83
Calderon, Ronald, 83
El Campesino, 117
El Canaveral, Mr., 88
El Cauelo drinking-water undertaking, 132
capitalism, 109-110
Carevic, Luis, 193
Carmona measure, 148, 158, 159, 168
Carrera, Fernando, 94
Carter, President Jimmy, 197, 269
Carter, Rosalynn, 206
Cassidy, Sheila, 204-206
Castillo, Hector, 77
Castillo, Jaime, 218
Castillo, José, 208
Castillo, Rolando Matus, 76
Castro, Baltazar, 114
Castro, Fidel, vi, 21, 27, 28, 33-34, 56, 90, 93, 121, 127, 128, 160, 168, 179, 190-191, 215, 223, 227, 250 *et seq.*
Castro, Juanita, 250
Castro, Lautaro, 212
Castro, Admiral Toribio Merino, 118
Catalan, Elmo, 85
Catholic University, 20, 37, 40, 51, 136, 139, 141, 158, 222, 231, 236, 241
Central Bank, 29, 47, 51, 57, 103, 219, 238
Central Unica de Trabajadores. See Unitary Workers' Federation
Centre for Economic and Social Development in Latin America, 19
Cerda, President Pedro Aguirre, 5
Ceresita paint concern, 57
Chacon, Juan, 213
Chamber of Deputies, 41, 45, 50, 51, 141, 143, 152-154
Chamndez, Marcos, 10, 11
Chicago Boys, 232 *et seq.*
Child malnutrition, 243-244
Chile-Bulgaria Committee, 16
Chile-East Germany Association, 16
Chile Films, 54
Chile National Airline, 120
Chile-North Korea Committee, 16

Chile-Red China Association, 16
Chile-USSR Committee, 16
Chilean Telephone Company, 132
Choikin, Sol, 195
Chonchol, Jacques, 8, 30, 72, 74, 103, 114, 139
Christian Democratic Left, 17, 18
Christian-Democratic party, 5 *et seq.*, 14, 17, 23, 24 *et seq.*, 30, 31, 38 42, 50 *et seq.*, 146 *et seq.*, 155, 189, 226
Christians for Socialism, 21. *See also* Young Church
Chuquicamata, 35, 37, 113, 132-133, 218, 219
Cienfuegos, Ivan, 57
Cimma, Enrique Silva, 16
Cirankievicz, Mr., 28
Civil Code, 269
civil war, 200-206
Clarin, 41, 95, 96
Club de Paris, 187
Code of Citizenship, 269
Codelia, Juan, 56, 75
Colby, William, 185
collectivism, 110-111, 172 *et seq.*
College of Agricultural Experts, 142
College of Barristers, 166
College of Journalists, National Council of, 57
College of Left-wing Journalists, 132, 180
Comintern, 28
Communal commandos, 86-87
Communist International, 10
Communist Party, 4, 6, 10-12, 47, 51, 53, 70, 185, 203, 207, 264 *et seq.*
Communist youth organization, 20
Comunidad Cristiana, 205
El Condor, 56
Confederación de Empleados Particulares de Chile. *See* Confederation of Employees in Chile
Confederación Nacional de Provincias Agrarias Unidas, 195
Confederation of Employees in Chile (CEPCh), 133, 221
Confederation of Production and Trade, 81
Constitution, 45, 46, 48, 50, 81, 137, 143, 151, 152, 168, 227, 269
Contraloria. *See* Auditor-General, Office of
Co-operativa Vitalicia, 219
Copper production, 104-150, 235
Corneille, Mr., 128
corruption, 117-118
Corsican terrorists, 212
Cortes, Baltra, 103
Cortes, Jorge, 84
Corvalan, Luis, 10, 66, 158, 202, 203, 221, 248, 250
countryside, expropriations in, 72 *et seq.*
La Cronica, 57, 58
Cruz, Luciano, 97
Cuba
  Communist Party, 191
  involvement in Chile, 190 *et seq.*
Cuba Aviación, 92
Cuban Liberation Directorate, 192
Cuevas, Exequiel Aroca, 36, 77
Cumsille, Rafael, 69

DGI, 191
DINA, 218
DIRINCO. *See* Directorate of Industry and Commerce
da Silva, Milton Santos, 193
Dawson Island, 202-203
de Castro, M., 219
de Ona, Beatrice, 27, 191
de Ona, Luis Fernandez, 27, 191, 192
de Ropert, Maria Contreras Bell, 35, 91, 121-122, 160
Debray, Régis, 29, 85, 174, 175, 180
Declaration of the Rights of Man, 169
del Canto, Hernan, 45, 55, 93, 96
del Valle, Jaime, 40, 41
Democratic Confederation, 148
denationalisation, 232
Diaz, Eduardo, 53
Diaz, Gladys, 199
Diaz, Father Luis Antonio, 21
Diem, Mr., 253, 257
Dienlevent, M., 217
Dieye, Abdoulaye, 214
Directorate of Industry and Commerce (DIRINCO), 60, 66, 68, 143
disappearances, 206-214

Domic, Juraj, 67, 69, 98
Donoso, Teresa, 205
drug traffic, 119-120
Duran, Julio, 6, 17, 23, 148, 149

ENU. *See* United National School
economic decline, 102 *et seq.*, 186 *et seq.*
economic recovery, 229 *et seq.*
Economist Intelligence Unit, 110
Ecuador Socialist Party, 132
Ediciones Zig Zag, 58
Edwards, Agustín, 59
Edwards, Sonia, 59
Elmo Catalan Brigade, 85
Empresa Nacional del Petroleo, 116
Empresa Nacional Quimantu. *See* Quimantu National Press
Enrique Ortuzar Commission, 218
Enriquez, Edgardo, 118
Enriquez, Edgardo (ex-minister of Education), 118
Enriquez, Miguel, 75, 90, 118
Eperva fishing enterprise, 113
Errazuriz, Maximiano, 56
Escarte. *See* Paredes, Eduardo (Coco)
Escuela Nacional Unificada. *See* United National School
Espinoza, Raul Mendez, 83
Estanco Automotriz, 119
Estensoro, Paz, 260
European Economic Community, 183, 237
Evian, General, 257
Evren, General, 271
exports, 233-234, 238
L'Express, 11
expropriations of property, 72 *et seq.*
Ezanco-Latin American Chamber of Commerce, 235

Faivovich, Jaime, 14, 156
Federal German Constitution, 226
Federation of Santiago Secondary-school Students, 138
Field, Frederick V., 195
Fierlinger, Mr., 28
Figueroa, Enrique, 77
Figueroa, Luis, 11, 97, 179
Filippi, Emilio, 114
Five Year Plan, 230
Flores, Fernando, 48, 68
Fomento Fabril company, 80
Fontanarosa. *See* Marambio, Max Joel
foreign currency reserves, 239
foreign intervention, 184 *et seq.*
Fornes, Enrique, 121
Fourcade, Anibal Palma, 66
France
  Chile's lesson for, 180-183
  Communist Party, 11, 180
  Constitution, 226
  Radical Party, 221
Franco-Latin American Chamber of Commerce, 240
Franz-Josef, Emperor, 253
Freedom Fund, 60, 130
freedom of expression, 50-61
Frei, President Eduardo, ix, 6 *et seq.*, 19, 22, 25, 30, 32, 42, 50, 73, 79, 102 *et seq.*, 120, 146, 150, 151-152, 167-169, 184, 186, 188, 217, 226, 239, 242, 245, 263
Frente de los Trabajadores Revolucionarios. *See* Revolutionary Workers' Front
Fuentealba, Renan, 146, 147, 152

GAP. *See* Group of Personal Friends
GRU, 192
Galleguillos, Daniel, 55
Gallo, José Antonio Viera, 42
Gallo, Viera, 77
Galtieri, President, 252
Gandi, Mrs., 253
Gardenas, President Lazaro, 260
Garreton, Mr., 19, 156
Garrido, Manuel, 95, 193
Gazmuri, Mr., 19
Giscard d'Estaing, President, 172, 256
Gleason, Thomas, 195
Godoy, Jorge, 79
Gonzales, German, 76
Gonzales, Gilberto, 76
Gonzalez, Manuel, 95
Gossens, Salvador Allende. *See* Allende, Salvador
Goulart, Joao, 28, 127
Graham Agency, 56

gremios, 143, 144, 156, 165
Group of Personal Friends (GAP), 18, 31, 68, 87-89, 90, 91, 122, 164, 191
Grove, Major Marmaduke, 3, 260
Grupos de Amigos Personales. *See* Group of Personal Friends
Guastavino, Luis, 118
Guevara, Che, 20, 179, 191
Guijón, Dr. A., 160
Gutierrez, Nelson, 72, 204
Gutierrez, Robinson, 95
Guzman, Jaime, 225
Guzman, Mario, 149

Hamilton, Senator Juan, 53, 147, 152
Henriquez, Cardinal Raul Silva. *See* Silva, Cardinal Raul
Herald of Freedom, 194
Hermosilla, Ciro, 46
Herriot, Edouard, 16, 28
Hiss, Alger, 194
Hitler, Adolf, vi, 10, 162, 223, 249, 252, 253, 261, 263, 264, 268
Hitler-Stalin pact, 10
Ho Chi Minh, 253
Holzapfel, Armando, 16
Hook, Professor Sidney, 267
Hourton, Bishop Jorge, 205
house-building, 107
Hoy, 220
Hua Kuo Feng, 224
Huentelaf, Moises, 76
Huerta, Admiral Ismael, 47, 48
Hugo, Victor, 253
Human Rights Charter, 81
Humeres, Héctor, 44, 80, 150

INDAP. *See* Institute for the Development of Agriculture and Stock-breeding
IRA, 212
ITT. *See* International Telephone and Telegraph Corporation
Ibanez, Arturo, 12, 23, 133
Ibanez, Bernardo, 197
Ibañez del Campo, President Carlos, 3, 6
Iglesia de Santiago, 205
Illich, Mr., 193
Incas, 4
industrial cordons, 63, 86
Industrial Development Agency (CORFO), 51, 57, 58, 60, 78 *et seq.*, 118, 130, 232
industrial production, 235-236
Industry and Commerce, Directorate of. *See* Directorate of Industry and Commerce
inflation, 238
Institute for the Development of Agriculture and Stock-breeding (INDAP), 72, 77, 103, 115
Institute of Pacific Relations (IPR), 194
Inter-American Institute for the Development of Free Trade Unionism, 197
International Association of Jurists, 214
International Labour Office, 197
International Monetary Fund, 110, 240
International of Blood, 192
International Telephone and Telegraph corporation (ITT), 132, 184-186, 191, 194
investments, 234-235, 239
Iran, Shah of, 257
Iribarra, Nelly, 76
Itinéraires, 199, 211
Iturra, Colonel Pablo, 85

JAP. *See* Juntas de Abastecimientos y Precios
Jaccard, Mr., 208
Jacobin Club, 143
Jarpa, Sergio Onofre, 42
Jaurès, Mr., 12, 180
Joffee, Philips J., 195
Joignant, Alfredo, 45, 77
Juarez, Sergio, 56
Juntas de Abastecimientos y Precios (JAP), 35, 37, 48, 62, 67, 68-71, 81, 88, 144, 154

KGB, 186, 196, 197, 264
Kadar, Mr., 256
Kennedy, Senator Edward, 197, 198
Kennedy, President John F., 198
Kéraly, Hugues, 203, 211-212, 220
Keraly, M., 199
Khruschev, N. S., 11, 109
Kim Il-Sung, 253, 258
Korry, Edward, 186

Kravchenko, Mr., 197
Kremlin, 28, 29, 100
Krivitsky, Mr., 197

Labin, Suzanne, 195
Labour Party, 183
Lacrampette, Hector, 157, 193
Larrain, Mr., 19
Latin-American Solidarity Organization (OLAS), 27
Lattimore, Owen, 195
Law Courts, 46
Left Radical Party (PIR), 17
Leighton, Mr., 218
Lenin, V.I., 7, 15, 47, 51, 70, 98-99, 117, 175, 179, 188, 266
Letelier, Orlando, 197, 198, 257
Levi, Albert, 76
Levi, Andre, 76
Liberal Party, 183
liberalism, 218-221
Loero, Teresa Donoso, 19, 21, 22
Louis XIV, 47
Lumumba University, 256

MADEMSA, 119, 121, 193
MAPU. *See* Movement for Unified Popular Action
MCR. *See* Movement of Revolutionary Peasants
MIR. *See* Movement of the Revolutionary Left
MPR. *See* Movement of the Revolutionary Shantytown-dwellers
Maachell, Antonieta, 75
McArthur, General, 261
MacHale, Tomas, 52, 56
Mackenna, General, 83
McLeod, Scott, 194
McNamara, Mr., 110
Madiran, Jean, 211
La Mañana, 55-56
Mannheim, Karl, 264
Mao Tse-tung, 171, 223, 253, 256
Mapuches, 4, 73-74, 114, 135
Marambio, Max Joel, 18, 75, 88
Marchais, Mr., 183
Marquis, Jacques, 211
Martin, Nelson, 91
Martinez, Amador Medina, 73
Martinez, Juan, 16
Marx, Karl, 20, 51, 102, 111, 176, 184, 196, 224, 252
Matos, Major Hubert, 203, 249, 250
Matos, Jorge, 249
Matus, Rolando, 87
Meany, George, 195-197
Medina, Guillermo, 134
Mena, Jorge, 76
Mendez, Paul, 80
Menendez, Nieres, 193
Mengistu, General, 28, 256
Mensaje (Message), 19, 220
El Mercurio, 14, 28, 54, 58-59, 61, 71, 84, 90, 119, 122, 131-132, 133, 191, 202, 219, 220, 241, 242, 246
Mickey, Commander. *See* Villalobos, Alejandro
Mill, John Stuart, 267
Millalonco, Juan, 95
Millas, Hernan, 114, 121
Millas, Orlando, 45, 187
Mint, the, 46
Minute, 199
Miranda, Hugo, 16
Mirists, 56, 64, 127. *See also* Movement of the Revolutionary Left
Mitterand, President François, vi, ix, 12, 15, 172, 182, 183, 223
Mobutu, Mr., 257
Monckeberg, Dr. Fernando, 243-244
Le Monde, 240
Montero, Admiral, 157-158, 164, 169
Montero, President, 3
Montes, Carlos, 74
Montes, Jorges, 249
Montesquieu, 264
Montoneros, 193
Montt, President, 2, 3
moral standards, 117 *et seq.*
Morales, Luis Bravo, 94
Morande, Maria Correa, 127
Moscoso, Carlos Liva, 57
Moss, Robert, 69
Movement for Unified Popular Action (MAPU), 8, 17, 18, 19, 30, 37, 56, 57, 68, 81, 87, 97, 116, 119, 146
Movement of Christians for Socialism, 193
Movement of the Revolutionary Left (MIR), 8, 17, 18, 21, 27, 30,

38, 47, 53 *et seq.*, 63 *et seq.*, 81, 82 *et seq.*, 158, 192, 193, 204, 211
Movement of Revolutionary Peasants (MCR), 72 *et seq.*
Movement of the Revolutionary Shantytown-dwellers (MPR), 18, 78
Movimiento de Accioñ Popular Unificada. See Movement for Unified Popular Action
Movimiento de Campesinos Revolucionarios. See Revolutionary Farmers' Movement
Movimiento de la Izquierda Revolucionaria. See Movement of the Revolutionary Left
Movimiento de los Pobladores Revolucionarios. See Movement of the Revolutionary Shantytown-dwellers
Municipal Works Corporation, 112
Mussolini, Benito, 223, 253, 264
Muzorewa, Bishop, 257

NBC, 255
NPE, 163, 164
Napoleon III, 253
Nasser, President, 258
Nathalia, Comradi, 78
National Columbia News Service, 25
National Confederation of Commerce, 141
National Confederation of Production, 141, 142
National Confederation of Small-Scale Industry and Craftsmen, 141, 142
National Nutrition Institute, 243
National Party, 5, 23, 41-42, 50, 55, 60, 146 *et seq.*
National Union of Associations of the Liberal Professions, 142
nationalization, 102
Navarro, Jose, 95
Navas, Sarah, 138, 157
Ne Win, General, 256
Nepal, King of, 255
Neruda, Pablo, 11-12
Neto, Agostino, 28
New York Times, 255
Nixon, President, 12, 45, 247
Notebooks on National Reality, 139
Nouvel Observateur, 220
Novoa, Eduardo, 42
Nunez, Enrique, 80
Nyerere, President, 253

OIR. *See* Presidential News and Radio Office
OLAS. *See* Latin-American Solidarity Organization
October Revolution, 250
O'Higgins, General Bernardo, 1, 124
Olivares, Sergio, 94
Opposition
political, 146 *et seq.*
popular, 126 *et seq.*
Organisation of American States, 217
Organized Vanguard of the People (VOP), 65, 80, 81, 82, 83, 88, 90, 146
Orrega, Paul, 195
Ortega, Abraham, 92
Ortuzar, Enrique, 225
Oscar Spichiquer powder store, 91
Osorio, Mr., 120
Ovando, General, 256
Overseas Private Investment Corporation, 184

Pacheco, Francisco Ismael Villegas, 83
Paillas, Enrique, 45
Palestro, Mario, 14
Palma, Domitilia, 75
Palma, O'Higgins, 91
Palma, Patricio, 66, 143
La Papelera, 32, 34, 60-61, 130-131, 144, 154
paramilitary groups, 82 *et seq.*
Pardo, Mr., 91-92
Paredes, Eduardo (Coco), 83 *et seq.*, 120
Pareto, Luis, 119, 151-152
Park, General, 257
Partido de la Izquierda Radical. See Left Radical Party
Paseyro, Ricardo, 11, 12
Pastenes, Ivan Papic, 120
Pasternak, Boris, 12
Patria y Libertad, 87
Patton, General, 261

La Payita. *See* de Ropert, Maria Contreras Bell
Pedro, 72
Penal Code, 45, 218
People's Courts, 64
Pepe, Commander. *See* Vera, Jose Liendo
Père Duchêne, 95
Pérez, President, 2
Peron, Colonel, 256, 260
Peugeot-Renault group, 235
Pham Van Dong, 258
Philips, W. *See* Joffee, Philips J.
Phillips, Patricio, 114
Pineda, Oscar, 95
Pinella, Rojas, 260
Piniero, Manuel, 191, 192
Pinochet, General Augusto, vi, 3, 10, 19, 66, 89, 124, 133, 134, 188, 189, 193
  AFL-CIO interventions, 195
  American intervention in affairs of, 194-195
  campaign against, 248 *et seq.*
  coup d'état by, ix, 25, 159 *et seq.*, 200, 260 *et seq.*
  economic recovery under, 229 *et seq.*
  liberalism under, 218-221
  present political situation under, 217 *et seq.*
  repression under, 199 *et seq.*
  social policy, 243-246
pistoleros, 193
Plan Z, 162-165
Pliego de Chile. See Roll of Chile
Pobladores, 55
Pol Pot, 249, 253
political opposition, 146 *et seq.*
Popper, David H., 194, 195
popular opposition, 126 *et seq.*
Popular Unity Front (UP), 5, 6, 14, 15, 18, 20, 22 *et seq.*, 30 *et seq.*, 200, 229
  corruption, 118
  drug traffic, 119-120
  economic disaster under, 102 *et seq.*
  end of regime, 155 *et seq.*
  expropriations in the countryside, 72 *et seq.*
  legality flouted by, 40 *et seq.*
  moral standards, 117 *et seq.*
  nationalization of La Papelera, 130-131
  political opposition to, 146 *et seq.*
  popular opposition to, 127 *et seq.*
  position of, 171 *et seq.*
  regimentation of the people, 62 *et seq.*
  violations of freedom of expression, 50 *et seq.*
  violence by, 85 *et seq.*
  workers' hostility to, 131-133
Portales, Diego, 1, 2, 3, 124
Posta Central de Primeros Auxilios, 193
Prats, General, 26, 36, 38, 47, 155
La Prensa, 56
Presidential News and Radio Office (OIR), 50, 143, 144, 154
Prieto, Pablo Urrutia, 75
Prieto, President, 1
Programme of the New Business Man, 230
Puelma, Jorge Baraona, 75
Punto final, 51, 95, 116
Puro Chile, 42, 93, 120

Qaddafi, Colonel, 256, 258
Quarterly Report, 110
Que Pasa, 222
Quezada, Raul, 76
Quimantu National Press, 58

Radical Democratic Party, 17, 148
Radical Party, 12, 15-17
Radio Agricultura, 52, 143, 144
Radio Alonso de Ercilla, 52
Radio Arica, 52
Radio Co-operativa, 53
Radio El Carbón, 53
Radio Presidente Balmaceda, 52
Radio Riquelme, 52
Ramona Parra brigade, 53, 85
Rand Corporation, 260
Raoul, Commander, 56, 64
Ravinés, Eudocio, 10-11
Red Brigade, 212
Red Cross, 214, 251
referendum, 217-218, 227-228
Retail Traders' Confederation, 69
Revolutionary Farmers' Movement (MCR), 18
Revolutionary Workers' Front (FTR), 18

Reyes, Francisco, 55, 56
Ricabarren, Luis Emilio, 10
Rillon, Mr., 209
Rios, Arnoldo, 97
Rios, President Juan Antonio, 5
Rivas, Alfonso Montoya, 53
Rivas, Juan Manuel, 76
Rivas, Luis Hernan, 76
Rivera, Jose, 90
Rivera, Ronald, 83
Rodriguez, Carlos Rafael, 191
Rodriguez, German de Jesus Cortez, 211
Rodriguez, Manuel, 133
Rodriguez, Pablo, 194
Rodriguez, Roberto Sapiain, 118
Roebuck, Dr., 212
Rojas, Manuel. *See* Savella, Andrés, 208
Rolando Matus Brigade, 87
Roll of Chile, 36, 143-145, 147
Roman Catholic Church, 19 *et seq.*
Rossi, Luis Valente, 52
Rousseau, Jean Jacques, 264

SUMAR, 112
Saenz, Doctor Cristobal, 114
Salazar, Dr. Antonio de Oliveira, 260, 264
Salazar, Heriberto, 32, 83
Salazar, Miguel, 138
San Martín, General, 1
Sanhueza, Fernando, 60
Santa Maria, President, 2
Santiago Court of Justice, 197
Santiago Gas Company, 57
Sartre, Jean-Paul, 17, 174, 175, 182
Savella, Andrés, 208
Savonarola, 124
Schatz, Jaime, 132
Schneider, General, 25, 26
La Secretaria Nacional de la Mujer, 245
Sepa review, 56
Sepulveda, General, 48
Sery, Leonid Mikhailovich, 196-197
El Shandu. *See* Berrios, Juan Marchant
shanty towns, 63-64, 176, 244
Silberman, David, 132, 210-211
Silva, Orlando, 94
Silva, Cardinal Raul, 20, 21, 22, 138, 215, 222
Silva, Victor Domingo. *See* Savella, Andrés
Siqueiros, Mr., 12
Social-Democratic Party, 183
social policy, 243-246
Socialism, 82 *et seq.*
Socialist International, 12, 17
Socialist Party, 4, 5, 12-15, 39, 53, 87, 88, 116, 140, 260
Sociedad Fomento Fabril, 235
Soekarno, President, 28, 159
Solidaridad, 206
Solidarity Vicariate, 206 *et seq.*, 219
Solzhenytsin, A., viii, 14, 117, 249, 258
Somoza, Mr., 257
Soto, Alfonso Cortes, 88
Souper, Colonel, 38, 155
Soviet Union
  agriculture, 109
  Food Supply Committees, 69-70
  involvement in Chile, 189-190
  People's Commissariat for Food, 69-70
Stalin, J. V., vi, ix, 11, 16, 17, 28, 171, 223, 249, 250, 252, 263
Stalin, Svetlana, 117
standard of living, 240-242
Statute of Guarantees, 14, 26, 29, 38, 50 *et seq.*, 60, 82, 90, 91, 146, 152, 153, 168
Stuardo, Julio, 53, 54, 56, 135
Suharto, President, 252, 253
Sule, Anselmo, 16, 17
Supreme Council of National Security, 84
Supreme Court, 46, 48, 55-56, 95, 143, 150, 151, 157, 166, 168, 212
El Sur, 57-58
Surazo, 57

Tagle, Monsignor, 22
Taraki, General, 256
tax reforms, 233
Télérama, 211
El Teniente copper mines, 38, 112, 133-136, 139, 154
Tery, President Belaunde, 260
Thatcher, Mrs. Margaret, 190
Tito, J. B., 227, 257
Toha, José, 30, 45
Tomic, Radomiro, 23, 24

Toro, Victor, 78
Torrealba, Ernesto, 46
Torres, Camilo, 20
Torres, General, 256
Torrijos, General, 260
Touré, Sékou, 256
towns, expropriations in, 78 *et seq.*
trade union rights, 221-223
Tres Alamos camp, 203
Tri-Continental Conference, 27
La Tribuna, 55
Trotsky, L. D., 12
Tupamaros, 193

UP. *See* Popular Unity Front
Ugarte, General Augusto Pinochet. *See* Pinochet, General Augusto
Ugarte, Nelson, 74
Ultima Hora, 48
Ultimas Noticias, 71
Unitary Workers' Federation (CUT), 7, 11, 21, 37, 63, 81, 97, 133, 157, 197
United National School (ENU), 37, 66-68, 137-140
United Nations, 251
  Charter, 66
  Children's Fund, 244
  Food and Agriculture Organisation, 72
  investigation of complaints against Pinochet regime, 214-216
United Press International news agency, 55
United States
  intervention in Pinochet's Chile, 194-195
  Senate Judiciary Committee, 195
University of Chile, 50, 53-54, 107, 139, 241, 245
Urra, Jose, 94
Urrutia, Thomas Arnold Gutierrez, 83

VOP. *See* Organized Vanguard of the People
Valdes, Patricio, 16
Valéry, 128
Vallejos, Pizarro, 216
Valparaiso Chamber of Commerce, 103
Van Lanker, Mr., 199
Vanguardia Organizada del Pueblo. See Organized Vanguard of the People
Vasquez, Raul, 76
Vekemans, Father Roger, 19, 22
Velasco, Fernando Castillo, 20, 139
Velasco, Mr., 218
Vera, Jose Liendo, 74, 86
Vera, Pedro, Oportot, 56
Vergara, Daniel, 52, 93, 162
Vergara, Sergio, 76
Vicaria de la Solidaridad. *See* Solidarity Vicariate
Videla, President Gabriel Gonzalez, 5-6, 253
Videla, Lautaro, 67
Viet Cong, 20
vigilance committees, 190
Villalobos, Alejandro, 55, 56, 64, 65, 85
Vilarin, Leon, 123, 140-141, 143, 145
violence, 82 *et seq.*
Voltaire, 267
Vuskovic, Mr., 97
Vuskovic, Pedro, 30, 118
Vuskovic Papers, 80

Wallace, Edgar, 28
Washington Post, 255
Water Service, 112
White Book, 14, 18, 47, 52, 89, 90, 94, 100, 162, 191
Wolff, Federico, 53
Women's Power, 128 *et seq.*, 149
World Bank, 110, 244
World Federation of Democratic Youth, 16

Young Christian Workers, 21
Young Church, 20, 21. *See also* Christians for Socialism

Zig Zag. See Ediciones Zig Zag
Zujovic, Edmundo Perez, 32, 82, 83, 146